Theopoetic Folds

John D. Caputo, *series editor*

Edited by ROLAND FABER
and JEREMY FACKENTHAL

Theopoetic Folds
Philosophizing Multifariousness

FORDHAM UNIVERSITY PRESS
New York ■ 2013

Library of Congress Cataloging-in-Publication Data

Theopoetic folds : philosophizing multifariousness / edited by Roland Faber and Jeremy Fackenthal. — First edition.
    pages cm. — (Perspectives in Continental philosophy)
    Includes bibliographical references and index.
    ISBN 978-0-8232-5155-1 (cloth : alk. paper) — ISBN 978-0-8232-5156-8 (pbk. : alk. paper)   1. Philosophical theology.   2. Theology.   3. Christianity and literature.   4. Poetics.   I. Faber, Roland, 1960– editor of compilation.
    BT40.T439 2013
    230—dc23

                                                                                2013003545

Printed in the United States of America

15 14 13   5 4 3 2 1

First edition

Contents

Theopoetic Folds

Introduction
The Manifold of Theopoetics

ROLAND FABER AND
JEREMY FACKENTHAL

Philosophic tradition has bestowed on us many beginnings in poetics and theopoetics. They appear in multiplying tensions, antagonisms of war and mutual affliction, paradoxes and unfinished businesses. The poem of Parmenides and the fragments of Heraclitus: moods of being and becoming. Aristotle's *Poetics* and the expulsion of the poets from the Platonic state: antagonisms on artistic imitation as insights or distortions of reality. The poem of Lucretius—a praise of Venus and the reverence of materiality: the war between science and myth. Kant versus Nietzsche, the *First Critique* versus *Zarathustra:* the battle between reason and life. Philosophy *more geomentrico,* as in Spinoza, versus philosophy in rhythms and verses, as in Goethe—mathematics versus poetics: Is it a question of expression or meaning, of style or essence?

In questions of nature and art, theory and aesthetics, theology is never far. When George Santayana divides philosophic history into three periods, he invokes *Three Philosophical Poets:* Lucretius for antiquity, Dante for the Renaissance, and Goethe for Romanticism. Three themes emerge: nature, religion, and self. Three attitudes toward the world become visible—immersed in nature's breadth, in divine complexity, and in the will to create. In the final analysis, one cannot be divorced from the other.

As in a supreme dramatic crisis, all our life seems to be focused on the present, and used in coloring our consciousness and shaping our decisions, so far as for each philosophic poet the whole of man is gathered together; and he is never so much a poet as when, in a single cry, he summons all that has affinity to him in the universe and salutes his ultimate destiny. It is the acme of life to understand life. The height of poetry is to speak the language of the gods.[1]

With Judith Butler, we could say that, whether for good or bad, we cannot understand the individual and social self without their theological history of construction and the philosophical deconstruction of their theological identities. Whether in the form of naturalism, pantheism, or atheism, *the history of the divine* reveals its involvement in matters of the world and the self as part of our ever-moving identities. The polyphony of the *poetics* of their interaction saturates the formulation of our quest for truth and beauty or their challenge. Even the crisis of their intersection that always accompanies their interaction will reveal their very *theopoetic* nature.

This book addresses the complex relationship between philosophy, theology, and poetics. It will circle around two central terms: *poetics* and *multiplicity.* With the term *theopoetics,* it suggests their current resonance in philosophy of religion, philosophic theology, and interreligious discourses. It arises in a resonance of its inherent complex oscillation of matters of language and reality, phenomenology and metaphysics, literature and theology, secular and sacred discourses in the maybe-surprising coalition between especially two traditions: continental philosophy (of religion) and process theology. It follows their traces with their present intersecting and interfering interlocutors: deconstructionism, poststructuralism, literary criticism, postcolonialism, feminist theory, and social theory, to name only a few. One of its centers of gravity, but by no means its only center, is Alfred North Whitehead's work, its current rediscovery in continental studies (Deleuze, Derrida, Levinas, Badiou, Kristeva, Irigaray) and its complex contestation by their suspicion not only of the death of God but of the death of metaphysics.

The aim of this volume is to recover the term "theopoetics" as a means of relating the above-mentioned interlocutors *differently:* as expressions of a multiplicity and of a theory of multiplicity in which we can neither gain any final unity nor presuppose any common ground that would avoid shifting with its instantiations. As on a Deleuzian "plane of immanence," the concepts of this volume will be moving into one another, restricting and opening their internal breadth and external closures on the shifting ground that really is their space of enfolding. Not all of these concepts originate exclusively, or at all, in the sphere of either continental or process philosophies and their theological companions, but all will intersect, divide, cluster, and coagulate repeatedly in a field with these focal points.

They want to distribute, radiate, and not hinder their processual conjunctions and disjunctions in their mutual encounters.

The term *theopoetics* has its one fascinating history of manifold connotations, none of them totally devoid of the other, each meaning rather lurking in the midst of the other. From the first Christian centuries, in which it meant *theosis,* the becoming divine of the world in God—already resounding with a panentheistic ring—to the twentieth-century theological antidogmatist movement at Drew University that sought the infinite multiplicity of the metaphor instead. Its process theological use (or at least the potential for it) remained long enough implicit only in Whitehead's understanding of the divine as the nonviolent, suggestive, attracting Eros and the all-encompassing companion in the world's suffering, who understands.[2] The rediscovery of Continental roots of the philosophical criticism of theological language and its new embrace, respectively, became another source of the claim of theology to be essentially not a dogmatic system of certain knowledge of God or ultimate reality and the human response to it, but either a response of infinite variability in face of the divine mystery or, in a different adoption of postmodern stances, a bulwark against a nihilism with the rediscovery of old knowledges of the divine enshrined in the diverse traditions of religious communities and their written witnesses.

As this multiplicity of voices is contributing to this volume, as though protected by a shadow of presence it remains conscious of at least one of its expressions, maybe best understood as a the fertile soil of its playfield, but not determining the game itself: namely, Whitehead's explicit statement that God be the "Poet of the world" and its explicit reason. These are his words from *Process and Reality:*

> The universe includes a threefold creative act composed of (i) the one infinite conceptual realization, (ii) the multiple solidarity of free physical realizations in the temporal world, (iii) the ultimate unity of the multiplicity of actual fact with the primordial conceptual fact. If we conceive the first term and the last term in their unity over against the intermediate multiple freedom of physical realizations in the temporal world, we conceive of the patience of God, tenderly saving the turmoil of the intermediate world by the completion of his own nature. The sheer force of things lies in the intermediate physical process: this is the energy of physical production. God's role is not the combat of productive force with productive force, of destructive force with destructive force; it lies in the patient operation of the overpowering rationality of his conceptual harmonization. He

does not create the world, he saves it: or, more accurately, he is the poet of the world, with tender patience leading it by his vision of truth, beauty, and goodness.[3]

Regarding the meaning of *theopoetics,* at least these three elements are worth mentioning (with no intention of exhausting the layers of valuable interpretation of this term or its variety of use). First, in this text, which names God a "poet," *the* Poet, God is not "defined" as anything—a person, a force, a substance, a cosmic law, and so on—except as that which in the poetic naming is refrained from because of its inability to be expressed in terms of physical forces, worldly causes or effects, and, even more importantly, as a fixed concept. In other words, the poetic of the poet, insofar as it is interested in the arousal of the desire of Truth, Goodness, and Beauty, does not, at the same time, force any dogmatic image of what that means on the world by arousing a response to the divine instigation that is as yet undecided, something the world and God have to wait for, something so valuable that its determination is never predetermined but, in divine patience, waited for and received in its expressions, not as from a cold recorder or a ruthlessly agitated despot, but as from a poet.

Second, as God is not in any way a force that can be confounded with earthly powers or coercive measures, be they only verbally suppressing and oppressively directing; the poetic understanding of creation is that of the divine not as an effective cause but as an attractor, suggestive of a seducer of beauty. Rather than exhausting the creativity of happening by being the creator, Whitehead's divine suggests variations, alternatives, options, for a better world (than as it was found) in any event to be decided by the creativity of these events of the world's happening themselves. In more technical terms, neither does God exhaust the creativity that creates nor is God the only "agent" of creative acts. If anything, God, rather than being suggestive in the first place, received the more or less creative answers into God, suffering from their incompleteness as compared with the infinite vision of Truth, Goodness, and Beauty that speaks forth from God's suggestions in all events, transforming and, thereby, saving their greatness, as implicit or neglected as it might have been, in their very act of happening into a poetic vision that will again become, and is worth becoming, the basis for a new alternative, divinely inspired future chain of cosmic events.

Thirdly, by differentiating God from creativity and, thereby, ultimate reality from its shortcut identification with the divine in the differentiation between creativity and poiesis, Whitehead created a terminology that removes God completely from the plane of power. From now on, so the promise goes, God should not be confounded with any articulation of power inasmuch as such an articulation in its very conceptuality brings with itself the coercion of forces, always as a mixture of constructive and destructive movements that are only identified with "God" for the price of making God a force among others and our imagination of God a projection of the cosmos onto the divine measure of the mystery of God, the essence of which is nothing but idolatry.

This volume testifies that the multiplicity of theopoetic reactions to a world of violence, amid which religious violence is not the least, is current, and relates to the very future of the ability to address questions of ultimate reality and the divine after having recognized the problems with the complicity of religious communities in the words and deed of such violence. This violence suggests the very absence of the meaning of the very suggestions of an ultimate meaning or a divine purpose to this whole process of the universe, in which the world is included seemingly only as its faint radiance of a sprinkle of light, enlightening a mass of pain.

> Religion has emerged into human experience mixed with the crudest fancies of barbaric imagination. Gradually, slowly, steadily the vision recurs in history under nobler form and with clearer expression. It is the one element in human experience that persistently shows an upward trend. It fades and then recurs. But when it renews its force, it recurs with an added richness and purity of content. The fact of the religious vision, and its history of persistent expansion, is our one ground for optimism. Apart from it, human life is a flash of occasional enjoyments lighting up a mass of pain and misery, a bagatelle of transient experience.[4]

It is because of the ambivalence of religion, its deeds, structures and its thought experiments, that it may remain a "synonym for 'hatred'"[5] if it is not able to enlighten the (religious and nonreligious) world (and itself) gradually and inevitably with a vision of such grand poetic outlook of saving harmony and creative appetite toward the peace it promises. It is in such a theopoetic expectation that this volume, with Whitehead and all others who strive for such a vision as relief of the pain of existence, strife, and violence and in view of the wonders of the vast universe, is determined to contribute to a future world of theopoetic peace.

Most of the essays included in this volume were first presented at the Theopoetics and the Divine Manifold conference, held in April 2010 by the Center for Process Studies at Claremont School of Theology (in association with the inauguration of Roland Faber as Kilsby Family/John B. Cobb Jr. Chair in Process Studies). The conference brought together a wide array of scholars, some of whom are heavily influenced by process thought and the philosophy of Alfred North Whitehead, and some who are not. Participants included philosophers, theologians, sociologists, poets, literary theorists, and musicians, each lending a nuanced perspective to the discussion that ensued. Eschewing the standard paper-response format, the conference was designed to promote discussion and critical engagement among the participants. We asked each presenter to deliver only the main ideas and perhaps some questions or interesting trajectories emerging from her or his paper, and this brief presentation was followed by a longer conversation among the whole group, thus fostering a creative exchange of ideas itself modeling the poetic interplay under discussion.

Conversation during these periods focused largely around the ambivalence in the term *theopoetics,* as it is not only open to many associations—referring to the theme of poetry and aesthetic theory, to theology and literature, to a multiplicity of imageries of repressed literary qualities, myths, and metaphorical theologies—but on a more profound level becomes the basis for questioning the fixed establishment of these fields. While residing in the dangerous realm of relativism, its discussions also demonstrated its potential to heal the desperateness of orthodox persecution. Like Derrida's *différance* indicates, the supplementation in theopoetics is not "confined" to any deity; instead, it is per se as poetics inclined to think multiplicity, is per se pluralistic, avoids the gap between logic and aesthetics, and seeks a critical connotation with theopolitics.

During the discussions, theopoetics appears as supplement, not an addition, but to the contrary, that which in all binary structures is always excluded. It adds itself to binary "essences," de-essentializing its counterparts only existing as the exclusion of its supplementation. As a (philosophical, interreligious, global, process or otherwise) supplement, theopoetics takes the essentializations to trial (process), the *totalizations* of systems that hide their *logos* in logocentrism. In its insistence on the ultimacy of the irreducible manifoldness of the world in ontological, aesthetical, and ethical terms, in its multiple ways of expressing this insistence on manifoldness even as a divine gift, this "poetics" invokes the love of the folded divine for the manifold of the process of becoming, and it becomes the creative expression of this love as a mutual happening and as the relationality of its "creatures."

At the end of the conference, Roland Faber asked presenters to think on the question, in what sense does or could the term *theopoetics* in its many connotations contribute to your work as you try to think on the edge of theology, philosophy, literature, or sociology? As a result, the essays of this book explore, in their own manner, the complex philosophical ways in which theopoetics is, should, and can be the instigation, harboring, and explication of multiplicity. The chapters include reflections on the relationship of theopoetics or poetics and philosophy, theopoetic thought that critiques and denies an appeal to mono-orthodoxy and logocentrism, the theopoetics of pluralism or multireligious outlooks, and theopoetic insight into hegemony of anthropocentric thinking over philosophical approaches to ecology that value all forms of life. The sections of the book are divided among these various trajectories such that each section brings together lines of thought that sometimes find convergence, sometimes diverge, sometimes provide mutual critiques, and sometimes supplement each other's work. Inclusion of these many and sundry strands of theopoetic thought further demonstrates the multiplicity of theopoetics itself, since none claims authority over any other but rather increases the multifarious folds in the field of theopoetics.

The first section, "Poetics," aims at elucidating the relationship between poetics or theopoetics and philosophy. Each of the four authors in this section takes a different approach in establishing and articulating this relation—Halewood through Whitehead's injunction against the bifurcation of nature, Phelps through the four truth procedures of Badiou's event ontology, Laurent through the multiplicity of selfhood and interplay of aesthetics, and Colapietro through the relation between polyphonic voices in the blues tradition and the pluralistic philosophies of Whitehead and Dewey. In the first chapter, Michael Halewood questions the division between reality and its qualities, arguing for a view of reality as inclusive of the qualitative, making use of poetry, rather than philosophical or scientific argumentation. He appeals to the poetry of Rimbaud and Stevens and the philosophy of Whitehead in order to show that reality should not be divorced from the qualities experienced in this reality and that ultimately poetry can and does play a vital role in inhibiting this divorce. Hollis Phelps's chapter grapples with Badiou's Plato-like assessment of poetry, noting that Badiou banishes poetry from any ontological statements. The first portion of Phelps's chapter traces Badiou's four truth procedures, describing the role of nomination in each, before moving on in the second portion to articulate an irreducible theopoetic moment in Badiou's philosophy and ontology, since Badiou himself regards events as poetic. In the final section, Phelps seeks to bring the theopoetic implications of Badiou's philosophy into conversation with Whitehead's notion of the poetic. In his chapter on the multiplicity of spirit, Sam Laurent notes Kierkegaard's opposition to Hegel's logic on the grounds that logic only articulates stasis and cannot account for the becoming of the human subject. Laurent provides a theopoetics of the divine–human relation by describing

Kierkegaard's anthropological view in which the spirit is included in human subjectivity. Using the work of Helene Russell and Mark C. Taylor, he cites selfhood as an ongoing process inclusive of multiplicity and theopoesis. Finally, Laurent draws from John Dewey to describe the role of aesthetics within the interrelational self, noting the ethical and religious import of the convergence of these theories. Vincent Colapietro's chapter articulates theopoetics as a genre of the blues, citing the ability of the blues to invoke a response that issues into a call-and-response exchange between music and listener. Colapietro explores how such modes work to destabilize secular forms of reasoning that tend not to avail themselves of the possibility of a transcendent experience or of theological/theopoetic insight by means of the blues or other musical expressions. After suggesting, through recourse to Whitehead and Charles Peirce, that the world expresses itself in a polyphony of voices and must, therefore, be articulated in an equally polyphonic manner, he unfolds an understanding of the blues as such a polyphonic utterance, one that requires human response as response to the other.

The "Polyphony" section engages religious worldviews based on pluralism and multiplicity from a theopoetic perspective. Matthew LoPresti's chapter explores theopoetics and the question of relativity, critically reflecting on the role of theopoetics in philosophy. Addressing whether or not theopoetics can be termed a relativistic endeavor and whether or not Whitehead's particular theopoetic notions make for sound philosophy, LoPresti ultimately highlights the ways in which theopoetics sparks imaginative insights in loci where orthodoxy has led to stagnation. Along the way, he assesses theopoetics' ability to speak to and from a variety of religious positions, including eastern religious perspectives. The chapter concludes with an appraisal of Whitehead's statement that God is the poet of the world, noting the significance and creativity of the divine–human relation and the value of transformative thinking that emerges from Whitehead's invocation. Bob Mesle, in his chapter on "The World as an Ultimate," argues for three metaphysical ultimates: God, creativity (or emptiness in the Buddhist tradition), and the manifold. Mesle explores Whitehead's own proposal of the three ultimates of God, world, and creativity, suggesting that the manifold be substituted for world, given its ability to encompass the multiplicity of the world. Drawing from Paul Tillich's discussion of symbols, Whitehead, and Hindu and Taoist philosophy, Mesle outlines a theistic—or non-theistic—vision in which the three ultimates of God, creativity, and the manifold promote a more holistic ethic that accounts for all the world's sacredness. Laurel Schneider describes theopoetics as a mode of theological analysis that begins in poetry and ends in theology. She uses theopoetics as a theological approach to overcoming linear, monotheistic presuppositions in favor of multiplicity. Her chapter names the limits of monolinear thinking and examines the positive contributions of indigenous modes of thought that claim a robust, lived multiplicity through understandings of creation as incarnation.

The section on "Sub-version" explores philosophical theologies and anthropologies that diverge from the logic of the One or from clear universals as statements of dogmatic finality. John Caputo's chapter begins with a description of radical theology (as opposed to confessional theology) as employing postmodern hermeneutics and deconstruction to uncover the underlying events of religion, rather than seeking some set of universal principles applicable to all religions. For Caputo, the postmodern form of radical theology is theopoetics, by which he means a way of articulating those events in human life that one would call divine. As a result, theopoetics gives an account of the event or events of the divine as a call that requires a response. In his "theopoetic response to monorthodoxy," Callid Keefe-Perry defines monorthodoxy as a fixed, singular worldview demanding acquiescence. Against monorthodoxy, he argues for a "heraldic theology" that creates space for divergent views without abandoning all claims to truth. In the first half of the chapter, Keefe-Perry develops the heraldic position using Christian theological positions and Christian thinkers, whereas the second half moves beyond Christianity to explore the implications of a heraldic perspective for an ethic that challenges monorthodox thinking in its many instantiations. In the last chapter of this section, Paul Fiddes seeks to insert the work of Iris Murdoch and Julia Kristeva into a discussion of the sublime. He proposes a combination of Murdoch's and Kristeva's employment of the sublime in order to encourage an attention to the other and, hence, to the good and an empathetic identification and forgiveness with and of the other. Such a view, he suggests, points toward a theopoetics of the divine who creates the multifariousness of the world with an excess of generosity and with an inherent relation to the divine itself. From this, Fiddes develops a philosophical and theological insistence upon humanity's attention to the other.

The final section of the book, "The Pluri-verse," seeks to destabilize anthropocentric worldviews, insisting instead on realizations of humanity as part of the manifold, the multiplicity of the world, and not as its hierarchical head. Catherine Keller traces the history of theopoetics, bringing together three strands of theopoetic thought: its early formulation in classical Christian theology (as "theosis"), its development in the 1960s at Drew University as an alternative *to* theology, and finally its articulation through a Whiteheadian, process lens as an alternative *within* theology.

Keller sees the unfolding process theopoetics as drawing from the other two—the orthodox/apophatic and the literary traditions—in its own polyphonic vocalization of theologies of multiplicity. Returning to Whitehead, theopoetics, for Keller, envisions the pluriverse as seeking truth, beauty, and goodness within the convivial cosmos. Luke Higgins similarly articulates a process ecotheology through a theopoetic enfolding of the cosmos. He brings to this chapter the work of Elizabeth Grosz, Gilles Deleuze, and Whitehead, offering an aesthetic valuation of the production of novelty for the sake of beauty and intensity over and above the evolutionary aim at novelty for the mere sake of survival. He suggests that such novelty issues forth from the folds of the "chaosmos" as life and art, and, drawing from Faber, posits the divine as this poetic enfolding of the cosmos. Ultimately, this valuation of the world's beauty and intensity brings one, he argues, to a position of ecological responsibility called forth from what he terms as a musical or poetic "riff" on the rhythms and pulse of creation. Roland Faber posits humanity as a stranger or graciously and patiently invited guest into a wildness in which we must become (or realize our position as) contingent. He proposes that we become *intermezzo* in order to release our grasp on eco-nature as an entity within our control and manipulation, a creation we attempt to coerce in order to ensure our own survival. Becoming intermezzo then incites a poetics of becoming one with and in the midst of the multiplicity of the world.

In his Gifford Lectures, Raimon Panikkar reminds us that the language of theology cannot be, and should not attempt to be, clear and precise, since such technical language always misses a part of that which it attempts to disclose.

Theological language should be as much as possible poetical language. Theology is not algebra and does not deal with lifeless concepts. The metaphor and especially the parable are theological tools. The dictum of the late Thomists—*formalissime semper loquitur divus Thomas* ("Saint Thomas always speaks a formal language")—besides not being true, already represents the decline of Thomism and all of the scholastic tradition. How dare we encapsulate in clear and distinct ideas what deals with the ineffable mystery of the real?[6]

The essays included in this volume aim at articulating, in various ways, the reasons why *poiesis* aids the tasks of theology and philosophy. As Whitehead poignantly suggests, philosophy "may not neglect," but must rather express and reflect upon "the multifariousness of the world . . ."[7] Following his impulse, the folds of theopoetics venture toward philosophizing the heterogeneous nature of reality, as the title of this volume intimates. This irresistible multiplicity, this Whiteheadian multifariousness, this cosmic origami in the Deleuzian sense, envelops an infinity of folds, not indicating merely a "many-ness" of isolated and essentialized singularities as opposed to a destructive and all-absorbing "one-ness," but rather expresses an inextricable relationality—a being-in-between and between the between, instead of a center or basis of "things." Adequate articulation of the nature of these folds requires *theopoetic* insight, which must always aim at expressing the complex diversity of the world, which in such multiplicity reflects its own indeterminacy and mystery. It is the mystery, says Deleuze, we all seek, the "magic formula" that avoids mere sameness or opposition.[8] It is the stunning underside of our seemingly seamless field of perception, experience and theorizing closures that is countered by its own suffering from simplicity and the neglect of unexpected novelty, the "depth as yet unspoken."[9] Yet it is not surrender to the nameless. When Whitehead supplements philosophy with poetry, it is not mere mystery but its appearance through its *meter* that leads us to the unspoken. We hope that the following chapters will unfold continued proliferation of philosophies and theologies that subvert anthropocentric, logocentric, and essentializing modes of thought, that supplant and supplement mono-orthodox and bifurcated positions, and that, rather than tending toward dogmatic finality, strive to give voice to polyphonies of the mutual immanence, the multifariousness of the world.

Poetics

Reality, Eternality, and Colors
Rimbaud, Whitehead, Stevens

MICHAEL HALEWOOD

Introduction

To invoke the notion of "eternality" might seem, in our post-Enlightenment yet scientifically situated culture, to recur to an outdated philosophical or theological moment. In this paper I will argue that the concept of eternality is worth revisiting precisely insofar as it might elicit some insights into the character of reality that neither dismiss nor passively accept the legacy of Enlightenment philosophy and science's proclamations on reality, time and space. Instead, I aim to use the notions of eternality (and of colors) to put into question the very divisions between reality and its qualities that infuse our culture of thought. As will be seen, eternality does not have to refer to a separate realm of existence but can enable the development of a conception of a reality that is suffused with the qualitative. While it might be possible to make such arguments from within the established philosophical and scientific positions, I will argue that taking poetry seriously not only produces novel conceptual approaches but is emblematic of the shift in thinking that is required of modern thought as it attempts to throw off the shackles of its constraining concepts.

To this end, in this paper I will read the work of two poets (Arthur Rimbaud and Wallace Stevens) and one philosopher (A. N. Whitehead) as producing together a practical and valuable account of reality that requires no more that itself to exist but is always more than that which exists.

Rimbaud

Arthur Rimbaud is quite clear that vowels are colors: *A* is black. *E* is white. *I* is red. *O* is blue. *U* is green. This is not simply a synesthetic manifesto, and he is certainly not making the minor claim that vowels are like colors. He declares that vowels *are* colors. Yet, even to put it in this way might appear to suggest only an equivalence, a sameness, just as 2 + 3 is the same as 5 (supposedly). Such a notion of perfect similitude is not, I would suggest, Rimbaud's point. That is why he does not even use a copula and simply assigns each vowel a color.[1]

So, what is the role of colors? Rimbaud writes:

A, black velvety jacket of brilliant flies
which buzz around cruel smells,
Gulfs of shadow; E, whiteness of vapours and of tents,
lances of proud glaciers, white kings, shivers of cow-parsley;
I, purples, spat blood, smile of beautiful lips

To divide these phrases up into their constitutive elements, especially into nouns and adjectives (vapours, tents, etc., which just happen to be white, for example) and to then claim that, in some way, colors grant qualities to things and thereby express the emotional, accidental, metaphorical, and hence resolutely human experience of the world, is to falsely breach what is, in reality, undivided. The blackness, velvetiness, and jacketiness of the brilliant flies all come at once. It is this togetherness that makes them what they are, grants them their specificity, invigorates them and the line in the poem. Qualities and the world are, in reality, inseparable. The expression of such qualities is a complex matter, and the apparent dogmatism of Rimbaud's opening line is tempered by his introduction in the poem's later stages of "purples," "viridian" and, most interestingly, perhaps, "violet."[2] These modes of colorfulness indicate the variety that inheres in the irruption of color in the world.

However, I started by saying that Rimbaud insists that vowels *are* colors. What has happened to this claim? In order to follow this, it is necessary to ask what role vowels have in reality.

It could be said that vowels are the breath of language; they are that which enables speech. Consonants on their own are an impossibility—as this Czech tongue-twister partially demonstrates: "Strč prst skrz krk."[3] But vowels on their own would glide into each other and never end. The friction and fricative-ness of consonants requires the openness and liquidity of vowels as much as the vowels require consonants simply to be able to end, become finite and grant sense. To state that consonants are nouns and vowels are adjectives would be too strong. But the requirement of each of the other and the impossibility of their solo existence does match the utter imbrication of the world and its qualities as detailed by Rimbaud.

To return to colors, they can now be seen as the manner in which to express the potentiality, as opposed to the mere facticity, of existence. They are the breath of the world. Importantly, however, vowels and colors cannot exist on their own; the granting of quality to the world requires the finitude of consonants and existence. This leads to the question as to what is the status of such "things" that render potentiality and quality in finity and yet that somehow maintain a discrete existence. To flesh out a response I will turn to Whitehead's notion of "eternal objects." However, before turning to this, and in order to contextualize their role, I will first look at Whitehead's important notion of the bifurcation of nature.

Whitehead on the Bifurcation of Nature and Eternal Objects

I will start with two long quotations:

> Another way of phrasing this theory which I am arguing against is to bifurcate nature into two divisions, namely into the nature apprehended in awareness and the nature which is the cause of awareness. The nature which is in fact apprehended in awareness holds within it the greenness of the trees, the song of the birds, the warmth of the sun, the hardness of the chairs, and the feel of the velvet. The nature which is the cause of awareness is the conjectured system of molecules and electrons which so affects the mind as to produce the awareness of apparent nature. The meeting point of these two natures is the mind, the causal nature being influent and the apparent nature being effluent.[4]

> Nature gets credit for what should in truth be reserved for ourselves: the rose for its scent: the nightingale for his song: and the sun for his radiance. The poets are entirely mistaken. They should address their lyrics to themselves, and should turn them into odes of self-congratulation on the excellency of the human mind. Nature is a dull affair, soundless, scentless, colourless; merely the hurrying of material, endlessly, meaninglessly.[5]

Here we have the condition of modernity where the real reality is reserved for the unseen yet fundamental operations of those entities (molecules, electrons, etc.) that constitute facticity and that are utterly devoid of intrinsic meaning and that are utterly divorced from the meaningful realm of human existence. This reduces nature to an inert, implacable basis that is deprived of any purpose or inherent quality. Furthermore, the realm of experience (of warmth, redness, softness) and description of such experience (in poems, art, etc.) is posited as solely a human affair and creation. This divorce can lead to the celebration of this latter realm as the indicator of the specificity of the human as that sole element of existence endowed with language, value, and consciousness. Or it can entail a reduction of such language, values, and consciousness, as well as the subsequent descriptions of these experiences, to mere "psychic additions."[6] Such phenomena thereby become simply interesting but less real aspects of a dislocated humanized culture, or worse—to the mere and irrelevant meanderings of an offshoot of existence that is entirely ineffective in accounting for or acting upon the world outside of the extremely narrow limits of art and inconsequential fun. Poets and poetry have nothing to say about the real world, as the qualities and experience of which they speak are not really in the world but are only to be found among the epiphenomenal occurrences that constitute the human realm. "Proper" philosophy and real science are impossible projects for poets and poetry.

This seemingly unbridgeable gap is one that Rimbaud refuses to recognize and that Whitehead insists is not only a misdescription of reality but is a limitation on thought and life. According to him, we must develop a fuller, more realistic, and more democratic account that does not commence by disqualifying any element of existence or of prioritizing one set of "facts" over another. A true empiricism (which is supposed to be the foundation of science) cannot ignore any element in the world, cannot, arbitrarily, dismiss any thing; it must account for every thing, for *all* the facts. And human experience is something that happens and, hence, cannot be so easily dismissed. "We may not pick and choose. For us the red glow of the sunset should be as much part of nature as are the molecules and electric waves by which men of science would explain the phenomenon."[7]

For the purpose of this paper, the task, then, is clear. To explain how colors really are in nature; how quality is an essential aspect of existence and not merely the quaint, artful reaction of humans to a world that they encounter but whose full explanation lies elsewhere. "My present point is that sky-blue is found in nature with a definite implication in events."[8] Yet to justify such a claim will be no easy task and will take some philosophical work. I have chosen to follow Whitehead's construction of his account of the place of qualities in nature through an analysis of his notion of eternal objects, especially in relation to the status of color in existence.

Eternal Objects

Whitehead introduced the term *eternal objects* in *Science and the Modern World*, although he does not develop a full theory of them, and they play a different role than that which will be assigned to them in *Process and Reality*. As such, care needs to be taken in using this text as providing firm and accurate statements of the status of eternal objects. At the same time, the early discussions of them do emphasize the specific notion of eternality that Whitehead is invoking:

> Every scheme for the analysis of nature has to face these two facts, *change* and *endurance*. There is yet a third fact to be placed by it, *eternality*, I will call it. The mountain endures. But when after ages it has been worn away, it has gone. If a replica arises, it is yet a new mountain. A colour is eternal . . . It comes and it goes. But where it comes it is the same colour. It neither survives nor does it live. It appears when it is wanted. The mountain has to time and space a different relation from that which colour has.[9]

Existence is not unchanging. Things come to be and things pass. In the formation of any entity there is another essential element that enables change and yet that grants specificity. Whitehead names this "eternality." Such eternality is not wholly abstract and does not constitute a separate realm from the entities of the world that endure and pass; eternality appears *in* the enduring entities of the world but is not limited to, or by, the existence of such entities. It is in this sense that it is eternal: It is out of time; it is not an element in the duration and passing of the things of the world. Colors are indicative of this notion of eternality.

Although some do not like Whitehead's notion of eternal objects, and even those who do are clear that they are metaphysical entities that cannot simply be named, denoted, or captured by language, the point of them, as with many of Whitehead's technical terms, is to nudge at the edges of our thought, to make us stop and reconsider, to jump us out of complacency. Poetry and philosophy have, therefore, a similar role: "Philosophy is akin to poetry . . . In each case there is reference to form beyond the direct meanings of words."[10] I therefore wish to suggest, in this paper, that colors express the role of eternal objects but I am not saying that colors are eternal objects or that eternal objects are colors. In this sense, I do not want to go as far as Rimbaud. But I do wish to trace the relation between color and the role of eternal objects in Whitehead's philosophy.

Again in *Science and the Modern World*, Whitehead would seem to make a direct link between colors and eternal objects: "[The] interfusion of events is effected by the aspects of those eternal objects, such as colors, sounds, scents, geometrical character, which are required for nature and are not emergent from it."[11] And: "An eternal object such as a definite shade of green, which cannot be analysed into a relationship of components, will be called 'simple.'"[12] However, by the time of the publication of *Process and Reality*, Whitehead is less plain in his definitions of eternal objects and the statement that colors *are* eternal objects has softened so that now[13] "qualities, such as colors, sounds, bodily feelings, tastes, smells, together with the perspectives introduced by extensive relationships, are the relational eternal objects."[14] There is no longer an identity between colors and eternal objects but there is a relationship. Stengers puts it thus: "a colour is not, in itself, an eternal object. It is the experience of colour which witnesses the ingression of an eternal object."[15]

So, eternal objects *do* have something to do with sense data, insofar as they help explicate the relation of actual entities to the general creativity of the universe, through their expression of potentiality. And this is the crucial and positive point. Here we have moved from the critique of those philosophies, theories, and approaches to science that bifurcate the world into the real causes and the human experience of such causes, to a position where existence is always and everywhere a matter of both potentiality and facticity in elements that cannot be pulled apart in reality. We do not see eternal objects; we never encounter them. But colors are a privileged site of access or witness to the ingression of eternality into the every day. In fact, potentiality is an integral aspect of fact. Colors exist in nature, in reality, in things—absolutely. We are back with Rimbaud. Whitehead is with Locke:

> Locke makes it plain . . . that by a "simple idea" he means the ingression in the actual entity (illustrated by "a piece of wax,"[16] "a piece of ice," "a rose") of some abstract quality which is not complex (illustrated by "softness," "warmth," "whiteness"). For Locke such simple ideas *coexisting* in an actual entity, require a *real* constitution for that entity. Now in the philosophy of organism . . . the notion of a real constitution is taken to mean that the eternal objects function by introducing the multiplicity of actual entities as constitutive of the actual entity in question.[17]

The crucial and positive role of eternal objects is to give specificity to an actual entity. A piece of wax is not just an inert piece of wax; it is a piece of wax in a certain way—it is warm in the hand, for example. Such warmth is not essential to the existence of wax per se; it could be cold in the hand. But, it *is* integral to the existence of that piece of wax at that time and that place. Yet, warmth and whiteness are not limited by the existence of that particular piece of wax. They are, in this sense, abstract and eternal. However, they do not exist separately from the individual occasions in which they occur. There is no separate realm of warmth, whiteness, or softness. But they are *there*. Poetry and philosophy have the task of enabling us to think of the inseparability of qualities and facticity in the individuals we encounter.

"Red," as eternal object, does not exist in a separate realm from reality. It is only to be found among genuine experiences of red things. This is the basis of Whitehead's empiricism. There are only those things that are presented, encountered, and experienced and nothing else. It is in these terms that eternal objects "tell no tales as to their ingressions." At the same time, the world is not limited to these items as presented in these situations. The world is in process, the reality of the universe *is* process. Each actual entity is an exemplum of this process, but it neither explains process on its own nor does it exhaust the potentiality of the universe. In this sense, Whitehead's empiricism might be called an un-Kantian "transcendental" in that each entity is an expression of the universe but does not stifle that which comes before and that which goes after. "An 'object' is a transcendent element characterizing that definiteness to which our 'experience' has to conform. In this sense, the future has objective reality in the present."[18] This is the role of eternal objects; they explain the pure potentiality of the universe but only insofar as such potentiality is materialized in those entities that make up the ongoing process of the universe.

And, to return to poetry, Andrew Marvell in his poem "The Garden" wrote of "Annihilating all that's made/To a green/Thought in a green shade."[19] The world does not emerge from the conceptualizations of a subject, as Kant maintained. The world transcends itself in a certain way, exhibiting, in the process, elements of abstraction and eternality and situating these in individual experiences and events, such as an act of thought in and of a garden. This is not a reactive, contemplative thought but an actual occurrence of the quality of existence in both the greenness of the garden and the manner of the thinking. The greenness of the garden becomes an integral element in the constitution of that thinker. Qualities, as exhibited by colors, are essential to experience and cannot be understood as separate in reality or in thinking about reality.

Having now established the philosophical basis of the relation of abstraction, eternality, facticity, and the expressions of colors, I would now like, finally, to return to poetry through a brief analysis of Wallace Stevens's *The Man With The Blue Guitar*.[20] As Steven Meyer has stated,[21] Wallace Stevens was fascinated by the work and ideas of Whitehead but he did not, unlike certain other poets, simply accept Whitehead's view and try to express it in poetical form. Instead, Stevens has a tensile relationship with Whitehead and tests his thoughts through his poems. I will try to follow aspects of this test and to focus on the role of color in the descriptions of becoming, being, and life.

The Man with the Blue Guitar

In his poem "The Man with the Blue Guitar," Wallace Stevens appears to consider the implications of Picasso's painting *The Old Guitarist* for our understanding of the character or existence and life and the role of poetry therein.

> 1
> The man bent over his guitar,
> A shearsman of sorts. The day was green.
> They said, "You have a blue guitar,
> You do not play things as they are."
> The man replied, "Things as they
> Are changed upon the blue guitar."
> And they said then, "But play you must,
> A tune beyond us, yet ourselves,
> A tune upon the blue guitar
> Of things exactly as they are."

These first few stanzas set out the problematic of the poem. The need to describe the process of change that constitutes things, "Things as they / Are changed upon the blue guitar." The role of colors as implacably founded in existence, as a full quality of reality: "The day was green." And the common-sense, commonplace, but contradictory desire of humans to be both objects and subjects; fixed, defined and self-identical, yet to also be things that grow and change. "But play you must, / A tune beyond us, yet ourselves, / A tune upon the blue guitar / Of things exactly as they are." The following thirty-two sections of the poem could be read as a consideration of how it is possible to account for both the fixity and process that constitute life and the integral role of colors in expressing the conjunctions and disjunctions that compose facticity, quality, and the ongoing becoming of reality.

This raises the question of whether a poem is really the place to indulge in such philosophy. Or, at least, what is the effectiveness of poetry in dealing with abstractions and in developing concepts? Stevens responds:

> Poetry is the subject of the poem,
> From this the poem issues and

To this returns. Between the two,
Between issue and return, there is
An absence in reality,
Things as they are. Or so we say.

It might be possible to view these lines as rendering poetry passive, as the subject *matter* of the poem, as that which the poem reflects upon and that remains in and of itself mute, even if the poem slightly alters the wider realm of poetry upon the poem's completion. A Whiteheadian reading would not follow any such analysis. Instead, activity would be granted to both poetry as the subjective form of the creative process that constitutes the unfolding of the poem and to the self-constitution of the poem. That is to say, there are no subtending subjects that experience or suffer qualification or change or development. Rather, poetry is that which becomes: It becomes a poem in the events that constitute both the writing and reading of the poem. Hence, poetry undergoes the same existential conditioning as all elements in the world do. As with all other actual entities, it becomes, and in its becoming it just "is where it is and what it is."[22] When Stevens refers to an "absence in reality," he is not talking of a lack but is referring to the genetic growth, the concrescence of the poem, which, as a creation of a moment and place of extension, is no mere object but is that process that constitutes reality. Becoming is just what happens; it does not have parts or stages, it is not divided in itself. What becomes is not clear until it has become, and it is impossible to perceive or describe the contemporary process of a becoming. "There is a becoming of continuity, but no continuity of becoming."[23] In order to focus our thought on this peculiar notion, he terms it an absence, a productive absence, that defines what a thing really is ("Things as they are")—that is the becoming that is the being of the poem: "Its 'being' is constituted by its 'becoming.'"[24] This entails that it is the task of the poem to become and, in the case of this poem, to account for the manner and operation of the becoming of that poem.

The manner of the becoming of the poem will include a description only of the "how" and the qualities inherent in this. And, to accomplish this, Stevens, like Whitehead, invokes colors as that which express the concreteness of the becoming of qualities in the world that, thereby, express the ingression of the abstract eternality into the real things of nature and reality. So, in a further reflection on the status of the reality of the absence that constitutes the poem's becoming, Stevens states:

Is it
An absence for the poem, which acquires
Its true appearances there, sun's green,

> Cloud's red, earth feeling, sky that thinks?
> From these it takes. Perhaps it gives . . .

The description of the becoming of the poem as an absence is not sufficient to account for the fullness of the becoming of the poem, considered from the poem's own point of view (in "formaliter," as Whitehead puts it).[25] The acquisition of its own "true appearance" is a process of the acquisition of qualities, in this case described in terms of colors, the "sun's green, / Cloud's red." This enables him to progress beyond the simplistic dualism of objects that are granted accidental properties, to an account of existence where actions, feelings, purpose, and value may and must be granted to all those things that become. The earth feels, the sky thinks, not in exactly the same way as humans feel and think, but the difference is a quantitative one not a qualitative one, and such phrases are not metaphors.

The poem, as an item in the world, comes from that world, becomes itself in its becoming and, in so doing, appropriates diverse elements of that world and brings them into a specific unity. Once completed, the poem then contributes to that world and offers itself as a possible element for future becomings: "it takes. Perhaps it gives."

Poetry is, therefore, immanent to the ongoing creativity of existence. Creativity is not, therefore, to be located in a transcendent realm, whether such a realm be considered as an author, God, or a separate realm of beauty (and hymns).

> Poetry
> Exceeding music must take the place
> Of empty heaven and its hymns,
> Ourselves in poetry must take their place . . .

Poetry is Stevens's term for describing the process of creativity in the world. This is a general category that is not created by humans but is one within which humans and their experiences and lives occur and are to be situated. "Ourselves in poetry must take their place." There is nothing so special about humans that they have a privileged site within creativity, within poetry, which enables them to celebrate themselves as the specific and foundational creators of words, poems, feelings, beauty, and the experience of colors. Such a bifurcation of nature must be resisted, and poems must not simply be "odes of self-congratulation on the excellency of the human mind," as Whitehead puts it.

This is not to suggest that poets are not themselves creative; it is not to dismiss the poet as author of the poem or to boringly invoke the overly cited "intentional fallacy" that claims that the day of the author is done. It is, rather, to insist that the creativity that constitutes the creation of a poem is a difficult, complex affair that is an exemplum of the wider creative process of the world, or poetry in general, as Stevens would have it. So, this difficult creative process that will enable the poem to become what it is will involve a bringing together of diverse data into a single whole. This coalescence must include qualities coming into facticity, and so, once again, Stevens turns to colors to explicate his point and the character of the process.

> And the color, the overcast blue
> Of the air, in which the blue guitar
> Is a form, described but difficult,
> And I am merely a shadow hunched
> Above the arrowy, still strings,
> The maker of a thing yet to be made;
> The color like a thought that grows
> Out of a mood, the tragic robe
> Of the actor, half his gesture, half
> His speech, the dress of his meaning, silk
> Sodden with his melancholy words,
> The weather of his stage, himself.

The author is implicated, is part of the process, but is not center stage, is not a unified creative force modeled on the notion of an external god-like entity. The poet is "Sodden with his melancholy word," is awash within the elements that compose the poem and is an aspect of that poem's becoming "The weather of his stage, himself."[26] At the same time, the poet is there, is somewhere, within the process, hunched over the "blue guitar" and has the potential to create; the poet is "The maker of a thing yet to be made." The whole point is that the process of the creation has to be undergone for the poet to become a poet, the poem to become the poem, poetry to play its role. And, once again, it is colors that enable the constitution of all of these elements. There is the penumbra, the range of potentials offered by the colorness that permeates the initial stages of the creation of the entity that is the poem and the poet: "the overcast blue / Of the air, in which the blue guitar / Is a form." There is abstraction here, in the sense that Whitehead's eternal objects are abstract, but there is also an abstraction in that the guitar itself is not a fixed entity but is a manner of enabling things to be produced, for things to be "as they are." As the process continues, the influence and operations of the colors intensify, are sharpened, and, ultimately, provide definiteness to the poems, its words, its concepts, and itself. "The color like a thought that grows / Out of a mood." Colors are the poem's thinking, which is not a human thinking but necessary for the thoughts and qualities of the poem to become apparent.

To neglect the processual character of the poet and the poem is to do violence to the world and to its characters. To use the "blue guitar" to try to describe the objectivity of human life is to falsely render the becoming that constitutes the being of the poem and of life; it is to try to divide that which, in reality, in concrescence, in *formaliter*, is not divided. It is to attempt to separate the quality from the facticity, the adjectives from the nouns, the colors from the things. So, as with Rimbaud and Whitehead, Stevens protests against those who vivisect the world and its creatures in order to describe them.

> Ah but, play man number one,
> To drive the dagger in his heart,
> To lay his brain upon the board
> And pick the acrid colors out . . .
> To bang it from a savage blue . . .

To reduce things "as they are" to fixed objects, as opposed to subjects involved in becoming, is not merely to make a metaphysical error; it is to condone the violence that those intent on finding the essence of real things justify in the name of science, accuracy, and knowledge. It is to insist on ripping apart what is, in its reality, a complex whole. Such violence condones its actions in an appeal to a mistaken pragmatism and can be seen in attempts to dissect the concepts and reality of sexual difference, criminality, alcoholism, IQ tests, SATs, and genetic determinism, among others. Rimbaud, Whitehead, and Stevens would not envisage such simplistic and aggressive approaches to the world and life.

Instead, they all stress the rather more complex task of accounting for the "buzzing of the blue guitar." Or, as Whitehead puts it: "We find ourselves in a buzzing world, amid a democracy of fellow creatures."[27] This lack of hierarchy, this refusal to place humanity outside of or beyond the creativity and becoming of the world entails that the becomings that punctuate that world will transgress the boundaries usually associated between subjects and objects, subjects and subjects, and objects and objects.

> Slowly the ivy on the stones
> Becomes the stones. Women become
> The cities, children become the fields
> And men in waves become the sea.
> It is the chord that falsifies.

That is to say, the chord is a grid that attempts to reduce the specific yet diverse becomings, resonances, and harmonics that emanate from the buzzing strings on the guitar into a fixed, abstract pattern that supposedly accounts for all that is involved in the sounds produced by pulsating strings but only reduces them to what Foucault has described as a "grid of intelligibility."[28] This is an operation replete with power and domination. It is in this way that the chord "falsifies." There is much more to an F-minor chord than the sheet music allows for.

The importance and impetus of the insistence on the complete integration of colors in the facticity of existence, as evinced by Rimbaud, Whitehead, and Stevens, is now apparent. The elision of vowels and colors, the ingression of eternality in finity as describing the process of reality, and the implication of poetry, the poem and the becoming of subjects, constitute no mere rhetorical device. It is a protest against the bifurcation of nature, the stultifying modes of thought that permeate modernity, and the forms of domination that take both of these for granted and use them to justify their procedures and expansion further and further into our lives. To resist the violence of facticity, the melding of eternality as potentiality with the becoming of real, democratic subjects must be clarified and insisted upon. Humans, cats, colors, grass, noses, the past, the present, the future are involved in a negotiation with, and embodiment of, eternality. As Stevens puts it:

> The cats had cats and the grass turned gray
> And the world had worlds, ai, this-a-way:
> The grass turned green and the grass turned gray.
> And the nose is eternal, that-a-way.
> Things as they were, things as they are,
> Things as they will be by and by . . .

Cats beget cats and this is an element of creation. The world has worlds. This equally is an element of the same creation. Grass becomes now green, now gray. Even its death is a part of creation. The nose in its tracing of scents, smells, and odors is in touch with aspects of eternality. Things were, are, and will be. The task is to dwell among these facts and factors without doing violence to their description of being.

Conclusion

The relation between philosophy and poetry is not a simple one. To reduce philosophy to poetry would be to lose its critical effectivity and to run the risk of relegating it to heartfelt but superficial claims and statements about the world. As Stengers[29] insists, philosophy must not be nostalgic. This is not in any way to suggest that poetry is inherently nostalgic or superficial. Rather, it is to stress that philosophy must deal with contemporary problems and concepts and not feed off, or long to return to, its supposedly glorious past. Often the very practice of philosophy seems to be historical in that the works, ideas, and concepts of long-dead heroes are ritually and continually invoked. Insofar as such invocations remain at the naive historical level of re-creating past systems of thought, or of attempting to unearth the real truth of these quasi-sacred texts, they are guilty of nostalgia and idol worship. To refuse such nostalgia as an element of philosophy is not to locate nostalgia as an integral element of poetry but is simply to warn that a lazy implantation of the concerns and procedures of poetry directly into philosophy would run the risk of invalidating the specificity of both poetry and philosophy. The historical aspect of poetry, in terms of a Whiteheadian analysis, would arise from his view that "History is record of the expressions of feelings peculiar to humanity."[30] Such expressions are both documented and widened in and through poetry. This is not an unphilosophical task, but it is not a wholly philosophical task. And it is certainly not a matter of heartfelt statements or nostalgia (and it is not simply to reduce poetry to the historical!). There needs to be a clear understanding of the specific concerns and roles of philosophy and poetry in order to bear witness to their respective critical and effectiveness and importance. Likewise, to reduce poetry to philosophy would, equally, be to limit its scope; it would deprive it of its ability to utilize language as a way of challenging and extending the boundaries of our thought, our experiences, and our lives. Hence, Whitehead is clear that the two are not the same but that "philosophy is *akin* to poetry."

This paper has attempted, without too much systematic or explicit argumentation, to identify examples of this kinship through an overview of a poem each by Rimbaud and Stevens with a philosophical interlude from Whitehead. The aim has not been to demonstrate, once and for all, the role and function of any Philosophy–Poetry couplet but to suggest that analyses based on their cooperative elements could develop productive ways of analyzing and understanding life and the world. Philosophy and poetry share the chance to demonstrate how language changes our thoughts and lives, as it is a concrete element of our thoughts and lives. Both approaches inspect and clarify both the importance and limitation of language; they bend words to make us think and be differently or, at least to temporarily halt us in our complacency and to hesitate before the limits and edges of the words and the things that we claim we own.

In this way, poetry can offer a way of refusing the bifurcation of nature and of providing novel and effective insights into the complexity of existence. Contemporary society and theory have tended to limit the role of poetry to an expression of human perception, knowledge, and emotion. Some welcome this limiting, as it marks the poet as the bearer of all that is specific and best about humanity. But, in doing so, they accept the reduction of the human to exist only in and through its own values and finite realm of existence. This tacit acquiescence to the claims that science alone is equipped to talk of the real reality leaves the poet with only the crumbs of emotionality. There is an epistemic and ontological violence here, as the circumscription of areas of expertise and witness always involve a diminution both of the possibility of that which we call human and the potentiality of reality to be more than it appears to be, and more than it is. Hence, poetry needs to assert itself as more than a vehicle of the specificity of humanity and as a forceful, active protagonist in the battle for elicitations of what constitutes reality. It has a philosophical, political, ethical, and "scientific" impetus and responsibility.

(Theo)poetic Naming and the Advent of Truths
The Function of Poetics in the Philosophy of Alain Badiou

HOLLIS PHELPS

The work of French philosopher Alain Badiou has only recently begun to receive considerable attention in the English-speaking world. Over the past ten years or so, many of his most significant texts have been translated into English, and his philosophy as a whole has been the subject of a growing body of commentary and criticism, including several book-length introductions and edited volumes. In the most general terms, Badiou's project, at least since the publication of his first magnum opus *Being and Event,* can be understood as an attempt to construct a contemporary systematic philosophy, the parameters of which revolve around the articulation of a mathematical, and hence rational and deductive, ontology and a nonobjective or generic theory of truth and the subject.

One of Badiou's constant emphases since the publication of *Being and Event* is his insistence on the plurality of truth, on the material existence of truths. That is, truths, when they occur through the productive activity of subjects, do so in one of four irreducibly singular registers: science/mathematics, art/poetry, politics, and love. Philosophy itself does not produce truths. Rather, its task is, on the one hand, to draw out the formal aspects of each of these four generic truth procedures, to bring to light what it is that makes these truths *truths,* in fashion similar to the way in which theology is a reflection upon an already-existing faith. Philosophy is, in Badiou's words, "the go-between in our encounters with truths, the procuress of truth."[1] On the other hand, philosophy has as its task the organization of the compossibility of science/mathematics, art/poetry, politics, and love, all of which serve as conditions for philosophy. Indeed, philosophy for Badiou is only possible on the condition that each of the four truth procedures are operative: "the lack of a single one gives rise to its dissipation, just as the emergence of all four [conditions] its apparition."[2] "The specific role of philosophy," then, "is to propose a unified conceptual space in which naming *takes place* of events that serve as the point of departure for truth procedures . . . [Philosophy] configurates the generic procedures, through a welcoming, a sheltering, built up with reference to their disparate simultaneity. Philosophy sets out to think its time by putting the state of the procedures conditioning it into a common place."[3] Otherwise put, the task of philosophy is to construct the formal category of Truth from the four material truths that condition it.

However, because of his emphasis on the irreducible singularity of science/mathematics, art/poetry, politics, and love as conditions for philosophy, Badiou has, on the whole, paid little attention to the mutual implication of each of these truth procedures. That is, although Badiou has provided extended analyses of the four truth procedures on their own terms, he has not, to date, provided any systematic treatment of the connection among the four truth procedures, of the ways in which these potentially cross each other. The problem has not gone unnoticed among interpreters of Badiou. For instance, at the end of an interview with Badiou, Justin Clemens asked him the following question:

> For you it seems absolutely crucial that love, mathematics, politics, they're absolutely separate, absolutely heterogeneous, they don't intermingle with each other in any way, yet in "What is love?" there are two sexuated positions, there's man who metaphorizes, and woman who knots the four truth-processes together. Insofar as these are a knotting—that is, in fidelity to an event of love a woman knots all of these—is one not in love when one is faithful to a political event?[4]

Badiou responded with the following answer, which acknowledges the problem but fails to give any adequate solution:

> The problem is the problem of the connection between the different procedures. It is a problem which is very interesting and complex. For instance, there are some similarities between politics and love, and I demonstrate this with technical concepts, numericity and the unnameable and so on; a singular connection between artistic creation and political thought also, and also a connection between love and science because love and science are the two procedures which don't know that they are procedures, in fact. It is not the same with

artistic creation. We know perfectly that it is a procedure of truth in rivalry with science. It is not the same, naturally, for other conditions. It is necessary to elaborate a general theory of the connections of the knots between different procedures but the difficult point is to have criteria for such an evaluation: however, it is possible once you have categories for the different steps of the procedures. I am working on this point.[5]

The interview took place in 1999, and if, at that time, Badiou mentioned that he was "working on this point," any adequate discussion of it has failed to materialize.

In this paper, I provide a provisional attempt to understand the connection between Badiou's four truth procedures, though in so doing I hope to complicate some of Badiou's own claims, specifically regarding the relationship between scientific/mathematical truths and artistic/poetic truths. Although I focus primarily on the connection between scientific/mathematical truths and artistic/poetic truths, I full recognize that the conclusions reached need to be supplemented with consideration of the relationship among the four truth procedures taken as a whole. My focus on the relationship between science/mathematics and art/poetry, however, is not just for the sake of expediency. On the one hand, as Badiou points out in the quotation above, the relationship between these two truth procedures is peculiar in that they are often considered rivals in regard to the question of truths. Indeed, as we will see, this is a rivalry that goes to the heart of Badiou's equation of mathematics and ontology. Nevertheless, it is a rivalry that simultaneously must be alleviated since, for Badiou, "the writing of philosophy is constantly obliged to span two ostensibly incompatible registers, that of mathematical formalization and that of poetic diction."[6] On the other hand, focusing on the relationship between science/mathematics and art/poetry also provides an opportunity to begin to think about a theopoetics at work in Badiou's philosophy, albeit a theopoetics that Badiou himself would no doubt disavow.

The first part of this paper discusses the separation Badiou institutes between science/mathematics and art/poetry in the ontological register of his thought. As I discuss in this section, mathematics, for Badiou, provides the ontological condition for philosophy and, in so doing, goes about its work without recourse to poem, which can only lead the thought of being qua being astray. The second part of this paper discusses Badiou's attempt to treat the poem as a truth procedure in its own right. Although Badiou banishes poem from ontology, such banishment, on his own account, frees it up for its vocation as a singular operation of truth, one that is concerned with manifesting the power of language. Indeed, as I show, insofar as the truth of poem lies in its relation to language, it functions within each of Badiou's four truth procedures as that which allows for the naming of an event. It is on the basis of this notion of naming that I think we can begin to sketch a theopoetics at work in Badiou's philosophy. I attempt to do so, albeit briefly, in the conclusion, where I draw on Whitehead's theopoetic understanding of God.

Mathematics against Poetics: The Place of Ontology

As mentioned above, part of Badiou's philosophical program consists in developing a mathematically based, and hence rational and deductive, ontology. The call for such an ontology, and the construction of that ontology itself, is condensed in the difficult and contentious claim, first made in *Being and Event,* that "mathematics *is* ontology."[7] Understanding the sense of this claim is part of the goal of this section. But it is important to emphasize that the discussion that follows in no way attempts to discuss in detail the main themes of Badiou's ontology (the priority of multiple-being-without-One, belonging and inclusion, the void as the proper name of being, the transfinite, etc.), even if many of these themes inevitably come up throughout this section and the rest of the paper. Rather, the purpose of this section is more formal in nature, in that I seek to isolate mathematics as a truth procedure through a reading of the disjunction that Badiou forces between it and poetic speech.[8]

A good place to begin for working out an understanding of this disjunction is Badiou's call for a "contemporary atheism," an atheism that attempts to think through and beyond the death of what he sees as the three "gods" that continue to hold thought captive: the God of metaphysics, the God of religion, and the God of the poem.[9] A full discussion of the death of the first two gods—the God of religion and the God of metaphysics—need not detain us here, since the substance of Badiou's claims should be familiar enough. Suffice it to say that Badiou, following Nietzsche, takes it for granted that the time of the God of religion, that is, the God of faith who governs the lives of individuals and the course of history, has passed. As Badiou puts it:

God is dead means that He is no longer the living being who can be encountered when existence breaks the ice of its own transparency. That so and so declares to the press that He was encountered under a tree, or in a provincial chapel, changes nothing. For we know that from such an encounter no thought can use its rights to advantage any longer, let alone do we grant someone claiming to see specters more than the positive consideration of a symptomatic manifestation.[10]

Badiou does not so much argue this claim as simply declare it: "I take the formula 'God is dead' literally. It *has* happened. Or, as Rimbaud said, it has passed. God is finished. And religion is finished, too."[11] Such a claim is, perhaps, not surprising for one who describes himself as "irreligious by heredity."[12] Likewise, Badiou, in line with much twentieth- and twenty-first-century philosophy—and, it is important to note, many significant strands of theology—rejects the God of metaphysics, that is, the ontotheo-logical God that does little more than guarantee the consistency of the concept. In order to finish up with this God, it is necessary, according to Badiou, to unbind the infinite from the One. As Badiou puts it, "The key point is to unseal the infinite from its millenary collusion with the One. It is to restitute the infinite to the banality of manifold-being, as mathematics has invited us to do since Cantor. For it is as a suture of the infinite and the One that the supposed transcendence of the metaphysical God is constructed."[13] Or, as Badiou puts it elsewhere, "There is no God. Which also means: the One is not."[14]

However, it is also necessary to declare the death of what Badiou refers to as the God of the poets. Concerning this God, Badiou writes:

It is neither the living Subject of religion, although it is certainly about living close to Him. Nor is it the Principle of metaphysics, although it is all about finding in His proximity the fleeing sense of Totality. It is that from which, for the poet, there is the enchantment of the world. As there is also its loss, which exposes one to idleness. About this God, we can say that It is neither dead nor alive. And It cannot be deconstructed as a tired, saturated, or sedimented concept. The central poetic expression concerning It is as follows: this God has withdrawn and left the world as prey to idleness. The question of the poem is thus that of the retreat of the gods. It coincides neither with the philosophical question of God nor with the religious one.[15]

Given his attempt to return ontology to its putative poetic foundations, Badiou's target in this quotation is, not surprisingly, Heidegger, even if Badiou elsewhere praises Heidegger as "the last universally recognizable philosopher."[16] Far from moving beyond metaphysics by turning to the poetic utterances of the pre-Socratics and select Germans, Badiou argues that Heidegger's thinking remains "enslaved" to what Badiou takes as "the essence of metaphysics; that is, the figure of being as endowment and gift, as presence and opening, and the figure of ontology as the offering of a trajectory of proximity."[17] From Badiou's perspective, Heidegger's "poetic ontology" lapses into a quasi-mythical discourse "haunted by the dissipation of Presence and the loss of the origin."[18] So much is evident in Heidegger's well-known claim, oft cited by Badiou, in his posthumously published *Der Spiegel* interview that "philosophy will not be able to effect an immediate transformation of the present condition of the world. This is not only true of philosophy, but of all merely human thought and endeavor. Only a god can save us."[19] Such a statement, taken in light of Heidegger's philosophy as a whole, manifests nothing more than a nostalgic longing for or "retroactive anticipation"[20] of the "re-enchantment of the world."[21] According to Badiou, "To say 'only a God can save us' means: the thinking that poets teach—educated by cognition of the Platonic turning, renewed by interpretation of the Presocratic Greeks—may uphold at the heart of nihilism the possibility, devoid of any way or means open to utterance, of a resacralization of the Earth."[22]

For this reason, Badiou understands the Heideggerian entanglement of ontology with the poem, with poetic speech in general, as ultimately concealing a religious impulse. More specifically, it allows for "the return of the religious."[23] That is, suturing the thinking of being qua being to thought of the poem irretrievably ties the thinking of being to the circulation of sense, which can only lead to a quasi-mystical and mystifying longing for Presence from within the finitude of existence. "Only a god can save us." According to Badiou, "As long as finitude remains the ultimate determination of existence, God abides. He abides as that whose disappearance continues to hold sway over us, in the form of the abandonment, the dereliction, or the leaving-behind of Being."[24] Or, as he puts it otherwise, "Finitude is like the trace of an afterlife in the movement that entrusts the overcoming of the religion-God and the metaphysics-God to the poem-God."[25]

Badiou's attempt to ground ontology in mathematics in disjunction from the alluring and mystifying power of the poetic utterance, then, is in large measure a way to bring the death of God—understood in three senses as the God of religion, the God of metaphysics, and the God of the poem—to its ultimate conclusion. For, as Badiou writes, it is only mathematics that allows for "break with superstition and ignorance. Mathematics is . . . that singular form of thinking which has *interrupted the sovereignty of myth*. We owe to it the first form of self-sufficient thinking, independent of any sacred form of enunciation; in other words, the first form of an entirely secularized thinking."[26] Or, in more polemical terms:

Mathematics provides philosophy with a weapon, a fearsome machine of thought, a catapult aimed at the bastions of ignorance, superstition, and mental servitude. It is not a docile grammatical region. . . . The mathematical realm does not acknowledge the existence of spiritualist categories such as those of the unthinkable and the unthought, supposedly exceeding the meager resources of human reason; or of those skeptical categories which claim we cannot ever provide a definitive solution to a problem or a definitive answer to a serious question.[27]

In this much, Badiou sides with Plato. Correlative to Plato's banishment of the poets from the ideal *politeia* because of the corrupting power of their art, Badiou casts out the thought of the poem from ontology because of poetic utterance's tendency to suture thought to the unthought, which all too easily leads to the restoration of "ignorance, superstition, and mental servitude." What poetic thought and speech is ultimately against, for both Plato and Badiou, is *dianoia* or discursive thought. In Badiou's words, "*Dianoia* is the thought that traverses, the thought that links and deduces. The poem itself is affirmation and delectation—it does not traverse, it dwells on the threshold. The poem is not a rule-bound crossing, but rather an offering, a lawless proposition."[28]

Hence, to ground ontology in mathematics, to claim that "mathematics is ontology," is to make a claim about discourse. Although Badiou stresses that the statement "mathematics is ontology" should be taken literally, he is quick to point out that the statement "does not in any way declare that being is mathematical, which is to say composed of mathematical objectivities."[29] He goes on to state, "It is not a thesis about the world but about discourse. It affirms that mathematics, throughout the entirety of its historical becoming, pronounces what is expressible of being qua being."[30] That is to say, "mathematics writes that which, of being itself, is pronounceable in the field of a pure theory of the Multiple."[31] Mathematics is able to take up this position because, contra the poem, it subtracts itself from the circulation of sense. The language of mathematics proposes "the rigor of the subtractive, in which being is said solely as that which cannot be supposed on the basis of any presence or experience."[32] What Badiou finds important, in this sense, is the sheer formality of mathematical language, its axiomatic prescriptions and discursive procedures, which allows it to think rigorously and in general terms the structure of any situation without recourse to the meaning of that situation. In Badiou's words, "Set theory, considered as an adequate thinking of the pure multiple, or of the presentation of presentation, *formalizes* any situation whatsoever insofar as it reflects the latter's being as such; that is, the multiple of multiples which makes up any presentation."[33] That is, mathematics is able to think what it thinks—being qua being—precisely because of the generality and universality of its language. Mathematics is, to use the words of Justin Clemens and Jon Roffe, "as pure as reason gets, i.e., mathematics is at once non-empirical, axiomatic, deductive, extra-linguistic, non-definitional, universalizing."[34]

It is worth pointing out that Badiou's understanding of mathematics, here, is not at all out of the ordinary. For instance, although he does not directly make the claim that ontology is mathematics as does Badiou, Alfred North Whitehead, himself both a mathematician and philosopher, expresses a similar view on the function of mathematical language.[35] As Whitehead points out, the uniqueness of pure mathematics lies in its endeavor to attain complete abstraction. As Whitehead puts it, "The point of mathematics is that in it we have always got rid of the particular instance, and even of any particular sorts of entities. So that for example, no mathematical truths apply merely to fish, or merely to stones, or merely to colors. So long as you are dealing with pure mathematics, you are in a realm of complete and absolute abstraction."[36] In contrast to natural, particular languages, which always maintain some immediate relationship with particular situations, mathematics "is the resolute attempt to go the whole way in the direction of complete analysis, so as to separate the elements of mere matter of fact from the purely abstract conditions which they exemplify."[37] For this reason, Whitehead avers that "mathematics is *thought* moving in the sphere of complete abstraction from any particular instance of what it is talking about."[38] In Badiou's terminology, mathematics as ontology thinks being as such as *"the presentation of presentation."*[39]

Nevertheless, we should be careful to avoid the assumption that the identification of ontology with mathematics amounts merely to the utility of mathematical language, as described above. In addition to the specific utility that mathematics allows with regard to the thinking of being qua being subtracted from sense, it is also the case that mathematics qua ontology is a truth procedure, which in this context means that it—and it alone—accesses being intrinsically. Badiou is, of course, well aware that ontology has throughout its history fallen under the jurisdiction of philosophy. Indeed, Badiou even emphasizes that the question of being qua being is primarily philosophical in nature. Nevertheless, according to Badiou, it now falls to mathematics to provide an "answer" to the philosophical question. In Badiou's words, "the science of being qua being *has existed* since the Greeks—such is the sense and status of mathematics."[40] If the ontological destiny of mathematics has gone largely unrecognized until now, this is because "it is only today that we have the means to *know* this."[41] We know this, according to Badiou, in the wake of Georg Cantor's mathematical rationalization of the infinite, a rationalization that is fundamental to Badiou's entire philosophical enterprise and, indeed, any attempt to take leave of the theme of finitude. For if the contemporary task of ontology is to unbind being from the One and deliver it over to the multiple dissemination of the infinite, then this is precisely what has been accomplished in post-Cantorian mathematics:

> Mathematics localizes *a plurality of infinites* in the indifference of the pure multiple. It has processed the actual infinite via the banality of cardinal number. It has neutralized and completely deconsecrated the infinite, subtracting it from the metaphorical register of the tendency, the horizon, becoming. It has torn it from the realm of the One in order to disseminate it—whether as infinitely small or infinitely large—in the *aura*-free typology of multiplicities. By initiating a thinking in which the infinite is irrevocable separated from every instance of the One, mathematics has, in its own domain, successfully consummated the death of God.[42]

In contrast to poetic thought and ontologies, which tend to push the infinite into the beyond of sense, into the unthought, mathematics, under the pressure of Cantor's construction of transfinite numbers, renders the infinite "fully transmissible within knowledge."[43] Mathematics, in this sense, provides the ontological condition for philosophy and, in so doing, seemingly goes about its work without recourse to the poem, which can only lead the thinking of being qua being astray. What, then, is left for the poem? It is to this question that we now turn.

Naming: The Truth of the Poem

As we discussed in the last section, Badiou, in a move correlative to Plato's infamous banishment of the poets from the ideal *politeia,* forces the poem and poetic thought and speech in general out of the ontological domain, a domain that belongs to mathematics alone. Badiou insists on the disjunction between mathematics and the poem at the ontological level because mathematics allows for the construction of a rational ontology based on a secularized notion of the infinite. In a statement that directly opposes the Heideggerian program in ontology and, perhaps, all poetic ontologies in general, Badiou thus states, "the science of being qua being *has existed* since the Greeks—such is the sense and status of mathematics."[44] However, there is much to suggest that this disjunction is less straightforward than it would appear on the surface, especially if we consider the role of naming in regard to truths.

To begin with, consider the case of Plato. Plato, as we know, banishes the poets and their art from the ideal *politeia*. According to Plato, poetry, as well as the mimetic arts in general, "produces a product that is far removed from truth in the accomplishment of its task, and associates with the part in us that is remote from intelligence, and is its companion and friend for no sound and true purpose."[45] Poetry and the mimetic arts, on Plato's account, appeal to the irrational, appetitive part of the soul rather than the rational, that is, "to the emotions of sex and anger, and all the appetites and pains and pleasures of the soul which we say accompany all our actions."[46] That is, "poetic imitation . . . waters and fosters these feelings when what we ought to do is dry them up, and it establishes them as our rulers when they out to be ruled, to the end that we may be better and happier men instead of worse and more miserable."[47] Because the poem has within itself "the power to corrupt," Plato argues that "we can admit no poetry into our city save only hymns to the gods and the praises of good men."[48]

Yet, as Badiou rightly points out, even Plato, whom Badiou holds up as the paradigm for understanding the disjunction between mathematics and poetry, could not maintain such a sharp distinction between the two. On the one hand, Plato allows for the possibility of allowing the poetry and the mimetic arts into the *politeia*. Immediately after the long discussion in the *Republic* on the necessity of banishing the poets, Plato thus has Socrates add the following caveat: "But nevertheless let it be declared that, if the mimetic and dulcet poetry can show any reason for her existence in a well-governed state, we would gladly admit her."[49] On the other hand, Plato himself often lapses into poetic utterance and imagery when the perceived limits of discursive thought are reached. As Badiou puts it:

> He could not do this because he himself had explored the limits of *dianoia,* of discursive thought. When it is a question of the supreme principle, of the One or the Good, Plato must admit that we are here "epekeina tes ousias," "beyond substance," and consequently that we are beyond everything that exposes itself in the incision of the Idea. Plato must avow that the donation in thought of this supreme principle—which is the donation in thought of a Being beyond beings—does not let itself be traversed by any kind of *dianoia.* Plato must himself resort to images, like that of the sun; to metaphors, like those of "prestige" or "power"; to myths, like the myth of Er the Pamphylian returning to the kingdom of the dead. In short, when what

is at stake is the opening of thought to the principle of the thinkable, when thought must be absorbed in the grasp of what establishes it *as thought*, we witness Plato himself submitting language to the power of poetic speech.[50]

Now, Badiou rejects the Platonic positing of being beyond being as little more than a feature of an ontology of presence, which contrasts with his own mathematical ontology.[51] Nevertheless, the problem of the limits of *dianoia* or discursive thought still remains—and this is where the poem comes in.

In order to understand what is at stake here, it is important to emphasize that Badiou's banishment of the poem from the domain of ontology is not, on his account, a swipe at the poem as such. The problem lies, rather, in confusing the procedure of mathematical-ontological truth with that of the poem, a problem that, at a basic level, results from the suturing of philosophy to one—and only one—of its conditions.[52] Badiou thus insists, "Examined from the vantage point of philosophy, both the poem and the matheme are inscribed within the general form of a truth procedure."[53] We could say that, similar to the way in which Kant "found it necessary to deny knowledge in order to make room for faith,"[54] Badiou sees the barring of the poem from ontology as freeing up the poem for its vocation as a truth procedure in its own right. The philosophical limitation of ontology to mathematics thus "liberates the poem, the poem as a singular operation of truth."[55] Badiou proposes, then, a limitation on the Platonic expulsion of the poem: The poem has no place in ontology, but it does have a place among the four truth procedures, meaning that it is an irreducible condition for philosophy.

What is it, though, that constitutes the singularity of poem, of poetic speech, qua truth procedure? How are we to understand "the poem's genuinely intelligible vocation"?[56] Badiou describes the poem in the following terms:

> The poem is neither a description nor an expression. Nor is it an affected painting of the world's extension. The poem is an operation. The poem teaches us that the world does not present itself as a collection of objects. The world is not what "objects" to thought. For the operations of the poem, the world is that thing whose presence is more essential than objectivity.[57]

The poem, according to Badiou, is not primarily concerned with a "description" or "expression" of the world, taken as an object of and for interpretation. Indeed, Badiou credits the modern poets—Hölderlin, Mallarmé,

Rimbaud, Trakl, Pessoa, Madelstam, and Celan, to name a few—with effecting "the destitution of the category of the object, and of objectivity, as necessary forms of presentation."[58] The poem, then, as a condition for philosophy, is not primarily concerned with meaning. Rather, on Badiou's account, it is an "operation," an operation of truth that invites one to enter into it to think its thought. "To enter into the poem—not in order to know what it means, but rather to think what happens in it. Because the poem is an operation, it is also an event. The poem takes place. The superficial enigma points to this taking place. It offers us a taking place in language."[59] That is, what characterizes the poem, and poetic utterance in general, "is its capacity to manifest the powers of language itself."[60]

Otherwise put, I have mentioned that both mathematics and poetry have the general form of a truth procedure. Indeed, Badiou even indicates that both have as their reference point the pure multiple, out of which both mathematics and poetry make truth. But whereas mathematics qua ontology makes truth out of the presentation of inconsistent multiplicity, the void, poetry "makes truth out of the multiple, conceived as a presence that has come to the limits of language. Put otherwise, poetry is the song of language qua capacity to make the pure notion of the 'there is' present in the very effacement of empirical objectivity."[61] As a making-present of the "there is," poetry situates the power of language at the threshold between absence and presence, disappearance and appearance. The poetic act, as the manifest power of language, is fundamentally a naming, even if it cannot name its power to name itself. Poetry pushes the limits of language so as to effect "a powerful anticipation, a forcing of language enacted by the advent of an 'other' language that is at once immanent and created."[62] Poetry addresses itself to the infinite "in order to direct the power of language toward the retention of a disappearance."[63]

Now, what is interesting in this articulation of poetry as the power of language "to make present the pure notion of the 'there is,'" to effect "the advent of an 'other' language," "to direct the power of language toward the retention of a disappearance," is that it dovetails with how Badiou often characterizes his notion of the event. Indeed, the similarity is far from accidental, since poetic speech maintains a particular and privileged relationship to the event. On the one hand, as a singular truth procedure, poetry is, of course, the domain in which poetic events occur and are worked out as truth procedures through the composition of poetic works.[64] On the other hand, and crucially, poetry is related to any event that occurs in any of the four domains precisely because "in summoning the retention of what disappears, every name of an event or of the eventual presence is in its essence poetic."[65] To quote Badiou on this important point:

When the situation is saturated by its own norm, when the calculation of itself is inscribed there without respite, when there is no longer a void between knowledge and prediction, then one must be *poetically* ready for the outside-of-self. For the nomination of an event—in the sense in which I speak of it, that is, an undecidable supplementation which must be named to occur for a being-faithful, thus for a truth—*this* nomination is *always* poetic. To name a supplement, a chance, and incalculable, one must draw from the void of sense, in default of established significations, to the peril of language. One must therefore poeticize, and the poetic name of the event is what throws us outside of ourselves, through the flaming ring of predictions.[66]

Now, for Badiou, the event, the occurrence of something new that induces a subject and allows for the possibility of constructing a procedure of truth, always breaks with the logic governing the situation in which it occurs. Because of this, the belonging of an event to a situation, its existence in that situation, is, strictly speaking, undecidable or unprovable from within the situation itself. In the technical language of Badiou's ontology, the event is "supernumerary to the site," meaning that it eludes the count-as-one of the situation.[67] To put the matter in different terms, the event occurs at the limits of *dianoia,* or discursive thought, meaning that the latter cannot grasp the event, since discursivity is one of the features of the situation. Because the belonging of an event to a situation is in essence undecidable, the only way to make an event effective for a situation, to make it susceptible to the production of truth, is to make a wager on its belonging to the situation, a wager that, from the perspective of the situation, must always be illegitimate and illegal. What is needed is what Badiou terms an "intervention," which he defines as "any procedure by which a multiple is recognized as an event."[68] However, in order for the event to be susceptible to interventional decision regarding its belonging to the situation, the event must also be named. In Badiou's words:

The act of nomination of the event is what constitutes it, not as real—we will always posit that this multiple has occurred—but susceptible to a decision concerning its belonging to a situation. The essence of the intervention consists—within the field opened up by an alternative hypothesis, whose *presented* object is the site (a multiple on the edge of the void), and which concerns the "there is" of an event—in naming this "there is" and in unfolding the consequences of this nomination in the space of the situation to which the site belongs.[69]

Naming, as Badiou makes clear in this quotation, is not to be confused with an event. Nevertheless, insofar as an event immediately disappears after it appears, nomination functions as the trace of an aleatory event—its "there is"—which allows an event to be submitted to decision and made available for the formation of a truth.

Now, once the event is named, it can become subject to *dianoia* or discursive thought, that is, to a formation of a truth. Such is the sense of Badiou's notion of fidelity to the event, which consists in a set of procedures or inquiries that attempt to draw the consequences of the event for the situation.[70] However, discursive fidelity is only possible on the basis of a prior interventional decision, which, as tied to naming, is irreducibly poetic, as is the construction of the subject language proper to the construction of a new truth.[71] What this means is that all events—whether they are mathematical, poetic, political, or amorous—require a poetic supplement in order to make them available for thought. Otherwise put, the construction of all truth procedures depends in some fashion on poetics, the power of language. What this means, in effect, is that the disjunction between mathematics and poetry, so important to Badiou's ontology, is more complicated than he himself lets on. Based on what we have said, it would seem that the positing of the disjunction between mathematics and poetry and the thesis that "ontology is mathematics" are poetic claims, since they rely on naming mathematics in general and particular mathematical concepts as significant for the production of ontological truth. Badiou seems to indicate as much when he notes that the disjunction between "these two regimes of thought," between mathematics and poetry, must be marked "within language."[72] Thus it would seem that Badiou's mathematical ontology, predicated on the disjunction between mathematics and poetry, is at least minimally conditioned by a prior and irreducible poetic intervention, on poetic truth.

Conclusion: Toward a Badiouian Theopoetics

In the final section of *Process and Reality*, Whitehead suggests that we understand God as "the poet of the world." To quote him fully on this point, "God's role is not the combat of productive force with productive force, of destructive force with destructive force; it lies in the patient operation of the overpowering rationality of his conceptual harmonization. He does not create the world, he saves it; or, more accurately, he is the poet of the world, with tender patience leading it by his vision of truth, beauty, and goodness."[73] That is, for Whitehead, God is not to be understood along ontotheological lines, as the necessary and sufficient ground of the world. Such a conception of God, according to Whitehead, can only be static, in that it separates God from the flux of the actual material world. Rather than being concerned primarily with creation, with grounding or establishing the world, Whitehead's God is, as Roland Faber emphasizes, concerned primarily with salvation. In Faber's words, Whitehead's God "is interested not in creation, but in *salvation*. In organic philosophy, God's role is not to *ground* or *establish* the world (ontotheologically), but to reconcile it (soteriologically)."[74]

The sense of this soteriological understanding of God is multifaceted, involving as it does the complexity of Whitehead's system as a whole. As Faber emphasizes, Whitehead's definition of God as the poet of the world means, at least, that "God appears as the source of the genuine future and of spheres of possibility, as the Logos of organic order, as the ground of subjectivity, as the intensive meaning of existence, as the guarantor of personal identity, as the eschatological meaning of the history of both life and the world, and as the contrafactual 'unity' of the process."[75] Although we cannot here go into detail concerning each of these notions, Whitehead's theopoetic understanding of God, I want to suggest, allows us to begin to sketch a theopoetic reading of Badiou's philosophy. To be clear, Badiou would, of course, have no interest in such a project. Although Badiou often uses theological concepts in a secularized fashion, he is, by his own account and in light of the death of the God of religion, the God of metaphysics, and the God of the poem, an atheist through and through. Thus Badiou claims, "I need neither God nor the divine."[76] Moreover, in reading Badiou theopoetically, I am aware that I leave myself open to the charge of distorting Badiou's philosophy in a way that perhaps unduly poeticizes it, especially given Badiou's painstaking attempts to limit the function of the poem. It is, I think, fair to say that I am reading Badiou against the grain here. But if the argument presented above concerning the role of naming, the role of poetic intervention, in each of the four truth procedures (science, art, politics, love) is sound, such a reading seems warranted. Indeed, given what I have argued above, my claim is that a poetic element is already at work, even if its role is not always explicitly thematized or even actively disavowed. It is on this basis that I think it possible to bring Badiou's philosophy into the realm of theopoetics, without, however, ignoring the difficulties that such a reading may pose.

As Faber emphasizes, Whitehead views novelty in radical terms. The radical nature of the new "appears precisely where its appearance is accompanied by the unexpected, the surprising (or even frightening) element of something otherwise inaccessible that can *in no way* be derived from the old."[77] To quote Faber more fully on this point:

The essentially new for Whitehead is that which is *wholly unrealized,* not merely that which "could be" (the form of possibility of an antic- ipatory prognosis), but rather that which is wholly uninvented. . . . That which is "uninvented" (or radically "invented") is, on the one hand, *possible* insofar as new events feel and then actualize that which is radically new in connection with their origin (real possibilities); it is, on the other hand, *impossible* because it simply does not in any way reside within the horizon of the possible *before* actually entering, *wholly unexpectedly,* into that horizon.[78]

Although Whitehead's events and Badiou's events are not exactly the same, since for Badiou events are extremely rare, their respective understandings of novelty have in common the notion that novelty is the radically new, as that which exceeds the horizon of expectation.[79] In Badiou's terms, the event is a "supernumerary" supplement, which entails that its existence be, strictly speaking, undecidable from the perspective of the situation. The decision to name the event poetically, then, is what makes it available for the construction of truth.

It is this poetic element, necessary for the production of all truths, that seems to imply a theopoetics, even if Badiou would not recognize it as such. Indeed, the act of naming literally saves an event from falling by the wayside, from its undecidability, making it available for the production of truths. Moreover, Badiou himself notes that there is a certain homology between his notion of processes of truth and the creative activity of God.[80] In light of this, it is important to point out that Badiou has been criticized precisely on this point, in that the notion of naming would seem to im- ply some form of transcendence, a transcendence traditionally associated with God. That is, as Badiou summarizes the criticisms leveled against the importance of nomination for his theory of the event, the act of nomina- tion seems to imply "a mysterious naming" that occurs "from above."[81] In light of such criticisms, Badiou has attempted, in *Logics of Worlds,* to develop things in a different direction, without explicit recourse to the act of nomination.[82] Instead of referring the efficacy of the event to the act of nomination, Badiou speaks of the effects of the event as the event's "trace," and attempts to develop a logic of the sites, not all of which are necessarily eventual as in *Being and Event,* in reference to the distribution of various intensities of appearing, in which the site is more directly related to the consequences drawn from it.[83] However, Badiou does not, I would claim, drop the poetic function of naming; naming is, rather, folded more imma- nently into the processes of truths themselves, as a type of self-reflexivity between the event and its subjective unfolding.[84]

Interestingly enough, this brings Badiou closer to Whitehead's own conception. For Whitehead, novelty, understood as the essentially new, cannot be accounted for solely in terms of the world, otherwise it would not be the essentially new. It is here that God comes in for Whitehead. God is the "source" of such novelty as the "absolute future" of the world.[85] Crucially, however, this conception of God as the "absolute future" of the world implies neither unilateral action nor transcendence, at least in the traditional sense: God's activity qua novelty is, rather, folded into the immanent becoming of the world as event. Likewise, if Badiou's theory of poetic naming seems to require, at least structurally, a more traditional top-down notion of transcendence, I would suggest that the revised conception in *Logics of Worlds* does not so much get rid of the poetic function as immanentize it as self-reflexive. We could, in this regard, conceive of events and their naming for truth along the lines of a theopoetic unfolding, in which subjectivizable bodies simultaneously give form to and are formed by the poetic articulation of truths. Doing so would, I think, be in line with the much more prominent place that Badiou seems to give to poetics as such, in both form and content, in *Logics of Worlds*.

This sketch of a theopoetics at work in Badiou's philosophy is, admittedly, all too brief, and much more work needs to be done. Nevertheless, if the analysis of the function of poetics in Badiou's philosophy given above holds, then I hope that it represents a fruitful place from which to begin the construction of a theopoetics both in and with Badiou.

Kierkegaardian Theopoiesis
Selfhood, Anxiety, and the Multiplicity of Human Spirits

SAM LAURENT

Søren Kierkegaard, a seemingly unlikely interlocutor for theopoetic discourse, and indeed not here wholly folded into this emergent school of thought, nonetheless shared with this contemporary movement a resistance to the hegemonic claims of enlightenment rationality. Against the monolithic historical dialectic posited by Hegel, Kierkegaard emerged as a voice of individualism, his emphasis on the individual and the process of selfhood affirming that, as Mark C. Taylor says, "he holds spiritlessness to arise from the dissipation of individual selfhood created by abstract reflection."[1] Rather than seek to encounter spirit on a societal scale, Kierkegaard seeks to draw forth a resurgence of spirit through individual dialectical movements that rescue authentic selfhood from the assured historical trajectory he feared in Hegelianism. Taylor sums Kierkegaard's move thus: "The purpose of Kierkegaard's diverse writings is to engender inwardness by making people aware of the depths to which they have fallen and by creating the possibility for them to begin the journey from despair to realized selfhood."[2] The creation of the possibility for such movement, claims Taylor, marks Kierkegaard's work as *poiesis*, not *theoria*.[3] Indeed, this essay will argue that Kierkegaard's sense of poiesis extends beyond the rhetoric of selfhood to the very process of being an authentic self in his thought. Identifying the aporia of logic as the inbreaking of possibility and uncertainty, Kierkegaard understands this process to be a turbulent one, characterized at various points by despair, fear and trembling, and anxiety. Selfhood is for Kierkegaard an active process of becoming. As such, elements of Kierkegaard's articulation of selfhood will be found to be in harmony with contemporary understandings of divine relationship to the world as *theopoiesis*. This harmony offers a vision of radically democratic creative processes that better society precisely through the individual's greeting of possibility.

By first attending to Kierkegaard's understanding of logic in relation to time, this essay will highlight the relationship between freedom and possibility at the core of his conception of selfhood. Treating logic essentially as a descriptive endeavor, Kierkegaard confines its operation to analysis of the past; the actualization of possibility that constitutes the present's interface with the future exceeds the capacities of logic. The work of actualization is for Kierkegaard a harrowing endeavor taken on by individuals who must leave the comfort of the known to confront the uncertainty of the future. Framed by Kierkegaard with the concepts of despair and anxiety, the experience of being selfhood underscores the riskiness of becoming, and instills each moment with the key dynamism of what Alfred North Whitehead would later call an "event." The process paradigm will offer a hermeneutic for reading Kierkegaard in which the relationships that shape the individual are what create the tension of anxiety felt by Kierkegaard's future-oriented subject.

The anxiety of selfhood then offers a framework on which to explore the relationship between the self and God. Drawing from Helene Talon Russell's recent work on Kierkegaardian selfhood, I will situate the experience of anxiety within a paradigm of the "divine matrix" as depicted by Roland Faber. The necessary multiplicity inherent in the experience of selfhood, as argued for by Russell, is in fact the engine of anxiety. In Kierkegaard's language, "anxiety is freedom's actuality as the possibility of possibility."[4] Thus, the dialectical tension of selfhood, a key rebuttal to Hegel's historical dialectic, relies on the presence of possibility, which for Kierkegaard and for process theology means the presence of God. Kierkegaard's poetic method of drawing his reader into engagement of possibilities reflects an anthropology reliant on theopoiesis. The spirit that Kierkegaard seeks to reinstill in society is operative at the level of these individual experiences of self-relation.

The final section of this paper then ponders the ethical implications of such a notion of selfhood as point of contact between God and world. Following through on Kierkegaard's argument for selfhood, I will suggest that society can be described as a collective of spirits. Further employing Faber's theology of the divine matrix, Kierkegaard's individually located spirit, a "human matrix," will be situated in an interconnected societal field of other such human spirits, each of which negotiates its future in an intensely relational context. Any movement of society necessarily comes about through negotiation of its multiple constituents. Furthermore, a notion of future progress in this Kierkegaardian theopoetic scheme relies on society's ability to benefit from the actualization of possibility accessed by individuals in their negotiation of selfhood. Kierkegaard's own emphasis on individual selfhood would seem to protect such access within society, but a theopoetic scheme offers a model of communication among individuals that relies not on an overarching narrative but, rather, as with the aesthetic thought of John Dewey, on the encouragement of creative endeavors to actualize new possibility. Social transformation will be shown to be a function of individual transformations, and therefore of a fostering of multiplicity within a society that holds social responsibility and individual freedom in a dynamic tension.

Logic and Poiesis

Kierkegaard's assessment of the spiritlessness of his age characterizes it as a "dissipation" of authentic selfhood. In particular, the human spirit is lost within social structures that, concerned with historical patterns, seek to assure a level of comfort to the individual via ordering of society. "When sociocultural forms function effectively," Taylor says, "people begin to feel at home in the world. But, Kierkegaard insists, though usually unnoticed, spiritlessness thrives in the homey atmosphere of the family parlor."[5] Such comfort leads to reflection taking the shape of a leisure activity, with a degree of detachment that Kierkegaard finds troubling. In particular, "the reflective quest for a universally valid truth leads one to become essentially an observer or spectator for whom subjective interest and individual decision cloud the objectivity of universal vision."[6] For Kierkegaard, this attempt at objectivity obscures the subjectivity of the individual. In particular, the notion of a historical dialectic operating on a social scale washes over the individual, fostering spiritlessness through subservience to reason. "Through this process, the individual becomes so identified with or integrated within the social totality of which he is a member that all sense of personal uniqueness and self-responsibility evaporate." As we shall see, it is precisely this sense of self-responsibility that Kierkegaard believes constitutes human spirit, and his critique of the preeminence of reason opens up space for a poetic articulation of spirit within society.

"In logic," Kierkegaard states in *The Concept of Anxiety,* "no movement must come about, for logic is, and whatever is logical only is."[7] Kierkegaard is here not decrying logic altogether so much as suggesting that it is not determinant of the future. "This impotence of the logical consists in the transition of logic into becoming, where existence and actuality come forth."[8] Becoming, for Kierkegaard, speaks to an interface with the future and implies a dynamism he finds logic unable to provide. This move comes about via a critique of Hegel's decision to entitle a concluding chapter of his *Encylopedia Logic* "Actuality." For Kierkegaard, this is a misstep, one that facilitates a passivity that he finds to be the absence of spirit in society. By naming his chapter thus, "he thereby gains the advantage of making it appear that in logic the highest has already been achieved, or if one prefers, the lowest."[9] In particular, Kierkegaard finds this to be a glossing over of contingency, "which is an essential part of the actual," and "cannot be admitted within the realm of logic."[10]

Here, a first point of connection emerges between Kierkegaard's thought and a theopoetic scheme; indeterminacy always characterizes the future. This contingency emerges from Kierkegaard's understanding of actuality. Kierkegaard scholar M. G. Piety explains the differentiation in Kierkegaard's thought between reality and actuality: "Reality refers, according to Kierkegaard, to the mere presence of a thing, without any reference to how it came to be there. Actuality, by contrast, is always the result of a process of actualization."[11] Thus, for Kierkegaard actuality is brought about by a process of becoming, which, as we have seen, necessarily admits contingency. Furthermore, Kierkegaard's reliance on contingency is for him a reliance on God, whose presence in the dialectical construction of selfhood will prove to be a constant source of possibility in the experiences of individual beings. Possibility as a function of God's self-presentation to the world operates for Kierkegaard in much the same way that God's mediatory activity at the initial aim forges a field of possibilities in Whitehead's work. "Pure mental originality," Whitehead argues, "works by the canalization of relevance arising from the primordial nature of God. Thus, an originality in the temporal world is conditioned, though not determined, by an initial subjective aim supplied by the ground of all of order and of all originality."[12] This resonance between Kierkegaard and Whitehead need not be taken as a complete harmonization; Kierkegaard's model of selfhood, which lends itself to a theopoetic understanding of personal existence, relies on a certain Platonic metaphysics of the sort Whitehead seeks to query in his work. Still, both move toward an embrace of contingency from the limitations of logic; for Kierkegaard this is the above declaration that logic simply *is* and does not *become*. Becoming is not characterized by necessity for Kierkegaard. As Mark C. Taylor observes, "Necessity characterizes purely atemporal relations of logical idealities and cannot be predicated of temporal reality."[13] Assuming that logic accounts for becoming overlooks the presence of contingency. Likewise, this dynamic describes

Whitehead's "fallacy of misplaced concreteness," which "consists in neglecting the degree of abstraction involved when an actual entity is considered merely so far as it exemplifies certain categories of thought."[14] The deduction of a logic inherent in already actualized—that is, past—events cannot lead to the presumption of control over future events. Such a logic inherently neglects the complexity of actuality and its constant exposure to contingency.

Whereas Whitehead diagnoses the fallacy of misplaced concreteness as the source of shortsighted epistemological claims, Kierkegaard expands his own recovery of contingency by articulating an inward dialectic within the experience of the individual person. This dialectic holds the world and possibility in a dynamic tension that posits the work of selfhood at the intersection of temporality and the eternal. From the initial point of connection with process theopoetics via an expansion beyond abstract logic, Kierkegaard's model of selfhood indeed inscribes each person in a theopoetic process. Through a reading of Kierkegaardian selfhood in discussion with contemporary process discourse, theopoiesis emerges as both site of and potential outlet for the anxieties of personal existence in society.

Multiplicity in Selfhood

"A human being is spirit," *The Sickness unto Death* begins, "but what is spirit?" Put neatly, if enigmatically, "spirit is the self."[15] But the difference between a self and a human being is, for Kierkegaard, central to understanding how the human spirit can reclaim the vitality of society. "A human being is a synthesis of the infinite and the finite, of the temporal and the eternal, of freedom and necessity, in short a synthesis."[16] This human being, by simply existing as a synthesis, has not achieved authentic selfhood. Selfhood, for Kierkegaard, is a much more daunting proposition. "The self is the conscious synthesis of infinitude and finitude that relates itself to itself, whose task is to become itself, which can be done only through the relationship to God. To become oneself is to become concrete."[17] Consciousness is for Kierkegaard the difference between being a human being and being a self; the self consciously relates its history to its future and assumes a conscious accountability for itself. The concreteness toward which Kierkegaard gestures highlights the nature of the human synthesis; the concrete emerges out of the synthesis of the finite and infinite, but not as a neat confluence; rather, concreteness is attained with great struggle, and disappointment. As a synthesis of finite and infinite, the human being is not itself infinite; it relates to a perception of the infinite self. Psychologically speaking, then, "this infinite self . . . is really only the most abstract form, the most abstract possibility of the self."[18] By its awareness of the infinite, the self despairs of its own finitude. "With the help of this infinite form, the self in despair wants to be master of itself or to create itself, to make his self into the self he wants to be, to determine what he will have or not have in his concrete self."[19] The exposure to infinitude inherent in the human being's dialectical composition generates the basic despair central to being human. The human being confronted with the concept of the infinite self "does not want to put on his own self, does not want to see his given self as his task—he himself wants to compose his self by means of being the infinite form."[20] God, for Kierkegaard, is encountered as this infinity, this realm of possibility that creates the tension between actual and ideal that vibrates through the self. This gesture toward selfhood—a selfhood at once inherited and forged—as a task encompasses the structure within Kierkegaard's thought in which a dynamic *theopoiesis* is readily visible. The concrete self emerges from the subject's negotiation of the necessity imparted by the physical world and the freedom of the infinite possibility offered by the eternal, infinite side of the dialectic. The concretion of a Kierkegaardian self is not unlike a Whiteheadian concrescence; the limitations of the given self determine the range of possibility for the new concrete self, which inherits a past and assumes responsibility for an indeterminate future. As indicated by Kierkegaard's language of despair, the negotiations of selfhood are, for the self, an experience of constant insecurity and dissatisfaction. This instability, I will argue, emerges from the multiplicity inherent in the human experience but does not call for a resolution of that multiplicity. Theopoiesis offers here a hermeneutic for reading the despair and anxiety of Kierkegaardian selfhood as not only the engines of individual creativity, but also as the seeds of social transformation.

Helene Tallon Russell's recent work on selfhood in Kierkegaard and Irigaray deepens the connection between a theopoetic understanding of the God–human relationship and Kierkegaard's construction of the self. Centering her examination of Kierkegaardian selfhood on the opening paragraph of *The Sickness unto Death,* Russell finds the dialectical poles the human being negotiates to be a foundational multiplicity undergirding the very experience of being human. "The pairs of constructive elements of existence—finitude and infinity, temporality and eternity, freedom and necessity—are not reducible to each other, nor reducible to a third term."[21] The self as conceived at this interface between the finite world and infinite possibility does not resolve the perceived gap but instead is constituted by the relationship such a gap calls into being. In a famously enigmatic sentence, Kierkegaard puts the self in exactly this relational position. "The self is a relation that relates itself to itself or is the relation's relating itself to itself in the relation; the self is not the relation but is the relation's relating itself to itself."[22] Russell's distillation captures the dynamism more lucidly: "a genuine self is complex, multiple, and internally related to itself."[23]

In her examination of Kierkegaard's dialectical construction of three spheres of living—the aesthetic, the ethical, and the religious—Russell focuses on the multiple poles navigated by the human being taking on the task of selfhood. It is the movement between the ethical and religious spheres that constitutes the rattling difficulty of selfhood illustrated through Kierkegaard's meditation on Abraham in *Fear and Trembling*. This work is, in Russell's words, "a praise of Abraham as the knight of faith. He is contrasted with the knight of infinite resignation, who is the model of ethical and universal norms."[24] The person who, standing in the ethical sphere (which constitutes engagement of reason and responsible participation in and service to society), then begins to partake in the religious sphere finds, in their encounter with the absolute, a singularly individual experience that does not translate into the established norms of the ethical sphere. "The religious person does not make decisions based solely on the universal norms of society, or on the logic of reason, nor on the external relations of human beings to one another. But decisions are made."[25] The religious sphere is, for the self, always a source of paradox, for it does not present an escape from the limitations of finite existence. Rather, the self exists astraddle the divide between the two spheres. "Kierkegaard views subjectivity as the activity of holding the ambiguity and multiplicity of many parts within the self."[26] By holding Abraham up as an archetype of this complex relational work in relationship with God, Kierkegaard conveys the discomfort of being in the position of a prophet. Abraham's decision to sacrifice Isaac as commanded put him at odds with the norm of his society, but such is the burden of the knight of faith. "Faith's paradox is this," says Kierkegaard, "that the single individual . . . determines his relation to the universal through his relation to the absolute, not his relation to the absolute through his relation to the universal."[27] Drawn from the aesthetic and ethical spheres toward the religious, the authentic self finds a true home in none of them, and thus experiences the despair of existing in constant tension.

Russell's language of multiplicity allows for a framing of this experience of selfhood within a theopoetic model. In particular, by positing the self as a synthesis of irreducible poles, Kierkegaard evokes a process of constant *becoming* rather than *being*, a constant unsettling exposure to uncertainty. While the self despairs at its inability to define itself within infinity, it also experiences what Kierkegaard calls an anxiety at the dynamism of existing beyond the limits of logic. Oriented toward the transformative possibilities encountered in the religious sphere, Kierkegaard's self feels the uncertainty that accommodates freedom—an anxiety at the possible consequences of this bold synthesis. The multiplicity of selfhood, brought about by the relationship of the imagined ideal self to the existing self, emerges as a microcosmic expression of the encounter of actuality and possibility in each moment, as the present. Anxiety is not fear or despair, but more a restlessness that pushes the self forward into the future.[28] Anxiety, like a dangling carrot, pulls the self forward from its existing, necessary self, toward an imagined possibility of itself. For Kierkegaard's psychological sensibility, anxiety functions much as the creative God–world relationship does for Whitehead, where it "introduces novelty into the content of the many."[29] Anxiety as experienced by the individual self is the difference that produces action, and which restores spirit to the subjective world.

> That anxiety makes its appearance is the pivot upon which everything turns. Man is a synthesis of the psychical and the physical; however, a synthesis is unthinkable if the two are not united in a third. This third is spirit. In innocence, man is not merely animal, for if he were at any moment of his life merely animal, he would never become man. So spirit is present, but as immediate, as dreaming.[30]

Spirit generates anxiety, acting as both "a hostile power, for it constantly disturbs the relation between the soul and body" and "a friendly power, since it is precisely that which constitutes the relation."[31] Thus, the relationship between the self and this constantly stirring spirit is one of anxiety, neither fear nor sheer hope but a state of perpetual uncertainty experienced in the midst of becoming.

Anxiety, then, might be read as a prefiguration of contemporary theopoetics in that it expresses a self enmeshed in, and indeed constituted by a relationality that itself always operates in flux rather than stasis. Indeed, Kierkegaard's understanding of the human-in-becoming as spirit gestures toward the dynamism of such a relational existence by defining the person not as a substance but as a relation. Such a vision of selfhood as a process of creative becoming can easily be labeled poetic, for the creation is more a particular arranging, a cosmological creativity than an ontological one. The move to theopoetics comes in the particular nature of the dreaming spirit; it is the capaciousness of a perceived infinity that allows for the imagination of transformative actualities. Kierkegaard's poetic method, highlighted earlier by Taylor, is in fact a highly *theo*poetic process, for it transcends the limitations of logic precisely in the encounter of God as source of new possibility. "This internal constant relationality is only possible in relationship with the divine," notes Russell.[32] Theopoetics ventures a description of divine activity in and through these relationships that will not only enrich the harmonization of Kierkegaardian selfhood with contemporary discourses of theopoetic multiplicity but will also deepen the ethical stakes of selfhood as such.

Roland Faber's *God as Poet of the World* offers a rich description of *Pneuma* that, when read analogously to the process of selfhood described by Kierkegaard, might help unfold the significance of "spirit" as a term for the human synthesis. "The Pneuma is the *divine matrix*. The Pneuma is that *mode of immanence* of the transcendent God (the divine superject) in the world through which God *longs for* the world, enters into it *kenotically*, and takes it up in *delimiting* it that it might become the body of Christ."[33] Beyond the semantic parallels of the Pneuma/Spirit of God and the spirit of the human being, the language of divine matrix offers a name for the vibratory intersection of human and divine, and in particular captures the fecundity of that place as ground of possibility for actuality. Viewed within the process of becoming, the divine matrix acts for the divine as the spirit does for the human. "The Pneuma is the *transpersonal person* in which everything has become itself *beyond* itself. Like all living persons, the Pneuma too is *not* determined by a given 'character' (form), being instead in what amounts to a virtually archetypal mode an 'entirely living nexus' of mutual immanence of all events."[34] The divine matrix then is the space in which the actualizing moment is infused with possibilities. Like the Kierkegaardian self, the divine matrix functions as relation. This divine matrix "stands not only for the immanence of the world in God, but just as much for the immanence of God in the world. In the Pneuma, these two immanences constitute a *single* continuum of communications between God and the world."[35] Kierkegaard's language of selfhood as a task, and especially one felt as anxiety and often despair, thus lends a particular vocabulary to the human experience of the divine matrix and points in particular to an active agency through which the becoming subject can enhance the communication of possibility into the world.

The locatedness of the self in time, as seen above, frustrates Kierkegaard's self, which would prefer to adopt an identity from the infinite possibilities of eternity, one not conditioned by a particular history. This issue of time finds particular resonance in theopoetic discourse, again with Faber: "The divine matrix is the bond in which God and world are mutually immanent, one in the other, in which world time and God's everlasting time mutually permeate each other, in which alpha and omega are positioned within a reconciled continuum."[36] This interface of the two "times" likewise constitutes the synthesis at the core of personhood and funds the anxiety associated with existing *as* that synthesis. While Kierkegaard's conception of time is, like that of process thought, a series of becoming moments, his understanding of eternity is rather classical. The eternal, in contrast to time, is "the present in terms of an annulled succession (time is the succession that passes by)."[37] The eternal has no past or future, for it is does not exist for Kierkegaard as a succession. The existence of the self at the intersection of temporality and eternity, a point or space that Kierkegaard calls "the moment," takes its meaning from this feature of eternity. "By the moment then, is understood that abstraction from the eternal that, if it is to be the present, is a part of it. The present is the eternal, or rather the eternal is the present, and the present is full."[38] Kierkegaard admits that this concept is difficult to comprehend, but what we get here is a sense that eternity is the realm of possibility encountered by the spirit in the temporal present.

The moment is that ambiguity in which time and eternity touch each other, and with this the concept of *temporality* is posited, whereby time constantly intersects eternity and eternity constantly pervades time. As a result, the above-mentioned division acquires its significance: the present time, the past time, the future time.[39]

Every actuality takes place in and through the presence of God. Kierkegaard's understanding of the self as performing its synthesis within a moment then further harmonizes with the event structure of process thought, though the world's time and God's time are inseparable in process cosmology. Nonetheless, the centering of the human experience and its sense of history around a point of intersection between the world and God in the present suggests that God here functions as a divine matrix, poetically enlivening temporality by its relationship to the ground of possibility.

Attention then turns to the future, "the incognito in which the eternal, even though it is incommensurable with time, nevertheless preserves its association with time."[40] The future exists for the human being as a dizzying realm of possibility unactualized in time, lying temporally ahead of the subject in time, but yet present in the interface with eternity. Recognition of one's participation in the succession of temporal events, of one's membership in the dialectical tension between freedom and necessity, the temporal and the eternal, the finite and the infinite, places the subject on a precipice that demands decision but that does not offer certainty for the future. "The possible corresponds exactly to the future. For freedom, the possible is the future, and the future is for time the possible."[41]

For Kierkegaard's spirit, the tensive location at the constant point of contact between time and eternity leads to a dynamic anxiety. Kierkegaard describes anxiety, then, as the very act of subjectivity at that intersection. "In a logical system, it is convenient to say that possibility passes over into actuality. However, in actuality it is not so convenient, and an intermediate term is required. That intermediate term is anxiety, but it no more explains the qualitative leap than it can justify it ethically."[42] Anxiety again emerges as the experience of the moment of contact between the world and God, but with the clarification that anxiety, between the poles of possibility and actuality, is constituted by these multiple points of engagement. In a beautiful, if quintessentially circular passage, Kierkegaard lodges anxiety in complex relation. "Anxiety is neither a category of necessity nor a category of freedom; it is entangled freedom, where freedom is not free in itself but entangled, not by necessity, but in itself."[43] The self is then compelled toward the future by the multiplicity inherent in its existence as a becoming relation. Helene Russell finds overtones of process thought in this structure. "The self is always in the process of becoming itself through relating reflexively to itself; it is a dynamic relational matrix."[44] The freedom of the self is entangled in the limitations of the history and location of that self. If "divine matrix" describes the role of God in mediating relationships to each individual subject, and is characterized by a mutual immanence that makes possible a continuum of communication, the human spirit exists as the finite, constant act of stepping into the corelation initiated by the divine matrix. The task of selfhood for Kiekegaard is then poetic creativity in response to God's presence as possibility, a "leap of faith" into the uncertainty of relationship with the infinite. For Kierkegaard, the solution to the tension and despair of being finite lies in imitation of Christ, the God-Man, "as the absolute paradox, formed by an absurd coincidence of opposites which unyieldingly resists all rational, historical, and religious mediation."[45] A theopoetic meditation on Kierkegaard's selfhood, by avoiding such movement toward resolution, might find its straddling of difference to be a potential energy for transformational action. Furthermore, the rich interrelational integrity of theopoetics, which itself maintains a tradition of creative action generated by difference, offers mechanisms for advancing social transformation by celebrating the very difference at which our selfhood despairs.

The language of difference in theopoetics emphasizes the mutual immanence of the human synthesis. To wit, Faber on God's relationship to the world:

> Here one also finds the *fundamental structure* of a relational communicative world revealed. *Basically* nothing is separated; everything is instead mutually immanent in ontological solidarity. *Basically* everything derives from something else and is oriented toward something else, everything positioned in *différance,* within the arc of becoming and perishing, subjectivity and superjectivity.[46]

The Derridian notion of *différance,* the irreducible otherness that is in fact produced by relationships, is a crucial part of this theopoetic understanding of the world. By applying the subjective vocabulary of Kierkegaardian selfhood to this theopoetic discourse, the goal is not to neatly claim the Danish philosopher-theologian as a proto-process thinker or to import his theological model into theopoetic discourse. This essay offers instead a reflection on the relevance of Kierkegaard's exploration of selfhood to the finite world in which the self exists. Keying on the notion of productive difference, the final portion of this essay examines a theopoetic understanding of the world mediated by the divine matrix, and actualized by a community of *human* matrices, a multiplicity of Kierkegaardian spirits whose difference energizes their creativities.

Manifold Anxiety, Creative Spirits

Whiteheadian terminology provides both terminology and conceptual structures for envisioning a society that seeks broader transformation while protecting the individuality of its members. For Whitehead, the notion of a "society" is predicated on a level of organization or commonality beyond the basic bonds of relationality that hold actual entities in what he terms a "nexus." A brief examination of these terms, informed by Kierkegaard's selfhood, will help to situate the self within a scheme of related entities. By treating the self as an actual entity engaged in a process of becoming, Kierkegaard's emotional vocabulary can be brought to bear on a process model of society, offering parameters for ethical engagement with the other and the novelty the other introduces into the world.

A nexus, for Whitehead, is a group of actual occasions that, via their immediate relatedness to each other, create a community of sorts. "A nexus is a set of actual entities in the unity of the relatedness constituted by their prehensions of each other, or—what is the same thing conversely expressed—constituted by their objectifications in each other."[47] This technical facet of Whitehead's scheme is important for the present examination of self and society, for it explicitly resists the foreclosure of the individual perspective when formulating larger collectives from individual entities. Within Whitehead's scheme, each entity experiences a universe uniquely its own; the particular relationships that constitute the sensory data for any discrete becoming are different, if even subtly so, for each particular place and time. A nexus is then simply a grouping of actual occasions based on their network of relations with each other, and as such is always somewhat of an arbitrary delineation, given that the network of relationality can ultimately be expanded to include the totality of space and time. If any particular order or organization pervades the nexus, then it can be classified as a society. "A Society is a nexus which 'illustrates' or 'shares in,' some type of 'Social Order.'"[48] Here, then is the sense of relationality that will serve as a baseline for discussing the relationship of the self to society. "To constitute a society, the class-name has got to apply to each member, by reason of genetic derivation from other members of that same society. The members of the society are alike because, by reason of their common character, they impose on other members of the society the conditions which lead to that likeness."[49] The atomistic construction of society in this scheme avoids the top-down consideration of spirit that Kierkegaard reacts so strongly to in Hegelian thought. To that end, if we take this Whiteheadian term as a model for understanding a community of theopoetic selves, the commonality of the society is generated by the relationships of the selves that make it up, not by a grander overarching logic. To be human is to be a synthesis of the finite and the infinite—to be enmeshed in relationships with other finite selves and also in contact with the transcendent source of possibility.

The self in a Whiteheadean society is then in that society by virtue of its very relationality; the self is entangled in its mutual immanence with other selves. The self's anxiety comes about as a result of the entanglement of the self's freedom both in the relationships that formed it and in the possibilities it envisions. I suggest, then, that human societies might best be described as collectives of spirits, each an ongoing synthesis of its relationships to the world and its relationship to possibility. All of these relationships are mediated by the divine matrix, the continuum of communication, and at each moment the society *becomes* a society; the inertia of the past shapes, but does not dictate, the future. As what would be termed a manifold by Faber and other contemporary theopoetic thinkers, society thus construed is defined not by an ontological unity—it is after all made up of a multitude of spirits that are all unique syntheses—but by the interrelatedness of its constituents. In a statement that Kierkegaard might find amenable to his own views, Faber highlights the irreducibility of such a structure. "Insofar as the Manifold is held beyond the Logic of the One that always tries to close the process down into static Law or eternal order, theopoetics harbors *a divine insisting on multiplicity that saves the Manifold from any controlling power of unification.*"[50] As such, a theopoetic reading of Kierkegaardian selfhood in society will insist on the presence of multiplicity not simply as a difference to be resolved but as the source of dynamism in the world. To lose multiplicity would be to experience ultimate entropy, to become a static "one."

A further implication of this theopoetic understanding of Kierkegaard's self is that the transformation of the spirit as it encounters what Kierkegaard calls the religious sphere will, through the mutual implication of a society, render an effect on the other spirits to which it is related. The inward act of selfhood, by virtue of its entanglement, holds the potential to become an outward proclamation. This is not news for Kierkegaard; much ink is spilled in *Fear and Trembling* especially on the dissonance between the inward transformation and a society that privileges the more comfortable ethical sphere. The theopoetic understanding of the Manifold, though, suggests that such individual transformations are in fact the potential kernels of social transformation; if the tension between the religious and ethical spheres of Kierkegaard's thought can be made less painful, it will be, as it has been with prophecies past, through the courageous outward expression of the inward transformation affected by the act of selfhood. This structure of transformation, we shall see, moves with far less predictability and assurance than does the Hegelian dialectic, but its guiding principles, dictated by the primacy of selfhood as the opening for novelty in society, are protective and indeed demanding of individual freedom. Anxiety experienced personally may spark broader transformations.

An illustrative model of this phenomenon can be found in the aesthetic thought of John Dewey. Strongly influenced by Hegel, much of Dewey's work focuses on societal transformation, but his consistent concern for the preservation and increase of freedom marks a sharing with Kierkegaard of concern for the discrete individual in any such system. As a human matrix, driven by the experience of difference as anxiety, the self described thus far finds itself a creative participant in society, a conduit for novelty enabled by its simultaneous participation in the actualized world and the realm of pure freedom. Dewey's pragmatic theory of artistic expression incorporates a similar movement of individual inspiration into societal discourse, and helpfully fleshes out the parameters of a society that aims to maximize its benefit from such fresh possibilities.

For Dewey, creative expression, which he broadly categorizes in all its forms as art, is itself a key component to nature, a product of inward tension directed toward external objects. "Art is thus prefigured in the very processes of living. A bird builds its nest and a beaver its dam when internal organic pressures cooperate with external materials so that the former are fulfilled and the latter are transformed in a satisfying culmination."[51] Such actions, inasmuch as they enter into the spatio-temporality of the world, become part of a larger phenomenon of experience. "Experience" for Dewey has an intentionally broad scope, serving to describe natural processes in a way similar to event-based metaphysics (though Dewey himself intentionally avoided metaphysical claims). Dewey scholar Thomas Alexander defines experience as "a process situated in a natural environment, mediated by a socially shared symbolic system, actively exploring and responding to the ambiguities of the world by seeking to render the most problematic of them determinate."[52] Later in his career, Alexander notes, Dewey grew frustrated by the misconceptions surrounding his understanding of "experience" and moved toward labeling the phenomenon "culture."[53] Furthermore, "instead of taking scientific discourse or formal logic as constituting the paradigms of meaning and communication, Dewey explicitly selects art and the aesthetic."[54] For Dewey the category of artistic expression offers the mechanisms for social progress, and such expression emerges out of individual experience, which is always situated in but not fully expressed by society.

The world, always perceived in the process scheme as the past, is for the Kierkegaardian spirit and the Deweyan artist the established order. Dewey's formulation of the desire of the subject implicates a measure of novelty as central to the thriving of what is in my line of argument termed the spirit. "The live creature demands order in his living but he also demands novelty. Confusion is displeasing, but so is ennui. The 'touch of disorder' that lends charm to a regular scene is disorderly only from some external standard."[55] Art, the organization of the inward energies into an outward expression of those energies, provides that touch of disorder, and thus prioritizes the creative freedom of the self within a society.

Beyond the affinity with the Kierkegaardian self, art's value is for Dewey assessed by its impact on the world. "The very meaning of an important new movement in any art is that it expresses something new in human experience, some new mode of interaction of the live creature with his surroundings, and hence the release of powers previously cramped or inert."[56] Art literally reconfigures the relationship between the spirit and the world, pushing against the limitations of the past. Furthermore, works of art are experienced by other subjects, and thus facilitate communication among the collective of spirits. The entry of art into the experiences of other subjects creates the possibility for it to trigger a revelatory or transformative experience for those who encounter it. The greater the experience and the more broadly it is felt, the more effective the art; such a valuation moves beyond subjective judgment and places the task of evaluating art in the hands of the experiencing public (who, in Dewey's thought, therefore ought to receive the necessary education for the task). Art then can be said to promote productive harmonies by cultivating the experience of something that moves beyond reason, that satisfies the anxiety of the self in ways that simple logical movement cannot. For Dewey, this necessitated not only a promotion of art but an openness to a broad array of artistic traditions, which he saw operative in his own time. "The new features are not mere decorative additions but enter into the *structure* of works of art and thus occasion a wider and fuller experience. Their enduring effect upon those who perceive and enjoy will be an expansion of *their* sympathies, imagination, and sense."[57] Again, recalling that art is for Dewey the expression of an experience that moves the spirit, the Kierkegaardian self, which encounters dissonance in its reentry into society, is ripe with the potential to offer forth an expression of its experience. Dewey felt that cultural barriers against new forms of expression only blocked the potential productivity of art. "This insensible melting is far more efficacious than the change effected by reasoning, because it enters directly into attitude."[58] Art, generated outside the causal chain of logic, carries a power unavailable to sheer reason, a power effected through the multiplicity of subjects within a relationally conceived society.

For Dewey, the language of God as source of possibility is entirely unnecessary; the relationship between human and nature provides the dissonance and energy that motivates art. Theopoetics, then, only partially harmonizes with Dewey's thought, but those harmonies do lend a depth to the model of self in society brought about by a theopoetic reading of Kierkegaard. The work of art, by triggering experiences in those who encounter it (experiences not dictated by the artist but emerging organically within those who experience the work of art) helps to reorient the values of society intent on cultivating progress for their spiritual collective. Crucially, the artist's expression does not oblige other selves to a particular experience of the work of art; at best, a work of art might lead others to experience the presence of possibilities that converge into a productive harmony.

By advancing the notion that social progress only comes through communication among the spirits, and by understanding that such communications often challenge the norms of society, Kierkegaard's theopoetic selfhood not only highlights the tensions involved in being human but also calls for the inscription of vulnerability into the definition of social boundaries. Understood as artistic expression, the invocation of novelty into the ongoing discourse of society is privileged within this scheme. Rigid restrictions on expression, generally intended to preserve a particular social order, import the fallacy of misplaced concreteness into the societies they govern. By recognizing the role of anxiety in motivating human action, and especially in inspiring artistic expression, this theopoetic conception of the self recognizes that the most pragmatic approach to such expression is to allow it to enter the critical experience of a society as the physical reaction to the dynamism of the spirit.

None of the thinkers invoked in this work would argue that an optimal society simply defers to individualism; indeed for Whitehead and Dewey a productive harmony is the optimal outcome of self-expression. Put simply, the expression of one spirit ought not foreclose the expression of another. In Whiteheadian thought, this principle is expressed as Harmony, struck on a spectrum between vagueness, in which the difference between actualities is insufficient to produce the contrast characteristic of beauty, and triviality, in which the relationships between actualities suffer a lack "of coordination in the factors of the datum, so that no feeling arising from one factor is reinforced by any feeling arising from another factor."[59] Conflicts between points of view are of course inevitable; indeed to overlook such dissonances would be to deny the complexity necessary in any such society. The members of a society constantly renegotiate and redefine the identity of their collective, and no society is truly isolated—all participate in a continuum of experience by virtue of their locatedness in a relational physical system. As such, the maximization of generic freedoms is in dialectic tension with the need to maximize *each* individual freedom; an untenable expansion of one individual's freedom impinges on those of another. Harmony, forged by productive tension within this process theopoetic scheme, is the value field within which societies maximally thrive. While Dewey holds out a hope in a radically democratic culmination of society, a theopoetic vision insists that a collective of thriving individual spirits offers the optimal space for living in relationship with God, without suggesting a final culmination to history. Whitehead inscribes this rejection of universal teleology through the same dialectic that forges the Kierkegaardian self: "The immanence of God gives reason for the belief that pure chaos is intrinsically impossible. At the other end of the scale, the immensity of the world negatives [*sic*] the belief that any state of order can be so established that beyond it there can be no progress."[60] Harmony among its constituent spirits is then the primary goal of a society that takes seriously the theopoetic nature of human existence. The key contribution of the Kierkegaardian self to this model is the insistence on a democratic foundation to that society, one that seeks to maintain the necessary capaciousness to allow each spirit to thrive, so as to maximize the potential for the progress of the whole. "The right chaos, and the right vagueness, are jointly required for any effective harmony," notes Whitehead. Kierkegaard's theopoetic selfhood points not to society as governed by an overarching spirit, but rather to society as a manifold collective of spirits invigorated by their encounters with God as possibility. The irreducible multiplicity within the self and among selves, and the differences it engenders, is indeed the transformative potential in our world.

Theology as a Genre of the Blues

VINCENT COLAPIETRO

Introduction

The topic of theopoetics provides the occasion for reflecting upon irre-pressible and irreducible differences,[1] but also upon unexplored and indeed previously unremarked conjunctions. So I want to seize this occasion as an opportunity to juxtapose theology and the blues, thereby considering a possibility, one itself of possibly broad and deep significance. Specifically, I want to consider theology as a genre of the blues. While certain forms of the blues unquestionably have their roots in theology,[2] theology itself draws from the sources and arguably inspiration of various dimensions of human experience (our experience *of* and *in* the world).[3]

No less than theology, however, the expression "the blues" is ambigu-ous. While it has as one of its main referents a musical idiom or, more accurately, an extended family of musical idioms, its meaning is hardly exhausted by this usage. As Albert Murray so acutely observes, the blues is above all else "an attitude toward human experience (and the alternatives of human adjustment) that is both elemental and comprehensive."[4] He unpacks the meaning of this claim, thereby illuminating the significance of the term in its deeper meaning, in asserting:

> It is *a statement about confronting the complexities* inherent in the hu-man situation and about improvising or experimenting or riffing or otherwise playing with (or even gambling with) such possibilities

as are also inherent in the obstacles, the disjunctures, and the jeopardy. It is also *a statement about perseverance and about resilience* and thus also about the maintenance of equilibrium despite precarious circumstances and about achieving elegance in the very process of coping with the rudiments of subsistence.[5]

Certain musical idioms singularly express this distinctive attitude, but the attitude is not reducible to these idioms. Such is the testimony of such authors as Amiri Baraka, Ralph Ellison, Toni Morrison, Angela Y. Davis, Albert Murray, Cornel West, and Eddie Glaude Jr.

Without question, certain genres of religious discourse and musical utterance at least appear to have a strongly transcendent function, since they seem to aim at transporting us to a sphere beyond the historical world with all of its humiliations, frustrations, and losses, also with all of its occasions for exuberance, exhilaration, and ecstasy. But we can count among the functions of religious language and blues idioms (musical and otherwise) the task of taking the here and now with the utmost seriousness, the acutest urgency. In this respect, neither this language nor the blues transports us from this world to a sphere beyond history; rather, they drive us ever more deeply into the heart of the present, in all of its complexity, confusions, and conflicts.[6]

Accordingly, they drive toward the reparation of the world, insofar as the world appears to be an arena in which our existence is threatened and our significance negated. The salvation of significance requires attention to the quotidian, including the seemingly insignificant or utterly trivial.

Yet seemingly insignificant details can possess resounding significance.[7] The hermeneutics of everyday existence demands nothing less than alertness to what all too many of us are disposed to treat as meaningless minutiae, as chance particulars.[8] The religious uses of language no less than the music of the common tongue[9] help us attend to such particulars, holding the promise of discerning what itself promises to provide sustaining significance. Accordingly, they provide in countless instances an effective hermeneutic of everyday life.

For my purpose, two examples seem especially telling. The first is encountered in the dedication of one of Charles Hartshorne's books, the second in one of the most important chapters of Alfred North Whitehead's magnum opus.

Fleeting Days and Abiding Worth

Charles Hartshorne dedicated *A Natural Theology for Our Time* (1967) to a number of thinkers, among them A. N. Whitehead.[10] Of them—men such as Fausto Sozzinni "and his brave Protestant followers in Poland and elsewhere," also "Gustav Theodor Fechner and Jules Lequier, Iqbal in what is now Pakistan and R. K. Mukerji in India, Varisco in Italy, Berdyaev in Russia . . . James Ward in England, and W. E. Hocking, E. S. Brightman, W. P. Montague, and A. N. Whitehead in the United States"[11]—he wrote: "their example may give comfort to those who would rather come as close as possible to difficult truths than enjoy facile half-truths in the best of company."[12] Then, in an act of *self-interruption,* Hartshorne asked rhetorically: "But—are not such men, scattered through history for one another the best of company?"[13] Immediately after identifying such thinkers as the best of company for one another and presumably also *for us* (at least insofar as we strive to come as close as possible to difficult truths), Hartshorne closed his dedication by quoting a Jewish ritual: "He will endow our fleeting days with abiding worth."[14] What indeed will endow our fleeting days with abiding worth or even simply a *sustaining* sense of their incomparable worth? At the outset, however, I simply want to stress Hartshorne's explicit invocation of the words of a religious ritual, though words bearing directly upon the *simultaneous* affirmation of the fleeting and abiding dimensions of our actual existence—that is, the actual occasions of our unfolding lives. This seemingly slight detail might be far from slight in its import and implications.

My second example concerns a figure even more central to this volume and, more broadly, to the project of articulating a theopoetics (at the center of which is the image of God as the poet of the world[15]). In one of the most pivotal chapters of his monumental work *Process and Reality* ("Process"), Alfred North Whitehead quotes two lines from a traditional hymn:

> Abide with me;
> Fast falls the eventide.[16]

Before quoting these lines he stresses: "The best rendering of integral experience . . . is often to be found in the utterances of religious aspiration."[17] Whitehead goes so far as to assert: "One of the reasons for the *thinness* of so much modern metaphysics is its neglect of this wealth of expression of ultimate feeling."[18] We can go some distance toward making our reflections *thick* (experientially freighted and thus humanly significant) only by actually turning to human experience in all of its invincibly disruptive force. The utterances of religious aspiration and (more generally) the practices of religious worship are—at least, they can be—instances in which this force of experience is itself felt. Hence, attention to them can provide us with an opportunity to confront—truly to experience—the disruptive power of these utterances and practices, thereby of that to which they (however cryptically or circuitously) bear witness. Above all else, however, Whitehead's suggestion ("The best rendering of integral experience . . . is often to be found in the utterances of religious aspiration") must be borne in mind.[19]

The Vital Connection to Human Practice

We have been somewhat prepared for such an emphatic assertion by the opening chapter of *Process and Reality*, the chapter devoted to "Speculative Philosophy." There Whitehead suggests, "Philosophy frees itself from the taint of ineffectiveness by its close relations with religion and with science, natural and sociological [or social]."[20] Indeed, philosophy "attains its chief importance by fusing the two, namely, religion and science, into one rational scheme of thought."[21] While the drive toward unity is here evident, the sites of confluence, the loci of intermingling, perhaps need to be problematized and indeed pluralized beyond anything imagined by Whitehead. The abiding need for philosophers and theologians to maintain or re-forge intimate connections with religious experience and practice is no less pressing or critical than that of sustaining or establishing close ties with scientific discoveries and practice.[22] The more attenuated is the connection between human practices in their historical thickness *and* our various discourses (but especially theology and philosophy), the more these discourses will be marred by "the taint of ineffectiveness" and, indeed, of thinness. The more intense, intimate, and intricate are these connections, the more vital and thereby enlivening are our discourses. Such, at least, is unquestionably the counsel of Whitehead, one worthy of our recollection here.

In the opening chapter of *Process and Reality*, Whitehead also writes: "Metaphysical categories are not dogmatic statements of the obvious; they are tentative formulations of the ultimate generalities."[23] For Whitehead, however, the ultimate generalities are inseparable from human practices. That is, the formulations of these generalities are bound up with our practices in their irreducible multiplicity and variable import.[24] Whitehead is explicit about this: Whatever is unquestionably found in human practice must fall within the scope of metaphysical description.[25] "When the description fails to include the 'practice,' the metaphysics is inadequate and requires revision."[26] Too often metaphysical systems and categoreal frameworks have been Procrustean beds, especially with respect to the full array of human practices. But nothing necessitates that this be the case. Indeed, Whitehead goes so far as to assert: "Metaphysics is nothing but the description of the generalities which apply to all the details of practice."[27] Practices provide, at least from his perspective, the bases for our generalization. The force and fecundity of these generalizations are measured, more than anything else, by the power of these generalizations to illuminate the details and indeed impasses, the fulfillments but no less the frustrations, of human agents entangled and implicated in a complex nexus of historical practices (hence, in evolved and evolving processes).

This presumably includes our religious practices and the distinctive uses of human language partly constitutive of this distinct sphere of human practice. In the framing of such descriptive generalities, metaphorical or figurative language is inescapable.[28] But, also in our attempts to describe what is entailed by the discursive practices in which such descriptive generalities occupy such a central place (such practices as theology, metaphysics, and more generally philosophy), metaphorical language is unavoidable. To suggest that theology is a genre of the blues is to indulge, unapologetically, in metaphor. But in noting this I am jumping ahead of the story. At this juncture, my concern is with not the discourse of theology but the disclosures of our experience. Nothing fully prepares us for these disclosures (often, very little does much to prepare us for them at all). Inseparably connected to this, little equips us with the theoretical or rhetorical resources requisite for bearing witness to these disclosures. "For we do not, after all," as Patricia Hampl notes, "simply *have* experience; we are entrusted with it. We must do something—make something—with it." She then adds: "A story, we sense, is the only possible habitation for the burden of our witnessing."[29] Whether or not the burden and (in countless instances) joy of our witnessing finds its most appropriate, let alone only, habitation in a narrative, our experience is not simply *had;* it is truly entrusted to us and in such a way as to make claims upon us. The acknowledgment of such claims must indeed be something we do, something we make, though a song or painting, dance or sculpture, might be as fitting (on many occasions, even more apt) than a story.

In the sense intended here (a sense deeply informed by Whitehead's own use of this word), experience is not anything subjective or subcutaneous. It is what goes on between and among the irrepressible multiplicity of dynamic beings so fatefully conjoined in the fleeting patterns of cosmic events.[30] It is quite simply only explicable in reference to what Martin Buber identifies as "the category of the between." Things as they manifest themselves in our experience are not primarily closed in upon themselves; rather they are radically (i.e., they are at the very *root* of their being) exposed to the lure, impact, and disruption of other things. Moreover, they in effect (and, in the case of humans and possibly other agents, often by design) refract the effects of these exposures and encounters (what could be more commonplace than even the most stately tree swaying in a violent storm, but what could be more significant than the observable respects in which actual encounters transform the things caught up in these transfigurative processes?)[31]

In a poetic register, James Agee illuminates the entanglement to which I am referring. We witness nothing less than "flexions . . . taking place everywhere, like a simultaneous motion of all the waves of the water of the world. . . ."[32] Each is intimately connected with "the bottom and the extremest reach of time"; each is identical with "all that surrounds him, the common objects of his disregard, and the hot centers of stars."[33] To bear unblinking witness to these commonplace flexions is to be propelled to ask:

> So that how can it be that a stone, a plant, a star, can take on the burden of being; and how is it that a child can take on the burden of breathing; and how through so long a continuation and cumulation of the burden of each moment one on another, does any creature bear to exist, and not break utterly to fragments of nothing[?][34]

These are, as Agee goes on to assert, "matters too dreadful and fortitudes too gigantic to mediate long and not forever to worship."[35] But our experience attests that such things, for however limited a duration, do *not* break utterly to fragments or nothing—indeed, they not only assume the burden of being but also do so in a manner inviting celebration (if only because they are in their innermost character unabashed celebrations of transient fragments).

Whatever reservations one might have about such rhapsodies, it is undeniable that things and events bear upon one another in evident and yet-to-be-discovered ways. The bearing of things and events on one another are manifest in and through our experience of these things and events. This makes of our experience nothing less than a medium of disclosure. If we accord our experience the status of a medium of disclosure (Whitehead, Smith, Faber),[36] then it is unquestionably the case that *reality manifests itself in multiple ways*. The multiplicity of these manifestations is, at least, as salient and telling a feature of the world and of our experience as are the possibilities for reducing (in some respects, though hardly in all or even most) this multiplicity to a unity. (Please note: The possibility of such reduction itself implies multiplicity, since there are multiple possibilities for reducing the many into *a* one.) Such reduction indeed always entails loss, if not also violence. A. N. Whitehead (e.g., in the chapter on expression in *Modes of Thought*), John E. Smith (e.g., "Being, Immediacy, and Articulation"), and others have illuminated in suggestive ways this aspect of Being or reality. The insights of some of the most rigorous thinkers square with those of some of the most primordial or archaic (in the sense of that which pertains to the *arché*) sources of human culture, the oldest religious utterances presently available to us. For the manifestations of reality are, in the one case as much as the other, unhesitantly framed as instances of *expression*. Reality manifests itself in multiple ways; that is, the world expresses itself in a polyvocal manner. To reduce the multiplicity of voices to a single voice—to bring into a harmony of harmonies the angles of vision from which we catch a glimpse of the world—is as much a betrayal of reality as an assault on humanity (or even on animality). However this might be, there are, indeed, various human cultures—hence, diverse religious traditions—at the center of which we hear a robust affirmation of cosmic expression (nothing less than the cosmos is articulating itself—in effect, speaking to us).

Does the World Speak?

But this claim flies in the face of that issued from one of the most influential voices in contemporary thought. In *Contingency, Irony, and Solidarity* (1989), Richard Rorty bluntly asserts: "The world does not speak. Only we do."[37] Yet he does not deny to the world a role in the determination of our beliefs, even if these beliefs are in his judgment couched in the contingent languages of ethnocentric beings. For Rorty readily admits the "world can, once we have programmed ourselves with a language, cause us to hold beliefs. But it cannot propose [much less underwrite] a language for us to speak. Only other human beings can do that."[38]

But does not the world of our experience in all its irreducible richness and ceaseless intimations suggest to us an array of images, in effect a language for us to speak? In any event, Rorty's position stands in sharp contrast to the one advocated by C. S. Peirce. For the sake of not only displaying this contrast but also presenting Peirce's views more fully, I will touch upon more than his claim that the world addresses us. My purpose in doing this is that indeliminable intelligibility needs, from a Peircean perspective, to be linked to qualitative immediacy and experiential compulsion. That is, the manner in which the world addresses us and in which we respond to the call of the world (response to both the things of the world and what appears to be beyond the world) can itself be rendered intelligible only in reference to (at the very least) the firstness of qualitative immediacy, the secondness of brute compulsion, and the thirdness of indefinite intelligibility. "There are," Peirce claims, "certain Forms of which we are immediately aware, [such] as Red, Beauty, Pitifulness, etc. No metaphysician can explain away this fact by any account of how they come about, however true it may be; for he will leave their peculiar suchness untouched; and suchness are all that they [these unique forms of qualitative immediacy] are."[39] Peirce's emphatic insistence on sheer suchness is, for our purpose, of paramount importance. But no less so is his claim that qualitative immediacy is not limited to human feeling or even human affectability. He rather caustically asserts, "One needs be as reason-proof as the stiffest metaphysician to deny the being as suchness [please note: the *being* as suchness] of other qualities than those that we immediately feel."[40] There are more qualities than those of which we are immediately aware; moreover, there is more to the qualities of which we are immediately conscious than what is conceptually registered or verbally expressed. "Of Matter [in contrast to Quality], too, we have direct experience in pushing against an obstacle in the dark, and in many other ways. As with [the] Form [of any Quality], we presume the existence of matter which we do not directly experience."[41] Finally, it "is the same with Signs. . . . Some address themselves to us, so that we fully acknowledge others that are not directly addressed to us, and that does not suppose still others of which we know nothing definitely."[42]

If Peirce is correct, then our world is one of qualitative immediacy, brute facticity, and largely unmapped intelligibility. It is one in which we are continually being addressed by others, in their qualitative uniqueness, irreducible otherness, and (for the most part) incomprehensible (at least, uncomprehended) significance.

The world addresses us in various ways, many of them so subtle or imperceptible as to escape our conscious notice or verbalized intelligence. That is, there is a sense—an experiential and thus vital sense—in which the world *does* speak. We dwell in a world and, as a result, there dwells within us a feeling that we have been addressed and being time and again claimed by utterances beyond the strictly human sphere. Our locus is that of one who has always already been addressed, one whose very being is bound up with having been and (at every turn) being addressed. In other words, the very structure of our lives is one of call and response. Thus, those musical practices in which this very structure is constitutive (most notably, the African American spiritual and its various offspring, including the blues) provide resources for understanding nothing less than the structure of our lives. On this occasion, however, I want to focus primarily (almost exclusively) on the blues. In my sense, the blues designates at once a quite local and specific phenomenon as well as a basis for generalization far beyond the times and places in which this distinctive mode of human utterance can be heard.[43]

The Blues as a Distinctive Form of Articulation

There is nothing triumphalist about the blues, though there is character-istically the defiant note of being the champion of an invincible cause. The blues and indeed allied forms of musical expression (e.g., "We shall overcome") are often triumphant, though never triumphalist. This is be-cause they are a resolute expression[44] not to be defeated in the worst sense of human defeat and degradation imaginable—being party to one's own self-abnegation and self-negation. There is, however, an essential equiv-ocation or, at least, uncertainty even in this expression of defiance. We shall overcome, but if we do not it will be the result of confronting impos-sible odds.

The power and indeed meaning of the blues are only intelligible if this genre of expression is set in a lineage. "The affirmation of self in the blues is," James Cone notes, "the emphasis that connects them theologically to the spirituals. Like the spirituals, the blues affirms the sombodiness of black people, and they preserve the worth of humanity through ritual and drama."[45] They are part of nothing less than a process of transformation or, even more precisely, transfiguration (to use here a theological term in its strict theological sense). "The emphasis was on free, continuous, creative energy as produced in song."[46]

"For the art—the blues, the spirituals, the jazz, the dance—was," Ralph Ellison suggests, "what we had in the place of freedom."[47] But Ellison's meaning might be better understood if we take these arts as themselves sites of emancipation, thus places of freedom. They are together "the place of freedom" in which the ongoing struggle for other forms of human free-dom (e.g., civil rights) is, in part, carried on. Without *this* place of free-dom, freedom in those senses would be neither imaginable nor adorable (in its original, undiminished meaning).

"Through the song," Cone argues, "black people were, able to affirm that Spirit who was continuous with their existence as free beings."[48] Though he is here referring to spirituals, the reference of his claim can easily be broadened to include other forms of musicking. Whatever is continuous with one's historical existence as a free being—whatever enables one to en-vision oneself as such a being and, then, to sustain one in one's exertions to realize (hence, to revise, time and again) that vision—is, on this account, divine. This makes of religion not a set of beliefs or a code of conduct but a form of life in which response to a call—or a series of calls, themselves only audible in reference to a history of self-inflicted deafness—is pivotal: Everything turns upon conceiving existence in this manner. At the very least, this means that "religion is wrought out of the experience of the people who encounter the divine in the midst of historical realities."[49] The blues is what a people (given the circumstances into which they have been thrown) is able to make out of its experience, an experience always problematically bearing traces of an encounter with the divine here and now. As a sensibility, it is unwilling to ignore or (worse) erase these traces, but it is equally unwilling to treat their meaning as transparent or their promise as necessarily attainable. It marks a living conjunction of radical hope and (at least) equally radically doubt.

Theology as a Distinctive Genre of the Blues

Theology is about more than consolation. More precisely, *religion* is more than this.[50] But the saving word is at the very least the sustaining word. In turn, the sustaining word is the always-surprising utterance offering "some small reassurance / that tragedy while vast / is bearable."[51] It is surprising above all because it proves capable of offering such reassurance. (The prefix *re-* is here important, though I do not have time to exhibit its importance.) These are the concluding lines of a poem by Lucille Clifton entitled "grandma, we are poets."

Please allow me to cite this poem in its entirety.[52] But first a word about its structure: This poem is a series of insertions—possibly interpolations and even interruptions—(each beginning with "say rather") woven into the lexical definition of *autism,* as found in two authoritative reference works. It is an instance of talking back. Here is the poem "grandma, we are poets" in its entirety.

autism: from Webster's New Universal Dictionary
and the Random House Encyclopedia
in psychology a state of mind
characterized by daydreaming
say rather
i imagined myself
in the place before
language imprisoned itself
in words
by the failure to use language normally
say rather that labels
and names rearranged themselves
into description
so that what i saw
i wanted to say
by hallucinations, and ritualistic and repetitive

patterns of behavior
such as excessive rocking and spinning
say rather circling and
circling my mind i am sure i imagined
children without small rooms
imagined young black men and
filled with holes imagined
girls imagined old men penned
imagined actual humans
howling their animal fear
by failure to relate to others
say rather they began
to recede to run back
ward as it were
into a world of words
apartheid hunger war
i could not follow
by disregard of external reality,
withdrawing into a private world
say rather i withdrew
to seek within myself
some small reassurance
that tragedy while vast
is bearable[53]

The words in italics are from *Webster's New Universal Dictionary* and *Random House Encyclopedia*. They are thus pronouncements from on high. The refrain "say rather" clearly indicates the disposition to speak back, in this instance, to authority, if only in the form of the dictionary. It is at the same time a deliberate interruption of the authoritarian voice. One acquires one's own voice, in part, by talking back, by refusing to accept externally imposed accounts or simply descriptions of one's character or condition.

The psychoanalytic theorist Adam Phillips suggests, "psychoanalysis is a theory of interruptions."[54] Religion might assume the form of a practice of interruptions. In countless historically instances, it has actually assumed the form of such a practice. Hence, what Phillips says about psychoanalysis might with equal force be said on such a form of religion: "psychoanalysis is as much about the *making* of gaps as about the making of links."[55] As a result, "the *fluency* of 'idealization'—usually a pejorative, and always a cover story—is replaced by the halting of ambivalence."[56] And, as a result of this, ambivalence is registered and interrogated, acknowledged and examined.[57] Two points are, however, critical to add here. First, the idealization of fluency as much as the fluency of idealization is called into question, checked time and again. In such *self*-interruptions, the question, "Just *who* is it that is tripping me up, stripping me of my fluency and this competency in this instance or situation?" becomes pertinent and pointed. Hence, the fissures and fragmentations not only within but also constitutive of the self are likely to become more legible. Second, there is a reflexive or recursive possibility regarding self-interruption: We can interrupt our tendency to interrupt ourselves—in effect, suspend it—and thereby regain a desired, situational fluency of response.

Let us turn from Clifton's poem (as it turns out, a poem about the poet her "grandma" and she herself happen to be),[58] as illuminated by Phillips's insights into interruption, to John Coltrane's *Alabama* (a track on *Live at Birdland*).[59] In "Daybreak in Alabama," Langston Hughes (or the character in this poem) announced:

When I get to be a composer
I'm gonna write me some music about
And I'm gonna put the purtiest songs in it
Rising out of the ground like a swamp mist[60]

When four young adolescents whose names we almost never recall (they are Denise Mcnair, eleven years old, and Carole Robertson, Cynthia Wesley, and Addie Mae Collins, all fourteen),[61] moreover *individuals*[62] whose time of life we also tend to efface,[63] were murdered on September 15, 1963, when on children's day at the Sixteenth Street Baptist Church in Birmingham, Alabama, terrorists set off bombs hidden in the basement of the building[64]—when this took place, Coltrane was already a composer. His composition is about not daybreak but heartbreak in Alabama. Hughes's poem imagined a composer captured by a sense of possibility:

And I'm gonna put white hands
And black hands and brown and yellow hands
And red clay earth hands in it
Touching everything with kind fingers
And touching each other as natural as dew[65]

In contrast, Coltrane composed a piece in which he sounds all but crushed by an acknowledgment of actuality, an unblinking attempt to register the full weight of irrevocable loss.

Moreover, the musical qualities of King's eulogy[66] are more than matched by the vocal qualities of Coltrane's "utterances." At one point, however, the drummer Elvin Jones begins to pick up the tempo slightly, and Coltrane in a gentle way halts the group—interrupts the process—and then begins again almost immediately. While King at the end of his eulogy invokes the traditional trope of a celestial ascension of the "little girls," Coltrane tarries with the negative and abides in the transience of lives so violently annihilated, the vulnerability of bodies so unspeakably mutilated.[67]

Talking back is an instance of interruption, but cultivating the capacity to be taken aback by what one is about to say or has just said, by what one is about to do or has just done, is an instance of self-interruption. Repetition can function, paradoxically, as an instrument of self-interruption. Religious language and even theological discourse can enhance, solidify, and even intensify this function. Our capacity to be stopped in our tracks, to be taken aback or turned around, is itself testimony (however immediate and unwitting) of being religiously alive and, hence, spiritually alert.

Conclusion

There is often heard and hence witnessed an *appeal*—a fantastic, somewhat pathetic yet also ennobling appeal—to that which holds the promise of granting our fleeting days abiding worth, that which *graciously* gives "some small reassurance / that tragedy while vast / is bearable."[68] The inherited, often inspired forms in which such spontaneous, passionate appeals are articulated—the words of a Jewish ritual or those of a Christian hymn, those of a traditional spiritual or even the intonations of a jazz composition such as Coltrane's "Alabama"—provide us with dramatic instances of the primordial forms of religious utterance. The dominant forms of secular reason amount to nothing less than a case against the legitimacy of such an appeal, while many of the enduring forms of religious life do not so much offer a defense as an exemplification of appeal to what transcends human finitude.

We are *called into being* by the graciousness of forces beyond anything we can even imagine or control, conjure or command. But the manner in which we are called into being always already prompts a response to that which issues this call. The very structure of our lives is that of call and response, wherein the possibilities for response are themselves (in some manner) attributable to "the poet of the world." This structure can be illuminated by *various* analogies and metaphors—indeed, it must be illuminated by a multiplicity of perspectives, (to borrow Nietzsche's own image from another context) "a mobile army of metaphors, metonyms, and anthropomorphisms." One such metaphor is the blues. Properly understood, the blues designates a relentlessly critical sensibility and, at the same time, an irrepressibly celebratory disposition. If the poet of the world is so by virtue of her ability to sing the blues, so we might be able in our efforts to offer a portrait of this poet. We might deepen our understanding of both the poet of the world and the most appropriate forms of theological discourse by attending carefully to that distinctive mode of human articulation called the blues. In my reflections I have neither shown this thesis to be true nor even rendered this claim to be plausible. I have only presented what I judge to be an intriguing, suggestive *possibility*—one among countless other possibilities. Even so, the mere suggestion of this possibility intimates an array of other possibilities—ones bearing on embodiment, sensuality, celebration, mourning, and thus ones bearing on loss and being lost, reassurance and being borne along, talking back and being taken aback, the moment and its immanent transcendence, the transcendent and its multiple loci.

For a blues people, "existence is [itself] a form of celebration"[69]—a revelation of breathing as a form of singing and in turn of singing as a transfiguration of breathing (what we take for granted as simply a physiological function). It is an affirmation hurled in the face of negations, above all, those pervasive, systemic negations of one's very being (of being somebody). It is a response to "You ain't nothing."[70] In the face of systematic annihilation, it is as often as not a fierce affirmation of one's own singular existence. This affirmation is both an act of rebellion and a call for recognition—better, a *demand* for acknowledgment.

The roots of the blues can be traced to a number of sources, not least of all spirituals (see, e.g., Cone). This might suggest to some that the blues is (at least, in part) a genre of theology (indeed, an arresting exemplification of some of the more memorable "utterances of religious aspiration"). I am, however, far more inclined to see theology itself as a genre of the blues, hence this distinctive sensibility and its characteristic modes of human utterance as more basic. In part, I am disposed to see the blues as more basic because they are more mundane,[71] more sensual, more skeptical of otherworldly hopes, and more hopeful for the effective work to be accomplished by earthy skepticism.

Doubt is a phase in the life of faith.[72] In turn, a robust faith can be a condition for a radical skepticism, what Peirce identified as a "healthy skepticism," one unflinching in its resolve to press the most unsettling questions. (What are we truly about? Just *who* are we, despite our presumptions and protests, proclamations and pretentions? To what are we truly devoting—thus sacrificing—our lives?) Such radical doubts, however, do not preclude resounding affirmations—not least of all the self-affirmations that are more than simply one's own insistence on one's significance. For one's life is nothing less than an utterance, whose "archaic" source is the poet of the world, but whose abiding resonance is the conjoint work of countless voices.[73] The conjunction of these voices does not rule out the singularity of one's own voice. One's life is, however, not an isolated or disjointed utterance, just as its source is not an external and absolute sovereign over a finite and finished process. Yet, in the moment, the question arises, how can anything whatsoever—"a stone, a plant, a star," a child, a family, a people—take on "the burden of being" and (in some instances) "the burden of breathing," without breaking utterly to fragments of nothing? How can the task of assuming this burden be transfigured into something celebratory rather than burdensome; moreover, how can the celebratory voices bear such eloquent witness to the fleeting moment, the annihilated self, the desecrated ideal and yet still be resolutely affirmative, unsentimentally passionate?

Polyphony

Poiesis, Fides, et Ratio in the Absence of Relativism

MATTHEW S. LoPRESTI

> In some measure or other, progress is always a transcendence of what is obvious.
> —**Alfred North Whitehead**, *Process and Reality*

> It is more important that a proposition be interesting than that it be true.
> —**Alfred North Whitehead**, *Adventures of Ideas*

Transcending the obvious is not always an analytical prerogative. Progress in speculative areas of thought is sometimes best begun with poetry. Why? Because progressive thought typically requires one to step outside of the comfort zones of "known" and "obvious" truths or tried and true methods. This needn't mean that one abandons reason for relativism; rather, it admits that one may successfully transcend the obvious by speaking in a transformative way that resonates with one's audience. Sophistry aside, this sort of transformative rhetoric can call for many things; for Alfred North Whitehead and much of process theology, it called for new concepts and neologisms. But unless one is to develop a new systematic theology, metaphysics, and so forth, theopoetic thought need only call for transcending the orthodoxy of the "obvious" in a way that resonates meaningfully with others when it comes to novel, nonanalytic religio-philosophical thought.

In such instances it is more important for the ideas expressed to be interesting than demonstrably true at the time of their inception. Thus, they can attract due attention as expressions that resonate with an audience. It is the job of the theologians and philosophers who are amicably touched by these types of ideas to work toward establishing rational bases for them.

Critics—who abound—play a crucial role by holding such ideas, theories, and so forth to the highest standards of scrutiny. If, over time, theopoetic ruminations fail to attract philosophers to do the heavy lifting of championing their rationality or reasonableness, then they will likely be abandoned and forgotten. Should such philosophers or theologians themselves fail to successfully argue and establish the validity of a theopoetic inspired notion, then unless we can properly establish the philosophical basis for it ourselves, we seem to be left with only the choice of dismissing it or embracing the unfathomable realm of relativism. We needn't be entrapped by this dichotomy, however, as there is always the possibility that future philosophers may prevail in making rational sense of things where we have failed. This should not greatly concern the theopoet though, as it is her job to fill the world with thought, words, and deeds, not to defend them.

The poet Rene Char once said, "A poet must leave traces of his passage, not proofs. Only traces bring about dreams."[1] In this sense, I argue it is not the task of a theopoet to defend her visions, for that task typically falls to another. As a philosopher of religion (and I suppose now as a philosopher of theopoetics), I have the task in this chapter to critically reflect on the role theopoetics plays in religious thought and the appropriateness of the term itself. While the last part of the paper explores Whitehead's theopoetic phrase—which has inspired this book, and which is an instance of his own creative, transformative, and at times theopoetic thinking about God and world—the majority of this paper considers whether or not theopoetics is rightly regarded as a relativist endeavor. This is a potentially fatal charge that should not go unanswered. David Hoy most succinctly defines relativism as "the view that nothing is absolutely true or right."[2] Relativism is thus a natural enemy of theology since theologies tend to presuppose a divinity (or at least a soteriological worldview) and thus an absolute perspective, namely, God's. Without this perspective, theology seems to lack an effective standard by which competing reference claims are judged. Should theopoetics be determined to be a relativistic endeavor, it would essentially be an antitheological endeavor. I argue, to the contrary, that theopoetics is supratheological. In other words, theopoetics is not antitheology; it is an antecedent to theology. Theopoetics is essential to the creative process of speculative theology and, while the process can at times result in relativism, this should in no way reflect negatively on theopoetics itself.

"Theo" and "Poetic" Reservations

Prior to articulating an important place for theopoetics in religious discourse, I must begin with two reservations that I have with the term itself. The first is with the use of *theo* and second is the reference to being "poetic." These will help to launch us toward a third and more profound reservation that others are likely to have concerning the relation between theopoetics and relativism.

In much of my scholarship I seek to motivate the field of philosophy of religion to acknowledge the paramount importance of beginning from a comparative perspective when understanding and developing viable philosophical or meta-theological responses to religious diversity. One sensitivity that this disposes me to is theocentric discourse when it comes to a divine or religious ultimate that traditions fundamentally orient themselves toward in their teachings. By *ultimate* here I mean an irreducible ontological aspect of reality. For many traditions this ultimate is a supreme deity, for others a pantheon. Still others are no less religious for lacking a primary role for a deity in their ontological narrative. Siddhartha Gautama, for instance, taught of the fundamental nature of reality as one of constant flux and relation through the concept of *pratityasamutpada,* or "dependent co-origination." The impersonal, unnamable Dao is an ontological and religious ultimate in Chinese traditions, and *nirguna Brahman* is an undifferentiated absolute in Indian traditions. Nevertheless, each of these traditions has what I believe most authors in this volume would regard as a rich, "theopoetic" literary heritage.

As a result of this diversity we ought to be cautious in any use of *theo*centric language when making claims that we might also wish to apply to nontheistic or a-theistic traditions. *Religio-poetics* might convey a degree of what I think the term *theopoetics* is getting at, but this term would be a problematic alternative since the strict division of religion from philosophy is not made in most non-Western traditions. *Onto-poetics* perhaps best encapsulates a similar meaning because of what I think is a fundamental (if not explicit) topic of ontology in most theopoetic musings. This sort of policing of language is meant not to suggest that only God-neutral language will suffice but rather to serve as a consistent reminder that if we use theocentric language in metareligious reflections that refer to whatever religious ultimate(s) there may be, then we should do so with a conscious awareness that our language and our categories may intentionally or unintentionally exclude traditions for which the notion of a deity is of little relevance or concern.

While any presumed emphasis on deities in theopoetics is rightly critiqued, and I believe that *ontopoetics* would be a more appropriate and less isolating term, for the sake of consistency with the other essays, I too will use *theopoetics* in this chapter, with the understanding that it refers not merely to the concerns of theocentric traditions but rather to all ontopoetic traditions.[3] Acknowledging this from the start is vital to encouraging cross-cultural and interreligious engagement. As a comparative philosopher of religion, it is my duty to draw attention to this for the sake of encouraging cross-cultural theopoetic ruminations and reflection prior to examining its other aspects. For example, it gives theopoetics more room to grow in accommodating expressions of divine multiplicity in a way that allows for, say, both a theistic and nontheistic religious ultimate to simultaneously obtain—a scenario that is central to my research toward establishing a philosophical basis for genuine religious pluralism.

As to the second reservation, let us begin with a positive case for using *poetic*. I'd venture to say that theo-*poetics* is, or at its best can be, childlike. This is not because it is simple but because of its fundamental allegiance to emotions that spring forth from wonderment. This wonderment is not culturally specific, nor does it depend on the concept of a deity. Rather, it is a wonder fueled by reverence for the divine forces in nature and respect for the Other. The theopoet is ideally free, like a child, to experience the world with few or no preconceived ideas to get in the way. Thusly, the theopoetic can work toward expressing one's intimate experiences, which may lie outside the bounds of the established frameworks of one's tradition, and thus are sometimes denied by strict binary logic or rigid, dogmatic faith. This is much the way that U.S. poet laureate W. S. Merwin speaks of poetry as primal experience. Poetry, he says, "is an attempt to say what cannot be said in ways that it has not been said before."[4] Such attempts to express the ineffable, he muses, are likely the origin of language itself. I take this to mean that the creativity and spontaneity of great poetry blooms outside the constraints of preconceived ideas, just as I argue that wondrous theopoetic ruminations best grow wild, that is, outside the bounds and tethers of established traditions that prune and shape the creative spark only in preapproved patterns. We will revisit this idea shortly.

Despite the apparent appropriateness of *poetic*, there is a downside. Namely, that the grandiosity of saying that some writings or thoughts regarding the divine are "poetic" also make for rather general and imprecise declarations. Does this then entail all cryptic utterances, or is it merely meant to suggest that, even though they may be in stark contrast to *logos*-guided utterances, poetic utterances are also valuable? For example, a metaphorical metaphysics can have value, not necessarily because it is bound by *logos* but precisely because of its *poiesis* (creativity), which in turn may someday inspire faith and find support in reason. Indeed, a major function of theopoetics, in my opinion, is to provide a transformative depth to religio-philosophical discourse that complements (and sometimes feeds) the spiritual roles of both faith and reason. Likewise, however, a reasonable concern for the scope of the "poetic" can assist us in identifying and purposefully contributing to theopoetics in general. *Poetic* in this paper should be taken as *poiesis* or creativity. In this sense I tend to think of theopoetics as a sort of "creative theology," which means that it is a *precursor* to the adventure that is speculative theology in which creative musings on the divine are to be given greater shape. At the very least, as this is an academic and critical paper, the insistence of *logos* to inquire after definitions and the logocentric concern readers may have will naturally guide us to confront the specter of relativism as it may pertain to theopoetics.

To initiate this we look to the perspectives of two popes with contrasting views toward other belief systems. One seems to have had an expanding mission and his successor a constricting mission and tolerance of belief systems that originate outside of their shared tradition. In the encyclical *Fides et Ratio*, Catholic philosopher Karol Wojtyla (Pope John Paul II) made the philosophical and theological case for the congruity of faith *and* reason, religion *and* science in part as a way of reaching out to the faithful and the logical so that they were not misled into thinking that they had little overlap. Indeed, part of this message is that some of the overlap can be found in the teachings of the church. On the heels of this two steps forward Catholic theologian Joseph Ratzinger (now Pope Emeritus Benedict XVI), who has vociferously argued against taking things too far and sometimes taking things far too near what he regards as relativism. This fear in his writings can be seen at times to be a fear of creative thinking,[5] and a major point of this paper is to argue that we can have creative theological or metatheological thinking without falling into relativism, just as we can have a marriage of faith and reason. Moreover, what we need to further advance our theological understandings of the world is openness to the plausibility of notions that stem from creativity as well as faith and reason.

Poiesis, Fides et Ratio, and the Question of Relativism

As a philosopher, Pope John Paul II spent many of his years concerned with the intimate necessary relation between faith and reason. On September 15, 1998, he released the Encyclical Letter *Fides et Ratio*. It begins with this blessing:

> Faith and reason are like two wings on which the human spirit rises to the contemplation of truth; and God has placed in the human heart the desire to know the truth—in a word, to know himself—so that by knowing and loving God, men and women can come to the fullness of the truth about themselves.[6]

Following its publication, John Paul spoke of his encyclical to a group of U.S. bishops visiting Rome, saying that his purpose was "to defend the capacity of human reason to know the truth."[7] Part of his concern is clearly echoed in the current pontiff's deep and troubled concern over the evils of relativism. For Pope Emeritus Benedict XVI, relativism it seems is a beast that must be defeated, given that our ability to know the truth and our "confidence in reason is an integral part of the Catholic intellectual tradition, but it needs reaffirming today in the face of widespread and doctrinaire doubt about our ability to answer the fundamental questions . . ."[8]

I agree that relativism must be combated, for it threatens both progress and tradition. When suspected, relativism must also be understood as much as it can be in order to distinguish it from helpful and progressive pluralisms. John Fagen, on an official Church website, summarizes "Truth" according to John Paul as:

> known through a *combination* of faith and reason. The absence of either one will diminish man's ability to know himself, the world and God. . . . [John Paul] explains the proper roles of faith and reason on man's path to truth . . . they compliment and support one another with complete compatibility.[9]

Theopoetic creativity, I argue, complements faith and reason. While truth may be known through faith and reason, the nascent expressions of spiritual truths (like the one in John Paul's blessing above) are typically conducted theopoetically. I argue that this is as true for the personal believer who later comes to an understanding of how her own tradition incorporates a theopoetic expression (e.g., "God is love") as it is for novel spiritual truths that become doctrinal components of an established faith at some point thereafter (as I believe a genuine religious pluralism will be in future instantiations of current religious traditions). Roland Faber suggests that theopoetic expressions "supplement" faith and reason. I believe they can and do add to these pillars of religious belief, but that it is more accurate to say that theopoetic notions actually tend to precede faith and reason. For faith and reason tend toward shaping a coherent set of beliefs and rules, which are influenced by the creativity of expression that inspires them. At its best, theo-*poiesis* initiates novel communion with the divine for others to emulate; long before discrete beliefs are formed or dogmas take hold, the wellspring of theopoetic creativity is tapped. As a supplement, theopoetics serves to refresh the hermeneutic between faith and reason, pushing it toward greater and greater correspondence with the human heart-mind's relation with the divine.[10]

We must also keep in mind, however, that just because mature theological thought may be rational, this does not mean that it is right. This is not an attack on reason but merely to say a systematic theology is not correct just because it may be consistent and therefore rational. Internal coherence of beliefs is not correspondence with reality; validity is not soundness. There may be, and typically are, authentic religious phenomena, beliefs, or practices that are not fully accounted for in any systematic theology. This is where a supplemental theopoetic exploration may be of more efficient use and of more practical use to the faithful—who, I believe, are compelled to question their particular conceptions of the divine.[11]

The religious concept of God has become a prisoner to the conceptual restraints of philosophy. Here we see the relevance of process theology for making sense of age-old theopoetic adages. With process philosophy, the concept of God is redefined in such a way to allow an understanding of him to flow freely from philosophy to religion and back again. For example, if God is more akin in His mode of existence to our mode of existence, then it becomes more possible to have a personal relation with him in process theology than in substance-informed theology. This goes a long way in making religion, in practice, more tenable to philosophical scrutiny when it comes to living up to religious aspirations like the dictate in Matthew 5:48 in which we are told, "You, therefore, must be perfect, as your heavenly Father is perfect." This is most clearly an absurd normative directive under the substance view of deity. Even if this is not a normative directive to alter our ontological mode of being (which it seems it is not), as a metaphorical or symbolic expression, it is at best unclear how we should act then as a being might act with absolute power and knowledge, regardless of his ontological relation with the world. The practical implication of a process conception of deity enables religious practitioners to genuinely model their actions after the divine qualities of persuasiveness rather than power, and recognize the limitations of our knowledge and make informed decisions nevertheless toward the greatest moral and aesthetic ends,[12] and so on. These are qualities of the divine that humans can emulate and thus partake in Godliness. It is in this way that process theology and process philosophy of religion offer an actual path for the emulation of God and thus offer a sensible explanation for the efficacy of emulation in bringing us closer to God in our everyday practice and in our everyday lives. It takes us from the theopoetic dimension to the practical living of our faith without violating our allegiance to the emotional, spiritual, and rational dimensions of the human condition. Thusly, we can actualize *poiesis* and *fides et ratio*.

The fear of relativism seemingly arises because theopoetic ruminations can make for spiritual pronouncements that are not intended to withstand immediate analytic scrutiny. In part, the relatively recent popularity of theopoetics may be seen as a festive rebellion against last century's infatuation with the falsification criteria of meaning, which zealously strived toward discrediting the vast majority of religious utterances as meaningless because they could not be falsified. To be sure, neither poetry nor creativity can be falsified. This does not, however, condemn us to a relativism that rejects truth and falsity as meaningful designations. Theopoetics is a style of thinking about God, Dao, Brahman, and so forth. It is not a theological theory in itself—because there is no inherent content per se—thus the binary logic of true or false does not appropriately apply. Instead, we can apply a criterion of truth qua authenticity to spiritual endeavors.[13] If a tradition, teaching, or expression achieves what it purports to achieve, then it is authentic. If it does not, it is pretentious. Avoiding pretension is the first of many hurdles facing the widespread acceptance of any theopoetic utterance.

Distinguishing theopoetics from relativism is necessary for establishing the philosophical legitimacy of this movement. Given my understanding of theopoetics, I hope to have shown that relativism is not applicable to theopoetics itself, but surely many theopoetic ruminations face charges of relativism in the early stages of critical analysis. In some cases those ideas that find champions among philosophers and theologians have a better chance of becoming understood in nonrelativistic terms in the future. Because the realm of religious thought is expected by believers to have traction in the world, we have a responsibility to look toward objective realist explanations of religious phenomena and ideas; thus relativism is philosophically and religiously untenable. Fortunately for theopoetics, religio-philosophical *poiesis,* or creativity, can never properly be regarded as relativistic on its own. Once these expressions are given form, however, insofar as one works toward determining how they may fit with other, more established and accepted notions, then the charge of relativism about the acceptance of particular ideas may follow. Independently, however, theopoetics does not necessarily inject relativism into religio-philosophical dialogue; it is merely part of a process that may result in relativism. As there is no necessary relation that ties them together, any identification of theopoetics with relativism would be unfounded.

Orthodoxy as Bonsai Tree: Religious Pluralism as Inspired by Theopoetic Creativity

If theopoetics is to have value for religio-philosophical discourse, it is not enough to argue that it avoids the sin of relativism. We should not overlook a positive view of what and how it contributes to faith and reason. If faith is man's internal response to the divine, and if reason is that by which man can know and reflect on this world, then I would say that what is termed as theopoetics in this volume is that by which man strives to *express* an external response to truths that are encountered through faith and reason[14]—but that often do not jibe with dogma, or with sanitized views that often define traditions.[15] This is not to reduce theopoetics to a type of mystical expression, though it can be. I do not mean to merely suggest a new name for old phenomena. Rather, I think that the category of theopoetic expression can include the unpruned heart of the faithful, many of the pronouncements of spiritual poets, the language of religious art, and many of the messages of mystics in a way that traces a common element in their thought as influential on their tradition. Those with a theopoetic strain of expression may intend to express religious or spiritual views that conflict with the orthodoxy of their day but, for whatever reason, have come to embrace their own will-to-believe. I believe that a relevant contemporary example is in the growing theopoetic ruminations that reflect a basic pluralistic view of other religious traditions (if not at least of other people and their capacity for salvation despite their lacking exposure to one's own tradition's religious narrative). This would be an example of meaningful and accurate theopoetic expressions about the world if traditions come to understand that the world can and does arguably accommodate a plurality of faiths (as compossibly authentic) and that people can and do achieve spiritual progress despite hailing from different traditions or cultures. The main obstacle to publicly embracing such theopoetic expression has been the false presumption that relativism must accompany any such view, and this is where we find much of the debate surrounding religious pluralism today.

If we think of religion organically, then a religion with a high sense of rigorous orthodoxy can appropriately be compared to a bonsai tree. A bonsai achieves its highly manicured shape and beauty through restricted growth and pruning to attain a desirable form that nevertheless looks completely natural in its growth. In this analogy, theopoetics then would be the untamed shoots that spring from the bonsai template as it grows. If left unattended, these offshoots would flourish on their own. These are not all always trimmed. If they yield complementary balance to the tree as a whole, then select sprouts may be encouraged to flourish as part of the new orthodoxy. If not, they can be judged heretical and cut off. Naturally, this analogy is limited. These heretical branches can and often do continue to grow and thrive if they are not entirely extinguished. While these cuttings can and often do leave scars on the bonsai itself, adding to its gnarled beauty, rooting out the capacity for human creativity is never truly achievable, no matter how greatly discouraged it may be. Recall that the root word for *heretic* is the Greek word *hairetikos,* which means "to choose" or "to freely think for oneself."

One persistently regenerative branch on the trees of various religions is that of religious pluralism. This is not a branch that links a particular tree with others but rather an acknowledgement that other traditions also offer potentially valid spiritual solutions to real problems. What is more, for these pluralistic branches, the allowance for the possibility that these other diagnoses and prognoses of the human condition and their prescriptions for soteriological action may not necessarily contradict those of one's own tradition. Achieving a theology wherein this can make clear doctrinal sense would be a Herculean task for most traditions, but such a cosmopolitan idea is more than acceptable in today's world, while persecution for this type of expression is increasingly provincial and rare.

Philosophers of religion have worked toward theorizing religious pluralisms from metaphysical, ethical, and phenomenological perspectives among others. These are surely legitimate and noble pursuits wherein inspired ideas are tested to see to what extent they can stand the rigors of rational analysis. If they can, it would then be the job of theologians from within traditions themselves to measure to what extent a speculative theology could be developed that brings philosophical analysis to bear on their tradition and vice versa. Theopoetics is that nascent realm of thinking imaginatively and adventurously about God, religion, the ultimate, our relation with the world, suffering, and any other number of religious themes wherein intellectual freedom, if not safety, for exploring such ideas is taken for granted. Philosophy works independently to test the rational grounds, if any, of theopoetic musings; in such instances philosophy rightly fulfills the role that Thomas Aquinas assigned to it as a handmaiden of theology. This is at least one hierarchical path for the relevance of theopoetics to the disciplines of many who are either writing in or will be reading from this book. Others, I suspect, imagine a more independent role for theopoetics in a way that doesn't necessarily reject theo-*logical* reflections on it or the rational analysis philosophers are so eager to apply to everything. It is in this capacity that I believe questions about relativism may *rightly* surface from philosophers and theologians alike.

Consider the relationship between theopoet and philosopher to be like that of an architect and a civil engineer. The architect provides designs and inspirations that the engineer must test and try to responsibly implement within the constraints of the laws of physics. In the end, masterful architecture may appear effortless and light, perhaps even spontaneous in its lines or form, but the physical construction is, in no uncertain terms, grounded in a thorough understanding of the stresses, strains, and construction materials if there is to be a lasting structure with any semblance of the original design. No real architecture defies the laws of physics, and no serious architect disdains the laws that must limit and ground her imagination. Similarly, at the end of the day no serious theopoet rejects reason—though theopoets may differ when it comes to considering the bounds of reasonableness. As a poet of design, an architect may lack the engineering skills to say explicitly *how* her designs are to be actualized. Similarly, a theopoet may lack the philosophical rigor to explicate *how* her vision could possibly be accurate, but neither scenario negates the possibility of the poet's vision or the necessary importance that the design be subjected to the rigors of reason before it can break ground or have meaningful traction in the world.

In looking at contemporary religious thought I think we can find a mounting theopoetic urge as a consequence of both pluralistic faith and a rejection of falsification criteria of meaning. That is to say, the fact that we currently seem to lack a philosophical, much less theological, acknowledgement of the soundness of a pluralistic religious hypothesis does not necessarily sway pluralistic thinkers—instead, they are currently left with theopoetic expressions while they and others take the necessary time to develop philosophical and eventually theological justifications for their pluralistic stances. This does not condemn them to relativism, but it does make it easy for unsympathetic scholars, theologians, and so forth to be dismissive of their plight. This is where I think myself and many other scholars come in to stand as champions for this relatively underdeveloped idea (despite its long history).[16]

Theopoetics, as I see it, offers fertile imaginings of a pluralistic hypothesis like the one argued for in my research insofar as it provides an inspirational understanding of what seems to be a growing *gut intuition* or *recognition of the heart of the faithful* that people of other faiths are neither stupid nor deceived by some web of lies. Rather, they are seen to be fellow pilgrims on an authentic path distinct from one's own. To many philosophers of religion (e.g., many in the Notre Dame school of thought, such as Alvin Plantinga) and theologians (like Joseph Ratzinger, now Pope Emeritus Benedict XVI) this may sound like relativism, but I think this sort of a reaction is

	% agreeing that . . .	
	Many religions can lead to eternal life	There is more than one true way to interpret the teachings of my religion
	%	%
Total affiliated	70	68
Protestant	66	64
Evangelical churches	57	53
Mainline churches	83	82
Historically black churches	59	57
Catholic	79	77
Mormon	39	43
Jehovah's Witness	16	18
Orthodox	72	68
Jewish	82	89
Muslim	56	60*
Buddhist	86	90
Hindu	89	85

Source: From the Pew Research Center's Forum on Religion & Public Life, "U.S. Religious Landscape Survey," © 2008, Pew Research Center. http://religions.pewforum.org/.

Note: Results based on those who are affiliated with a particular religion.

*From "Muslim Americans: Middle Class and Mostly Mainstream," Pew Research Center, 2007.

condescending to lay religious people around the world. Just because lay people may find it difficult to express, with philosophical rigor, a view that other traditions may have spiritual lessons that are worth learning, or offer understandings of the human condition that their own tradition lacks (or does not emphasize) and are worth acknowledging as authentic, does not mean that they are relativists. It seems to me that these (potentially hundreds of millions of) people simply lack a theoretical framework for articulating these pluralistic sentiments in a deeply and genuinely pluralistic way. (See accompanying table.)[17] Statistics like this[18] give practical urgency to the task of articulating and amplifying genuine religious pluralism, and this is what philosophers, such as myself, try to do and what I believe others are trying to express (among other things) via theopoetics.

A practical definition of a genuine religious pluralism, then, is any theory that combats the intellectual and theological elitism of theologians and philosophers of religion who reduce laypersons' genuine pluralistic beliefs to nonsensical relativisms, heresies, or faithlessness and instead makes charitable sense of what so many people already "know" in their hearts to be true—namely, that there is more than just one authentic religion. To the dogmatic theologian or untrained philosopher of religion (or vice versa), any attempt to articulate such a pluralism would be a futile exercise in relativism. However, a careful version of religious pluralism that has a sound basis in a coherent metaphysics, such as John B. Cobb Jr.'s deep religious pluralism, is clearly distinguished from relativism and offers a sensible narrative for the multiplicity of veridical traditions.[19]

Theopoetics is an effective means for pushing the boundaries of theological thought and I and others like me thus look to test and support them with philosophical justification. The example of deep religious pluralism hopefully shows that it is far more than just a pluralistic attitude; it offers a theoretical justification for having a pluralistic attitude (like those expressed in the poll above) in the first place. Testing the success of a theory such as this is not so much a determination of its truth as a measurement of the degree to which it can resonate with people who choose to enrich and inform their lives with one of the myriad religious traditions but also feel that other traditions offer authentic paths as well. To test it, then, is to examine whether it actually functions as a theory that offers a meta-theological narrative that can be widely accepted by people of various traditions while largely respecting these traditions' understandings of themselves. (After all, this is not physics, so, while a coherence standard of truth plays a role, a correspondence theory of truth is less of a viable option than, say, Deutsche's authenticity standard of truth.) Whitehead writes that, in the end, it is more important for ideas to be interesting than true, and if such ideas can and do prove to be authentic expressions that can spiritually enrich the lives of the faithful, then I believe that this is a suitable credo for theopoetic reflection.

As a philosopher I am particularly attracted to those theopoetic ruminations that pose questions that either are left unanswered or imply unorthodoxies. I find that these add new life to the discipline of philosophy of religion in exciting ways: Some of them directly raise questions of God; others reflect more on personal suffering or the lamentations of a community. These agonies illustrate living religions full of petitions and thanksgiving. As many contemporary faiths admit, God still continues to speak to us and is capable of being an active part of our lives. This does not necessarily mean we must entertain the notion of new prophets springing up, in deference to our Muslim brothers and sisters, but it does mean that we can become inspired to speak of God or of our human experience as it relates to the divine in novel poetic ways—ways that may lie outside the rigidity of endorsed theology, but they may nevertheless ring true to the heart of the faithful. Such creative expressions such as these contribute to the vitality (and thus also the variety) of contemporary religious expression. Those expressions that resonate with the spirituality of a critical mass of believers will go on to affect the theological developments of future centuries. Theologians, in a sense, are left to pick up the pieces and make sense of new or renewed theopoetic emphasis in such a way that a coherent continuity of tradition is maintained. It is noble work to search for systematic reason and cause in the beliefs and practices of the faithful. Over long periods of time, theopoetic ruinations may become systematized or suppressed. Recognizing this process enables us to see that *theopoetics is the seed of speculative theology.*[20] Indeed, the fruits of theopoetic rumination may take ages to mature, so that what today seems doomed to relativistic fantasy may someday, with the right philosophical basis, provide a meaningful worldview to a living tradition.

The Seminal Theme of Creation in Theo-*poiesis:* "God as Poet of the World"

A few lines of poetry can distill what might take hundreds of years for theologians to rationally parse. Throughout history and across traditions theologians have constantly strived to catch up to and make sense of what we can call here theopoetic ruminations. The Rig-Veda is the oldest known collection of religio-poetic ruminations (ca. 2000 B.C.E.). It took Brahmanical theologians a millennium of reflection to formulate the earliest Upanishads (ca. 900 B.C.E.) in which philosophical interpretations are mingled with further theopoetic extrapolation. The book of Psalms, from the Abrahamic traditions, is a theopoetic example insofar as they can at times defy established theo-*logical* doctrines. Indeed, it is by virtue of this that the psalms are still vital to the inspiration of these living traditions. These psalms are lyrics that were to be sung along with instrumental music, as denoted by the Greek origin of the word *psalmoi.* As a prayerful medium of literary expression, the psalms are expressive of the human condition, but they do not necessarily make for good theology. The problem of God's transcendence versus His immanence, for instance, has long been an issue in Abrahamic theology, and, while various psalms emphasize one aspect or another of what Whitehead refers to as the Absolute and the Contingent nature of God, Psalm 113 succinctly contains them both. The reference to problematic theological issues is not a situation unique to this psalm (much less the psalms in general), but the point is that there are sanctioned hymnal prayers that have been embraced by the orthodoxy of Abrahamic faiths, and yet they tend more toward a theopoetic venture.[21] Indeed it is this particular problem that partly inspired and informed Alfred North Whitehead's speculative theology of the di-polar nature of God. While his speculative theology was part of a larger systematic metaphysics, he still relied heavily on what I and others would call theopoetic turns of phrase to jar us out of established thought patterns and creatively transform our conceptions of God and the world. Whitehead offers us such a phrase in asking us to consider "God as poet of the world." This notion is foundational to Faber's theopoetic ruminations toward theoplicity and is here critiqued so as to reflect on the dangers and opportunities of the theopoetic imagination when we try to come to terms with the holiness of the divine multiplicity.

"God as poet of the world" finds its context in Whitehead's work where he writes of God acting as a being who "saves." We should consider what Whitehead means by "saving" in the context of the preservation of value in the world. For Whitehead, God functions as one who saves the value of the world in His "tender care that nothing be lost."[22] In the same place where Whitehead writes of God in this way, he also contrasts the function of *God saving the world* with the more traditional function others have given to God in his *creation of the world.* These are two different uses of the word "save." In the first, *strong* sense of "save," God literally and supernaturally saves, that is, preserves, value in its actual immediacy as eternally novel. In the second, *weak* sense of "save" God saves the world as "the poet of the world, with tender patience leading it by His vision of truth, beauty, and goodness."[23] That is to say, God lures the world toward ever-increasing aesthetic ends. The strong literal saving of value is not necessary for the weaker, where God is both historian and poet. Rather than implementing raw causative power, God works to harmonize antecedent value in the world with potential value in a way that is more akin to an artistic creativity that lures the world toward ever-greater aesthetic fruition in each moment.[24] The etymology of *poetry* leads us to *poiesis,* which means production, formation, creation, and thus as the poet of the world God functions more as an aesthetic conductor than as an architect. This conductor, for Whitehead, is also part divine historian insofar as He retains a perfect memory of every antecedent novel occasion, thus enabling Him to best harmonize the cosmos. But this "saving" of the world is quite different from His first role as the savior of value. That is, He saves us from "perpetual perishing" by retaining not just the memory of these occasions: By retaining each occasion in its actual novelty, he also retains value in all its freshness. God captures this value with his omniscient intellect. In other words, God not only keeps all of them in their every detail in His unfailing memory, but they objectively reside there. The implication is thus that value in the creative advance accrues because of this strong saving function of God. For Whitehead, then, the world in every episode of valuation is supersaturated with value because each creative advance adds to the coffer of cosmic value. This is a problematic role that Whitehead sees God playing, however, because value is only concomitant with the phenomena of arising phenomena: To capture it is to kill it. Were such accrual even possible, it would be akin to hoarding, which at its best is an unseemly goal in a processional world. At some deep cultural level, we in the West know this to be true if we look at the tales we tell. For example, the dragon that sits upon its gluttonous pile of treasure is not a sage to be praised but a monster to be slain.[25]

This example helps us to see the dangers and the opportunities for theopoetic expression. If the process God is a poet of the world in this theopoetic sense, then he truly does lure us toward an aesthetically oriented future by imagining a better world rather than miraculously causing it to emerge. This seems to be the best theopoetic interpretation of Whitehead's phrase, though it has remained unexplained by him as well as by Faber. As mentioned before, such articulation is not the role of the theopoet per se. But Whitehead is more than that, and those like Faber might be better off by distinguishing when they are speaking theopoetically and when they are not.

The theopoet inspires us to imagine relations between the divine, self, and the world in new and transformative ways; scholars like myself try to make rational sense of them. As a philosopher, I have problems with the Whiteheadian epigram that, in the end, it is more important for ideas to be interesting than to be true. Nevertheless, I see this as a fitting theopoetic credo, and I have no problem understanding and agreeing with the pragmatic value of this perspective in the service of creative thought. As a movement of speculative spiritual philosophy, theopoetic rumination should inspire a creative adventuring of ideas, stoke dialogue where orthodoxy may have become stagnant or bogged down in polemics, increase human flourishing as it relates to the divine, and certainly nurture further novelty of thought. More than just *inspiring* new philosophy or theology, efficacious theopoetic expressions are *creative (poiesis) of transformative thinking*. As fellow poets of the world, theopoets strive to commune with both an audience and the divine (either in nature or as Godhead) through poetic language. It is up to the rest of us to wrestle with the implications these expressions have, if and when they stand the test of reason over time.

The World as an Ultimate
Children as Windows to the World's Sacredness

C. ROBERT MESLE

Roland Faber is insistent that *"theopoetics is about multiplicity!"*[1] Of the many meanings of multiplicity that Faber explores, two are helpful to note at the start. First, he fights against the reduction of process theology to a single Whiteheadian orthodoxy. In this paper and elsewhere, I support that effort by working to keep alive creative dialogue between various theistic and nontheistic visions of God and the World. Secondly, Faber also urges us to resist any reduction of God to One, to "God as being 'someone' creating, a 'self' being subject of self-creativity, a 'force-field' of creativity, a 'divine' matrix—and *affirm nothing but the salvation of the manifold, that is, insist only as/on infinite manifoldness.*"[2] On both counts, I believe my own directions share kinship with Faber's much more extensive and comprehensive efforts.

More deeply, perhaps, I share a motivation I find expressed in the closing pages of Faber's *Theopoetics,* regarding love. Why use the language of *God* at all? Indeed, why bother to talk of God at all? Faber writes that his concept of *polyphilia* is a "restatement of what could be called '(divine) Love.' I understand this Love to be the only, and in this sense, irresistible, reason to retain God-language . . ."[3] It is also my own deep commitment to love as an ultimate, even methodological, motive and criterion that drives all of my own discussions of God. As you will see at the end, even when I argue against God, it is out of a respect for the infinite relational love that I believe the divine poet envisioned by Whitehead, Cobb, Suchocki, and others would have felt for the manifold creatures of the world, an approach to theology taught to me by my father, exemplified in the life of my mother, and inspired by my encounter with my children and grandchildren.

The inspiration of encounter with my children and grandchildren will form the skeleton of these reflections. But for all their personal power, I offer them only as an example of what may inspire others. Surely the theological symbol of divine omnipresence reminds us that there is nothing in this world, no creature so small or mean or profane, that may not serve as the occasion for grace—an ecstatic awareness of the sacred depths, what Tillich called the depth dimension, of reality. While only you can witness to whatever may have occasioned your own encounters with grace and sacredness, I will start with Sarah.

After Sarah, our first child, was born, I rushed from the delivery room to make the traditional phone calls reporting Sarah's size, weight, and so forth. Afterward I returned to the delivery room, where I held Sarah for the first time. In that moment my life changed forever. It was as if the entire universe suddenly fell into place with Sarah at its exact center. Yes, that center included my wife, Barbara, and our families, but everything was different now. After years of existential struggle about the meaning of life, suddenly such questions disappeared in one radiant moment of transformation. Sarah Matters![4] Her "mattering" requires no theological or philosophical justification. Thereafter, every such argument began and ended with the clear, unshakeable affirmation that Sarah Matters. All else must fall into place around that central affirmation. When our son, Mark, was born, he joined Sarah in the center of my life. His value, like hers, needs no further justification.

Yet, of course, for thoughtful people further reflection and clarification are required. You might, for example, be concerned that I am one of those parents who selfishly and destructively dote on their children in ways that are harmful to them and other children. I hope that is not the case. For every person can at times have Sarah's or Mark's face. I remember vividly seeing an elderly woman carrying a heavy bag of groceries and suddenly seeing her with the face of Sarah as an old woman. If that were Sarah as an old woman, what would I want some young man to do? So naturally I offered to carry her groceries for her. Thus, it is not that other children or other people do not matter but that in my life Sarah and Mark became windows through which I see in a new way the sacredness of all children, all people, all living creatures, and all that is.

"Any future theology I do must put the welfare of children above the niceties of metaphysics."[5] Liberation theologian Robert McAfee Brown's principle for theological reflection was published in the *Christian Century* shortly after Mark's birth, and it has shaped my thinking, writing, and teaching ever since. Under its influence I often think that it would be nice if we could simply stop worrying about metaphysical enterprises and get on with being kind, compassionate, and just. Yet, it seems that we cannot escape having worldviews, and as long as that remains true, it will matter to the welfare of children what kinds of metaphysics we share. So whenever I teach or write about metaphysics, I try to return often to the question, Does this matter for the welfare of children and other living creatures?

We are all, of course, someone's child, and every rock is a child of the universe. Yutaka Tanaka cites a Taoist story that I believe approaches this same deep valuing from a different perspective.

> Dogguozi asked Zhuangzi, saying,
> "Where is what you call the Way to be found?"
> Zuanzi [*sic*] replied, "Everywhere." The other said,
> "Specify an instance of it. That will be more satisfactory."
> "It is here in this ant."
> "Give me a lower instance."
> "It is in this panic grass."
> "Give me a still lower instance."
> "It is in this earthenware tile."
> "Surely that is the lowest instance?"
> "It is in that excrement." To this Dongguozi gave no reply.[6]

There is much about the vision of the mystics, in the meaning of Brahman or the Tao, which I do not understand. Yet I am confident that it is this larger vision of unity, expressed in the Tao, in Brahman, in the concept of divine omnipresence, and in the ethical vision of concern for all, that may come to any person in unexpected ways, that for me is captured most powerfully in my encounter with my children. Where you find it, only you can say. But it is there, waiting to lay claim on each of us, to transform us into persons driven by love of all that is. No doubt it finds expression in the ethical vision of Jesus in Matthew 24:45: "'Truly, I say to you, as you did it to one of the least of these my brethren, you did it to me.'" And so I repeat Brown's sound principle, "Any future theology I do must put the welfare of children above the niceties of metaphysics." With this concrete moral guide as our anchor, let us turn to questions of metaphysical ultimacy.

Among John Cobb Jr.'s many creative transformations of apparent contradictions into complementary contrasts is his proposal that Buddhist–Christian dialogue could be transformed by recognizing two Ultimates: Emptiness and God.[7] In *Beyond Dialogue*, in 1982, he argued that God stands as an ultimate because God is the ultimate *actuality*. "God's non-identity with ultimate reality in no way subordinates God to it, for God is the ultimate *actuality*. God as the ultimate actuality is just as ultimate as is Emptiness as ultimate *reality*."[8] I shall make essentially the same argument regarding the World. Whether in speaking of Tillich's Being Itself, Brahman, the Tao, or Creativity, the concrete World, which is the actualization of these ultimates, must itself be respected as ultimate. Cobb has briefly affirmed that Whitehead offers compelling reasons to treat the World as a third ultimate. It is that proposal that I wish to explore here, from the perspective of a nontheistic, process-relational religious naturalist.[9] A further goal is to help build bridges between theistic and nontheistic process relational thinkers.

To connect the concrete Mattering of Sarah, Mark, and all living creatures with the realm of ultimates, it will be helpful, I think, to reflect on Paul Tillich's concept of symbols as developed in his little classic, *The Dynamics of Faith*,[10] and in *Theology of Culture*.[11] I invite you to consider Sarah and Mark as symbols in Tillich's sense. Tillich notes five primary characteristics of symbols. Like signs, symbols point beyond themselves, but, unlike signs, symbols participate in that to which they point. A national flag, for example, is not like a street sign: "the flag participates in the power and dignity of the nation for which it stands."[12] To attack the flag is to attack the nation itself. In just this way, Sarah and Mark are symbols for me because they participate in the "mattering"—the ultimate intrinsic value—of the larger, transcending realm of value of which they are parts. To deny their worth is to deny the worth of every child.

Clearly, Sarah and Mark are much more powerful symbols than a flag because the flag's value, however powerful, is derived entirely by association. We can rightly say, in certain contexts, that the flag is, of course, just a piece of cloth, and we can intellectually know that it has no intrinsic value. Yet no moral person would ever say this of a child.

Here we touch on a central polarity in Sarah's and Mark's Mattering. In one sense, I would insist that Sarah's and Mark's value is intrinsic; it needs no larger theology or philosophy, or even God, to justify it. Sarah and Mark simply Matter. Period. To say otherwise is to risk denying that their value is intrinsic. It is to risk losing the Kantian sense of their dignity as persons, or the utilitarian conviction that their happiness counts equally with all other persons. To make Sarah's and Mark's value contingent is to risk making every child's value contingent, just as we Westerners have so destructively made the value of every nonhuman creature contingent on our human needs and desires. That is a path we must reject.

Yet, to see Sarah's and Mark's value as purely isolated and individual is to see them as Cartesian substances, which "exist independently," and "need no other thing in order to exist."[13] That is a path any process relational thinker will reject. The polarity between intrinsic worth and worth derived from a larger unity is at the heart of my thoughts in this paper and will lead us directly to understanding the World as an ultimate.

Before going on, however, we need to look at the other features Tillich attributed to symbols. Tillich saw the main function of symbols as "opening up levels of reality which otherwise are hidden and cannot be grasped in any other way,"[14] and also as unlocking "dimensions and elements of our souls which correspond to the dimensions and elements of reality."[15] "So every symbol is two-edged. It opens up reality and it opens up the soul."[16] Sarah and Mark certainly do this for me. They open up for me the existential depths of value as nothing before had ever done. Never before had I had such a transparent window through which the deep value of every person could be seen so clearly. Never before had my own egocentrism and selfishness been so challenged by confrontation with the infinite value of others. But unlike some of the more negative existentialist visions, it was not a confrontation that declared that I was meaningless along with everything else. Exactly the opposite was true. In discovering that I could no longer live in the illusion that I am the center of value, I also rediscovered my own value as one more person who might wear the face of Sarah or Mark, and who therefore shared in their infinite, intrinsic Mattering. To see that Mark and Sarah Matter is to discover in a whole new way that I, too, Matter, as do you.

I will say only a few words about the last character of symbols that Tillich describes, the fact that "symbols cannot be produced intentionally. . . . Like living beings, they grow and they die."[17] Tillich obviously meant to speak about words, crosses, and flags rather than children, so I will resist the temptation to play with this theme of birth and death. I can only say that it was no intention of my own that Sarah and Mark reached into my heart and put themselves in place of it. To say that another way, my wife often cites Elizabeth Stone's wisdom that "Making the decision to have a child . . . is deciding forever to have your heart go walking outside your body."[18] But while having children was a decision, their impact on my life was no decision at all. It hit me out of the blue.

I want to return, now, to that central polarity between the brute fact that Sarah and Mark Matter, an existential truth requiring no intellectual justification, and my rejection of a Cartesian individualism that sees them as existing independently, requiring nothing but themselves to exist. How do we solve this problem? How do we follow the honorable process tradition of turning the apparent contradiction into a constructive polarity?

First, let me restate my own experience of the finality of value captured in the phrase *Sarah Matters* or *Mark Matters*. I have asserted that their

Mattering needs no justification beyond itself. Yet I have also said that, at least in part, they achieve this precisely in the way Tillich describes, by opening up dimensions of reality and dimensions of my soul that can be opened up in no other way. In *Theology of Culture* Tillich captures this with great power.

> We can call this the depth dimension of reality itself, the dimension of reality which is the ground of every other dimension and every other depth, and which therefore, is not one level beside the others but is the fundamental level, the level below all other levels, the level of being itself, or the ultimate power of being. Religious symbols open up the experience of the dimension of this depth in the human soul.[19]

How is it possible for Sarah or Mark or you or anything at all to open up such depth dimensions of reality and the soul? Tillich's answer is important. He urges us never to speak of anything as "merely a symbol," or "just a symbol."[20] Sarah, Mark, and you are not "mere symbols." Nor are you symbols by way of abstraction. It is precisely by being concretely *yourself*, precisely by your being an *actual instance* of this very depth dimension of reality, that you can be *both* intrinsically valuable *and* windows to the infinite expanse of that depth dimension of value of which you are actualizations.[21]

I am arguing that Tillich's analysis of symbols, when applied to children or you or other creatures in the manifold, leads us to see that the creatures who (and which) *actualize* the ground and power of Being must themselves stand in the realm of ultimacy as manifestations of Being. Indeed, I doubt that it makes any sense to speak of Being Itself as having value apart from actual beings. *We value Being Itself, if we do precisely as that which makes the actual beings possible.* But I think this discussion can be given sharper focus by shifting from Tillich to Whitehead. Whitehead tells me more clearly what I am encountering when I confront the infinite value of any creature.

First, Whitehead insists that each drop of experience constituting the world "has significance for itself."[22] It has its own intrinsic value, requiring no justification deeper than itself. Indeed, there is nothing deeper than itself. As Whitehead explains, "'Actual entities'—also termed 'actual occasions'—are the final real things of which the world is made up. There is no going behind actual entities to find anything more real."[23] "The ontological principle can be summarized as: no actual entity, then no reason."[24] No deeper justification for the value of actual experiences can be given because Whitehead's "'ontological principle means that actual entities are the only *reasons;* so that to search for a *reason* is to search for one or more actual entities."[25] That is, there can be no creativity apart from its instantiation in actual entities.

Yet, its value is not that of an isolated, independent, Cartesian substance. Whitehead shows us that each actual entity or society of entities, including each person but reaching far beyond the boundaries of human beings, exists precisely and only by arising out of the whole infinite web of reality and value. Yes, each actual entity, each actual experiencing subject, does have value *for itself.* Yet its value, its existence, can only be actual as it becomes *one more face of the infinite web of relationships extending infinitely back in time, and moving infinitely forward in the creative advance.* A full understanding of the becoming of any single actuality would reveal the value emergent from all that infinity that has gone before, and the potential for infinite values yet to emerge.

Whitehead's principle of relativity implies that each new actuality, like a new moment in the life of a person, can only come to have feelings of its own value because it first prehends or grasps the values of others who have gone before, and by anticipating the contributions it might make to future experiencers who share its feelings.[26] As Bernard Loomer understood, the true good emerges from deeply mutual relationships.[27] For any person or any other creature to have its own intrinsic value is precisely for it to be one more face of the infinite web of value out of which it arises. This brings me to another story.

Barbara and I live in the Iowa countryside, surrounded by woods and fields, with a beautiful five-acre pond down the hill. When our daughter, Sarah, was due to have our first grandchild, Barbara and I were packed and ready to leave at a moment's notice in hopes of making it to Chicago for the birth. The call came at 5:30 a.m. on September 7, 2006. We leaped out of bed, and, while Barbara packed the last few things, I took our two golden retrievers, Abe and Ellie, for a last walk down by the pond.

The moment was magical. The full moon was deep red, sitting exactly atop the hill to the west. Dawn's rosy fingers were just beginning to reach up from the east. A beautiful mist covered the pond where the summer-warmed water kissed the cool September air. As we walked across the dam I looked into the mist with my heart full of anticipation of the new life about to join us, and something important happened to me. To explain it, I must first back up a little.

At that time I was preparing to teach the Bhagavad Gita, which includes one of the greatest accounts of revelation in all religious literature. The God, Krishna, reveals himself to Arjuna as Brahman, the ultimate reality. Brahman, the infinite, eternal, all-inclusive reality, is so great that even the

Gods themselves are only a few of the many faces of Brahman. Each of us, too, is one face of Brahman. Let me share just a few key lines from this great text.

> Look, Arjuna: thousands,
> millions of my divine forms,
> beings of all kinds and sizes,
> of every color and shape. . . .
> The whole universe, all things
> animate or inanimate,
> are gathered here—look!—enfolded
> inside my infinite body. . . .
> Arjuna saw the whole universe
> enfolded, with its countless billions
> of life-forms, gathered together
> in the body of the God of gods. . . .
> Arjuna said . . . I see you everywhere, with billions
> of arms, eyes, bellies, faces,
> without end, middle, or beginning,
> your body the whole universe, Lord.[28]

This passage was very much on my mind and in my heart that morning. Looking into that mist, I had my own small vision of Brahman—not with billions of heads and arms, but a few. Then, for just a moment, I saw a tiny, new face press out of Brahman.[29] Soon it withdrew into the cosmic whole—as we all eventually do. I stood with tears of joy pouring down my face. Later we learned that our new grandchild was a boy, Elliot. As with our own children, when I look into his eyes, what I see smiling back at me is not just Elliot, but Brahman.

It was a mystical moment, linking me unexpectedly with one of the most ancient of religious traditions, in which the awesome mystery of our deepest reality and interbeing reached out and drew me in. Whatever is, is Brahman, including you and me, and any God or Gods there may be. The traditions of India teach us that if we all understood fully our inter-relatedness in Brahman, the world would be a better place for children and other living creatures. I agree. Elliot Matters. He Matters because he is one face of the ultimate web of reality, Brahman, which itself is the depth dimension of all reality and all value, which I understand Whitehead to be struggling to describe. As a process-relational philosopher, I will wish to have further discussions of the nature of the reality named Brahman, but for now I see it as a beautiful symbol for why it is that Sarah, Mark, Elliot, and you and I all Matter.

It should be obvious why this leads me to treat the World as an ultimate. It is largely a matter of where my personal loyalties lie. Let us be honest. Few, if any, of us build deep personal loyalties out of metaphysical visions. Rather, those visions sometimes express and give depth to—and occasionally transform—those loyalties arising out of our autobiographies. I am drawn to Whitehead because his vision of reality makes such good sense of my own experiences—the very standard Whitehead proposed for testing his ideas. So, let me say in another way why Whitehead's philosophy confirms my experience of the World, including Elliot, as a metaphysical ultimate.

Whitehead, of course, reserved the category of "ultimate" for creativity.[30] "Neither God, nor the World, reaches static completion. Both are in the grip of the ultimate metaphysical ground, the creative advance into novelty."[31] But Whitehead gives us good reason to count the World as an ultimate in the last chapter of *Process and Reality.* For example, "It is as true to say that, in comparison with the World, God is actual eminently, as that, in comparison with God, the World is actual eminently. . . . It is as true to say that God creates the World, as that the World creates God."[32] "Also, the World's nature is a primordial datum for God; and God's nature is a primordial datum for the World."[33] At the very end of his essay on two ultimates, Cobb agrees that Whitehead justifies treating the world as a third ultimate.

Actually, Whitehead's text supports our speaking of three ultimates, and there are types of spirituality oriented to the third one as well. This is the world. Whitehead writes that there is no creativity apart from God and the world. There is no God apart from creativity and the world. And there is no world apart from God and creativity. This passage makes clear that these three cannot be ranked in a hierarchical way. If there can be no creativity apart from God and the world, then creativity is not in some way superior to or, in my language, more ultimate than God or the world. Equally this counts against the theistic tendency to rank God at the top and the world and creativity as subordinate.[34]

Cobb suggests that many "primal communities have focused on the world and that this emphasis was belittled by the axial religions that all tended to focus strongly on the distinctiveness of the human."[35] Jeffery Long makes a similar argument in his essay, "A Whiteheadian Vedanta."[36] Long distinguishes between Nirguna Brahman and Saguna Brahman. Nirguna Brahman is "Brahman as unqualified and unconditioned by form."[37] Saguna Brahman is "Brahman as qualified by the limitations of time and space, as the sum total of all actual entities. So Nirguna Brahman corresponds to Whitehead's understanding of creativity as nonfactual and form-less. Saguna Brahman corresponds to the two realities Whitehead calls . . . God and the world."[38] On this view, God and the World stand on footing roughly equal to expressions of Saguna Brahman.

We might add to this the distinction between the Tao as undifferenti-ated, and the Tao as differentiated into the manifold of the world. In a slide presentation at the Process Summer Academy at the East China University of Science and Technology in the summer of 2009, Professor Yang Fubin explained that "the *Dao* itself has two essential aspects discriminated as *Wu* (无, Being—without—form) and *You* (有, Being—within—form). The former is invisible and abstract, employed by *Lao Zi* to indicate the state of the *Dao* before it comes down to its actuality, whilst the latter is visible and concrete, employed to indicate the outcome of the *Dao* as manifested in the things which surround us."[39] This is simply the distinction between the Tao that cannot be named and the Tao that can be named.[40]

Whether in the case of Brahman, the Tao, Emptiness, or Whitehead's Creativity, Cobb's argument that God is not subordinate to Creativity be-cause God *actualizes* Creativity seems to me to apply to the World as well, in each case. Brahman or the Tao as manifest in actuality in the manifold of the world is not less ultimate than that which it manifests.

Cobb allows for the World to be the third ultimate. I have sidestepped that language so far by speaking of the world as *an* ultimate. If I am not theistic, clearly, I think there are only two. Yes, I confess. The first portion of this paper was, in fact, a personal testimony and metaphysical argument that the World can stand on its own, without God, as a ground of sacred ultimacy. I have tried to show how it is that each creature in the world can have its own infinite worth and be a window to such infinite worth in a purely nontheistic religious naturalism.

At the same time, I still think that my vision of religious naturalism fits into the process tradition of turning contradictories into compatibles. My goal now is to clarify why it is that I have always seen theistic and non-theistic process-relational forms of thought as close allies, not opponents. John Cobb offered his proposal for accepting God as one of two ultimates to Buddhists, most of whom are not theistic. But while I am sure he hoped that some would be won over to process theism, I suspect he also hoped to show nontheistic Buddhists why they need to see process theists not as op-ponents but as partners with whom dialogue holds possibilities for mutual transformation. In the same spirit, I present the idea of the World as an ul-timate as a way of persuading theists and nontheists alike that they can en-ter into dialogue that can be mutually transforming and noncombative.

Here, then, I turn back to a personal story that underlies my agreement with Faber that Love is the reason to talk about God. My father taught me to evaluate theologies by always asking, "What would a genuinely loving God be like? And what would a truly loving God be doing in the world?" I continue to support the process-relational vision of God because in it I see what I think a genuinely loving God would be like, doing what a truly loving God would be doing in the world. My own spiritual commitment to the World arises very much from my father's teaching. If I ask myself whether such a God would want me to care more for God or for the World, the answer seems clear. A truly loving God would want my first loyalty to be to the World that God so deeply loves and with which God rejoices and suffers. In Tillich's language, if I ask "What would be the ultimate concern of the process relational God?" the answer seems clear—the World. I think some motive like this inspires Faber's vision of *theoplicity* and *polyphila,* when he argues that *"only theoplicity can be polyphilic . . ."*[41]

It is important to be clear that for me, personally, the primary question is about love and compassion—about ethical and spiritual ultimacy rather than metaphysical ultimacy. I think there are good metaphysical reasons to view the World as an ultimate, but that is never the main question for me. It is the creatures constituting the World in all its concreteness that draw my ultimate (though of course flawed) compassionate love. It is Sarah, Mark, Elliot, and you. It is the children and other creatures who I think have the greatest need of my love.

Jesus said that "the Sabbath was made for man, not man for the Sabbath; so the Son of man is lord even of the Sabbath."[42] Following that lead, a more theological way to explain why the World takes priority for me is that I don't think the process-relational God would have issued the first great commandment: "You shall love the Lord your God with all your heart, and with all your soul, and with all your mind."[43] Or perhaps, God would not have broken the great commandment into two parts, where the first is to love God and the second is to love your neighbor. At the very least I think a genuinely loving God would have reversed the order. I think this God would be saying something more like, "Love each other and the creatures of the world 'with all your heart, and with all your soul, and with all your mind.' That is who I love most, and I will always be working with you for the World's welfare—whether you think I am here or not. As long as you care for the World with compassionate wisdom, we are working together." I suspect that for many people any persuasive argument for putting the commandment to love God first is based on the fact that it will better enable us to live out the second—to love our neighbors. But if the commandment to love God is really a means to that end, we ought to make that clear. I cannot imagine the process-relational God truly wanting us to love God more than we love the children of the World. Would any of us who have children want people to care more for us than for our children?

Such a view of God, I hope, allows theists and nontheists to roll up our sleeves and join arms in common cause. Given this view of divine love, the theist has no need to be concerned about viewing the World as a third (but equal) ultimate, and the nontheist has no cause to be concerned that such theism will draw love and loyalty out of the world where it is so desperately needed. This is not to say that the theists will feel that their personal relationship with a profoundly loving God is not important, or that the nontheists would not be better able to love the world if they shared such spiritually empowering love. Nor does it mean that the nontheists will lose all concern that aspects of theism may still draw energies into less productive directions. But my hope is that these could remain friendly concerns, a family argument shared while working in a common vineyard, helping to keep each other continually open to the others' compassionate wisdom. It seems to me that this is what actually happens in our process community.

While there will be some family conversations over the virtues of various theistic and nontheistic approaches to process relational thought, I have no doubt that we share commitments to a wide range of political, social, economic, environmental, and ethical work to be done. We share concerns for global warming, for the destruction of coral reefs, for genuinely democratic dialogue and political structures. We share concern for social justice for the poor and oppressed, for women and minorities. We are likely to vote in favor of gay rights. We are likely, I think, to share a Buddhist compassion for all sentient life. And while we older folk have usually not overcome our carnivorous habits, I see my younger vegetarian and vegan students drawn to a process-relational vision that values all sentient life.

I return, finally, to Sarah, Mark, Elliot, and you. Elliot Matters. You Matter. For me, our philosophical reflections are not required to justify the ultimacy of his or your claim on us; they only help us to understand the grounding of that claim. There are no disputes between theists and nontheists over whether Elliot Matters. It is, for me, the beginning and end of the discussion.

The Gravity of Love
Theopoetics and Ontological Imagination

LAUREL C. SCHNEIDER

"I understood love to be the very gravity holding each leaf, each cell, this earthy star together."[1] This concluding line from a prose piece by Joy Harjo follows, as a kind of explanatory note, on a longer poem entitled "The Woman Who Fell from the Sky." That longer piece is Harjo's version of one of the most widely shared narratives by the same name of the eastern woodlands Native peoples of North America. Harjo's poem is more than a restatement or interpretation of an original. It is a storied response to a particular present, a specific time and place. Among the eastern tribes, "The Woman Who Fell from the Sky" (dubbed the "earth-diver narratives" by anthropologists) is a never-twice-the-same story about how this world of earth, water, sky, and creatures came to be. It generally starts with a young woman who runs off with a star (or other sky person of uncertain character). Eventually she becomes too curious or willful, leans too far out of the sky world, and falls (or jumps) with her twin babies into this watery world. By falling through the sky into the arms of this world's creatures she becomes an essential element, a necessary ingredient, of *this* world's creation.

Even in brief summary it is evident that "The Woman Who Fell from the Sky," along with the other earth-diver narratives like it, disrupts the logic of linear consequence, or at least it disrupts the temporal linearity of absolute beginnings. *By falling into the arms of the creatures of this world, she helps to create this world.* But even more disruptive to linear logic than a creation-by-fall, in a complex tease of tenses this creator-woman falls even before she started falling: In some versions she was a creature of this world already before it is created by her falling. And she fell then, too. She fell in love with a star/bad boy wizard/eagle/trickster. According to some, she disobeys her mother and follows him to the sky world. She conceives twins, gets curious (or bored, or rebellious) and falls or jumps through a hole in the sky. A group of water creatures see her hurtling toward them and recognize the peril that she is in. They consult with each other, catch her before she can hit the surface, and pull up a bit of earth on which she and her children can stand. The rest, of course, is history.

Historical credibility depends upon the a priori concepts that prefigure horizons of possibility for what can count as real. Whether a world, for example, can be created out of nothing. Whether a world can be created on a sunny morning by its own creatures who spot a young woman tumbling from the sky. Logics of consequence are only disrupted if they apply in the first place. This fundamental insight grounds a range of theopoetic sensibilities, allowing them to illuminate the fissures and creative openings in otherwise foreclosed narratives. Theology has long depended upon the a priori conditions of credibility that make poetries of origin credible.

What is more, how theology understands itself and navigates its own constitutive multiplicity depends a great deal on the tools that it uses. During the millennia of European domination of Western Christian thought (and of Christian domination of European thought), it is not surprising that the codes of rationality forged in that cultural context also served to shape the particular scope and criteria of plausibility in Christian theological inquiry. What is more, the past few centuries of global shifts in populations and colonial overlapping and overtaking of cultures make clear that no theological approach has ever stood alone in a vacuum of influences. The interdependence of cultures (and religions) also makes clear that interdependent modes of reasoning help us to get at the deeper plurality of the world, indeed the deeper plurality of Christian thought itself.

It bears repeating here that "multiplicity" is not the same as "the many." It does not refer to a pile of many separable units, many "ones," and so it is not opposed to the One or to ones. "The multiple" (it is ironic how the English language seems to want to make it into a singularity), or "multiplicity," results when things—ones—so *constitute* each another that they come to exist (in part, of course) *because of* one another. Essential separation becomes incoherence. So does essential wholeness, or oneness. The whole is constituted by its parts, but then, the parts are also constituted by their participation in the whole. As Jean-Luc Nancy points out, the Latin "*plus* is comparable to *multus*. It is not 'numerous'; it is 'more.'"[2] Multiplicity is what happens when something is more than the sum of its parts but also, by virtue of its necessary participation as a part of other somethings, is not itself therefore completely whole. The multiple is therefore more but also less than whole, or One. And of course, as we have seen, the One fails to be only one, over and over again. Nancy puts it this way:

> The One as purely one is less than one; it cannot be, be put in place, or counted. One as properly one is always more than one. It is an excess of unity; it is one-with-one, where its Being itself is co-present.[3]

This is a mathematical statement, but it is also a qualitative one. Mathematically, "one" is a relational number. It is fully dependent on its relation to and distinction from all other numbers (two, three, and so forth). One has no actual meaning without at least one other. The One comes into being in relation to Other(s), or not-ones. This is the conundrum of the One; why it cannot get away from the One–Many divide, even when it is conceived not as a simple one but as a totality. Nancy's point is that a "pure" One is impossible because as such it implies no other, no relation. And so the pure One is less than one because it "cannot be . . . counted" since counting requires the defining company of others. This is the mathematical contradiction of the One. At the same time, as Nancy suggests, there is a qualitative contradiction in the One that comes from its moreness, its excess of totality that results from its necessary coming into being in relation.

Jean-Luc Nancy, focusing on the impossibility of totality (substantive or empty), describes pure multiplicity as the "One-minus." Gilles Deleuze likewise argues that "the multiple" implies subtraction, "always $n - 1$." And Alain Badiou characterizes multiplicity as "without-one."[4] All three are attempting to think multiplicity beyond the One–Many divide by exposing the mathematical (logical/nominal) and spatial (relational) interdependence—or compromise—of the One with its others. There is also an interdependence, or compromise of the One and its others in terms of time. This is the issue of stasis and change. One can only remain One if no change (time) fractures it. In time, the One is without oneness. It is, as Badiou suggests, "without one." One then and One now can only remain one if there *is* no then and now. From this it is easy to see why the negation of time in eternity became such a firmly rooted doctrinal assertion about God in Christian philosophical theology.

It is one thing to see that the One–Many divide is a projection of the logic of the One. It is another thing entirely to imagine *thought* in some other dimension. Can we imagine multiplicity as a mode that opens a possibility for thought beyond the One–Many divide? We must try, at least, to begin. Again. Any other option, it seems to me, will keep us slipping back into the groove of opposition to the One, which thereby reinscribes the One–Many divide and its conclusive logic. This is no small task, although the circumstances in which we find ourselves now may demand it. Rosi Braidotti agrees. New modes of thinking that better reflect actual embodied complexity require monumental effort, she claims, because "we live in permanent processes of transition, hybridization, and nomadization, and these in-between states and stages defy the established modes of theoretical representation."[5]

Thought like this requires sea legs. It must find its rest not in the landlocked stability of conclusions, but in the rhythms of Aionian motion, in the flow continuous. This exercise is not, therefore, about a search for some kind of "pure" multiple, or a "pure" multiplicity, precisely because that effort remains fully within the mode of the One–Many divide, requiring an aim and a dialect of reduction and abstraction. Alain Badiou has already made this point. Pure multiplicity, he argues (against Heidegger and Deleuze), is fundamentally Platonic. It is ideal and mathematical because only mathematics can make a multiplicity without imposing an interpretation (a unity) upon it.[6] Unfortunately, in his excellent criticism, especially of Deleuze's claims to a fully immanent philosophy, Badiou is conflating multiplicity with the many, and so makes his point still from within the logic of the One–Many divide. His use of the word *pure* here may be the signal of that entrapment. It may also be that the word *multiplicity* is itself too deeply tied to the mathematics of the One–Many divide (which is, in part, Badiou's point) to allow us to use it to move into what Braidotti calls a more nomadic mode.[7]

It is entirely possible that Deleuze is right and there is no *ontological* "logic of multiplicity" that is readily available to philosophy or to theology as they have constructed themselves, steeped as both disciplines are in modes of thought that require reduction and simplification, that frown upon contradiction, and that valorize the universal.[8] But an ontological logic of multiplicity may be available both to philosophers and theologians if they are willing to do three things: to dispense with Eurocentric requirements for European precedent in argument (already I am advocating a departure from accepted understandings of the terms of logic!), to risk meaningful contradiction, and, finally, to consider with Miguel de Beistegui the possibility that "the ontology of the multiple can only be locally circumscribed."[9]

Meanwhile, from other non-European directions, less plodding modes of thinking multiplicity—not tied, in other words, to the heavy genealogical constraints of dialecticism that burden European thought—come concepts of fluidity, disorientation, change, presence, and shape-shifting that may go much further than the philosophers in *thinking* multiplicity beyond the One–Many divide. Furthermore, some might say, with good reason, that the tellers of parables have never lost sight of multiplicity and becoming as modes of thought. It is just that their ranks have been thinned by monotheistic evangelism, colonizers' guns, and the unification of global capital (not necessarily in that order), all of which depend upon the dualistic logic of the One–Many divide for success. And philosophers have begun to see dull poverty of imagination, if not a masquerade of control, at the dualistic true–false center, or mirror, of the One. It is certainly the case that many cultural traditions with their varying modes of reasoning are already embedded within Christianity. The Bible alone contains texts that celebrate different and sometimes conflicting accounts of the world, exposing a range of rationalities that are expressed in a variety of genres. But even more important for theology's work today is the complicated multitude of cultures within which Christianity is rooted. As Thomas Reynolds neatly points out, "being religious—being Christian—already entails being 'beyond' one's own local faith perspective, [it entails] being interreligious. Pluralism affects religious affirmations from the root."[10] Pluralism here refers to the polysemic intersections, dissonances, relations, and syncretic accretions of multiple stories, experiences, presences, cultures, religious traditions and modes of reasoning that lead to Christian theology's positions and aversions. Theology that has grown over the course of millennia cannot help but result, in hindsight, in a kind of "polyphonic bricolage."[11]

This assumption of an *originary pluralism* from which Christian theology properly begins, along with the mature awareness of the limitations of Euro-Christian modes of reasoning, form the primary set of presuppositions upon which a theopoetics of the manifold depends if it is actually to redress the deficits resident in dominant Christian theological reasoning today. I have argued that Christian theology suffers from a sensible lack—an anorexic denial even—of humor and of poetry; it wastes from an overreliance on apodictic and deductive modes of reasoning to the exclusion of other pathways.[12] One such other pathway that is informing my own study is illuminated by the work of several Native American writers: Joy Harjo (Muskogee), Gerald Vizenor (anishinaabe), and Thomas King (Cherokee) especially. Although King's work is largely responsible for my introduction to this mode of reasoning, my discussion in this paper relies primarily on chancy coincidences of insights from Harjo and Vizenor.[13]

Harjo is a Muskogee poet from Oklahoma, though of course the Muskogee people lived for a thousand years in the southeastern woodlands of what is now Alabama and Mississippi before Andrew Jackson drove them on death marches to what is now Oklahoma. Her poetry, like that of several other Native American writers, deliberately blurs lines between the Euro-modern notion of poetry "as art" and a less bifurcated view of poetry as metaphysical creativity, as invocational, as a power that participates sacramentally in the worlds that it helps to bring into being. This blurred understanding of poetry ignores early Protestant distinctions between art and the sacred, a distinction summed up by the eighteenth-century poet and literary historian Samuel Johnson, who said that art, if it is any good, necessarily embellishes what the artist sees. Understood this way, all art is fiction, and that is Johnson's point. "Poetry pleases," he claims, "by exhibiting an idea more grateful to the mind than the things themselves afford," whereas religion must concern itself exclusively with the truth. This is the reason, Johnson argues, that religion makes for bad art, and vice versa.[14]

Aside from the more or less obvious apology for Protestant iconoclasm resident in Johnson's early modern bifurcation of art from truth (which is not a small aside, but the Protestant dimension is not the direct subject of this paper) the dominant logic resident in that division makes the challenge of thinking theopoetically today all the greater. If poetry is art, and art is fiction, then poetry is fiction. The irony or, more accurately, the problem in this equation is that it only works if fiction means a lie, or misrepresentation (both of which occur as synonyms in mainline thesauri). The equation falls apart if fiction means a particular mode of invoking, creating, or constructing the real.

In "A Postcolonial Tale," Harjo writes "Everything was as we imagined it. The earth and stars, every creature and leaf imagined with us."[15] She writes poetry in a more or less conventional sense of the word. But her "embellishments" on what she sees in the world are not exactly fictional in the modernist, dualistic sense that requires art qua art to be other than real or even representational, something other than presence—a deferral of presence at most. Within a logical framework that grants to nature an independence from human imagining (whether in the Newtonian sense of objective substances governed by universal laws or in the post-Kantian, postmodern sense of a nature/world so wholly independent from human imagining that it can only *be* imagined, which is to say fictionalized, or misrepresented) the possibility that imagination has substantive effect is nonsense. It is a lovely embellishment, a fiction, to say that *everything was as we imagined it* and actually mean *the earth and stars, every creature and leaf imagined with us.* Because of course we cannot *actually* mean that, grant it some kind of objective truth. But process metaphysics edges into the territory of such possibility. Native modernity has always already been in that territory. In the territory of Cartesian metaphysics, however, such a statement can maintain a claim to "truth" only by reducing it to the emaciated, sundered level of art-as-misrepresentation, or to a level of subjectivity in which the word *truth* may apply, but only in an individual, psychological sense. Thanks to Freud, psychology provides Cartesian metaphysics with an outlet for fiction's stubborn comingling with truth in the form of profound subjectivity and of delusion (in either case, it is "true for me" without any necessary reference to an external, shared world) while allowing it to have certain real effects.

Harjo and others like her simply do not begin with the presuppositions of European modernity and Newtonian mechanics. The rationality she inherits perceives a world that is more malleable than the mental–physical poles of western thought allow; it is less law-abiding than that. And poetry not only describes some of that unruliness; it also implicates—folds—us into it. But this implication means that theopoetics of the manifold, or poetics that engage ontic possibilities according to "other" metaphysics, must also find a way to relinquish a good portion of the Protestant iconoclasm that undergirds conventional meanings of the term *poetics* (not to mention *theos,* not to mention *metaphysics!*) and allow the metaphors of poetics to have more agency and kataphatic resonance than the concept of poiesis heretofore has allowed. Poetry is poiesis in actuality and as such casts possibility backward and forward precisely because it pokes holes in anything solid and ushers productive ambiguity in not just in language, as if language is merely a mode, but in actuality, at least in those realms that understand that stories must be told in season, and carefully, because the story itself, the poem, makes and breaks the world.

The challenge of framing theopoetics of a divine manifold that does not simply slide back in to the logic of the One is a challenge of undoing the early modern bifurcation of the linguistic from the material, which means a return—for Protestants in particular—to the touchy matter of the sacramental. Theopoetics is the possibility of a touchy, material, sacramental rationality, which is how I would describe divine poiesis, although I think that Roland Faber's definition from his postscript to *God as Poet* is helpful here: "a creative event of construction and synthesis (Whitehead would say 'concrescence')." He also suggests that God's poiesis "is a relational act of tender patience and saving love."[16] For these definitions to gain traction out of the deep grooves of the logic of the One, however, we need the deep materiality of process thought modified by the trickiness of imaginative concretion. In other words, the potential resident in Whitehead's understanding of the imaginative as origin of self-determination[17] may still be shackled by his own bifurcation of the mental and physical poles so that understanding the imaginative as origin of world-determination (as nexus of self-determinations that are thereby not really *self-*determined) still may elude us. This is a matter of emphasis, rather than correction, and it exists as a problem, as Whitehead argues, because of the Cartesian emphasis on "the disastrous separation of body and mind."[18]

Regina Schwartz gives a very tidy summary of the problem that faces theologians in particular, which is also a problem of the metaphysics that produced modernity. She is approaching the "disastrous separation" in terms of its effect on sacramentality, which can be a helpful way for those of us within and on the margins of process philosophy to think about theopoetics within an ontologic of multiplicity. She calls the problem the logic of secularism, but it is also, no surprise to us, the logic of the One in practical terms. She writes:

> Because sacramental thinking is completely alien to the way modern secularism has conceived matter, space, time, and language, in a sense it had to be almost dismantled for modernism to be born. "God's body cannot be here and at the right hand of the Father," said a logic of physical space that trumped the sacred space of sacramentality. "Man [sic] cannot eat God" said a logic of human physiology that, turning a deaf ear to the liturgy of sacramentality, went so far as to equate the claim of participation in the divine with cannibalism. "A priest cannot sacrifice God" claimed a logic of authority that denied the mystery of sacramental agency and accused man of trying to exercise power over the divine. "A sign can only stand for, that is, stand in for what it signifies, which is necessarily absent" said a logic of representation that defied the participation of the sign in its referent.[19]

How can a process theopoetics break out of this web of exclusions and maintain its coherence in a world still governed by that logic? It may not be able to do both. But what takes place in the work of poets and other artists like Harjo could provide some wisdom: There is a presupposition in that work of creative relationship between the artist and a world that never listened to the secularists of early modernity like Johnson to begin with—a world that never divested itself of divinity and so never had to justify or mourn the loss of the gods in the world the way the moderns did. At work in Harjo's writing is a mode of reasoning that is not beholden to Thomistic or Kantian limits. It is a mode of reasoning that Gerald Vizenor, an anishinaabe philosopher, has dubbed "native modernity."[20] Among other things, with this concept Vizenor suggests that the philosophical moves of European and American postmodernity are beginning to approach Native modernity, which has already long understood the malleable, fluid, and interdynamic aspects of narrative construction of reality.

Concerned primarily with survivance—by which he means "an active sense of presence" of Native peoples beyond the tragic nonactuality of a nonhistory called by the misname *indian*—Vizenor argues for a much trickier nomenclature for the "storiers of native modernity." He builds his argument on Louis Dupré's observation that "cultural changes, such as the one that gave birth to the modern age, have a definitive and irreversible impact that transforms the very essence of reality. Not merely our thinking about the real changes: reality itself changes as we think about it differently. History carries an ontic significance that excludes any reversal of the present."[21] Native survivance is not merely a tattered picking-up of the traditional pieces in the brutal aftermath of colonial devastation, a nostalgic "reversal of the effects by returning to premodern premises."[22] In this exercise in theopoetic thought, I am picking up on Vizenor's picking up on Dupré to think about theopoetics as a kind of ontic signification that takes seriously the reality-changing trickiness of our work.

Native modernity, as Vizenor develops the concept, emphasizes the vitality of old stories told in new ways, and new stories told in old ways, that indicate chance presences or ontic significations that *effect* (not just affect, although that too) the world. *Life* occurs in the stories we tell and hear, and this seems to me to be something of significance for theopoetics even as it echoes certain aspects of process metaphysics. It includes a recognition of a responsive creativity between world and art. Art—speech—imagination— does much more than describe, embellish, or lie about what is already there. Art—speech—imagination—storytelling—also creates what is there. *This* is the anathema to Euro-modern thought and the logic of the One. It involves multiplicity that is far beyond the realm of numerical reckoning, and into the realms of shape-shifting, responsive, and excessive process— the capacity for reality to respond to our words, for us to respond, rhizomatically, to the world. That is what a theopoetics of the manifold is talking about, especially when it is paired with process thought.

But process thought, while still self-consciously employing a mode of reasoning that traces itself through the ontological intuitions of Plato, Leibniz, and Descartes, nevertheless recognizes that a different metaphysical result is needed—especially since Kant. John Cobb writes that "Whiteheadians have been convinced that the cosmology and metaphysics that are now needed are quite different from those that were dominant in the past" and process thought, for Whiteheadians, he claims, is that different metaphysics.[23] Native modernity already functions and thinks from different cosmologies and metaphysics, and there are some interesting points of intersection that cannot be reconciled into a "same" but that can provide some interesting entwining. Process metaphysics does not require a sensibility of poetry in quite the same way that Native modernity does, although there is no reason why it shouldn't: The structure of prehensions and actual occasions, especially in nexus and the gathering of events in new potentialities all resonate with the responsive and motile quality of reality that comes through Native modernity.

For example, Harjo's thinking of love as the "very gravity that holds each leaf and star together" is not that far from John Cobb's thinking of forgiveness as the creativity that persists even in the narrowest of circumstances, a divine lure and structural openness of every actual occasion to a new outcome. In both cases, a form of natural theology is suggested—gravity as love/love as gravity, new moments as forgiveness/forgiveness as the next moment. But in neither case is natural theology in a *reductive* sense adequate to describe what is going on in the different cosmologies/metaphysics being engaged. A part of what is distinctively shared, at least as I am suggesting it here, between Native modernity and process thought, is an openness to actual presences (as actual occasions according to Whitehead, or as chance associations, conversions, and reversions according to Vizenor) that make a kataphatic difference without reversion or reduction to a problematically substantive stasis.

Harjo begins "A Postcolonial Tale" with the stanza "Every day is a reenactment of the creation story. We emerge from / dense unspeakable material, through the shimmering power of / dreaming stuff."[24] The mode of reasoning at work here is utterly serious about the claim, also in this poem, that "earth and stars, every creature and leaf imagined with us." And yet this is not a reductive rationality. She concludes with "No story or song will translate the full impact of falling or the inverse/power of rising up." If natural theology is to apply here at all (and we may not even want to take up that contested charge), it means something altogether other than a mechanistic conflation of "nature" with design. The chancy, excessive, poetic dimensions of reality disrupt the mechanisms of Newtonian nature, making gravity a kind of desire (or vice versa) and love its material memory, its occasion and its objective immortality. Gravity, here, is not a metaphor *for* love, an exchangeable similitude, but its inexplicable presence, its actuality. Every day we reenact creation, become in the context (out of) the dense dreaming stuff, make ourselves and the world into presence by becoming present. This is a narrative, imaginative, ontically significant claim, and it is unintelligible to the "dominant metaphysics" against which, Cobb tells us, Whiteheadians also strive. It could be sacramental, if we see divine manifolding at play here—and how can we not?

According to Native modernity—which I am saying is the mode of reasoning that best describes what is going on in Harjo's theopoetics—

imagination and reality comingle just as they do in process metaphysics. In Native modernity this comingling is less mechanical, more lyrical and unpredictable (and so more tragic, perhaps, than recuperative and therapeutic), but in both cases (Whiteheadian and Vizenorian) "presence" is not the impossibility that it is for Kantians (and self-described post-Kantians), and this is what makes the metaphysics of process thought and of Native modernity overlap in creative ways.

For one thing, presence, or "being-with," to adopt the phrase that Jean-Luc Nancy prefers, is not a static notion; it requires becoming-present, or presentation. *Presence* is a tricky term for philosophies steeped in the logic of the One, because—as Kant intuited—no thing in itself can fully present itself without remainder, contradiction, or trickery. In the logic of the One, the only resolution to this problem is to deny presence(s) any epistemological or ontological certainty at all. Hence the caricature of postmodern philosophy's supposed nihilism: There is nothing that can be absolutely asserted, and "presence" requires too many substantive assumptions that simply cannot be supported in the context of so much possibility of error. Whatever one sees or experiences in the supposed presence of another can never certainly refer to anything outside of the narrative one inhabits; in the caricature of European postmodernity, this means that ultimately reality consists only of competing interpretations of texts.

As I am suggesting here, other modes of reasoning exist (other than the logic of the One, that is) that have never required "presence" to instantiate static, unverifiable substance prior to linguistic or narrative implication. They do not assume language, narrative, and story to be inert building blocks and tools for reporting, memory, or instruction. In other words, these other modes of reasoning do not assume language, narrative, and story to be disembodied, without agency on their own. Perhaps there is a fundamental tendency in book cultures toward the negligent idea that language and narrative can be reduced to utility and thereby bound (as in shelved). The error lies in forgetting the innate agency of stories, their capacity to be bound *for* something, for mischief and creation beyond any storyteller's ability to predict or manage. Ontic significance coimplicates story and presence(s), assuming a world-creating aspect to narrative that cannot be restricted or entirely managed. But this idea is intelligible only within a mode of reasoning that begins with multiplicity or, more specifically, does not presume a prior logic of the One wherein an ontological separation between truth (as one) and fiction (as multiple) must be rigidly maintained.[25]

It is significant that some European and Euro-American philosophers have finally begun to turn energetically toward theories of multiplicity as a starting point for postmodern rationality. They are doing so in part because the general global milieu for writing has allowed the possibility of different modes of reasoning (along with very different kinds of stories) to circulate and pollinate hybrid species of thought. They also have begun to reach some of the logical limits of negation in postmodern thought and seek more supple grounds for thinking about reality without reactivity about presence and ontology. This has led them to theories of multiplicity and a new willingness to entertain ideas of presence. Unlike the logic of the One, the logic of multiplicity is an openness that is not blank because it is not mesmerized by possession but is poised for passage, for shape-shifting. Just as porosity is meaningless in a void, multiplicity must be an affirmation of what is, even as the pores of what *is* receive and exchange possibility, and in so doing shift and pass away. A posture of divine multiplicity must not get stuck either in a paralytic stupor over that which is always already inexorably (and heart-breakingly) passing away, or in a naive embrace of what is always already to come, an "eternal sunshine of a spotless mind." Both positions resist openness, both oppose the "is" and the "isn't" as if the passing-away does not constitute the coming or as if being does not constitute its own absence. Mary Daly charged Paul Tillich of necrophilia in his favoring—to the point of obsession, perhaps—the angst of existential nonbeing over wonder at beings that surge all around. She argued, years ago, for a posture of multiplicity that she called biophilia, charging the theologians of existentialism with too little love of life *lived,* mourning instead of what they could not hold onto, or control. The "Verb of verbs," as she described divinity early in her philosophical career, is an ontological expression of existence-in-flux that demands openness to the new even as what is now passes away.[26] And Keller adds, "Let us draw the tehomic inference: the God who is not a Being does not exist over against nonbeing, as the opposite of nothing . . ."[27]

The natal Open is also the porous Deep. Keller names three "capacities"— *implicatio, complicatio, explicatio*—for the tehomic divine that, following Deleuze, she takes from the medieval theologians Giordano Bruno and Nicholas of Cusa. *Implicatio* refers to the creative, interconnected fluidity of the Deep.[28] She discusses the *plis*—fold—at the etymological heart of the three terms, which I take to be more like the folding of batter than the folding of sheets, though I would hate to diminish the potency of such rich language through an overly tedious translation. Porosity, I want to suggest, is related to this provocative suggestion of Keller's—the porousness of the divine is, in the dialect of multiplicity, a kind of open *implication,* an unfolding, complicating interconnection that confounds the One–Many divide.

Native modernity, as I have already said, starts with this assumption, taking from it the structures of plausibility that incorporate ambiguity (which is a kind of multiplicity) into the core of its mode of reasoning. Without ambiguity there are no stories, and without stories, as King asserts, there is no truth. Which means that truth, in truth, is multiple. It also means that, without stories, there is no world and, if we are to follow Whitehead (and Faber), without world, there is no God.

Sub-version

Theopoetics as Radical Theology

JOHN D. CAPUTO

In this paper I argue that radical theology is only possible as theopoetics, where theopoetics means a poetics of the event contained in the name of God.

From Theology to Radical Theology

The first step is to show that theology, by which I mean at the start confessional theology, is inevitably delimited and displaced by radical theology. To see why this is so, let us distinguish between religious actors and theological reflection. The actors belong to a first-order operation of religious beliefs and practices. Some of these practices are cultic in which, as Hegel says, the community deepens its sense of a common spirit, its sense of identification with God, with the Spirit, and in which it engages in a common reading of the sacred scriptures around which the community is organized.[1] To these works of worship we must also add the works of love, of making the words of worship into deeds. But in addition to its practices, there are also first-order beliefs—the catechism, the five pillars of Islam, the Ten Commandments—the basic assertions and creeds that circulate in a more or less common and popular form among the faithful. The vagueness of the popular belief is the reason the community requires theological reflection, which is a second-order operation where the community does its thinking. Theology conceptualizes the beliefs of the community, regulates its practices, and subjects its scriptures to a critical reading that establishes the guiding interpretation that defines the community and its traditions. But theology does not have unilateral authority, for in all such theological reflection the community must in its turn be able to recognize itself. Theological reflection must reflect the community. The theologians report back to the community and receive authentication by the way in which they make explicit what was all along implicit in the community's beliefs and practices. When they do not, either the theology simply disappears because it has no purchase on the community or the community attaches itself to the theology and then splits (schism).

Confessional theology is a local process, one that goes on in a concrete, historical community, where there is a "confession" or "profession" of an inherited and specific faith (*croyance*) commonly shared by the community. But it proves necessary—under the sheer force of questioning—to press on to a still-further order of reflection that continues the work of analysis and conceptualization but one without ties to a confessional community, one that to such extent questions in a more free and unfettered way. It is necessary to cross the borders of confessional theology and engage in a more "radical" theology. Radical theology does not report back to the confessional community or seek its authentication there, and it reserves for itself the right to ask any question, without regard to whether it fractures or divides the community or causes schismatic conflict and confessional breaks. Radical theology emerges both as a demand of thought, which has the right to ask any question, and as a demand of praxis, which seeks to suspend any claim that privileges an inherited legacy, which is an accident of birth (a historical community).

But then, we might ask, to whom does the radical theologian report? In principle, to everyone, to "humanity" at large, which gives radical theology a more universal look or cosmopolitan flare. The first form this took was in early modernity in the Enlightenment, where radical questioning took the form of the "rational theology" of the seventeenth- and eighteenth-century Rationalists. One thinks, for example, of Spinoza's principles of biblical criticism or of Kant's analysis of religion within the limits of reason alone, in which Kant concludes that the universal and rational element of religion is ethics, reducing the rest to superstition. But, as modernism is complicit with classical metaphysics and strong transcendental principles, the version of radical theology that I defend is not modern but postmodern, and it is not rationalist or transcendental but quasi-transcendental and hermeneutic, proceeding from the radicality of what I like to call a radical hermeneutics.

Postmodern radical theology sets out in search of a different kind of universality, not rationalist but hermeneutic, let us say the universality of hospitality, where the universal means being willing to talk to anyone so that there is nothing that cannot in principle be discussed. Hermeneutic universality means accepting universal risk, being willing to put one's own presuppositions at risk, as Gadamer said,[2] and to give a hearing to anything that puts them into question. Universality means not that we all speak with one voice (modern univocity) but that we all get a chance to speak (postmodern plurivocity). That is the universality implied in Derrida's notion of the right to ask any question, implying the right to pose any answer, which he variously describes as the characteristic trait of philosophy, the university, or literature.[3] If the radicality of the modern is to seek a single universal and common root (*radix*) of the multiple contingent and historical particulars, the very idea of the postmodern is to deny that there is any such thing. Postmodernity puts such mono-radicality in question, uproots this common root, so that postmodern radicality lies in a kind of ultra-rationality that passes through the rational while leaving its trace behind in the rational. Postmodern theology thus is not premodern, prerational, or antirational; instead, it proposes a way to further question standard form (modernist) rationality and radicality. Postmodern theology recognizes the multiplicity of "singularities," which are never simply particulars included under a universal, even as it thinks the origin is divided, never a simple source, so that its root system is, as Deleuze liked to say, rhizomatic.

Thus the premise that theology always "reports back" to the religious community is repeated with a difference in radical theology where this time the religious community is a "community without community," that is, completely open ended, since what the radical theologian has to say is addressed in principle to anyone willing to listen, with or without a confessional affiliation, so long as they are not stampeded by the word *theology*. But I must admit straight off that this is a bit of a fiction, which is why I slipped in "in principle." In fact we always begin where we are and when we reflect we always reflect our beginning. So the fiction embedded in the hermeneutic universality of radical theology is exposed by conceding that radical theologians are just like everybody else. They have not been granted a special pass on the human condition. They do indeed have a community to report back to from which they are seeking "authentification," and they do in fact submit to a vast and complex system of protocols and censorship.

To begin with, radical theology typically reports back to a specifically Western community. It is normally situated within Western monotheism and has recourse to Western philosophical discourses steeped in deep-set notions of presence, essence, idea, substance, subject, up to and including the very notions of "religion" and "philosophy," and the whole constellation of what Heidegger liked to call "metaphysics," meaning not an academic discipline but the entire Greco-European historical-cultural-intellectual framework. Secondly, despite its best efforts, such theology will inevitably reflect a certain confessional pedigree, background, and tradition. I for example make no bones about having broadly biblical and specifically Christian concerns, mostly because it is where I am, meaning that the confessional complex I have inherited and about which I am the least ignorant. So despite the protests of radical theology, it will not be able to avoid reflecting some determinate historical confessional tradition. In fact, it should stop protesting. Finally, almost any kind of theology today, confessional or radical, will be the product of an academic theologian, which means that it "reports back" to a rigorous system of academic protocols. Theology is written by career-minded, university-hopping academics for professional conferences, journals, and academic presses, by academic candidates in search of employment, tenure, promotion, and a long list of academic honors like endowed chairs, research grants, and prestigious lectureships. However much we like to think that thinking belongs to the order of the gift, that it is a vocation, and I am not saying that it is not, it *also* is rigorously inscribed within the economy of "academe," with the result that its freedom and hermeneutic universality are something less than it likes to think. Its unfettered freedom is profoundly fettered to having to make a buck, something to which the throng of young, jobless PhDs we have produced can testify better than can I.

Inasmuch as hermeneutics is always interested in hermeneutic presuppositions, another way to sort out the differences between confessional theology and radical theology is to pick out their differing presuppositions. The presuppositions of the confessional communities are the founding scriptures and the continuing traditions of the community. Such foundations are historical. The presuppositions of rationalist theology are transcendental and ahistorical, invoking a so-called "pure" reason. Inasmuch as postmodernists are dubious in the extreme about the latter, the presuppositions of postmodern theology are hermeneutic or deconstructive. Hermeneutics in the sense of Gadamer or Ricoeur presupposes the "truth" of the religious tradition or classic, its enduring viability, its continuing power to fuel the tradition in ways that are ever changing yet ever "true" to it. The "truth" of the tradition does not lie in a changeless body of propositional beliefs but in an enduring but ever evolving form of life. Hermeneutics in the more radical sense is a little dubious of such truth and so presupposes only what Derrida calls the "secret," where the secret is that there is no Secret, which produces a more problematic notion of truth. It insists upon the radical contingency of any historical tradition as a particular effect of the play of traces and as such denied a privileged access to the essence or *Wesen* of things and hence to any deep truth. It settles for more contingent truth and is more nominalistic about beliefs and more pluralistic about traditions. It treats our beliefs and practices as relatively stable and hence relatively unstable and provisional unities of meaning inscribed in *différance* or, as Derrida liked to put it later on, inscribed in the desert sands of *khora*, of khoral spacing, and productive of "chaosmic" results. If the assumptions of hermeneutics are always those of risk and hospitality, deconstruction thinks we are always already put more deeply at risk and asked to undertake a more unconditional hospitality than we imagine. A deconstructive or radical hermeneutics is more braced for trouble than garden-variety hermeneutics. But deconstruction must not be mistaken as merely destructive or skeptical. At its heart, deconstruction arises not from negation but from a deeper affirmation of something, I know not what, a faith (*foi*) in something that Derrida variously calls an event, a call, an exigency, a summons, an injunction, an imperative. That is why I describe a more deconstructive theology as a theology of the event, and my claim is that a theology of the event can only be undertaken as a poetics of the event, which is the spine of a theo-poetics, which is the point I am trying finally to establish.

The radical theologian does not report back to the concrete, historical confessional communities, but that does not mean it does not relate back to them in any way at all, that the two simply pass each other in the night. It is a salutary point for the radical theologian to recall that "confessional" theology is more or less the only theology that exists, addressing the only kind of religion that exists, the concrete confessional or historical traditions of religious beliefs and practices. While radical theology is addressed to a wider community, if the radical theologians are not also talking to the confessional traditions they run the risk of talking only to themselves about an inexistent conceptual construction. In their effort to speak to everyone they may well end up speaking to no one but themselves. So there ought to be a critical interaction between the two. Radical theology must find a way of bleeding into confessional theology even as confessional theology must expose itself to the disturbance of radical theology.

In my view, radical theology, as a second-order work of reflection, an even more radical work of reflecting on the reflection engaged in by the confessional theologians, is trying to produce something of a double effect on confessional theology. On the one hand, its effect is one of displacement and delimitation. Radical theology is not the theology of a rival religion trying to compete for membership with the confessional communities. It resembles more a hovering spirit that haunts the living confessional traditions, a ghost that spooks their closed confessional assemblies. It is not trying to produce a competitor, a rival body of beliefs (*croyances*). It is trying to affect the "how" of confessional traditions, not produce another "what." Radical theology discloses the historical contingency and multiplicity of the confessional traditions, exposing thus the deeply cultural valence of any body of historical beliefs and practices, making the actors in the several traditions acutely conscious of and uncomfortable with the extent to which their traditions are the effects of history rather than an intervention from on high, of the extent to which the "gift" of their personal faith is an accident of birth. In so doing it exposes the local and mythic content at the core of confessional theology. It thus tends to distance and disengage the actors from their scene and to attach a coefficient of historicizing irony to their beliefs and practices, the realization that, had they been born at another time and place, they would be acting out very different roles, singing songs to other gods, and taking their cues from other local stories. So the first effect of radical theology is subversive, disarming the apologetic armatures of the various confessional traditions so that one can continue to belong (or not!) to the confessional community only with a very considerable amount of unease. One may or may not continue to participate in the community. One's own loyalty to the community, and maybe even the community as a whole, are put at risk (spooked) by radical theology.

On the other hand, while the work of radical theology is critical and subversive of what the actors embedded in first-order beliefs and practices are doing, its effect is not, or is not ultimately, negative. Indeed it can have a radicalizing effect on the practitioners in the confessional traditions, by weakening the creedal structures and deepening the sense of the event. So in displacing it also opens up. If it endangers, it also saves. It puts into question but it is not negative; questioning is not a negation but a way of exposing the actual to the event. Nothing is worth our trouble if our only aim is to make trouble for it. In the end, radical theology is deeply affirmative—not of the confessional beliefs (*croyances*) and practices, but of a deeper faith (*foi*) in the event they contain.[4] Thinking on my account is always the thought of the event, and theological thinking is the thought of the event contained in the name of God, in all the names of religious beliefs and practices, of what we in the West call in Christian Latin "religion."

Events

What, then, are these events? What are we affirming? To what are we responding? By what are we addressed? To what are we saying yes? In what do we have a faith not fixed in creedal terms?

Events have two characteristic features: First, events are what we cannot see coming and, second, events are not what happens but what is going on *in* what happens. The event is what is to come that is already going on in what is happening and making it restless with a future that we cannot foresee. Another way to put the same point is to say that what is happening is what exists, while the event is what insists. Events are insistent but inexistent; they solicit and disturb. In the "philosophy of religion," what happens, what actually exists, is "religion," religions in the plural, what we call here the concrete confessional communities and cultural-historical traditions, both the first-order religious beliefs and practices and the second-order theological traditions in which they achieve conceptual articulation. The theological reflection that goes on within the confessions is critical and conceptual work, to be sure, but it remains within the system of religious belief (*croyance*), explicating what happens without tapping into the event. We might say, using an expression of Husserl's, that both the first-order beliefs and practices as well as the second-order theological reflection that goes on within the confessions together belong to a common "natural attitude" or naive belief in the confessional body, to a straightforward "doxic" attitude toward its founding sources. That falls short of the radical event-driven reflection undertaken in radical theology as the natural attitude falls short of the transcendental attitude. From the point of view of radical theology, a confessional theology is working within a tradition that is already "constituted," in which it has a naive belief, since what "constitutes" a religious tradition is the event to which it arises as a response. Hence the work of radical theology is to "think" (used as a transitive verb) the event, to explicate the more radical faith (*foi*) in the event that is taking place in what is happening in the historically constituted traditions of belief.

One good way to see how this unfolds is to say that the event is an event of *desire*. What do I desire? What do I desire with a "desire beyond desire?"[5] We need to distinguish two orders of desire. In the first place, we mark a straightforward or first-order desire, which is conscious and present to itself, which desires something identifiably itself, whether in "terrestrial" goods, like money or prestige, or even in "celestial" ones, like "heaven" or "eternal salvation." This desire has proper names with which we can name our desire and so up to a point can know what we desire and desire what we know. I distinguish such desire from a "desire beyond desire," the mark of which is that it lacks any proper names, that it does not know what it desires, that it desires something *je ne sais quoi,* something I know not what, something going on *in* what I desire. In desiring this or that identifiable good, something is getting itself desired, in the middle voice, so that the first-order desire simulates while also dissimulating something desired beyond desire. That is the disturbance. The reason I do not know what I desire is that there is always something *coming* in what I desire, always a radical exposure to the future, that is disturbing my present desire, so that to say I desire some identifiable thing, this or that, here and now, or even in the "hereafter," is to say I desire what is promised in and by this or that. In a thinking of the event, nothing is ever identifiably itself, which is why events produce displacement. Nothing can be contracted to itself and one can never claim to "know" "what" it "is," not because of some limitation on the part of the knower, but because this thing itself is not what it is. It is not yet what it perhaps can be. It is solicited, made to tremble, by what it promises to be which resonates in it as I desire. Everything is at once a promise made and a promise unkept, and what we desire is not what it is but what it promises to be, or rather what is being-promised in the desire. First-order desire is directed at something formed and constituted, while a desire beyond desire is elicited by the event that constitutes and forms the first-order object of desire. Desire beyond desire is sparked by the eventive or eventative force that is getting evoked in and by the determinate object, by the event that is troubling first-order desire.

One of Derrida's favorite examples of how these two orders of desire interact is "democracy," where it would be the height of injustice, a mark of the most undemocratic injustice, to identify "democracy" with any existing democratic state. For "democracy" is not what it is, not the pretense of democracy made by any existing democracy, but what it promises to be, what is being promised in and by and under the word "democracy." This Derrida calls the "democracy to come (*à venir*)," where the *à venir* is not the "future present," that is, some future state of democracy that will eventually become present, if we are lucky.[6] The "to come" is the demand, the exigency, the call, the promise of democracy that presses in upon the present and makes the present tremble with insecurity, solicited and shaken by the call of the *à venir*, the call to which we respond in trying to make democracy happen.[7] If deconstruction is the analysis of the event, we might think of the analysis of the event as the process of subjecting a given empirical reality to an infinite pressure. By *infinite* I do not mean the classical infinite—if that is what we mean, then deconstruction is always dealing with the finite. But deconstruction opens up the infinite in another sense by which I mean the pressure of the infinitive—the *à venir*. That is the white light of an infinitival exaction that refuses to content itself with what presents itself in the present, so that we are only content with the radical discontent provoked by the promise, by what is coming, by what is to come, which is the event. In the identifiable content of anything we desire there stirs the restless discontent of the event, which is what we desire with a desire beyond desire.

In any (finite) identifiable content, there is contained something that it cannot contain, which is the source of the (infinitival) discontent. When these considerations are brought to bear upon the question of theology we can see that the concrete confessional traditions, the communities of belief, are communities of desire of the first order. In them the infinitival event is contracted to a finite and historical content, an identifiable form that has a proper name, one that is inextricably embedded in the contingency of its particular cultural form of life. That means that the confessional traditions have a built-in tendency to close ranks, to close the circle of what they contain, and to resist the unnamable and uncontainable by which they are inwardly disturbed. Radical theology, on the other hand, is interested in the discontent, in the event disturbing the content, in a deeper faith in what is being promised in the content of these proper names, which threatens to be closed off and contracted in the confessional theologies. Radical theology thinks the infinitival and uncontainable that is going on *in* the concrete confessional traditions, what is getting itself desired in their desire, which we desire with a desire beyond desire.

That means that the event is also decisively marked by a certain *excess* or uncontainability. The limit of the confessional religions is that they contain something that they cannot contain, something uncontainable; something that exceeds what is as the promise exceeds presence, something "undeconstructible." What is undeconstructible (*s'il y en a*) is not something actually infinite and indestructible but that infinitival to-come in the name of which deconstruction takes place. The undeconstructible is what demands the construction of something in its name whose deconstruction it simultaneously demands, the way justice demands laws that enshrine justice and at the same time demand—in the name of justice—the deconstruction of the very laws that were constructed in the name of justice. Justice demands what must be and cannot be; justice demands laws whose possibility depends upon the very same thing that makes it impossible to ever meet this demand. Whatever law comes to be in the name of justice is annulled by the very demand for justice that brought the law about in the first place.[8] As "in the name of justice," so "in the name of God." The subject matter of radical theology is God, not so much God as the name of God, not so much the name of God as the event that is sheltered—both concealed and kept safe—by that name. Its *Sache*, as Heidegger liked to say, its stuff and substance, is the promise and the uncontainable excess that is harbored by the name of God, what is asked and solicited, called and recalled, desired and demanded in and under the name of God (for better or for worse).

Hegel and the Invention of Radical Theology

The event that is promised, that is to come, the uncontainable excess of the event, may also be called its "truth." The event is an event of truth. The truth of the democracy to come is the truth that is trying to come true *in* democracy. Just so, the name of God is the name of an event that is trying to come true in and under that name. It is at this point—truth—that I call upon the approach to religious truth taken by Hegel, who is, by my lights, the father or (if Tillich is the father) the grandfather of radical theology. Hegel is the first one to offer a new analysis of Christian theology and a new paradigm for the philosophy of religion by formulating a new idea of religious truth that constitutes for me a predecessor form of the theology of the event and consequently of theopoetics.

Before Hegel—which is not to say that this paradigm does not persist today—the distinction I am making between confessional theology and radical theology was treated as a distinction between "revealed" theology and "rational" theology, each of which provided access to a stratum of truth proper to itself. Revealed theology had to do with all those truths that humankind by its own lights, by the light of unaided human reason, was unable to know. Thus the Trinity and the Incarnation are the contents of *theologia sacra* whose ultimate presupposition is faith in the Word of God. Rational theology (*theologia rationalis*) gets what is left over, the relatively small core of "rational" truth that is not off-limits to reason, the bit that unaided human reason can come up with working on its own—which mostly reduces the philosophy of religion to a bad infinity of endless anthologies on the proofs for the existence of God, the immortality of the soul, and the problem of evil. "Rational" theology meant the tradition of seventeenth- and eighteenth-century scholasticisms that reached their most famous systematic form in Christian Baumgarten, which Kant labeled "onto-theology," a term later on made famous by Heidegger, who to the unrelieved joy of almost everyone wanted to "overcome" it. Kant rightly and famously criticized these rationalist excesses and proposed instead a "radical" theology, one that cut through to the taproot of religion in reason alone, albeit in practical reason, in the sole fact as it were of pure reason, the unconditional givenness of the Moral Law. In the Moral Law we can have a rational faith, with the result that in Kant religion is reduced to ethics and the rest is superstition.

Hegel, on the other hand, took the opposite view. He was interested in exactly what rational theology left out—above all in the Trinity, incarnation, crucifixion, resurrection, and ascension—in which he said everything truly interesting about Christianity is to be found.[9] He thought rational theology removed the pulp from the juice. So far from treating these defining Christian themes as supernatural mysteries that we could never have learned by the unaided use of human reason, which therefore needed to be handed down to earth by an Über-being in the sky, Hegel treated them as a *Vorstellung*, an imaginative-sensuous presentation—or what for me will be the stuff of a "poetics"—of something that required conceptual clarification. "Christian" then would refer to something not of "supernatural" but of "representational"—or, as I will argue of *poetic*—provenance, as a certain imaginative presentation of the world. "Christianity" is a determinate historical formation whose so-called mysteries are not mysterious because they "transcend" natural reason and require a dispatch from a supernatural source on high, but because they elude rational argumentation in the same way a work of narratival imagination eludes a formal argument. They acquire their "force" not from having a Divine Warranty, enjoying all the "good faith and credit" of God himself, as if God were the Central Bank, but from supplying the matrix of a viable form of life, of which there are of course innumerable alternatives. So Hegel branded the theologies of the rationalist philosophers as arid, abstract exercises of *Verstand*, which was something of a term of abuse for Hegel for anything that has its pulp removed. To call them *Verstand* was to pronounce them barren boring treatments of religion trading in one-sided formal bloodless ahistorical concepts.[10] Everything that is truly interesting about religion, everything substantive and enlivening, Hegel said, is being left out—all the warm blood and vitality, all the "spirit," all the "revelatory" force, all the *Sache* of Christianity. Hegel was a serious Christian philosopher for whom Christianity is the revelatory religion par excellence, the complete revelation of the consummate truth, and Hegel insisted that we take its most characteristic teachings—its *theologia sacra*—with the utmost seriousness *as philosophers*, for these are the carriers of its "revelation," the bearers of its truth.

Hegel's point is that something is getting itself said and done in these religious figures, that while still in figural form—artistically constructed narratives, textual allusions, symbolic references, theological leitmotifs, miraculous events, and so forth—is latent with true conceptual content. One is reminded of the distinction in contemporary physics between "picture" theorists and "equation" theorists, between the visualization of the Big Bang on the Science Channel and the mathematics behind it. So what is "revealed" *in* the religious imagination is made conceptually clear in philosophy, namely that the Absolute *an sich* ("God," the "Father") is a one-sided abstract understanding of the fullness of the truth of the Absolute.[11] Ultimately, the Absolute is *an sich und für sich* that is itself pictorially figured in the "Trinity" (the life of God), incarnation (birth of God), crucifixion (death of God), resurrection, and ascension (the afterlife or people of God). All of those dogmas have to be "thought," conceived in a *Begriff*, grasped in the grip of the philosopher's concept, where they take the form of *Philosophie, absolutes Wissen, Wissenschaft*. The good news for the "Good News" is that Christianity is the revelation of the absolute truth. The bad news is that the "Good News" is the absolute truth in a pictorial form, a stage in the development of truth, a relatively true but therefore still relatively untrue form of the becoming true of absolute truth, of its complete and consummate revelation. Each and every "doctrine" of Christian revelation is true, is a stage of truth in the making, where truth is a work in progress, and so each element merits philosophical respect and demands a philosophical analysis. The truth needs philosophy, but philosophy needs religion.

Hegel thus invented radical theology. At one and the same time he made the "revealed" theological content of Christianity the subject matter while also cutting off its Gnostic drift. He reveals the truth of revelation while undermining the mythic supernaturalism of classical theology. He demystified the two-worlds dualism institutionalized in early Christianity under the influence of Neoplatonism, most famously and triumphantly by Augustine, by which mainstream confessional theology has allowed itself to be trapped ever since. In its place he puts what we would today call, using the language of Deleuze, a plane of immanence where differences are marked by distinctions of degree, by gradations of intensity, and stages of becoming, with the result that "sacred doctrine" or "divine revelation" acquires worldly (meaning this-worldly rather than otherworldly) significance. Religion is about what Derrida called the promise of the world,[12] and the world is no longer divided between time and eternity, being is no longer divided by the natural and the supernatural, and knowledge no longer divided between reason and revelation. Instead, revelation is treated as a stage of our experience of the becoming true of the truth, a moment in the passage from the sensuous through the pictorial to the conceptual grasp of truth. Hegel has undermined the subordination of philosophy to revealed theology and made the contents of revelation part of the business of philosophy. Hegel thinks that religion is a *Vorstellung* of absolute knowledge, a dark mirroring of transparent truth, the trace that the self-thinking thought makes in the world.

From Hegel to Theopoetics

When Hegel insists on bringing philosophical conceptuality to bear upon religious *Vorstellungen,* the postmodernists complain that Hegel is being overbearing. Kierkegaard introduced the first postmodernism when his Johannes Climacus quipped that, according to the metaphysics of absolute knowledge, God came into the world in order to consult with German metaphysicians about the makeup of the divine nature. There is thus a considerable *gnosis* still clinging to Hegel, an unmistakably Gnostic insistence on knowing, *Wissen* and *Begriff.* So what I am calling a theology of the event is at best a heretical version of Hegel, a variant postmodern Hegelianism, a kind of hybrid or even headless Hegelianism without the Concept according to the strange logic of the *sans.* If my religion comes without religion, my Hegel comes without the *Begriff.* I regard the notions of Absolute Knowledge, Absolute Concept, and Absolute Spirit as so much metaphysical inflation, the *parole soufflée* of Idealist metaphysics. My own idea is that religion is a *Vorstellung* of which there is no Concept, a figure that does not admit of metaphysical elucidation. My *Vorstellung* has nowhere to turn for a Final Explanation of itself. Alternately one might say that when it comes to religion, the concept (lowercase) is that there is no Concept (uppercase), only *Vorstellungen,* only the several "presentations" or "figurations" of truth, but without a Truth to monitor their staging. So we might speak of a truth without Truth. The radical in radical theology can always be fitted out in the strange logic of the *sans,* where it reappears in a ghostly *sous rature.* Here is where I call upon a poetics for aid in my distress, a poetics that, as for Hegel, is midway between an aesthetics (art) and a logic (philosophy), but with a difference.

On the view that I take, in the wake of Hegel, a "revelation" is not a supernatural intervention from another world that interrupts the course of history and nature with a disclosure of which the world itself would not be capable. A revelation is "beyond reason" not because it exceeds all human faculties but because it exceeds the faculty of reason by way of other faculties. It is beyond reason the way any work of imagination lies beyond reason: It eludes reason's formal-logical skills while opening up the world in another way, in a more singular and preconceptual way. If we say a revelation is *tout autre,* that means it breaks in upon us not from *another* world but comes as *another worlding* of the world, another world-disclosure, another way the world itself opens up, is reconfigured, is "revealed" in an unforeseeable and unanticipated way. A revelation reveals by dis-closing a singular and idiomatic world, a life-world, a form of life, a linguistic and cultural framework, everything we mean by the disseminated but concatenated complex of the "world." A revelation interrupts our lives, unsettles settled beliefs and practices, not because it comes from outside space and time but because it interrupts the spacing and timing of the given world with a new form of spacing and timing, a new and unforeseen way to be, another messaging of the world itself. A revelation takes the world by surprise not because it is "super-natural" but because that is the way history works (its *physis,* so to speak). To live in history is to be structurally subject to surprise, to unforeseeability, to the future. The interruptive disclosure that breaks in *upon* the world in a revelation is the disclosive interruption that *is* the world. That is what we mean by the "world," by the idiomatic and singular constellations that the world is endlessly undergoing A revelation is a provisional and local fulfillment of the promise of the world, of the promise that gets itself made in and through and as the world, and it does so in a way we didn't see coming, which is what we mean by time and history.

In short, a revelation is an event, *l'invention de l'autre, de l'impossible,* and like every event, one we did not see coming, whereas in orthodox Hegelianism the Spirit is absolute knowledge and can presumably see everything coming. The in-breaking power of the Sermon on the Mount does not consist in being a supernatural revelation delivered by a celestial being come down from the sky, proffering some account of things that lies beyond the ken of humankind. It lies "beyond the reach of reason" in the sense that it lies outside the circle of its "logic." It represents an insight into a form of life structured by the "rule of God," let us say, by the ruleless and unruly rule of the gift as opposed to the logical rules of an economy. The Sermon on the Mount does not belong to the circle of a "logic" but to the open-endedness of a "poetics." It is a shocking re-envisioning of human life, of an unprecedented form of life. But by a *poetics* I do not mean poetry or verse, free or rhymed, or any form of poetic ornament or adornment of some preestablished belief. A poetics is not an aesthetics adorning a prior religious belief or practice (*croyance*) but a creative-discursive evocation (*poiesis*) of an unnamable faith (*foi*) to come.[13] A poetics needs to be resourceful in order to produce a discourse uniquely fitted to the event. Hence it is a nonformalizable constellation of puns and pictures, parables and paradoxes, of reversals and antinomies, of tropes, figures, narratives, of striking and even outrageous images, moving stories, miraculous events, visions, disseminations, evocations, solicitations, imperatives that nominate and record an event. A poetics is a repertoire of strategies, discursive and rhetorical, constative and performative, semantic, syntactical and pragmatic, all loosely assembled, like the mobile army of metaphors and metonyms to which the young Nietzsche refers, an army on the move, trying to gain ground on the plane of immanence.[14]

In a poetics, all of the aphoristic and anarchistic energy of what Derrida calls *différance* join forces with what Hegel means by a *Vorstellung,* as a sensuous-pictorial embodiment of the truth, not a conceptual-logical one. A *Vorstellung* is a world-picture, a world-praxis, a world-formation, a world-creation, an event of *poiesis,* of the creative and recreative, by which I do not mean the origin of the universe in the Big Bang, or the *creatio ex nihilo* of the second-century theologians. The "world" in the poetics of the "world" is the life-world, a form of life, a vision, a disclosure, a paradigm, a revelation, and the "poetics" is the constellation of discursive strategies and practices in which and through which the world is forged or formed. A "revelation" is the idiomatic trait, the structure of singularity of a world, the singular way the world is revealed in the formation, rather the way we speak the "world" of Milton or Shakespeare, of Renoir or Picasso, the way the world is revealed in different ways in different writers or painters, or in different languages, where a given language is, as Merleau-Ponty once said, a singular way to "sing the world." A revelation is a world-disclosure, a constellation of elements—linguistic, cultural, economic, social, political, ethical, religious, and who knows what else. That is why there is no such thing as "revelation" in the singular, but there are many revelations in the plural, each of them "special," each a special showing of the possibility of the impossible, as many as there are cultural forms of life.

In my hybrid headless Hegelianism, the *Vorstellung* is a presentation or representation, a figure or an image, not of the *Begriff*—I have no head for the *Begriff*—but of the event. A poetics is not an aesthetics of the work of art, nor a logic of the concept, but a poetics of the event. The event is not what happens but what is going on in what happens, what is being promised and mourned, called and recalled, desired with a desire beyond desire, contained without being contained, in what happens. A genuinely radical theology is a poetics of the event, a theo-poetics, not a theo-logic, a poetics of the event that is harbored in the name of God, which is a "natural" name, that is, occurring in a "natural" (meaning "historical") language. A theopoetics is a deployment of multiple discursive resources meant to give words to the event, but without miscasting it as a gift from the sky (supernaturalism) and without laying claim to the high ground of the Concept (Hegelian metaphysics), without asserting one knows the secret, the code, the rule that governs events. There is no event of events, only so many events, so many eventive traditions, so many promises, so many calls, so many figurations. The traditions that we in the West describe in Christian

Latin as "religious" are so many ways of poetizing the event, so many ways the event takes the form of narratives, parables, figures, images, and sensuous presentations of the promise, of the gift, of the call, all more or less taking the form of the "possibility of the impossible,"[15] which is a venerable name of God in the Abrahamic traditions.

I treat religion not as a *Vorstellung* of a metaphysical substance or spirit but as a way to poetize what is called the "event" by several continental philosophers—Heidegger, Derrida, and Deleuze foremost among them, although I also think much of what Badiou has to say about the event can also be cautiously incorporated into this account (without the meta-mathematical preamble). I displace the philosophy of the Spirit with the poetics of the event. A theopoetics is a poetics of the event or cluster of events that is contained in the name of God, the event that is "harbored"— meaning both concealed and kept safe—by this name. An event is contained in a name without being able to be contained by that name, so that the name is a kind of *khora akhoraton*. The event is nominated without being finally named even as events are effects of names, the comet's tail of memories, hopes, and promises being made in and by the name. The event is called, called for, called up, even as we ourselves are called upon, all in the name of God. The event belongs to what it itself summons up, an appellatory, messianic, vocative, valorized space in which we are called upon or visited by *the* impossible. Theopoetics is a poetics of the possibility of the impossible, one of the most familiar and seductive names of God in the Hebrew and Christian Scriptures, which is why radical theology is itself inextricably tied to Western Jewish, Islamic, and Greco-Christian monotheistic traditions. In theopoetics, the several "religions"—if it is not time to give up on this word—are so many ways to "poetize" the world, and they differ from one another in ways that are broadly similar to the ways that languages differ from one another. It would make no more sense to ask what is the true religion than to ask what the true language is. They differ as do different modes of "being-in-the-world" (Heidegger), different "forms of life" (Wittgenstein), different modes of inhabiting the plane of immanence (Deleuze), where different languages do different things (Rorty).

Conclusion

In a theopoetics, "God" is an echo of events transpiring on the plane of immanence. Religious phenomena resonate paradigmatically, in a telling and "revealing" way, with events, which are the becoming true of the truth and the subject matter of a certain post-phenomenological poetics. For when there is truth, there are events, and when there are events, there are promises and prayers—and then there is "religion." Religion, we are arguing, is a *Vorstellung* of an event, of a cluster of events, which concretely figure a desire beyond desire. The task of the philosophy of religion, the continental one, the one that descends from Hegel, is to provide a poetics of the event, to hand-tailor a discourse that is neither poetry nor logic but uniquely sensitive to the event that is being nominated and enacted in the name of God. That discourse is theo-poetics.

Having thus uprooted the *logos* in theology, radical theology properly so called turns out to be an improper theology, a theology without theology, not because it is without *theos* but because it suspends its *logos*. It is not an a/theology but a theo-a/logic, theo-logy as theo-poetics. Radical theology thus is only possible as a theopoetics of the event, or, if you prefer, theopoetics is radical theology.

Toward the Heraldic
A Theopoetic Response to Monorthodoxy

L. CALLID KEEFE-PERRY

> In the study of ideas, it is necessary to remember that insistence on hard-headed clarity issues from sentimental feeling . . . Insistence on clarity at all costs is based on sheer superstition as to the mode in which human intelligence functions. Our reasonings grasp at straws for premises and float on gossamers for deductions.
>
> **—Alfred North Whitehead,** *Adventures of Ideas*

> A theopoetic impulse . . . seek[s] to roughen up unified appearances by differentiating the various deep-lying, multiple voices hidden under various powerful contenders of an alleged "orthodoxy" of content, method, and direction of thought.
>
> **—Roland Faber,** *God as Poet of the World*

All across the spectrum of religious thought, theologians and lay people alike fall victim to the pitfalls of a position that presupposes that a "correct form of belief and practice" (orthodoxy) will always manifest as a "uniformity of belief and practice" (monorthodoxy).[1] Conversely, I suggest that there is nothing that necessitates the collapse of those two positions into one, and I offer that there is another stance that actively insists on the reality of truth while maintaining the present provisionality of *all interpretations* concerning the ultimate, challenging any assertion that right practice always requires same practice.

This chapter will attempt to explicate the qualities of common, totalizing, monorthodox theologies and worldviews, exploring how such positions exert their influence in religious settings, often self-interestedly. A corrective to monorthodoxy will then be considered by means of the development of a "Heraldic" theology, encouraging a dialogical and manifold articulation of experience and Divine revelation. In the first portion of the chapter I explore monorthodoxy primarily within the Christian tradition, extending in the second to a consideration of monorthodox thought beyond the traditional boundaries of the church, suggesting that there might be an imperative, theopoetic response to such positions: a "roughing up of the unified appearances" that adherents to monorthodoxy claim are universal.

Monorthodox Thought

In a zealous desire for a clarity against which Whitehead's opening epitaph pointedly argues, many beliefs are formed into rigid positions, often relying on absolutism and an interpretive stance that assumes understanding is fixed and complete. While this is perhaps most visibly evident in claims of biblical inerrancy and the authority of religious leaders to correctly, and wholly, interpret scripture, it is not the mark of only a particular type of Christian. Indeed, a monorthodox perspective is found whenever the "true" religion is depicted as some continuous, uniform behemoth, when in fact it is as varied as its history and the faith of those who make it up.

When clergy and other arbiters of theology proclaim an understanding of a revealed God that is complete and/or closed, they position themselves to take on the role of gatekeepers of faith: If one is to come before God, it must be done in such-and-such a way or it is not done at all. This happens just as much when Progressive arguments claim that Christians as a whole must do something, as it does when someone proclaims a Christian exclusivism that asserts that individuals will suffer damnation unless they believe a particular theological point. In either case, taking such a position, even if well intentioned, allows for far too easy a slide into aggression and, in some cases, oppression. The presumption of a wholly understandable, closed, teleological revelation maps well onto means of continuing control and systematic domination.

While the intentions of this type of methodological approach are likely to orbit around ideas of theological purity, adherence to proper theology, or the correctness of tradition, it is also unfortunately true that these methods can easily be bent toward discrimination, tyranny, and injustice. As Walter Brueggemann has noted, "you cannot build a great empire on dialogue. You can only build an empire on monologue. You have to have a voice of certainty to amass a concentration of power."[2] Thus, while it is doubtful that adherents to monorthodox positions consider it their direct objective, the result of such a vaulted, monophonic theology can be the accumulation of social power that excludes others from participation in any dialogue that might bring about some change in damaging, dominant social mores or theological stances.

From the vantage of a Christian monorthodox position in which a concentration of power has been amassed, an individual's calls for reform and repentance carry with them the perceived weight of divine authority and insight. That is, since the claim is that individuals can be in near-complete awareness of God's will, those same individuals can make claims to having their desires also be God's. Interestingly, the certainty and clarity of God and God's support is often asserted by those already in positions of significant social capital and cultural weight, a state which does not appear to be the normative mode within the biblical record, which typically inverts social structures,[3] giving voice and power to those previously without it. Wanting to avoid being bound up in the negative implication of an authoritative, potentially self-serving position that asserts singular truth and the capacity of individuals to know it, a conceivable Christian response might be to displace the authority of traditionally centralized power with that of those on the fringes of society. However, a continuation of this stream of thought quickly shows this response to be untenable.

Carried too far, the suggestion could be made that only the disenfranchised can extol virtue and value. This is unnecessarily exclusive and does not address what would occur should marginalized voices be brought to center. Under a "margins-only" schema the only options would be either to remain excluded or to be silent upon recognition. Neither of these seems desirable, or in resonance with the biblical injunction to "teach all the nations." What it called for, then, is not a censure of individual claims to truth but a reframing of what it means to claim knowledge of ultimate truth, to confess experience of the divine, and to spread the Good News. Some of John Howard Yoder's work in missiology suggests such a paradigm, one that allows for individual proclamation yet refrains from coercion and the amassing of personal influence and power in the name of God.

The Herald

[The] Herald announces an event. . . . Yet, no once is forced to believe. What the herald reports is not permanent, timeless, logical insights but contingent, particular events. If those events are true, and if others join the herald to carry the word along, they will with time develop a doctrinal system, to help distinguish between more and less adequate ways of proclaiming; but that system, those formulae, will not become what they proclaim.

—John Howard Yoder, *The Royal Priesthood*

The Herald is one for whom the presence of God has become a reality that is personally undeniable. As a result, this experienced perception of God becomes an event that propels the Herald toward a reporting of the experience of the event(s) that transpired. The Herald is the bearer of *kerygma*, "an act of linguistic communication, as well as an occurrence or event meant to change the hearts and minds of those who experience it."[4] In contrast to monorthodox articulations of doctrine, revelation, and repentance, which strongly adhere to the certainty of a particular perspective as ultimate, Heraldic notions of proclamation accept that communities may need to regularly reexamine their own interpretations and expressions, moving from compunction to living a new way.

Yoder's offering calls for a Heraldic position wherein proclamation is not about adherence to "a doctrinal system" but rather an articulation of the Herald's experience of "contingent, particular events." His articulation of the Herald paints the picture of a postcolonial, invitational stance acknowledging that knowledge of truth comes about through interpretation in the context of community and can persist without coercion. Furthermore, while Yoder's Herald proclaims some particular interpretation, it is an admittedly time bound and provisional one. This allows for a permeability of thought and *praxis* adapted as required to meet the dialectic needs of the community in which one resides. Truth need not change for the articulation of it to shift: That revelation can be interpreted multiple ways does not necessarily change the revelation itself.

By simultaneously admitting human fallibility in interpretation and the power and Truth of a divine message, communities of faith can attempt to perceive and proclaim what the Good News is for *them,* in their place and their time, without feeling like they are rewriting scripture or performing mass, communal *eisegesis.* This model does not call for a de facto abandoning of doctrinal positions or traditional expressions of faith for those of some other group. It asks only that some measure of a hermeneutic of humility be enacted when engaging in interpretation of that which possesses an entirety beyond human grasp. Human interpretations are limited, and it seems we cannot hold onto perfect representation for any extended length of time. Those that are people of faith may strive after faithfulness and God; however, a claim to have reached some level of certainty about the entirety of God seems misguided, especially for those of the Jewish and Christian traditions, wherein scripture in Isaiah 55:9 reads that "For as the heavens are higher than the earth, / So are My ways higher than your ways / And My thoughts than your thoughts."

It is only through fractured human experience that people sense anything. Rather than this being considered a negative, though, the acknowledgment that cultural conditioning can influence experience, interpretation, and expression of God can open up possibilities for theological discourse. A community that is catalyzed into self-reflection, dialogue, and renewed expression would reach a place akin to Bonhoeffer's view of the "communion of saints," as a group of "persons in profound and God-centered and God-inflamed relationship with one another, where revelation of the other is the revelation of the holy, and vice versa."[5] It is this kind of catalysis that a Herald's proclamation engenders.

The Herald is not some messianic senator but a *kēryx* messenger desiring to enter into multiplicitous "God-centered and God-inflamed relationships" that will leave her vulnerable to attack from scientism and realpolitik. As Yoder writes, "what makes the herald renounce coercion is not doubt or being unsettled by the tug of older views. The herald believes in accepting weakness because the message [she carries] is about a Suffering Servant whose meekness it is that brings justice to the nations."[6] The Herald's example serves as a model for others to bear witness to their own experience. He asks how else things might be considered or portrayed and what would happen to practice and doctrine, were new interpretations considered. She raises these questions and encourages others to do the same, offering her own expressions of "contingent, particular events," aimed at evoking resonance in the experience of others.

Rather than becoming an idol in the cult of celebrity, the Herald offers his experience to the community in such a way that "he guides their eyes from himself to the spirit that quickens him."[7] The quickening spirit, then, though it be fleeting, is that which inspires further proclamation, consideration, and proactive deliberation regarding what is needed to best express and encourage the way God is drawing communities out into the world. The Heraldic stance is one that embraces the richness and variety of ways in which the Divine can be expressed and experienced, encourages individuals to speak the truth as they understand it, reminding them that their interpretations, doctrines, and claims to know God fully are somewhat less than complete. While people of faith strive toward the Divine and will ever consider new interpretations to guide them toward faithfulness, God will always have "a name written that no one knows but himself."[8]

The Herald's announcement is not that there is a new royal dictate or some new truth but that she has experienced some event she feels compelled to share. Still, her goal is not to individually develop and promote doctrinal systems and formulae but to speak of an experience she understands to be true, sharing with others and calling out to see if others discern it to be true, if it evokes change or response. This is similar in approach to what some theologians refer to as a "process hermeneutic," which asserts that interpreters must "be prepared to treat the text as open-ended and evocative, pointing beyond itself not only to an extra-linguistic word, but more proximately to propositions . . . that engage the imagination."[9] The Herald points toward an experience of the Divine revealed in such a way that he has come to believe it to be true, and brings this sense of truth to others for their consideration: not as the way that it *must* be for them but as the way that the Herald has experienced it to be.

A Heraldic approach to interpretation acknowledges that any human proclamation of religious experience, faith, sin, or judgment is bound by the marks of fallible interpretation, context, and community. Rather than attempting to disregard this fact, the Herald acknowledges that this is simply part of the human condition and proceeds with this knowledge in full view. There is something sublime in our limitations, something about our finite sight that is nonetheless in the image of an eternal God. In speaking this way, the Herald is impelled by the theopoetic impulse "to roughen up unified appearances."[10] That is, in affirming her own experience, the Herald does not just share her story but invites others to share theirs, raising questions to any monophonic theology that suggests a wholly accurate, complete, and closed interpretation of revelation and the Divine.

Monorthodox theologies seem the result of an "insistence on hard-headed clarity," an impulse that yields easy answers[11] and contributes to a form of cultural rationalism that encourages people to shy away from the creative and the risky in favor of certain and finished ideas that are sometimes at odds with individual experience. Aspiration toward the certain yields abstraction. If there is to be a move away from abstraction, it will necessitate a corresponding shift toward the particular and embodied, a transition that still seeks clarity but does not claim that the clear and true understanding of the individual directly corresponds to some universal clarity at which others must similarly arrive. In his own inimitable way, William Blake asserts this in a concise line: "to generalize is to be an idiot; to particularize is the alone distinction of merit."[12]

A Heraldic approach to theology suggests that separate communities of faith will come to separate interpretations and that, as the communities interact, each will be changed. This does not imply that they will become more like one another, or that they will necessarily agree with one another more and more as time goes on. It does, though, suggest that communities will find means of interpreting revelation and theologically expressing themselves that better allows for (a) individuals within those communities to come to a greater faithfulness and the means to articulate it and (b) *other* communities to see that new sight can be gained. In the latter sense, it is important to note that the models provided by other communities need not be replicated in entirety for them to be inspirational. This can be clarified by means of an example.

In an interview at the 2009 American Academy of Religion Conference, James Cone acknowledged that, while he was pleased with the wider attention *Black Theology and Black Power* received, it was essentially written for "his people, because they were dying in the streets."[13] Regardless of the intended particular focus, his clear voice paved the way for others to consider *them*selves in the light of what Cone had written. Forty years after its initial publication, one would be hard pressed to get through seminary without coming across Cone's work somewhere, regardless of one's race. What Cone had to say, people needed to hear.

While the particulars of his situation led him to write particular content in a particular voice for a particular audience, the power and truth in his articulation has led to countless others finding inspiration in it. Some portions of *Black Theology and Black Power* are difficult to read for those who are white, yet in spite of this difficulty it offers a powerful example of a Heraldic voice unafraid to challenge normative views and willing to allow for a development of position. As a professor of theology at Union, Cone has not simply continued to reiterate the contents of his first book but has continued to seek words with which to express his current sense of things, allowing him to reexamine his own stance, moving toward a fresh expression of theology issues pertaining to gender, sexuality, and class, as well as race.[14]

Cone's call for a new way to think and act was a critique of a church he saw as standing in apostasy. His call was indeed a call to a new orthodoxy. It was, however, particular and did not universalize experience. What can be true and needed for one group to more fully seek out God is not necessarily something applicable to all others. Communities will come to different understandings of experience depending on where they stand. Just because an experience or expression is not universalized does not mean that it cannot reflect some part of a larger truth. Indeed, sometimes it is the case that, in an attempt to generalize an expression beyond the reach of experience, interpretation may lose some significant measure of its appropriateness. Another example speaks to this point.

In a 1990 critique of Reinhold Niebuhr's analysis of sin, Daphne Hampson writes, "the argument is not that Niebuhr's analysis is false, but that it is inapplicable to the situation of *all humanity,* while failing to recognize that this is the case."[15] She critiques his attempt to extrapolate universal truths about sin and yet simultaneously acknowledges "that Niebuhr's analysis contains deep insights."[16] While his expression of sin results in some resonance for Hampson, where Niebuhr saw his expression as true for *all* humanity, she notes that what he "described was a peculiarly . . . male propensity."[17] His conceptualization of sin as tied to pride did not ring wholly true to Hampson, who operates within her own experiences and interpretive lenses. Regardless of Hampson's critique, given his name's conspicuous presence in copious articles, syllabi, and conferences, Niebuhr's theological expression and interpretation appear to have articulated enough of an aspect of truth to bear further consideration: Ideas that Niebuhr put forth have found their way into earnest sermons and congregations. He also articulated himself in such a way that the experience of women is often glossed over: This, too, has found its way into the notes of pastors and ministers.

A Heraldic approach suggests that a multitude of varying voices will be raised in an equally diverse number of communities, and that each will have come to rest (still contingently) in different doctrinal stances, settling on those which seem to best articulate the experiences and hopes of that community. Each will have its own interpretation of orthodoxy and will understand that other communities will as well. The context(s) of community deeply affect each hermeneutic, and it is understood that interpretation is not the same thing as that which is interpreted.

In attempting to develop universally applicable answers to religious questions, theologians have sometimes too narrowly defined what is acceptable, too quickly cut off possibility, and too rationally declined an abundant invitation to consider that there is power in the experience of the particular. That is, in the effort to find a unifying answer that is eternally applicable and wholly complete, theologians have been driven to a form of abstraction that has often distanced them from the events that originally inspired their craft. At least, this is what the Herald would assert, with support from the theopoetic thought of Stanley Hopper and Amos Wilder.

A Theopoetic Invitation

Stanley Hopper's speech "The Literary Imagination and the Doing of Theology" is reflective of much of his work from the early 1970s and is the first piece of scholarship to make direct English use of the term *theopoiesis.*[18] In it he asserts that we must seek a "radical revisioning of our way of seeing and thinking."[19] He prompted that the question was not how to develop new, socially relevant theologies, but "whether theology, insofar as it retains methodological fealty to traditional modes, is any longer viable at all."[20] Furthermore, he argues that any successful attempt at reinvigorating a vibrant religious dialogue will essentially abandon attempts to logically systematize religious thought. Instead, he advocates shared expression of spiritual experiences that "evoke resonances and recognitions."[21]

The shift from theologies, which he characterizes as utilizing hollow language, will require first "the unlearning of symbolic forms" and then "the activation of a new archetypal image."[22] Drawing on "What Is Called Thinking?," Hopper cites Heidegger's statement that "we Moderns can learn only if we always unlearn at the same time . . . we can learn thinking only if we radically unlearn what thinking has been traditionally."[23] His claim then is that people must unlearn modern approaches to theology, arriving at that which is "not theo-logic but theopoiesis."[24] As Hopper's student, Amos Wilder succinctly puts it, "the dimension too often missing is . . . that of rooted-ness, creaturehood, embodied humanness."[25]

Hopper's argument is that, to the degree that modern theology has rigidly attempted to prove something absolutely and as distinct from experience, the whole project has been a fool's errand. In his words, any "theology founded upon the mathematical models of propositional logic is founded upon a profound metaphysical error."[26] In some ways this can be seen as an energetic response to the death-of-God theologies that were in vogue at the time: Hopper had to find some means to condemn the "hollow language" of theology that was under fire at the time and then maneuver in such way so as to allow for some new resurgence of authentic Christian expression. While Hopper's claim of logical theology as "profound error" can be seen as extreme given contemporary approaches to contextual and constructive theology—especially ones that allow for the power and validity of voices beyond the normative ones, and the general progressive acceptance that theology is done provisionally and for a certain people at a certain time—the theopoetic insistence for a more creatively engaged, particular, embodied expression of Divine experience yet remains powerful.

The suggestion, therefore, is that, by supporting and validating the experience of others' conditions outside of our own, we might come to know more, not just of them but of ourselves and God. Imaginatively articulating one's sense of the Divine and encouraging others to do the same affirms that new expressions of experience can serve some greater role than political correctness. In keeping with Levinas's assertion that "it is in the face of the Other from which all meaning appears,"[27] Jason Derr writes that "to engage in the theopoetic is to tempt the radical nature of ourselves, it is to follow in the footsteps of the God-Speakers that could upset the Republic, could speak from the margins of our hungers and unspeakable truths."[28] The Herald engages others, speaks of her experiences, and encourages new articulations of the divine—and interpretations of scripture—not because she believes that that task will be accurately completed in her lifetime but because there is something gained from meeting others in incomplete spaces. The study and production of language about, and for, God is not to "get it right" but to engender more noticing of God and each other, and that of God in each other and Creation. Indeed, "the point is not to use the mind's eye to grasp and classify objects into discrete categories according to 'universal definitions,' [but to become] sensitive to differences and aware of empathetic connections between beings, subject to subject."[29] In his 1976 book, *Theopoetic: Theology and the Religious Imagination,* Amos Wilder asked this of his readers, hoping that it would forward a shift toward such a sensitivity:

> My plea for a theopoetic means doing more justice to the symbolic and the prerational in the way we deal with experience. We should recognize that human nature and human societies are more deeply motivated by images and fabulations than by ideas. This is where power lies and the future is shaped . . . Imagination is a necessary component of all profound knowing and celebration; all remembering, realizing, and anticipating; all faith, hope, and love. When imagination fails doctrines become ossified, witness and proclamation wooden, doxologies and litanies empty, consolations hollow, and ethics legalistic . . . Philistinism invades Christianity from within wherever the creative and mythopoetic dimension of faith is forfeited. When this happens doctrine becomes a caricature of itself. Then that which once gave life begins to lull and finally to suffocate us.[30]

Wilder's support of the deeply personal expression of experience does not deny the relevance of doctrine or theology; it merely warns against the dangers of allowing those things to become self-serving and more supportive of "that system [and] those formulae" than of the experience of the quickening spirit that inspired them. That is, when monorthodoxy exerts influence over communities, encouragement of individual articulations of experience is stifled unless those articulations support that which has come before. Questions calling forth a response about the divine shift from eliciting a response drawn from experience to one drawn from a pool of information that has been inherited and is assumed correct because of its inheritance. When a certain amount of *de facto* societal authority is given to clear, factual responses, the temptation of the church is to follow suit, providing rote answers to questions instead of using those questions as the catalyst to share stories and build intimate community, seeing if God is doing a new thing among the people. It is as if "we tend to use information to feed the emptiness created by the absence of our imagination."[31]

Conversely, the Herald engages communities in such a way so as to empower them to value their own experiences and take the risks of using their own voice and dialect to speak out for acknowledgment and justice. A Heraldic hermeneutic would be a theopoetic one, that is, one that values particular stories and images and leads to more conversation, exploration, and engagement rather than less. What Scott Holland writes of theopoetics is equally applicable to the words of Heraldic proclamation: "It is a kind of writing that invites more writing. Its narratives lead to other narratives, its metaphors encourage new metaphors, its confessions invoke more confessions, and its conversations invite more conversations."[32]

A community encouraging a Heraldic practice of theology would be further and further removed from a monorthodox, scientistic discipline of proof and proposition and closer to a passionate exploration of how God is seen to be ever renewing in all that is in each life, home, and community. Furthermore, it is in each of those places that the Herald's new proclamations, interpretations, and expressions will be tested, for not every instance of proclamation is appropriate or valuable. Experience can be afforded more attention without giving all interpretations of experience prima facie equivalence to truth. That is, given that the Herald's proclamation is the unique expression of personal experience that she nonetheless believes will speak to others, what is the community to which she speaks supposed to do with her message? Do they accept her interpretations in entirety? Put another way, what does Yoder's condition "if others join the Herald to carry the word along," look like, and by what means will they "with time develop a doctrinal system, to help distinguish between more and less adequate ways of proclaiming?" A consideration of the role of community in developing a hermeneutic stance is of use in exploring this issue.

A Communal Hermeneutic

In his book *Is There a Text in This Class: The Authority of Interpretive Communities,* the literary theorist Stanley Fish makes the clear argument that "strictly speaking, getting 'back-to-the-text' is not a move one can perform, because the text one gets back to will be the text demanded by some other interpretation and that interpretation will be presiding over its production."[33] What he suggests is that all attempts to "just read what the text says, without interpretation" are flawed because, as Fish cheekily notes, "like it or not, interpretation is the only game in town."[34]

What Fish offers is an understanding that "while there is no core of agreement in the text, there is a core of agreement (although one subject to change) concerning the ways of producing [interpretation of] the text."[35] When a community has come to a new interpretation that its members agree upon, Fish argues that what they have come to is not "The Meaning" but an agreement that, for their community, such-and-such will be the meaning: They have agreed on an interpretation, not archaeologically uncovered Truth. While Fish goes further than most theologians would be comfortable in that he discredits the idea that there is such a thing as the truth of a text, the proposal here is not that there is no such truth but that human attempts to interpret and express it will always somehow fall short of the mark. Knowing this, it is vital that communities be aware of the contingent nature of theological explanations and of interpretations of revelation, whether they come from a Herald, a clergy person, or an academic journal.

Given the proclivity of human communities to convince themselves of many things so as to avoid cognitive dissonance, the issue of valid interpretation becomes problematic: To some degree there is an interpretative corollary to the founder effect.[36] Communities tend to want to dialogue among themselves or with other communities they already know to express things in a manner similar to their own. Even given the contingent nature of interpretation, since people are inclined to place continued trust in the veracity of preexisting interpretations and tend to distrust encroachments on their extant fields of meaning, communities of religious interpretation can become increasingly monorthodox. When communities seem to want so badly to stay just the way they are, how can they possibly change? At least one corrective, by way of the analogy of the founder effect, is apparent and deserves acknowledgment.

Just as the inclusion of other people into a previously closed community increases the genetic variability of the offspring, so too does the presence of new perspectives invigorate new intellectual and interpretive life. Communities can develop hybridized doctrine and experiment with new ways of expressing themselves and their faith while not having to abandon central beliefs. Another, less positive, parallel can be drawn when it is considered that it is often the case that when closed communities are less than receptive to outsiders there is an increased likelihood that inbreeding can lead to possibly unhealthy offspring. Communities of interpretation are just as dependent upon new input as are the reproducing humans that constitute them.

The charge here is not to seek out the Other simply for the sake of social justice but to encounter the Other so that, in the meeting, interactions with one another might help to inform and reform developing interpretations. Shared expressions of experience and hope are invaluable because "concepts of person, community, and God have an essential and indissoluble relation to one another."[37] The call is not to accept everything heard as truth. This would be nigh on impossible, given the diversity of perspectives that abound. Instead, the encounter is to be one in which people have the opportunity to have interpretive lenses reformed and to more fully see in the Other some further call to move more deeply into faith. Indeed, these opportunities for reflection and interpretive reorientation can arise within the community itself.

Though members of a certain community may all consider themselves the same religion or denomination, it is unlikely that they all interpret scripture and experience in the same way. Unfortunately, though, if adherence to polity and tradition is emphasized for the sake of adherence, the likelihood of hearing differing experiences and expressions is greatly reduced. Communal movement toward a Heraldic stance means making liturgical and dialogical space to earnestly consider divergent views, with an acknowledgment that these views may very well come from within the tradition itself. Heralds need not come from foreign lands to bring new thought that shifts that which has come before. Whenever and wherever it is that such shifts occur, another opportunity has come to reconsider interpretation. This begs the question: Does this mean then that anything that makes a community happy is an acceptable interpretation—or that there is no such thing as right? Not at all.

As process theologian Russell Pregeant writes, not "all texts or strains of meaning [are] worthy of positive valuation. Although it is theoretically possible to create a positive pattern of meaning out of any set of complexes, the dialogical and persuasive character of Biblical authority mitigates against any hermeneutic of unqualified consent."[38] At some level, people of faith may be called to simply trust that something about the character of scripture, and the divinity that inspired it, will eventually lead toward goodness and truth. Indeed, regardless of one's religion, the reality of the limitation of human interpretation is a valent issue with which all people must grapple. For people of faith this grappling must generally come to a place wherein they trust that somehow the wrestling will eventually yield useful interpretation(s). And this trust can be a difficult thing to come by, given the surrender of any notion of an absolute, objective interpretation. In spite of this, it seems that, at some point, some measure of faith is required to accept the imperfection of our sight and directly reengage the text. If this is not done, a richness of faith, experience of unity, and the personal encounter with some mediated perception of the divine will all remain inaccessible, driven off by a distancing maneuver of doubt given life by the misguided notion that faith must seek certainty.

The text, and its interpretation, can be distanced for a time with a hermeneutic of suspicion, but eventually they must be accepted and brought close again, or no transformation or religious experience can take place. Knowing that interpretations are contingent and limited does not mean they must lack in power. As Richard Kearney asserts, "religions are imaginary works, even if what they witness to may be transcendent and true."[39] It is still possible to be deeply affected by actors upon a stage, though all know it is not "real" as such. While any interpretation is possible, something about scripture, when approached in faith, and with room made for a theopoetic multiplicity of voices, allows us, "in a post-critical[40] moment, [to] be caught up in the text, lost in the text, [so that] . . . the text functions as transformative mediation of meaning."[41]

A community that allows itself to become lost in the text in light of new perspectives may find itself destabilized. In the transitional moments of communal reflection, it is again useful to recall Yoder's reflection on the Herald: People will "develop a doctrinal system, to help distinguish between more and less adequate ways of proclaiming; but that system, those formulae, will not become what they proclaim."[42] It is important that communities of faith learn the difference between tradition, which has been handed down across time and defines who and whose they are, and traditionalism, which is the doing of what has been done because it has been done before. Traditionalism breeds monorthodoxy. That being said, it is not worth purging traditional thought simply because it is traditional. What is important is that individuals find a balance between their history, personal experiences, and an allowance of others to voice theirs, accepting that while there will be a difference in perspective, perspective is not all that there is. The truth is indeed out there; it is just that knowing exactly the whole of what it is proves to be quite a challenge.

Some accord must be found between a community's desire to remain true to its heritage and to appreciate Whitehead's warning that "religions commit suicide when they find their inspiration in their dogmas. The inspiration of religion lies in the history of religion."[43] *History* for Whitehead here functions as a reference to embodied experience, the same type of event that inspired the Herald in the first place; when communities take seriously a catalyzing, theopoetic voice from beyond their prescribed tradition, they step ever further away from monorthodoxy. The danger then becomes that, in an earnest attempt to be inclusive or progressive, a community may unwittingly throw the baby out with the bathwater, experimenting in a manner that is potentially damaging to individuals or the knit of societal fabric. Given human limitations, this seems bound to happen. The hope, though—the hope of many faiths—is that somehow, in spite of these failings and limited sight, incomplete interpretation, and proclivity toward exclusion, attempts to develop interpretations that lead to compassion and faithfulness will find a measure of success.

A Challenge to Any Totalizing Claim

In his very short fiction piece "Of Exactitude in Science," Jorge Luis Borges sketches the folktale of an empire in which detailed cartography became so highly valued that the whole of the empire's territory was papered with a map whose scale was 1:1.[44] Their love of maps came to drive them so greatly that they covered over the land that was the origin of the map with a paper that eventually smothered them. In his book *Simulacra and Simulation,* Jean Baudrillard builds upon this story to suggest that contemporary society exists in such as state as Borges's empire. He argues that we place such value in our representation of things that we no longer are capable of interacting with the things that they represent: The tree itself is so covered with the map of the tree that light can't get at its leaves nor we at its fruit. While Baudrillard's case seems too extreme in its extent to serve a theologian, it does offer a warning that can function to keep communities from overvaluing their interpretations at the cost of the source. The Herald's goal is not to singularly establish representational and unifying doctrinal system but to report "contingent, particular events," allowing the community to wrestle with, and seek transformation within, their journey to discover what they will come to believe and be.

Whether it be God or some other conception of goodness to which to aspire, human attempts to work toward it will always result in various claims to authority and interpretations of things given authority in the past. When the theopoetic proclamation of a Herald has catalyzed a community into conversation with its constitutive parts, and those beyond its boundaries, some new sense of interpretation and doctrine will eventually merge. Not all community members will personally experience or express it the same way, but some new understanding or insight into how or what they are called to be and do has been developed that the community self-acknowledges as different than before. The Borgesian warning, then, is to remember that the process is yet ongoing. Owning to our own imperfection and the vastness of the divine, any community's interpretation of any revelation, regardless of its presently perceived specialness or naturalness, will be perpetually provisional until that time at which we are capable of seeing with God's eyes. Maps are but representations, and Heralds will continually direct attention to that fact, calling for repentance in a way not often heard.

While normative perspectives on repentance are likely to revolve around ideas of sin having to do with remorse, regret, and penitence, it is interesting to consider the etymological origins of the Greek word from which is often translated into English as "repentance." For example, in Mark 1:4, the rendering of "repentance for the forgiveness of sins" comes from μετάνοια (*metanoia*), which Strong's *Dictionary of Greek* lists as a derivative of μετανοέω (*metanoeō*), the verb we see in English as "to repent" and is given as "to think differently or afterwards, that is, reconsider (morally to feel compunction)." In this light, the Herald calls for repentance, not as a euphemism for some particular doctrinally inspired behavioral adherence but as an invitation to powerfully reconsider one's perspective. Heraldic proclamations that "shift interpretive stances," "refocus lenses," and "reorient within new stories" are all invitations to repent and to reconsider.

When repentance is construed with toeing a party line, or simplified to exist solely as uniform lists of acceptable, appropriate activities, the result is that polity replaces prophecy, and those who exert control over it are given marked privilege. Such gatekeeping positions are buttressed through claims to piety and fixed adherence to doctrine, both indirect indications of an understanding of a revelation that is closed, correctly interpreted, and fully appropriated. For this position, orthodoxy is also monorthodoxy, that is, there is a specific and fixed right way to be a community of faith and act in accordance with that community's faith—and that way does not adapt to communities of difference. The Herald questions this, wondering aloud when her experience falls within proscribed perceptions, and calling for communities to consider if they draw lines inspired by the search for justice or those meant to reaffirm traditionalism.

Such questioning could allow communities of faith to maintain their present traditional practices and doctrinal stances while simultaneously providing means by which those positions could gradually develop without fear of apostasy. The Herald does not domineeringly assert that others are wrong; he places himself in a vulnerable position outside normative positions of strength and speaks experience to power. This would not immediately provide safe or welcoming grounds for marginalized voices, but it *would* insist upon the contingency of the proclamation and the provisional nature of interpretation, and the doctrinal systems upon which interpretations are built. This, in turn, establishes the *possibility* that an unusual, dissimilar belief—that is, one outside of a closed, monorthodox system—might be as in line with a faithful way forward as older, more traditional practices.

The voice of the Herald is one that stands in theopoetic opposition to a closed, monorthodox perspective wherein a single valid interpretation is understood to be correct in entirety. The Herald would agree with Carl Raschke that "what anti-postmodernists brand as the danger of embracing relativism amounts to nothing more than a refusal to acknowledge the overwhelming fact of cultural heterogeneity and social pluralism."[45] The contemporary reality of our increasingly global culture is a natural polyphony that need not be viewed as an enemy. Indeed, it may well hold a profound opportunity to recall how tenuous our "hard-headed clarity" is and what power and transformation can come from a voice beyond the edge of what has come before. The Heraldic approach to theological and doctrinal expression is seeking not to simply create "an-easier-to-get-along-with-Christian"[46] but to engender a broader model of proclamation that discourages the development of any monorthodox perspective that supports monophonic oppression and coercion. Monorthodox thought is as readily found beyond the formal boundaries of the church as it is within. The term is as applicable to *worldview* as it is to *theology*, marking any situation in which orthodoxy is presented as a powerful and uniform collection of action, belief, and direction of thought.

The move toward the Heraldic calls not just for another iteration of postmodern deconstruction but for an affirmation of the constructive power of particular, imaginative, and embodied articulations of experience: a power that follows Faber's theopoetic impulse to "roughen up unified appearances" and responds to Wilder's plea to accord a greater value to "the symbolic and the prerational . . . way we deal with experience." Heraldic interpretation functions as a critique of modes of thinking that demand acquiescence, encouraging communities of faith to seek out further callings to faithfulness and justice that may come from places other than on high. The Herald affirms the irreducible manifoldness of the world and calls others out into it, to experience, as Rilke wrote, what it means to be "lavishly flung forth."

The Sublime, the Conflicted Self, and Attention to the Other
Toward a Theopoetics with Iris Murdoch and Julia Kristeva

PAUL S. FIDDES

Three Versions of the Conflicted Self and the Sublime

The idea of the "sublime" is widespread in aesthetics and philosophy today. Indeed, it may—as Jean-Luc Nancy suggests—have maintained its popularity for several centuries, as "a fashion that has persisted uninterruptedly into our own time from the beginnings of modernity."[1] The sublime, as modified by Kant and the Romantics, has become a cipher in our late modern period for what brings thought, reason, or beauty into question. It goes under such other names as "the void" (Jacques Lacan), "difference" (Jacques Derrida), "chaos" (Gilles Deleuze), "otherness" (Emmanuel Levinas), infinity, or even death (Freud). The "sublime" in recent thought is the thrilling event of nothingness and absence that overturns the realm of representation, presence, and stability, so that Jean-François Lyotard finds "narratives of the *unrepresentable*" everywhere in the philosophy of our age.[2]

Everywhere too are *studies* of the sublime, and here the names of Iris Murdoch and Julia Kristeva are surprisingly absent or very infrequent.[3] This is a pity, because both Murdoch and Kristeva have important insights to make for understanding the phenomenon of the sublime, and they offer significant modifications to a prevailing tendency of thought. Of course, a great deal has been said about Kristeva's psychoanalytical explorations of the second term in my title, the conflict in the self, but very little about the place of the *sublime* in this experience of fragmentation. Again, much has been written about Murdoch's concern with the third term of my title—"attention to the other." Commentators have rightly focused on the insistence of this philosopher and novelist that we should notice the "other" as he or she really is, and that we should look attentively at the world around us; but there is little comment about her connection of "attending to the other" with the experience of the *sublime*.

So, let us begin on the task sketched by my title by considering the conflict in the self and its relation to the sublime. Here I propose to look at three versions of the conflicted self, including Murdoch's and Kristeva's and beginning briefly with the person to whom virtually all writers on this topic appeal—Immanuel Kant. Kant's sublime is a drama of struggle, and the main actors are imagination and reason, with understanding as an understudy.

For Kant, *reason* always demands that we make a whole of our experience: Reason always works toward totality, though it can never achieve it. *Imagination* seems to have an inner compulsion to seek out those situations in which it *cannot* answer these demands of reason. Though it works in a happy harmony with the *understanding* in the realm of cognition, in another realm—the aesthetic—it comes into conflict with reason.[4] It finds what Kant calls experiences of the sublime where it struggles and fails to make a whole out of things. Imagination strives after infinity and has some apprehension or intuition of what it is—whether it is an infinite series of things in human cognition (the "mathematical sublime") or whether it is prompted by awesome and terrible objects in nature that seem to have no limits—seas, mountains, skies full of stars, deep ravines, waterfalls (the "dynamical" sublime). Imagination has an *apprehension* of the infinite but cannot *comprehend* it. Faced by the sheer boundlessness of things, the imagination feels terror, and yet it also feels a kind of "negative pleasure"[5] because finally it will enjoy the sense of the superiority of reason that makes such demands upon it, and which is therefore greater than any phenomena in the world. Here is Kant's brief summary of this mental conflict according to his *Critique of Judgment:*

> Precisely because there is a striving in our imagination towards progress *ad infinitum,* while reason demands absolute totality as a real idea, that same inability on the part of our faculty for the estimation of the magnitude of the things of the world of sense to attain to this idea, is the awakening of a feeling of a supersensible faculty [i.e., reason] within us.[6]

For Kant, this is quite unlike the sense of the "beautiful," where the imagination works in harmonious free play with the *understanding.* The same imagination that assists the understanding to see and grasp objects in the world that come to us through our senses (phenomena) also runs free—without concepts—in fields of taste or aesthetic judgment.[7] There is no rule we can formulate to categorize an object that appears beautiful: We cannot identify it as either good or purposeful.[8] Beauty is a matter of form only. It is independent of any moral judgment or even any emotion. Our sense of the beautiful, for Kant, is the freedom of mere playfulness, over against moral freedom.

A second version of the conflicted self is to be found in one of Kant's most profound interpreters and modifiers, Iris Murdoch, who wrote two significant essays on the theme of the sublime and the beautiful.[9] In Kant, the self is in conflict with *itself*, the imagination struggling with the demands of human reason, a situation very like the experience of respect (*Achtung*) for the inner moral law.[10] For Murdoch the self is in conflict with something *outside* itself, nothing less than the moral demands of a transcendent and sovereign Good. As in Kant, the demands are mediated through phenomena in the world that evoke a sense of the sublime.[11] But, as a Platonist, she is clear that the Good exists beyond the self; we cannot commune with it, and it is certainly not a *personal* God, but we must *serve* it for hope of no reward, being "good, for nothing."[12]

Now Murdoch makes a leap of originality. The sublime is not to be contrasted with the forms of the beautiful, as in Kant, but is to be found precisely *in* them. The sense of the sublime is marked by the boundless, the endless, the being without limit, before which we feel awe and even terror. This, Murdoch claims, is exactly the sense evoked by the boundlessness of forms in the world, by the multiplicity of contingent things, and by the diversity of people who fill the world. The sublime shocks and amazes us, but (as she puts it) "what stuns us into a realization of our supersensible destiny is not, as Kant imagined, the formlessness of nature, but rather its unutterable particularity."[13] Kant, she thinks, was afraid of the messy details of the world and all the bodies in it. To know the world as a reality other than ourselves is to love it. And this love is truly moral, since for Murdoch virtue is apprehending that other persons exist, and letting them be as others. Through the sublimity of the many contingent details of the world, focused especially but not exclusively in works of art,[14] the self is brought into conflict with the Good, and we can break out of an artificial world we construct around ourselves.

The sense of excess here has some resonances with the way that Lyotard reconstructs the sublime in Kant. He suggests that 'the sublime can be thought of as an extreme case of the beautiful" in which there occurs "the proliferation of forms by an imagination gone wild."[15] But, unlike Murdoch, Lyotard finds that this excess of form giving results in the *overwhelming* of forms. Personifying the Kantian faculties of Imagination, Reason, and Understanding, Lyotard tells the story of the birth of the Sublime in his own myth: Reason (male) rapes/violates Imagination (female), and the Sublime is conceived. Imagination dies giving birth to the Sublime.[16] Apart from the persistence of a patriarchal violence here,[17] the myth is intended to express the fact that postmodern art "denies itself the solace of form." Murdoch certainly perceives the dangers of consolation in art: When a particular object is regarded as containing the whole of reality, we are discouraged from dying to the self.[18] But, for her, the self is turned toward the Good and stripped of its self-centeredness by paying attention to a multiplicity of forms that remain in their own integrity. They deliver the shock of the negative sublime, but this is intended to lead to love of others, and finally to the "supersensible destiny" of the Good.

In Murdoch's novel, *Nuns and Soldiers*, Anne Cavidge is a former nun who has lost belief in a personal God and left her convent to serve the Good in the world, though she scarcely knows how. Like many of Murdoch's characters, she comes up against the contingency of the world in the form of the many small stones that litter its beaches and landscapes, and her ability to swim is symbolic of her willingness to plunge into the boundless ocean of the world. At first she is appalled by the stones on the beach, reflecting: "What do their details matter, what does it matter whether Christ redeemed the world or not, it doesn't matter, our minds can't grasp such things. . . . Look at these stones. My Lord and My God . . . there they are."[19] While she remains under a negative impression of the sublime, she is preoccupied by her self and nearly drowns in the sea, but coming up out of it "she saw, close to her now, the sloe of dark, shifting stones . . . [and] Anne's feet were *again upon the stones.*"[20] Later she has a vision of her own, personal Christ, and he shows her a symbol of the world—not a hazelnut as in the similar visions of Julian of Norwich—but a small, elliptical, gray stone.[21] Toward the end of the novel she feels that she can at that point "call upon the name of the non-existent God" as she touches "the dense . . . stone in whose small compass her Visitor had made her *see* the Universe, everything that is."[22]

For most of the story Anne is staying with an old schoolmate, Gertrude, and the novel begins with Gertrude's husband, Guy, facing an imminent death by cancer. Before he dies, he urges Gertrude to find happiness by marrying again, and much of the plot of the novel is generated by the question of whom she might marry in the close circle of her friends and admirers. Might it be, for instance, a work colleague of Guy's, an upright, well-mannered Polish man who carries the nickname of "the Count" and who has long secretly and honorably loved her? The successful candidate turns out to be the most unlikely one of all—a feckless and penniless painter called Tim Reede, who has been living for years in an on-off relationship with his punkish girlfriend Daisy. Guy has been a father figure to Tim, and so Daisy persuades Tim to go and see Gertrude after his death to try and borrow some money. Gertrude, however, wants to help him without injuring his pride and so lends him her cottage in France to live and paint in over the summer. There, in the enchanting countryside, Tim and Gertrude fall in love.

Two locations in the country around become occasions for prompting their love—a great "Face" of rock with a crystal clear pool at its base, and a fast-running canal that disappears underground. Both are described in ways that seem to recall the Kantian dynamical sublime but that quickly modulate into what one might call the Murdochian sublime: That is, they have the aspect of the boundless and unlimited that evokes awe and even terror, but they also have the beauty of fine detail. We read of the Great Face, for instance, that "he looked upon it with awe . . . he fled";[23] "the numinous power of the rock shook him."[24] But he also draws its multiple lines and shifting contrasts of light, a profile that is full of diversity and plurality, and observes the floor of the rock basin as "covered with small crystalline pebbles."[25] It is this contingent detail that actually makes him frightened and brings on a sense of panic. In a period of separation and misunderstanding between Gertrude and Tim before they finally come together in marriage, Tim reflects on the Great Face that "there was absolute truth in the thing, something of wholeness and goodness which called to him from outside the dark tangle of himself. . . . That it should have been accidental [i.e., contingent] did not dismay him."[26] We notice that this is a "thing" in the phenomenal world embodying "absolute truth": Later, we shall draw a contrast with the Lacanian Thing, which inhabits the Void.

Again, during the miserable time of separation, the breach in their love, Tim moves from a Kantian mood of the negative sublime to a Murdochian sublime. Here is a description of his feeling of the first, echoing Kant:

> Sometimes the void gleamed like the sea . . . the external world disappeared. . . . he was a tiny scrap of being . . . a point in empty space . . . the sense of emptiness was occasionally almost pleasurable. It was always awful. . . . pure freedom . . . the cosmos itself, gentle, terrible final . . . also a vision of death.[27]

After taking a decisive step of leaving Daisy, the mood changes. The detail of the world impinges on him again: We read, "the white light seemed to be with him again but was different now . . . he could *see* the trees . . . he could *see* in the distance the line of the lake."[28] "He could *see* the Autumn leaves," and he begins to make collages of them in a period he calls "the time of the leaves": We read that "little works of art lay around—masterpieces which were lying about free of charge. . . . though he was still afraid to go back to the National Gallery."[29] Finding the sublime in the detail of the world, he will soon be ready to see not only the art in the gallery[30] but also Gertrude as she really is, and to recognize her love for him. The story makes clear how, for Murdoch, the essence of both art and ethics is the same, namely love, or a respect for the other and a genuine noticing of the other. As she puts it in her essay on "The Sublime and the Good": "Love, and so art and morals, is the discovery of reality."[31]

For all that, there is always the danger of mere consolation in art, a temptation that Murdoch is always ready to admit. There is just a hint of truth in Daisy's view of the paintings in the National Gallery, that they constitute "a fantasy world where everything's easy and pretty," echoing Plato's judgment that "art is a lie."[32] But when used as a pathway to the Good, the sublime-in-the-beautiful is truth. As the newly married Tim returns to work, his drawings are "coming to him out of a faintly discernible background of relentless *form* which he could apprehend as taking shape behind them."[33] The sublime for Murdoch does not destroy form but clarifies it. Here Murdoch differs both from Kant and from the postmodern appeal to the sublime. The postmodern mood follows Kant in placing the sublime in opposition to the beautiful, although the recent appeal to the sublime breaks down not only art and forms in the world but also—unlike in Kant—reason itself. Murdoch, however, wants to affirm sublimity *in* the beautiful.

Turning now to Julia Kristeva, we find our third version of the conflicted self. Here it seems we are back more firmly in the world of Kant, with the sublime as a symptom of a conflict within the self itself, rather than between the self and an external and transcendent Good. The self is riven by many conflicts, as Kristeva perceives it. But this is Kant psychoanalyzed, or perhaps a drawing out of the already incipient psychological character of Kant's thought. Here, for Kristeva, Freud is mediated through Jacques Lacan. The phenomenal level, the consciousness, is a world of language, a symbolic realm in which the self holds only a fragmented identity. For Lacan, therapy is centered on getting the individual to come to terms with his or her alienated identity. The infant, growing into a sense of individual identity, has had to exchange its preconscious sense of wholeness for a kind of being that is inscripted by language and by a society shaped by language.[34] Entry into the symbolic, into the world of words, comes at a price: This phenomenal world fails to satisfy, and we long for the "real

Thing," lost in the world of the preconscious. We have a desire for the "lost object," and yet this can never be possessed. There is a central impossibility, a Void or Thing at the heart of the symbolic realm that can never be represented but that must be recognized if meaning is to be generated by signifiers.[35] And those signifiers, according to Lacan, are essentially male in orientation; the symbolic realm unavoidably privileges male symbols and is inevitably patriarchal.

Now, Kristeva has taken on much of Lacan's analysis but wants to draw attention to the role of the woman in all this. For Freud and Lacan, the key point of entry into the symbolic is the Oedipal moment, which is all about the relation of father and son. Daughters and mothers are sidelined, given walk-on parts in this psychodrama. For Kristeva, the key moment for the growing infant is the necessary separation from the mother, or what she calls the "abjection" of the mother, taking up a term from Bataille and a load of theory from Melanie Klein. In the development of human subjectivity, the child must break from the mother: To attain a sense of self-identity the mother must be abjected, sacrificed, violently rejected. This point of separation is the boundary that the growing subject has to pass over to reach the realm of language and meaning, where subject is separated from object.[36] According to Kristeva, a person moves from deep, precognitive immersion in the life of the body to a social life.

Yet that preconscious realm remains as a living factor in symbolic life, capable of disturbing the patriarchal realm of symbols. A primary maternal body cannot be entirely suppressed, and this is associated with the realm that Kristeva calls the "semiotic."[37] As distinct from the symbolic, the semiotic is prediscursive, expressing an original libidinal multiplicity over against the monolithic tendencies of culture; it has the capacity to irritate and subvert the symbolic. Poetic language, for instance, relies upon multiple meanings and so challenges the law of unity. For Kristeva there is something "in play" beyond or outside rational discourse, something that goes "beyond the theatre of linguistic representations."[38]

Where the semiotic breaks into the symbolic, there is a resurgence of infantile drives arising from the *jouissance* of the subconscious. This moment of extreme, disruptive pleasure includes sexual pleasure but can also be experienced through art and literature. Kristeva suggests that the language of poetry recovers the maternal body, a field of impulse, full of diversity. Poetic speech is characterized by rhythm, sound play, and repetition, movements that reflect primal movements of love and energy. Here Kristeva envisages the semiotic as flowing from a realm that she denotes as the *chora,* taking the concept from Plato's *Timaeus,* where it refers to an unnameable space that exists between Being and Becoming. She develops the concept of *chora* as a womb-like, nurturing space of origin, as the pre-linguistic receptacle of subconscious drives and archetypal relations with the mother *and* the father. The *chora,* she writes, "precedes and underlies figuration and . . . is analogous only to vocal or kinetic rhythm." Poetry, in its rhythms of sound and idea, reflects the *chora,* which is a place "constituted by movements."[39] To this idea of a primal movement I want to return, as it is full of potential for theology.

The essential conflict in the self for Kristeva is thus between the symbolic and the semiotic, at the hinge of which is abjection, a moment of horror and terror. So we come to the place of the sublime, the experience of terror and pleasure, in this psychoanalytic rewriting of Kant. At the very beginning of her book *Powers of Horror,* Kristeva tells us that abjection is "*edged by the sublime.*"[40] This perception colors everything that follows, but what can it mean? First, it means that abjection is nameless, just as Kant thinks that the sublime cannot be comprehended by the imagination. Anything that is abject is felt as a threat to be repelled, yet (Kristeva confesses) "I feel that it *belongs* to me"; it cannot then be objectified over against me, given a name or even imagined. It is not object but abject. It is, says Kristeva, "a 'something' that I do not imagine as a thing" and it "does not respect borders." It simultaneously "beseeches and pulverizes the self."[41] The prime instance of the abject is the rejected mother, as we have described her: She is no longer an object of our knowing but coded as an abject.

Second, the abject is "edged by the sublime" because it is the source of excessiveness. Confronted by something felt as sublime, writes Kristeva, "the object dissolves in raptures of bottomless memory."[42] The sublime triggers a boundless expansion of memories; echoing Derrida's notion of a *parergon* (an "addition" or a "frame"),[43] she says that it is "something added that expands into an impossible bounding." The time of the abject is one of "veiled infinity from which revelation bursts forth."[44] It is a mark of psychosis, and particular of the "dark sun" of melancholia, to try to regress behind the moment of abjection, to attempt a recovery of undisturbed unity with self and mother. Facing up to the fact of abjection is to shatter the wall of repression, and so one can—in a certain sense—take "joy" in the abject while not knowing it or desiring it. There is what Kristeva calls a "sublime alienation," which *can* take perverse forms such as taboos in religion, or the attempt to "purify" what is felt to be unclean. Excessiveness, then, is a highly ambiguous state, tending to life or death.

Third, the abject is sublime because it leads to *sublimation.* As Kristeva puts it, confronted by the abject, there is an attempt to name it, to keep it under control,[45] and so to sublimate it. The sublime triggers *sublimation.* This insight is perhaps the most significant for our discussion, and it is here

I believe that Kristeva makes the greatest, but most neglected, contribution to the theme of the sublime. "Sublimation" has a double meaning. First, it is about *elevation:* To sublimate something is to raise it to the level of the sublime, as the reason is raised (*erheben*) by Kant above the sublimity of nature. Second, sublimation has the Freudian sense of *transfer,* the *sublation* of deep, primal impulses of the libido by redirecting them into other pursuits, such as artistic efforts and poetry.[46] In particular, the unconscious drive toward death is sublimated in objects of art and love. Kristeva merges the two meanings, elevation with transfer, following Lacan's concept of the "ideal."

The Sublime and Sublimation

For Lacan, the mind sublimates its sense of the Void, or the loss of the Thing that is buried deep in the unconsciousness. An object or person acquires a sublime quality when it is raised to the dignity of the Thing or stands in for the Thing.[47] As sublime, it becomes an ideal, pointing to the Void at the heart of the symbolic world. The ideal object might be an artwork, or it could be a person—and here Lacan takes as a key example the sublime figure of Antigone in Sophocles's tragic drama. For Lacan, the self-willed victim Antigone possesses "unbearable splendour . . . a quality that attracts and disturbs us" and that captivates the chorus.[48]

He has, to be sure, come under a good deal of feminist criticism for using the myth of Antigone to describe the "other" that threatens the identity of a masculinized self, the only "I"; he appears to use the idealized woman simply to support the delusion of male autonomy.[49] Indeed, let us admit that Kristeva has fallen under the same criticism, for agreeing with Lacan that the lost Thing is to be located in the pre-Oedipal state, before the separation of the child from the mother so that the mother takes on the role of a threat to identity. I should anticipate my later argument by acknowledging that there are all kinds of problems with her notion of abjection, not least what seems to be a feminist capitulation to violence and a patriarchal society,[50] but I want to suggest that Kristeva's real contribution lies beyond this critique.

Meanwhile, I want to introduce Kristeva's novel *Murder in Byzantium,*[51] with which we can explore themes of abjection and sublimation in an imaginative way. Her detective novels feature Stephanie Delacour, a Parisian journalist and amateur detective whom Kristeva describes as her alter ego. She is sent as a reporter to the imaginary country of Santa Varva, a corrupt seaboard state that appears to be in Eastern Europe but that is presented as the global village. Everything that happens in the world—

terrorism, rampant capitalism, mass-media distortions, the drug culture—happens in Santa Varva. In one strand of the plot there is a murderer at large who calls himself the Purifier and who is killing members of a cult called the New Pantheon, which mixes religion, drugs, and the mafia. The police chief, Rilsky, reflects that the murderer "is the purifier of abjection. . . . not only does he measure the horror, but this figure confronts it with a certain jubilation."[52] Later, Stephanie reflects that the murderer is in quest of his "pre-masculine embryo," an "imaginary infinite" that is the secret abyss, his joy, his love. He wants to return to the preabjective, pregendered time that is "the mathematics of the infinite,"[53] and so becomes a murderer without limitation of victims, signing his work with the sign of infinity in their own blood.

In another strand of the plot, a professor named Sebastian Chrest Jones disappears while researching the Byzantine Princess Anna Commena, a brilliant intellectual who wrote a history of the reign of her Emperor father, Alexias. Sebastian is obsessed by two ideals who attain the state of the sublime for him: Anna and a crusader called Ebrard, whom he believes to be his ancestor, and Anna's lover. Sebastian has disappeared from his university post in order to retrace their steps through his home country—and Kristeva's—namely Bulgaria. Stephanie reflects, "Sebastian is in love with Anna. He is a dangerous man . . . he's pursuing a dream,"[54] and later the narrator adds, "Stephanie was right, Sebastian was in love with Anna Commena; but he loved her as though he were Ebrard . . . the transfusion into his presumed ancestor had become such a strong hallucination and so intoxicating that he hardly took notice of real living people."[55] Ebrard is "the ghost or ideal Sebastian, who went back in time"[56]—in fact back not just in history but to the pretemporal state of the psyche.

The two plots are linked romantically, since Stephanie's lover and co-sleuth is the police chief Rilsky, who also happens to be Sebastian's uncle. They are linked psychologically, as both Sebastian and the murderer are prompted to their violence and their idealization by loss of their fathers and "the illusory hope of returning to the authentic origin where the mother is awaiting. . . . that unknown mother squashed by the Powers-that-Be,"[57] a state known especially by exiles in society—among whom Kristeva includes herself.[58] Like the murderer, Sebastian "projects himself into the black sun" of melancholia[59]—"ah, the sweetness of Byzantine sorrow"—with which Stephanie herself toys: "My own Byzantium is the color of time. . . . Byzantium is nowhere; it is no place."[60] The plots are also linked dramatically, as Sebastian has killed his lover, Fa, who turns out to be the sister of the murderer, and he is killed in the denoument by the murderous brother, in the ruins of the Bulgarian church where he locates his ancestor. Sebastian, we learn, has killed Fa because, in becoming pregnant without his knowledge or consent, she has "dared to become an origin without him," supplanting the authentic origin he seeks.[61]

The novel is a lot of fun, but one can see immediately how it is a vehicle for Kristeva's psychoanalytic philosophy, and particular of the sublime and sublimation. Indeed, Kristeva sees the writing of novels as a form of sublimation in itself. In addition, we see Sebastian and Stephanie in different ways trying to overcome the oppression of the symbolic order, so that she feels an odd sympathy with him: Both, as exiles in society, speak a "language of silence."[62] Stephanie reflects that in times of "emptiness," she feels the conflict between the symbolic and the semiotic that I have suggested is characteristic of Kristeva's sublime:

> I do not express myself in either words or sentences, even though I like to trace out rhythms and visions . . . More and less than words and sentences, it's the underside of a language that I sense flowing in my mouth.[63]

This novel may seem very different from Murdoch's. But in *Nuns and Soldiers* there is the same sense of the ambiguity of the ideal—of the artwork or the person raised to the level of the sublime. In the face of the loss of the father figure, Guy, both the Count and Tim idealize Gertrude: To the Count she is a "sudden, radiant source,"[64] and Tim believes that "Gertrude would save him."[65] Murdoch is always suspicious of consolation, and especially the making of others into savior figures who will relieve us of the burden of our own dying to self. So Anne asks Christ in her vision, "What shall I do to be saved?" and her "nomadic" Christ replies: "You must do it all yourself, you know."[66] As we have already seen, even the things of beauty in the National Gallery can become false consolation, reflecting Kristeva's statement that, while beauty never disappoints the libido, if it is used to *deny* loss, then it is perishable and mere artifice.[67]

For all the similarity, Murdoch finds the sublime experience of the ambiguous ideal to be pointing toward a Good that exists objectively, beyond the individual. For Kristeva, the sublime ideal points to a preconscious experience of separation and splitting in the psyche that has to be faced and dealt with. There is, however, a further dimension of sublimation, beyond idealization, that Kristeva perceives, and which I believe to be highly significant for the healing of the person—that is, *forgiveness*. On the way to this, we should think a little more about the third term in our title, "attending to the other."

Attending to the Other and the Sublime

Kant, so Murdoch claims, is not much concerned with the other.[68] For him, the sublime reinforces the self and especially Reason. By contrast, Murdoch is concerned with the sublime as the occasion for giving attention to the *particular other* and so for embracing a death of the self. "Love," writes Murdoch, "is the extremely difficult realization that something other than oneself is real."[69] As Guy expresses it, lying on his deathbed in *Nuns and Soldiers,* "death and dying are enemies," and the problem with Christianity is that it "changes death into suffering."[70] That is, religion can get so absorbed in the glorifying of suffering, even dying, that it neglects actual *death,* which is putting an end to the self, or a life built around the self. In the appearance of Christ to Anne Cavidge, he tells her that "my wounds are imaginary . . . if there was suffering it has gone and is nothing . . . though it has proved so interesting to you all."[71] Instead, "Death is a teaching. It is one of my names." So the "little bit of safety" of Tim's self has to be smashed open by exposure to the details of the world.[72] Emerging from the underground tunnel into which he has been swept as in a kind of death, he sees the grass and trees around him "with a clarity that remained with him ever after."[73] For Murdoch, the sublime is the beauty of particular things and persons in all their diversity, which we are to *see* and love.

Julia Kristeva, on the other hand, seems to inherit a Kantian assertion of the self. She accepts the Lacanian analytical theory that in phobic or depressive regression, the mother is felt to *threaten* the self, which must struggle into its identity through abjection. But the violence of this act (criticized by other feminists) is softened by attention to an "Another" who appears deep within the psyche. At the moment of dawning consciousness, on the verge of language and so of separating from the mother, the self imagines an image of a *father,* a father who belongs to the earliest, pre-linguistic life of the individual.[74] This is indeed the pre-oedipal "father of prehistory" in Freud's theory, and so not yet a gendered figure. But the key move that Kristeva makes is to privilege *this* kind of "father" or "mother-father" over the definitely *male* father who appears subsequently in Freud's famous Oedipal triangle. Unlike Lacan, *this* is the decisive moment evoked by the experience of the sublime—not the Oedipal pact, which seems to concern only fathers and sons.

The image of the father that arises in the growth of subjectivity is not the demanding Freudian superego but a self-giving father. The subject, says Kristeva, enters the realm of "trinitary logic."[75] As the subject has to face separation from the mother, it shares in an exchange of gifts of love that is symbolized in the mutual self-giving of the Trinity—Father, Son, and Holy Spirit. In later life, then, the self can become aware of others and share imaginatively in an interchange with them.[76]

The sublimation prompted by the terrors of the sublime is thus a transfer to the imaginary father-mother, not an Oedipal pact but a tale of love. Most important, this entails forgiveness. In an essay on Dostoyevsky's *Crime and Punishment*, Kristeva stresses that forgiveness is a form of sublimation, substituting the pair eros/forgiveness for eros/death.[77] Like Murdoch, Kristeva stresses that a preoccupation with suffering is unhealthy, a sign of dependence on the symbolic realm of divine law.[78] Rather, the sublimation of forgiveness "opens up a strange space in time" that is a counterpart of the unconscious, so that the unconscious may "inscribe itself in a new narrative that will not be the eternal return of the death drive."[79] Against Lacan, she insists that the unconscious is not structured as a language, not part of the symbolic order. Instead, it is semiotic, marked by identification with the other.

Forgiveness renews the unconscious and rebuilds the personality, affirms Kristeva, because it is empathetic. She writes: "Whoever is in the realm of forgiveness, giving and receiving, is capable of *identifying* with a loving father, an imaginary father, with whom he is willing to be reconciled, with a new symbolic law in mind."[80] This is not a matter just for the inner life of the psyche but for relation with others in society: Forgiveness, she writes, gives "shape to relations between insulted and humiliated individuals . . . [so] giving shape to signs."[81] Thus the sublime experience of facing up to abjection can lead to forgiveness, which in turn challenges the old law of the father. Kristeva writes: "There is no beauty outside the forgiveness that remembers abjection"; so, she continues, "*forgiveness is essential to sublimation.*" Identification with the other is always "unstable and unfinished" so that the "suffering body of the forgiver (and the artist) undergoes a 'transubstantiation.'"[82] The language of "unstable identity" and "transubstantiation" betokens, I suggest, empathy. This empathic forgiveness, she proposes, is symbolized by the Orthodox doctrine of the Trinity in which there is "a permanent instability of identity between the persons . . . each person of the Trinity identified with the others in an erotic fusion."[83]

In *Murder in Byzantium*, as in Murdoch's novel, attending to others involves "seeing" them as they are. Sebastian kills Fa because "he no longer saw her";[84] we are not surprised to learn that when he was a child he liked to crush the eyes of butterflies. Yet Sebastian knows that the culture of Byzantium, based on icons, was all about seeing: "the eyes, this is the key to Byzantium . . . so many debates about the visible and invisible. . . ."[85] Viewing Byzantine art at Boyana in Bulgaria, he reflects that "for the people of Boyana the *image* of someone or something meant nothing less than being in a living relationship with that person or thing," and he understands the roots of this in the Orthodox Trinity: He thinks "there is a whole history of love between the Father and the Son no less than between model and image. . . . the walls of Boyana impressed on Sebastian the economy of love of another age, another way of seeing."[86]

There is not much, at least explicitly, about forgiveness in this novel, but there is a great deal about the empathy as well as the seeing involved in love. Love happens in the "silence" that belongs to the inner Byzantium, not in much speaking.[87] Love is the "intense sensation of proximity, this osmosis between two bodies."[88] Toward the end, Stephanie reflects on her love affair with Rilsky that

> the silence that we love and in which we love each other. . . . preserves my lucidity and yours, incommensurable will and yet not shut off: you're me and I'm you, but we remain quite different inside this reciprocal echo chamber . . . what name shall we give "it"? Nothingness is too melancholic . . . silence is a humble term that doesn't rule out language . . . all the while remaining attentive to my body and yours.[89]

Such a love is one of empathy ("you're me and I'm you"), but this very process is one in which the self or the "incommensurable will" is not lost, for "we remain quite different inside this reciprocal echo chamber."[90] For both Murdoch and Kristeva, eros is a force that can lead us to notice each other as well as some primordial power. As Stephanie reflects, it is hard to name the place of silence, yet "all the while remaining attentive to my body and yours."[91]

For Murdoch, sexual love is a form of the energy of eros, which can sink toward a degraded state or be purified and point toward a higher eros of loving the Good for no reward.[92] Unlike Kristeva, eros always falls under the suspicion of becoming a false ascesis or an illusory stripping of the self, driven by the fantasy of "being in love." The contingency of all that is not the self is *for a moment* unveiled with a sublime radiance, but it does not last. It must lead on to true ascesis, a flaying away of the self for the sake of the Good. But even this "refined" eros, as a "force that joins us to Good," is not empathetic: There is no question of reciprocal response of the Good. Consequently, as Peter Conradi puts it, "love with the separate world and the separate people it contains" is "a darker, colder, more impersonal commodity."[93] Murdoch does raise the issue of forgiveness in *Nuns and Soldiers,* but it seems a mechanical process of adjustment: Daisy forgives Tim, but there is nothing empathetic about it. She remarks "one bit of wood doesn't ask another bit of wood to forgive it,"[94] and Murdoch comments that they forgave each other "out of a kind of hopelessness."[95]

What then can we conclude from the connection of "attending to the other" with the sublime? For Murdoch, the experience of the sublime prompts an attention that is a cold, dispassionate kind of love, but that includes attending to a Supreme Good that is not confined to the human self. For Kristeva there *is* no transcendent Good except what lies in individuals and in society, although Trinitarian symbolism is a powerful means of evoking it. Any kind of God, even the Platonist nameless Good, is an illusion.[96] But the sublime provokes an attention that is a highly empathetic form of love and forgiveness.

The Sublime and Theopoetics

It will come as no surprise that I want to combine *Murdoch's* kind of sublime, where attention to the multiple details of the world prompt attention to the Good, with *Kristeva's* sense of the sublime, where sublimation means empathetic identification and forgiveness. I aim to integrate two kinds of *attending* to the "other," two kinds of spiritual practice. But how shall we achieve this combination? First, by living in the narrative world created by the two novels I have been describing. I have not included them simply to *illustrate* philosophical ideas, as if they are optional extras to the argument. As we inhabit the lives and the thoughts of the characters, as we read both novels together, there begins to stir within us an inkling of how their worlds *might* connect. We begin to see the possibilities of a spiritual practice that is embodied in taking the two narratives together, and that cannot be totally contained in any theory.

But we can also *begin* to think theologically. In so doing, I must resist theological projects that fail to combine the two modes of the sublime that Murdoch and Kristeva together show us. Slavoj Žižek, for instance, adopts a Lacanian reading of the sublime as an indicator of the traumatic emptiness or lack at the heart of the symbolic realm.[97] Desire for the other (woman, or God, for instance) is the result of this primary deprivation; an object of love becomes sublime when it is raised to the place of the inaccessible Thing, as in courtly love. But, Lacan argues, as soon as woman is encountered in her body, she changes from a sacred object to a trangressive *abject,* and sublimation is brought to an end.[98] Following Lacan, Žižek thus maintains that religious discourse, claiming that God is love, has to avoid the fleshly associations of love, to enable sublimation to continue. Divine love, the totally self-giving love of *agape,* frees us from the realm of the law and must be distinguished from *eros,* the love that satisfies the body and the self.[99] Above all, for Žižek *Christ* is *agape;* he is sublime because his mortality stands in place of the overwhelming glory of God. His abjection in the cross does not contradict the logic of sublimation, since he is not (according to Žižek) presented here as an object of beauty; it is his consequent transformation through resurrection into a sublime object of desire that enables his follows to enter into the inexhaustible dimensions of the sacred Thing.[100]

We detect some echoes of Kristeva here, but her stress on love and forgiveness as empathy means that, for her, an *agape*-love cannot be separated out from *eros* in the experience of the sublime. Moreover, she finds (building on the Trinitarian thought of Hans Urs Von Balthasar)[101] that *abjection* is to be found in the erotic fusion of the Trinity itself, as separation or splitting (a "hiatus") enters into the very relations of the Father and the Son. Anyway, the old distinction between *eros* and *agape* has long been rejected by many theologians, who stress the eros of God for the world;[102] God opens God's own self in desire for creation and in dependence on it, though not as an external necessity but as a free choice, as one who desires to be in need.[103] As the theologian Eberhard Jüngel expresses it, *eros* and *agape* belong together in the being of God as love, as an event of "a still greater selflessness within a very great self-relatedness," since in giving himself away to the beloved, any lover is related to himself anew.[104] Žižek, an atheist arguing for the indispensibility of Christian symbolism, unfortunately misreads the symbols here. His project also fails Murdoch's analysis of the sublime, since for him sublime objects do not represent any transcendent "thing in itself" such as the Good, but only a human lack.

We are brought, I suggest, to what might be called a "theopoetics,"[105] a vision of God as the poet-maker of the universe, creating all its particular details in an excess of divine generosity and love and relating to them in compassionate imagination. Indeed, just as a poem is generated within what Kristeva identifies as the inner space of the person, her very own Byzantium, we may think of the whole of created reality (this universe and probably many others) as existing within God. It exists not in a mind but in the space made by the interweaving of the divine persons who—as Augustine and Aquinas hinted[106]—are nothing other than movements of relationship. As Leibniz proposed, and as is increasingly affirmed by modern science, relations do not exist in a Newtonian receptacle of space and time, but space is what is created *by relations* themselves.[107] So, we may say, finite beings share in the movements of love and justice that are happening within God, like movements of relationship between a father and a son.[108] And because these are movements of giving and receiving in love, it is *also* appropriate to say that they are like relations between a mother and a daughter, deepened and opened to the future by the rhythm of a shared love.

This triune imagery of space *within* God picks up what Kristeva calls "trinitarian logic" in the preconscious state and relates it to her description of immersion in the deep rhythmic movements of the *chora*. This rhythm, she affirms, is a constant semiotic challenge to the old law of the symbolic realm of society; it is embodied in the revolutionary power of poetry. So, I suggest, we can only think of God in terms of our participation in rhythmic, triune movements of love and justice, which are greater than we are: Like the *chora,* the movements that open the space for us to dwell cannot be objectified or conceived as a supreme subject—and certainly not three subjects. The idea of God as an interweaving of relations is of course kataphatic, but it is also apophatic, since we are not thinking of personal subjects who *have* relations but only movements of relation themselves that defeat all attempts at observation and objectification. This is a participatory kind of thinking, not a subject–object relationship. God as sublime disrupts all human, objectifying speech; thus far there is a truth in the postmodern experience of the negative sublime, and we should be wary of theologies that dismiss it as inauthentic.[109] Yet this sublime also makes possible an *analogy of beauty* with relations in the created world—analogy, that is, with various kinds of relations but not with created *beings* who have relations.

This kind of theopoetics takes up Kristeva's emphasis that the sublime means *sublimation* in empathetic forgiveness. For Kristeva, of course, "trinitary logic" is only useful symbolism for exploring the psyche. Here I am combining her insights on *sublimation* with Murdoch's insistence that the experience of the *sublime* turns our attention toward a Good that is a reality beyond the individual self. For Murdoch this Good is not a person; but then, I am myself only using the metaphor of personal relations to enable us to *engage* in the rhythms of a God who cannot be objectified as a Person or Supreme Subject. As in both Murdoch and Kristeva, spiritual growth involves increasing attention to the other, and a theologian will understand this to be both the created and the uncreated Other. Experiencing the sublime, rejoicing in the beautiful and participating in movements of unconditional forgiveness, we who are the creations of the divine poet of the world can become poets too.

The Pluri-verse

Theopoiesis and the Pluriverse
Notes on a Process

CATHERINE KELLER

> Cosmos like a dark record that spins and sings
> in the dead of the night
> or romantic radio borne to us on the wind.
> Each thing sings.
> Things, not created by calculus
> but by poetry.
> By the Poet ("Creator" = POIÊTÊS)
> Creator of the POIEMA.
> **—Ernesto Cardenal, "Cantiga 2," *Cosmic Canticle***

> It is within the net of interwovenness—the process itself—that God appears as the "poet of the world," as its surprising creator (the ground of its novelty), its compassionate companion (the ground of its interwoven nature), and its saving radiance (the ground of its harmony).
> **—Roland Faber, *God as Poet of the World***

Do we really want to trade process theology for process *theopoetics*? Doesn't the irreplaceable value of process theology lie in its capacity to get in there and argue with classical theism, to expose the fallacies of an imbricated metaphysics of substance and formulate firm doctrinal alternatives? A theopoetic priority may be subtly pursued, of course, with poetic indirection, and without any polemical opposition of the poetic to the rational. It may even de-emphasize the *poetry* of poetics. But won't it *ipso facto* soften that confident, counterorthodox process lucidity? And thereby weaken its voice *as* theology? Certainly the more rationalist among us worry quietly (and these are gracious, noncoercive, *process* rationalists) that this theopoetic proclivity may effect little more than decoration, distraction, abdication. It may cede strength to the certainties of the religious right and the atheist left, now, when the eco-democratic alternative so needs spiritual planetary enlivening.

Without the process-theological *answers* to the mind-numbing certainties of the received omni-God, I don't know how, for example, I would teach my annual Introduction to Systematic Theology for seminarians. I don't know how I would have come to identify myself as a theologian at all. Doubts, criticisms, and evasions might have gotten the better of my Christianity. Without John Cobb as text and as teacher, honoring the criticisms, I couldn't have made sense of the tradition. I couldn't have cared enough about the life of the Christian tradition to dispute its patriarchies. Even if I had, I wouldn't have mustered the conceptual fortitude to stay with it, to poke around in its run-down cathedrals and its desert shacks. As I encountered process theology, it signified a school, a community of discourse, convivial in its presumption of collaboration—as this very volume, flowing from yet another conference, suggests. Its systematicity always addressed the interrelations of systemic power, of economics and ecology, of political oppression and cultural repression. All the while it was offering the coherence of a metaphysical alternative for theology in its time of accelerating disarray.

Gary Dorrien—not a process theologian—may be right to declare process theology the leading, indeed the "only vital school" of liberal-progressive theology.[1] I find myself happy in the present context to write as part of its "we." Nonetheless, we are hardly strong enough to merit weakening! And if theopoetics *does* weaken the capacity of process theologians to make confident arguments in debates, in teaching, preaching and pastoral care, then I would not indulge in it. If, either by its discursive playfulness or its philosophical mysticism, it dilutes the force of the process counterorthodoxy, then I will stop now. Inasmuch as theopoetics would *replace* theology, I share these fears. But inasmuch as theopoetics serves in the Derridean sense as a "supplement," not a suppression or a supersession, then, far from undermining theology, it enhances its future likelihood. That future, at least in a form any of us would desire, cannot be guaranteed. But the theopoetic impulse ipso facto expects no guarantee. It works to uncork the effervescence of language, the force of metaphor, icon, and story, which every systematic form (including the process form) of theology cannot but discipline.

Metaphysics does not entail but does tempt literalism. Even a metaphysics of creativity will in its repetitions damp down the risks of creative indeterminacy. Without the energies of metaphor unleashed in and through the disciplined imagination, however, progressive theology may not long persist. In the face, the Janus face, of fundamentalism and secularism, we will always be outdone at the game of objectification—by belief or reason. But theopoetic lines of thought do not stand or fall by literal truth. And in their kinship both to negative theology and to poststructuralism, they foster sustainable negotiations with certain cutting-edge discourses. In this way a process theopoetics, far from dissipating process thought qua *theology*, works to endow its future. Roland Faber's occupation of the newly endowed Kilsby Family/John B. Cobb Jr. Chair of Process Studies symbolizes the incarnation of that theopoetic future for process theology. His formidable exegesis of Whitehead's trope of "God the poet of the world" will serve as the *sine qua non* of any process theopoetics.[2] But I want to argue that the theological intensity of theopoetics only becomes apparent as we reclaim its entire semantic spectrum.

Far from any recent bit of jargon, the term *theopoetics,* as it turns out, runs as deep and tangled as Christian theology itself. As *theopoiesis,* it originally belongs to the ancient mysticism of human ascent to the unknowable, immutable infinite. This root in classical apophaticism would appear alien to the entire process theological attempt to lodge *becoming* in the divine. Yet it will appear also inimical with the emergence of "theopoetics" as such, as a mid-twentieth-century strategy to dislodge any fixed logos. This second version arises quite independently both of the ancient meaning and indeed of process theology—though simultaneous with the latter. Indeed the tension between these divergent theopoetic lineages—let us call them the ancient apophatic, the modernist mythopoetic and the process cosmological forms—threatens a three-way repulsion. I am nonetheless hoping that the tension may prove fruitful for the present conversation. It is my guess that, for the sake of a theology at once honest and attractive enough to persist in the present millennium, this spectrum of theopoetic discourse can and must find conviviality—life-together—in its differences.

Theopoiesis: Becoming Divine in Eastern Antiquity

The term *theopoiesis* appears in the first centuries of Hellenistic Christianity, most frequently in its contracted form *theosis,* normally rendered "deification." The term *theopoiesis* retains the fuller sense of "making divine," indeed the more eerily ambiguous (at least to postmodern ears) meaning of "making God." It roots in Christian Neoplatonic absorptions of Plato's "likeness to God so far as possible." Clement defines *theopoiesis* as "assimilation to God as far as possible."[3] Irenaeus developed the concept more fully from scripture: "God the Logos became what we are, in order that we may become what he himself is." Most famously and punchily, it crystallizes in Athanasius's christological formula: "God became Man so that Man could become God."[4] In other words, the high Nicene christology was originally accompanied by a high anthropology. It can only be read in the context of a rigorous ascetic practice inflected from the start by varieties of Platonic mysticism. It provides a certain internal resistance to the theology of dualistic transcendence characteristic, for instance, of Athanasian orthodoxy.

Basil of Caesarea's fourth-century version lends theopoiesis particular luminosity:

> When a sunbeam falls on a transparent substance, the substance itself becomes brilliant, and radiates light from itself. So too Spirit-bearing souls, illumined by Him, finally become spiritual themselves, and their grace is sent forth to others. From this comes knowledge of the future, understanding of mysteries . . . distribution of wonderful gifts . . . endless joy in the presence of God, becoming like God, and, the highest of all desires, *becoming God*.[5]

A mysticism of participation is here in play, whereby a reflective brilliance does not merely bounce back or ascend but spreads laterally and relationally. Is its intuition, after all, alien to that of Whitehead (at one point a serious student of the patristics), who calls God "the mirror which discloses to every creature its own greatness"?[6] In yet stronger contrast to the Nicene dualism, the great theologian-poet Ephrem of Syria highlights a radical reciprocity: "He gave us divinity / we gave Him humanity." The becoming-divine of the human is inextricable from the becoming-human of the divine: "Blessed is He Who came in what is ours and mingled us into what is His."[7]

It is only honest theologically to register the shocking boldness of the claim of divinization, so muffled by later receptions of the orthodox lineage, above all by Protestantism, that it sounds like the stuff of heresy. Yet the ancient theopoiesis would also influence the Methodist theory of "entire sanctification." Charles Wesley "as a poet-theologian in the tradition of St. Ephrem" renews, as Christensen argues persuasively, this patristic sensibility in the poetry of his own hymnody. For example:

> He deigns in flesh to appear,
> Widest extreme to join,
> To bring our vileness near,
> And make us all divine;
> And we the life of God shall know,
> For God is manifest below.[8]

There is, however, no direct connection between the occasional outbreaks of the message of theopoiesis in the medium of poetry.

The entire theosis tradition refers to a set of key scriptures, above all the phrase of 2 Peter 1:4, "partakers of the divine nature," but also Psalm 82:6: "I declare, 'Ye are gods; you are all sons of the Most High.'" Moreover, Jesus's citation of that verse has him, according to the author of the gospel of John, responding to the accusation that "he, being a man, made himself to be God."[9] Jesus disarms the charge by claiming and redistributing it: "I say, 'Ye are gods.'"

What then might a process theopoetics tap from these roots of the term? Certainly process theology has not been shy in claiming a high-logos Christology—and with it the "God manifest below." Cobb's logos of "creative transformation" situates the possibility of human transformation in a cosmologically scaled narrative. But why then has process thought hardly explored theosis/theopoiesis? No doubt because it is embedded in the classical substance metaphysics, which process means to replace; and in its perfectionism it draws the individual soul toward a changeless immateriality. Process pulls in quite the opposite direction. Might we nonetheless, in accord with the logos/wisdom of the Johannine mysticism, consider revising this ancient vision of transformation? It is not without postmodern resonances. Hear this word from a continental philosopher who perhaps more than any shaped the emphatic feminist discourse of embodiment: "the religious aspect of our becoming has not been considered enough as a way to achieve a greater perfection of our humanity. Human identity and divine identity have been artificially separated. And we generally fail to recognize that becoming divine corresponds to becoming perfectly human."[10] Luce Irigaray, for whom full human becoming means "becoming divine," had swerved from her Nietzschean post-theism into a surprising rereading of Mary's son and the incarnation he instantiates. Yet she comes to her vocabulary of mystical perfectionism in apparent innocence of the entire theosis tradition it so precisely echoes.[11] Her compatibility with process theology, indeed with ecofeminism in general, has been explored elsewhere. Here let it just signify a possible conviviality of theopoetic thinkers.

Through the Whiteheadian dissemination of the incarnation to every creaturely becoming, might theopoiesis escape its confinement in the gilded icon of divinized Man—in its anthropocentrism as well as its androcentrism? In fact, the classical panentheism that characterizes precisely the Eastern Christian tradition already conditions the immanence of divine transcendence upon God's presence—as the logos—in all creatures. Moreover, the reciprocalism we noted in Ephrem's poetics may be read as anticipating the mingling of creaturely concrescence with divinity in the process God. For Whitehead it takes not the form of an exchange of metaphysical substances but of the entanglement of free becomings, divine and creaturely. But here the divergence suddenly widens. The divine in its "consequent nature" incessantly feels, prehends, and takes in the world—becomingly. No ancient theologian could let the making-divine unfold in the mutual making of God and world that the process model imagines: It is "as true that God creates the world as that the world creates God."[12] Such a poiesis takes on a new and risky meaning. Is such God-creating really only code for making God up? By a certain reading of theopoetics, the answer would be yes—and so much the better!

Theopoetics in Midcentury New Jersey

The notion of *theopoetics* sprang into play, in English, as though a neologism of the 1960s. And, by what to the present writer appears as a strange coincidence, it is at Drew that it was sprung. In his little 1976 *Theopoetic*, Amos Wilder observed: "I believe that I had picked up the term 'theopoetic' and 'theopoiesis' from Stanley Hopper and his students, no doubt in one or another of the remarkable consultations on hermeneutics and language which he had organized at Drew University . . ."[13] These conferences occurred in 1962, 1964, and 1966 and were methodologically situated "at the intersection," as David Miller has recently explained, "of left-wing Bultmannian biblical interpretation, the thought of the late period of Heidegger's existential phenomenology, and the Religion and Literature movement."[14] Yet by the time I arrived at Drew, long after a crisis had driven most of that faculty elsewhere, there lingered no echoes of the term. I thought I had coined it.

Hopper's splendid definition merits a new hearing: "What theo-poiesis does is to effect disclosure through the crucial nexus of event, thereby making the crux of knowing, both morally and aesthetically, radically decisive in time."[15] Through intensive readings of religious texts as literature and literary texts as religious, the poiesis of theology was disclosing itself as inseparable from poetry. Gradually a psychological depth dimension rendered the perspective mythopoetic. The effort to explode any prosaic *-ology*, any objectivization, of the Christian referents was linked in the early Drew conversations to Heidegger. If the "nexus of event" seems to refer to Whitehead, it would today tend to signify a quite different conceptual web of, for instance, the philosophies of Deleuze, Badiou, and Derrida, hardly innocent of Heidegger. But then these are being brought to bear upon Whitehead's own event nexus.[16]

Hopper's theopoetic legacy reappeared recently—at Drew—in a beautiful lecture by David Miller. He offered the cunning distinction between theopoetry and theopoetics. The former would be the assertion that all theological language is really already metaphor: This is "the poeticizing of an extant religious faith or theological knowledge."[17] He notes that his teacher, Hopper, deployed metaphor in Wheelwright's sense of "diaphor," in contrast to the weaker sense of metaphor (as "epiphor"). The latter allows the "reinscription of objectivization and of the onto-metaphysical tradition in which Being is viewed as a being or God as an idol."[18] In this stronger sense, the poetic is not made of similes, of similarities, but of difference, fragmentation, and multiplicity. In this context it is worth noting that Nelle Morton carried this Drew theopoetic legacy to Claremont in retirement, where it was reborn for a subsequent generation of moods and motives: Her "goddess as metaphor" meant metaphor first of all, and diaphorically, as iconoclasm.

Theopoetics, in other words, has everything to do with the art and form of poetry. But it is not reducible to a literary style. It does not camouflage the tawdry sanctuaries of dying belief with lovely bouquets of language. Indeed, as Miller shows so well, the modernist poets whom the theopoetic crowd find disclosive wrote the midcentury cutting edge of this subversion: like Wallace Stevens ("The steeples are empty and so are the people"); like Pound, writing poetry on how poetry finds itself in a "destitute time." What is theologically at stake here exceeds, in other words, the ancient questions of how to use human language to speak or not speak of God.

Theopoetics, in Miller's radicalization, does its work "after the death of God": Its developed lineage includes the work of Thomas Altizer and Mark C. Taylor. "It involves a poetics and not a poetry, i.e., a reflection on poiesis, a formal thinking about the nature of the making of meaning, which subverts the -ology, the nature of the logic, of theology." To this process theologians may say amen. We think our theologies have also been performing that subversion head on: We do not pit an illogic but an alter-logic against the logic of identity, essence, substance, noncontradiction, exclusion. Miller nails the difference thus: "In theopoetry, as opposed to theopoetics, theology does not end with the death of God, because there is no death of God." But then it follows for him that "theopoetics begins when theology ends."[19]

Oh dear. I had begun this essay by asserting that any theopoetics that claims to supersede rather than supplement theology itself will (logically enough) be done with process theology. Miller is sounding the call for the end of theology as the only honest response to the death of God. Hard indeed to see how that would not follow. But we must wonder, nonetheless: How is the *theos* of theopoetics exempted? Perhaps theopoetics, because it knows that it is making its gods up, does not go down with the really existing God. From this point of view, wouldn't the hopeful notion I had suggested at the outset, of theopoetics as supplement—inasmuch as it presumes some indispensable life and meaning still at play in whatever is worth deconstructing—then count after all as mere theopoetry? I don't think I can dodge Miller's opposition. I can, however, point it out. Does it reproduce the logos of noncontradiction that one hoped to be grieving along with its ontotheological theos? If we cannot ask back, "which God is it that died, and therefore which logos," by what logic are we drawing this opposition between "Gods"—the *theos* of theopoetics versus that of theology? That the tradition of the death of God awkwardly also calls itself "secular" or "radical *theology*," precisely at Syracuse where Hopper and Miller migrated when Drew Theological School exploded in 1969, symptomatizes the dilemma.

Still, sometimes one cannot elude a sharp boundary between the end and the novum; sometimes one cannot prize open a "third genre," an indeterminate *khora* as the space of the subversion of its own logic. What Whitehead calls a "contrast," the creative alternative to incompatible opposites, may not be possible. Yet I suspect that any process theopoetics must make the effort. Miller's substantive definition of the God who died is quite particular: "fixed and ultimate meanings accessible to knowledge or faith." It would take a gross literalization indeed to foist that definition of *God* upon all uses of the term, from biblical texts and on. He is rather questioning the dependency upon the unquestionable referents, or Heidegger's ontotheology, or Derrida's Transcendental Signifier, which has framed the space of premodern theology and hence of modern thought.

Process theology, when it considers the question, shares the critique of the dependency. And we presume, albeit heterogeneously, the constructedness or poiesis of God as signifier. But recognizing the constructedness—the poetics—of *theos* does not mean that therefore humans construct that God ex nihilo. What poet, what poetics, claims such an arrogant posture for itself? Yet a supersessionist approach to theopoetics implies just such a construction out of nothing, if that of a philosophical nihilism. If instead we recognize that our constructions spin themselves out of a chaos replete with the recycling images, stories, and questions of the prior *logoi* of *theos*, how would we draw a fixed boundary between theology then and theopoetics now? When theopoetic thinkers write not poems but prose about theopoetics, do we really imagine ourselves free of logos? Aren't we, rather, arguing, asserting, negating, criticizing, and propositioning each other in an effort to practice a credible counterlogic, not a transcendent illogic?

Even so, I think process theology does not escape Miller's challenge. We have been, all along, tempted toward our own reifications of "God," firm enough to displace the classically fixed attributes. We may mutter "a set of metaphors mutely appealing for an intuitive leap" like a refrain; we may perform the shift of language from fixed substantives toward a becoming nexus of events. But we are doggedly pushing on toward a *better* theology, one that need not claim permanent meanings or objectifiable referents. We are knowingly constructing that becomingly noncoercive, ecofeminist, and relationally sensitive God, God the Poet. So we are often understandably restless with that "death of God" drama, prone to relegate it to the past of late Euro-modernity. Indeed we want to get on with the work of theology in the world. Yet in order not to trip ourselves with impatient literalisms, we had best stay autocritically tuned to our own theopoiesis. We do not want to find ourselves decorating even a loveable and poetic God's coffin with theopoetry. For the sake of intellectual honesty and dialogue with fetching Nietzscheans, we might want to leave ourselves open to the charge that we worship an undead God. We might want to turn a cheek to it.

Theopoetic Indeterminacy

At the same time, we might reframe Miller's postulate thus: theopoetics begins not where theology *ends* but where it *negates* itself. This is actually where it *comes to be*: where it negates itself *becomingly*. For in the event of its self-negation theopoetics repeats the tradition of negative theology. But with a difference. Negative theology was always indissociable from a set of linguistic constructions whose claim was not eliminated by negation but deconstructed, or, in its own language, opened to infinity. The impact of negative theology has not accidentally registered all along the Abrahamic theopoetic spectrum, right up through the intensive interactions with the late Derrida. Nonetheless it operated under philosophical cover of the hyperousiologial Neoplatonic One. Today it might understand the affirmation that is made possible by the negation not as a truer version of changeless truth but as the construction of a language that is already always unsaying itself.[20] It may relativize its own utterances not as an act of self-abnegation but as the affirmation of its own unknown future and the beauty of its innermost history of becoming.

Negative theology originated in Christian discourse among the Cappadocians, particularly with Gregory of Nyssa, the aforementioned Basil's brother. The making-God of the human is figured upon an apophatic infinity. For the movement toward the divine infinity as the process of theosis is necessarily an infinite process. Indeed, Gregory was the first Christian theologian to name God infinite. This infinity shatters the bounded and knowable perfection of the immutable One. The Hopper-Miller line of theopoetics had, with Heidegger, welcomed the radical edge of apophasis, especially in Eckhart's divine nothingness. When Derrida, in a closely related tradition, first took up negative theology, it was in order to free deconstruction of its onus, criticizing in "How Not to Speak" Denys's Neoplatonic *hyperousia*.[21] Later he would welcome in this tradition its dissidence, its rejection of "all the inadequate attributions. It does so in the name of a way of truth and in order to hear the name of a just voice."[22]

As a whole the ancient tradition of negative theology knows that we finite creatures cannot *know* the infinite God except in the cloud of its own unknowability. That is itself worth knowing. Even Aquinas exercised this risky modesty—so importantly deployed by Elizabeth Johnson as a feminist maneuver: "we cannot know what, but only that God is."[23] But the link of theopoetics to apophasis now would have to radicalize the unknowing: If we do not know *what* then how can we know *that* God is? The Thomist doctrine of analogy, neatly balancing negative and positive ways, acquiesces in epiphor. But the apophatic theologians read differently. For instance, Nicholas of Cusa's *docta ignorantia* (important to both Faber's and my versions of process theology) produces knowledge relentlessly— but only as tuned, with loving irony, to a "precise truth" that "shines forth incomprehensibly in the darkness of our ignorance."[24] With Cusa we do not bluntly "know" anything; we may "conjecture," in knowing ignorance. But such theology builds into itself the principle of its *own* negation; it recognizes that the monosyllabic *God* is one among many inadequate terms for an infinity about which we learn more, the more we learn to abstain from certainty. Indeed his speculative cosmology is loaded with scientific truths that would not be "discovered" for centuries.

Germane to the present argument, Cusa takes up the tradition of theopoiesis.[25] But it takes on a twist rarely noted: Now it is not merely the human but the universe that is "made" in the image of God. Therefore, the crucial biblical intertext gains new meaning: "every creature is, as it were, a finite infinity or a created god." For the infinite unfolds in finite form in and *as* the creation: "it is as if the Creator had spoken: 'let it be made,' and because God, who is eternity itself, could not be made, that was made which could be made, which would be as much like God as possible."[26] The theopoietic keynote of Clement—to become "as much like God as possible"—here unfolds into cosmology. In Cusa the panentheism of God in all and all in God means at the same time "each in each and all in all."

So the anthropocentrism of classical mysticism breaks into a boundlessly ecological creation. In this Cusa anticipates Whitehead: "Everything is in a certain sense everywhere at all times."[27]

Process thinkers have not, on the whole, been attracted any more to the mystical epistemology of negative theology than to the metaphysics of theosis. Besides the problem with its Neoplatonism, apophatic gestures might work to unhinge our already embattled and marginalized model of God. But I submit that the confidence we enjoy in the alternative God-talk of process theology—with its enmeshed network of noisy allies among feminist, womanist, ecological, liberation, postcolonial, relationalist theologies—will not be diminished by this apophatic impulse, but revivified. For once we have anyway crossed that threshold of critical thinking for which the death of God is a historic trope, is it really any lack of knowledge or of certainty that undermines the strength of our own perspectives? I am speaking here not of how to popularize and spread a vision, but of our own faith in it. Isn't it, rather, the pressure to pretend to a certainty that we lack, to stifle the doubt that presses against faith? On principle, of course, this uncertainty is evident to process thinkers, theorists of a radically open future. Whitehead, after all, was constructing his system in the light of quantum uncertainty, as well as of metaphysical metaphoricity. Perhaps that systemic indeterminacy becomes so evident as to become invisible, paradoxically morphing into its own guarantor of the system. It would then benefit from an occasional shot of the "luminous dark" to render it once again, in the sense of *Modes of Thought*, "important."

Like the death of God atheology, like deconstruction, mythico-literary theopoetics has shown little interest in cosmology—another omnitudinous logos after all. And yet the ancient logocentric theopoiesis paid similarly fleeting attention to the visible and invisible integrities of the creation. The swerve represented here by Cusa opens a delicate bridge from the theopoiesis of premodern theism to a cosmology rife with implications for the current cosmos—and the brilliant darkness of its newly discovered, utterly mystifying, "dark energy." Without the apophatic gesture, however, there persists, in science and in religion, the habit of the abstract reterritorialization of both God and world by a triumphalist Logos.

The Poet of the World

"The divine process," writes Roland Faber, "is not an 'exemplar' of a cosmological rule, but rather the event of the new, of the inaccessibly inscrutable, indeed an interruption of categoreal continuity."[28] He can be read here as addressing that temptation within process theology to a smooth system, with its signifiers all too knowingly accessing their objects, even their supreme Object. When he collates divinity with *différance,* Faber does not, as we shall see, return God to the classical status of the exception, external to a creation "He" produces outside of Himself (*non de deo sed ex nihilo*). On the contrary, this difference signifies a self-deconstructing otherness. Yet it does not destroy rationality, or even the categoreal scheme of *Process and Reality.* "Paradoxically, acknowledgment of the other beyond categoreal exemplarism, rather than leading to a collapse of the principles, instead discloses them almost dialectically in their inner reconciled state."[29] Faber in this way continues the Whiteheadian struggle to capture in language a difference between God and world, or one and the other, without reinscribing the settled boundary between them—or erasing their difference. This differential nondualism is terrain that panentheism is having always to recapture.

"Here a key point is attained for theopoetics," Faber argues, "since now it is the negative theology of God's alterity—albeit a God who in God's orientation toward the world, rather than disappearing into speechlessness (and irrelevance), instead through God's own transcendence possesses poetic character in creating the world in a reconciled light."[30] No one has better illuminated the relevance of the apophatic to process theology than has Faber: The unspeakable becomes the very site of the theopoetic. We might as well acknowledge that, with the publication of *God as the Poet of the World,* a third primary sense of the theopoetic has occurred. The term does, in his thinking, come attached to the ancient teaching of theosis, which is not his portal to Catholic mysticism or to the modernist mythopoetics, which is not his portal to continental philosophy.

Noting that for the negative theology of the mystics, "God is the 'One' beyond all categories (of being)," Faber points to its emphasis on God's alterity.[31] This translates for him into "God's in/difference." One must not lose that inaudible slash, else "in/difference" will be confused with the chilling *apatheia* to which process theism has after all offered the passionate alternative. Thus "this negative assertion paradoxically requires that because God is indeed nothing beyond all differences, God thus appears only in differences." Without this requirement our appeal to the mystical unsaying might appear as one more guise of "the logic of the One" (Laurel Schneider). Faber's divine in/difference morphs into difference itself, the difference so radical as to be comprised by the "essential relationality" of all differences. It follows for him, then, that "*Theopoetic in/difference is the origin of, that is, insistence on, difference.* Like the latter, it too—as Derrida puts it—is 'older' than ontological difference. Because it does not refer back to any sort of 'foundation,' it is not comprehensible in categories of 'ground,' 'presence,' 'being,' or 'existence.'"[32] Difference is not merely a device for shattering unity; it fans luxuriantly into creaturely multiplicity.

As I hope I have shown, this negative theology enfolded in process theo-poetics does not point at an obscure mystery hidden behind the many, accessible only through mystically altered states. Its eros insists upon the unfolding of multiplicity itself: the creation. As Cardenal reminds us: the *poema*.

Why Are We Doing This?

An incongruent theopoetic field stretches right from the complex origins of orthodoxy into the wake of its God. Ancient theopoiesis and literary theopoetics have little in common beyond their negation of the proxi-mate idolatries. Yet, in that negation, tinged by biblical metaphors moving with diaphoric intensity, they are already more darkly harmonious than they would comfortably acknowledge. They converge in the cloud of an ancient and current unspeakability, where the *logos* of *theos* falls in and out of silence from the beginning. The cloud does not dissolve the incom-mensurabilities; it does, however, obscure any fixed point of opposition. I am suggesting that inasmuch as process theology embraces its own theo-poetic potential—and with it an apophatic attention to its own linguistic poiesis—it may lure both prior discourses toward a third space. A space only reached by moving in and through that cloud.

Process theopoetics only goes there, into that obscurity, with the ac-companiment of an entire chaosmos—a living multiplicity of multiplici-ties of creatures enfolded in and unfolding from one another. The ancient ontological theopoiesis can of course hardly support the emphatically open future, the keynote of evolution and the creative emergence of the world—let alone of its divinity. The world's divinity—that ambiguity at least has ancient resonances. But, even with such radical masters as Eckhart, Cusa, and Bruno, the substance metaphysics, with its changeless and unifying divine necessity, overwhelms delicate spaces of creaturely spontaneity and divine reception. The process dynamism of becoming is grounded, or un-grounded, therefore, in the torrential creativity of the universe, the many becoming—many ones.

If we imagine the divine luring its world, its own body of spontaneous differences, to become, it is not as the enactment of a plan but as the desire for a greater conviviality.[33] But this "life together" suggests that the mini-mum coexistence by which creatures exist requires an ability to respond. Such an ethic of responsibility, deprived of the routine anthropocentrism, is not therefore reducible to so-called nature. The human and nonhuman creatures thrive in the greater convivialities they crave; and the human may name this supreme conviviality *God.* These boundless entanglements of our symbioses exceed—as does *God*—our capacity to know and name them (as twenty-first-century natural science makes increasingly clear). But they would in a sense exceed the divine knowing as well—not because God suffers from an epistemic incapacity but because all-knowing is a knowing of what has come to be, not of what will yet become. The deep, the *tehom,* of the creativity of the universe may signify that reservoir of divine unknowingness, open to infinite surprise. Otherwise divine love would be void of all eros: It would already possess everything and so have nothing to desire. It is not that desire presumes a lack but that it provokes the new.

Or so we might conjecture.

No theology in history has been more tuned to the evolving symbioses of all creatures than process theology: Whatever science knows is brought into play, at the very edge of what is not yet known. Of course, the non-human creatures are much less antsy about knowledge. They practice an intelligence wired into a world of wordless processes. We have barely begun to recognize, or is it to remember, their wisdoms. Our species has perhaps still a bit of time left to learn how perilously ignorant we have been of our fellow creatures, as fellows, as creatures, and of our dwelling in them and they in us. Might they teach us how not to speak—and so to speak otherwise? A new intercreaturely apophasis, a pause in the global English of our self-defeating dominion?

At least they do call us now to recognize not just the incarnation of the cosmic logos but its intercarnationality: the word of a universe so multiple as to melt any logic into poetry. So many verses, kinds, and styles, species and galaxies of universe, as to be named already by William James a *pluriverse.* With Faber and, from a different angle, Miller, I agree that theopoetics does not boil down to poetry, to any genre of literature or language, let alone to metaphoric units fixed in models all too objectifiable by theology or science.[34] A deeper aesthetic is in play—yet not without art and, of course, poetry, and not without the metaphors, indeed the diaphors, of the divine. "God as Poet of the world" is a (poetic) trope for the responsive initiatives of that artistry, leading by its "vision of truth, beauty and goodness."[35] In *Adventures of Ideas,* its peaceable aesthetic finds its foil not in the turbulence of desire or the adventure of uncertainty but in the flattening of difference along "the easy road of Anaesthesia." As the theos of panentheism it hosts the conviviality of all the uninhibited and intertwined becomings.

The aesthetic significance of the very word *becoming* has often been missed: In English the verb has an odd transitive form, related to the adjective *comely.* We say, "That shirt *becomes* you"—as though beauty results from something becoming part of another, from some participatory genesis. (The shirt is so right for you, that shirt is you!) In other words, if theopoiesis means the human becoming divine through the divine becoming human: God *becomes* us. That God is comely, becoming, in us—clothes us in beauty. It is in *becoming* that we become divine. Beautiful—were we able to notice, to play along. All the more so, as we recognize what a multitude of creaturely becomings, human and mostly not human, make each of us up (and all our shirts) at any given moment. Attention to this crowd of clamoring others pushes us into the cloud of our unknowing—where new knowledge tempered to the multitude, the ecosocial manifold, has its chance. The ecology of the multiplicity demands a new planetary justice, polydox and political, barely possible.[36] Our evolving theopoetic viewpoint cannot guarantee a harmony of the good, the true, and the beautiful. It will require us to produce our own counterpoints and polyphonies. The scales may be too close or too distant. But they reveal a convivial cosmos sponsoring beauty not as a mere means to various greedy ends but as the festivity of all becomings.

A theologian does not need to be a poet, often should not be. We have all sorts of debates, ministries, dialogues, pedagogies, prayers, and protests to pursue. Nonetheless, the metaphor of theopoetics itself will wash out quickly if it is not occasionally renewed by the poetry that circulates as the art of all languages.

"Philosophy is akin to poetry," wrote Whitehead, as though paraphrasing the immediately prior proposition: "Philosophy is mystical. For mysticism is direct insight into depths as yet unspoken."[37] So his apophatic avowal is immediately yoked to the rhythms of "poetic metre," as they express the vibrations of which his cosmos is made. Such a poiesis is an art tuned like all arts, human and nonhuman, to the eerie beauty of the world. I am trying to conclude upon a transient harmony, and perhaps a sustainable polyphony, of all the three main currents of theopoetic potentiality this paper has examined. Each—the ancient apophatic, the modernist mythopoetic, the process theopoiesis—has narrowly survived its Christian birth. Let me seek closure in return to an actual poem, the one with which we began, by the great poet-priest-activist Ernesto Cardenal, in his gorgeously didactic *Pluriverse:*

Creation is a poem.
Poem, which is "creation" in Greek and thus
St Paul calls God's Creation, POIEMA,
Like a poem by Homer Padre Angel used to say.

Each thing is like a "like."
Like a "like" in a Huidobro poem.
The entire cosmos copulation. [. . .]
Listen to the murmur of things . . .
They say it, but say it in secret.[38]

As pluriverse complicates universe, the verses multiply boundlessly in this
POIEMA (and almost boundlessly in Cardenal's four-hundred-eighty-page
epic *Cosmic Canticles*). The poet-priest cites scripture as the poetry of the
POIEMA itself, citing a priest citing a poet to bring out the likenesses (no
mere epiphor, in this lush tropical intertextuality) of apparently incompatible desires. The orgiastic poiesis of the copulating cosmos strips away the
pious proprieties of theology, but, as Marcella Althaus Reid might have
noted all the more indecently, will not surrender its theos or its logos. Here
the nonhumans murmur apophatically, "in secret," which is Greek *muos,*
as in mystery, mysticism. What logos do we utter, what theos becomes—
apart from them? For the sake of the noisiest and most convivial planetary
democracy[39] we can muster, will we listen?

Consider the Lilies and the Peacocks
A Theopoetics of Life Between the Folds

LUKE B. HIGGINS

Alfred North Whitehead famously describes God as the "poet of the world" in the context of offering an alternative to traditional theological doctrines of creation that consider the world a mere product of unilateral divine will or presence.[1] A process approach to *theopoetics*, then, will inherently subvert any account of aesthetic expression in which the latter is considered no more than a derivative effect of some preordained divine plan or purpose. In other words, to attribute to God this role of cosmological poet is to affirm a plurality of indeterminate, self-creative agencies in the world whose aim at aesthetic richness is both conditioned by, yet also irreducible to, divine inspiration. Given the explicitly cosmological context of Whitehead's speculative philosophy, how might we understand this kind of aesthetic agency in the more-than-human realm? What might be at stake for ecotheology in conceiving God's mode of relationship with creation—specifically in its diverse, living, ecological manifestations—in these particular theopoetic terms?

If—as I will argue—theopoiesis is uniquely (though not solely) manifest in the emergence and evolutionary elaboration of *life*, this already suggests that life itself—in both its human and nonhuman forms—may best be conceived not as a mechanistic execution of divinely preordained essences or laws but an indeterminate enfolding/unfolding of intensive connections and alliances whose *telos* (to the extent that one can be spoken of) can only really be described in a language of aesthetic valuation. Whitehead defines life most fundamentally as a "bid for freedom" that exceeds the functional identities of the structured societies within which it is embedded—a point developed particularly in his concept of the "entirely living nexus," understood to arise only in the unique environment of the living organism's interstitial spaces. Elizabeth Grosz's Deleuzian aesthetic philosophy (as set forth in her book *Chaos, Territory, and Art: Deleuze and the Framing of the Earth*) validates this basic insight of process philosophy, arguing that life's evolutionary advances, particularly in and through sexual differentiation and selection, take place through a kind of "useless" or excessive production of novelty aimed less at mere survival than beauty, intensity, and enjoyment.[2] For Grosz, aesthetic innovation is fundamental to the creative processes of nature's living, evolving ecologies. Rather than conceiving art as an exclusively human phenomenon derivative from our linguistic capacities, for Grosz the dynamics, or forces, that give rise to art are already present in the most primordial initiatives of life—an insight grounded especially in her reading of Deleuze and Guattari's *A Thousand Plateaus,* with its discussion of the refrain and the becoming-expressive of territory.[3]

I argue that the emergence of the world's complexly diverse ecologies is conditioned by a theopoetic enfolding of the cosmos—what Roland Faber calls theoplicity,[4] which allows creation to engage in its own "intensive enfoldment" of time/space around itself such that a kind of virtual "screen" can intervene between local assemblages or event-nexuses and the wider "chaosmos" of which they are a part. Deleuze and Guattari's and Grosz's understanding of the territorializations and deterritorializations that occur along vibratory, contrapuntal lines of rhythm and melody might be constructively compared with Whitehead's understanding of the complex, ecologically interlocking structured societies that make the canalized spontaneities of the entirely living nexus possible. In both cases, life and art emerge out of complexly folded, "filtering" structures that both separate and enable new forms of passage between local, intensive, living "centers" and the larger chaotic Universe of which they are a part.

These "frames" or "filters" both shield a given territory from the "winds" of chaos and selectively draw on those chaotic forces for the territory's own unique, creative innovations. This can lead to an understanding of a "theoplicitous" exchange between God and the world such that God's receptive enfoldment of the world makes possible a becoming-expressive within God that culminates in the gift of God's "refracted" vision to each occasion (referred to in process theology as the "initial aim"). Conversely, creation must empty its attachments to an immediate "forcefield" of drives, habits, and reflexes in order to open to the virtual depth of God's aesthetic vision for it—a vision that simultaneously enables a deep receptivity to the larger chaosmos and insists that it become something unique for itself *through* this receptivity.[5] This theopoetic process enables local event-assemblages to "filter" and thus "extract" virtual, aesthetically expressive becomings from the chaotic currents of the larger Universe or the "chaotic nexus" (in Faber's language). Coming to terms with the inextricability of theopoiesis and the poiesis inherent to the life of creation (in all its diverse forms) makes it possible to envision the ecological responsibility to which faith calls us less in terms of mere obedience to some preestablished divine (or natural) law and more as a divinely inspired musical, or poetic, riff on creation's rhythms and melodies.

Between House and Universe: The Becoming-Expressive of Life in Deleuze and Guattari's and Grosz's Biophilosophical Aesthetics

In her development of a Deleuzian aesthetic philosophy, Elizabeth Grosz explores how art's inherent excesses of creative indeterminacy—normally linked exclusively with human culture and subjectivity—actually drive some of the most primordial biological processes. Instead of following the modern reductionist assumption that aesthetically expressive features of the natural world (including that of plants but especially animals) are mechanistically shaped by the survival-driven laws of natural selection, Grosz entertains the alternative hypothesis (inspired not just by her reading of Deleuze but also Darwin's oft-neglected theory of sexual selection) that the behavioral and bodily patterns that constitute a particular organism in relation to its territory emerge as a *result* of the "becoming-expressive" of a field of intersecting milieus. In Deleuze and Guattari's words, "Territory is not primary in relation to the qualitative mark; it is the mark that makes the territory. Functions in a territory are not primary; they presuppose a territory-producing expressiveness . . ."[6] In other words, nature's capacity for aesthetic expressiveness is not a mere product of certain predetermined functions or essences; if anything it is the reverse that is the case—it is melodic and rhythmic lines contrapuntally resonating between complexly overlapping milieus in the environment that "congeal" into (relatively) stable behavioral, or bodily, functions.

In this context we can begin to understand art most fundamentally *not* as mimesis or representation of some underlying selfsame nature— rather, it is nature's differential excesses that "crystallize" into expressively functional (and functionally expressive) patterns—of which art refers to some of the more deterritorialized forms. In this way, the underlying *telos* of life can be understood not merely as a practical drive toward survival or self-propagation (as more orthodox proponents of the neo-Darwinian synthesis would argue) but rather as something more akin to the "useless" drive toward intensification and enjoyment that characterizes artistic creation. It is important to point out that characterizing this aesthetic drive as useless or in excess of mere function, is *not* to advocate the idea that art is useless in the sense of being frivolous or secondary to the real, underlying processes of life. It is to say something like the opposite: that the drive toward aesthetic harmony and intensity is in a sense the very reason for the being of life itself—that life's practical functionality is itself *emergent* from this drive toward aesthetic richness.

An examination of Deleuze and Guattari's chapter in *A Thousand Plateaus* entitled "On the Refrain" can provide deeper insight into this process whereby a becoming-expressive of milieus gives rise to more or less stabilized territories. Deleuze and Guattari lyrically describe three stages by which a territorial refrain (1) first emerges within a larger chaotic flux, (2) consolidates an expressive territory, and (3) opens itself up to creative deterritorializations or lines of flight.[7] In the first phase, the musical, rhythmic repetitions of the refrain are fairly fragile—they sketch a calming, stable center at the heart of chaos but are in danger of breaking apart at any moment. Next, a more stable "home" or territory establishes itself in this field of intersecting milieus through a process of "weaving" a kind of "filter" or membrane separating an inside from an outside. This filter operates not just to shield and protect an internal space but also to relate it selectively to the flux of the larger, external world. In this way the establishment of territory "involves an activity of selection, elimination, and extraction in order to prevent the interior forces of the earth from being submerged, to enable them to resist, or even to take something from chaos across the filter or sieve of the space that has been drawn."[8] Finally, the "circle" that constitutes this territorial refrain is "cracked open" in a new region created by the territory itself. The powers of expression that come into being with the territory are released along a new line of flight, allowing them to take on life of their own with novel aims and "reasons for being" that go beyond the functional workings of the original territory. This deterritorialization constitutes a kind of rhizomatic resonation with the larger Universe that allows for a radically new becoming. "One launches forth, hazards an improvisation. But to improvise is to join with the World, or meld with it. One ventures from home on the thread of a tune. This time, it is in order to join with the forces of the future, cosmic forces."[9]

Grosz brings into her discussion one of the key insights of Bergson's biophilosophy (one of Deleuze's most significant influences)—the recognition that life emerges not so much by *adding* some unique (usually transcendent) presence or agency to an otherwise predictable, material cosmos but rather by *subtracting* something—bracketing, delaying, or placing into shadow certain elements of the Universe's overwhelmingly chaotic presence, such that it is able to extract only those elements of the cosmos that it can use for its own emergent purposes.[10] This bracketing or "harboring" capacity constitutes, on one hand, life's resistance to chaos, but, perhaps more importantly, it is also life's basic strategy for selectively utilizing the creative powers of chaos for its own innovations. In short, the "sieve" or filter that establishes a territory by keeping chaos at bay, paradoxically *also* functions to relate that territory in wider, broader ways to the larger, chaotic cosmos.

The temporal aspect of this process is particularly interesting—by slowing down, selectively delaying its reflexive responses to the immediate fluctuations of the wider world, a lifeform can thus intensively layer or fold its relationship to its past in more complex ways, allowing itself to be provoked by that past in more original, indeterminate ways. Instead of being mercilessly pushed and pulled by every minor flux in the world, the "shelter" that a lifeform weaves for itself allows it to develop relatively stable rhythms, or refrains, that enable it to "canalize" these unpredictable inputs from the "outside" into channels and reserves, offering the lifeform a more flexible agency in the way it shapes its responses to its world. The point is not for lifeforms to impose predetermined structures of order on an otherwise chaotic environment but for organisms to selectively "reclaim" particular sections of the living energy of chaos, using them for new, spontaneously emergent designs and purposes. In this way the construction of expressive territory is best understood as a strategy for resonating more intensively with the wider temporal-spatial sweep of the cosmos—not in order to lose itself or *fuse with* this cosmos but in order to become something unique, novel, *via* the cosmos.

In this way, it may be hard to strictly separate the forces that culminate in life and those that culminate in art. Both art and life can be understood as a kind of virtual "enveloping" of material chaos that enables it to resonate across its multiple milieus, extracting or liberating sensations that can go on to have a life of their own apart from the limited "functional" contexts of the systems from which they came. In Deleuze's words, "Art erects a plane, a sieve over chaos, not to control or contain chaos but to contain some of its fragments in a small space to reduce it to some form that the living can utilize without being overwhelmed."[11] Art in particular emerges when particular fields of this becoming-expressive of life deterritorialize—take on a life separate from the territory from which they initially emerged.

However, it is important to realize that this only happens because the territory *is already* intricately bound up with—indeed, woven out of—the larger deterritorialized cosmos.

In summary, the life of art and the art of life depend on a kind of convergence of—and selective passage across—two elements, one of which is ordered and the other of which is chaotic; one of which contracts/folds, the other of which dilates/unfolds.[12] In Deleuze and Guattari's words, "if nature is like art, this is always because it combines these two living elements in every way, House and Universe, *Heimlich* and *Unheimlich*, territory and deterritorialization, finite melodic compounds and the great infinite plane of composition, the small and the large refrain."[13] It is these complex structures, common to both life and art, that allow a pluralistic cosmos to creatively and ecologically differentiate itself in such a way that the novelties of local becomings continue to resonate with the larger Universe of which they are a part.

Deleuze-Guattari's writings draw extensively on the insights of Estonian biosemiotician Jakob von Uexkil, who describes natural ecologies as a kind of melodic counterpoint wherein various species serve as musical motifs for one another. The spider "plays" off the fly, constructing a web that is "contrapuntal" to the fly's bodily structure and movement. Similarly, the life of the tick can be understood as physical, behavioral "counterpoint" to a "musical score" provided by the mammal upon which it feeds. A meadow of flowers is perceived by the honeybee as a kind of "honeybee composition" made up of "bee-notes." These musically patterned relationships are precisely made possible by the organism's capacity to filter or selectively relate to particular features of its larger temporal-spatial environment. In a sense, the territorial "expressions" of an organism are *nothing more* than the playing out of these musical relationships. So, for instance, it is not the case that a certain pre-given, primary "essence of tick" comes to have secondary relationships with a world. Rather, what the tick is, most fundamentally, is a, "harmonic world, of its own rhythms and melody composed by its umwelt—the conjunction of mammal-twig-sun, in which it is a connective, an instrument."[14] This musical capacity to resonate with selective aspects of an organism's environment is precisely what allows for a proliferation of biodiversity in which organisms develop increasingly specialized niches or "life-worlds" for themselves that overlay one another, forming into complex, macroecological webs.

For Grosz, it is particularly in the phenomenon of sexual differentiation and sexual selection that the natural world evolves aesthetic expressions aimed more at intensity and enjoyment than any practical "use" or functionality. It is here that "life comes to elaborate itself through making its bodily forms and its archaic territories pleasing (or annoying), performative, which is to say, intensified through their integration into form and their impact on bodies."[15] She highlights Charles Darwin's often-overlooked observation that sexual selection does not always function in concert with natural selection but often conflicts with it, exposing an organism to dangers it would otherwise not incur. For instance, the male peacock's lavish plumage, even as it attracts female partners, puts it at a much stronger risk for predatory attack. "Sexual appeal imperils as much as it allures; it generates risk to the same extent that it produces difference."[16]

Grosz highlights Darwin's own connection between the emergence of *music* in particular and the operations of sexual selection. Birdsong is a particularly strong example of rhythmic and melodic elaborations whose capacity to evoke pleasure, satisfaction, or annoyance is the key component in their ability to attract mates or repel competitors. Darwin observes that there is something about the vibrations of music that are inherently pleasure producing apart from any specific survival function they might have. For Grosz, music's capacity to evoke enjoyment is linked to its role as a kind of "vibrating fiber" connecting the local bodily structures, habits, and behaviors of an organism and its larger, deterritorialized universe. Rather than understanding sexuality merely in terms of its ends or goals—namely the competitive reproduction of offspring—Grosz (inspired by her reading of Darwin) considers whether it might be approached more fundamentally in terms of the forces of bodily intensification and pleasure it makes possible: "Vibrations, waves, oscillations, resonances, affect living bodies, not for any higher purpose but for pleasure alone. Living beings are vibratory beings: vibration is their mode of differentiation, the way they enhance and enjoy the forces of the earth itself."[17] In a footnote, Grosz quotes Charles Hartshorne as one of a small number of thinkers who support Darwin's contention that music is first and foremost pursued for the purposes of pleasure: "[Bird] songs illustrate the aesthetic mean between chaotic irregularity and monotonous regularity. . . . It is often persisted in without any immediate results and hence must be largely self-rewarding."[18]

In short, Grosz sees in nature's excess of expressive forms a drive toward intensity and beauty that can't be explained merely by mechanical evolutionary laws aimed at nothing more than self-propagation. "The haunting beauty of birdsong, the provocative performance of erotic display in primates, the attraction of insects to the perfume of plants are all in excess of mere survival. . . . [They] affirm the excessiveness of the body and the natural order, their capacity to bring out in each other what surprises, what is of no use but nevertheless attracts and appeals."[19] In a parallel sense, she describes art as rooted in "a superfluousness of nature, in the capacity of the earth to render the sensory superabundant, in the bird's courtship song and dance, or in the field of lilies swaying in a breeze under a blue sky . . ."[20] In this way Grosz affirms a kind of aesthetic excess or "uselessness" at the heart of life's most basic operations and innovations. These indeterminately novel, aesthetically driven becomings are made possible by a selective folding or filtering of the larger temporal-spatial flux, which only then enables it to be utilized for new creative innovations.

Chaotic Nexus and Structured Society: A Poiesis of Life in the Folds

Whitehead's understanding of the role of aesthetic valuation in cosmic evolution converges in some fascinating ways with Deleuze and Guattari's and Grosz's accounts. Like Deleuze and Guattari, Whitehead challenges the Platonically derived assumption (important aspects of which are inherited by modernity) that the complexly varied orders in the cosmos result from an imprinting of a passive material substrate by eternal, transcendent essences (whether naturally or theologically conceived). Challenging some of the core assumptions of the modern scientific worldview, Whitehead argues that at the heart of the world's most fundamental processes (both inorganic and organic) is a seeking after experiential "intensity" and "harmony" aimed at higher degrees of "satisfaction." In this way, Whitehead brings a language of aesthetic valuation to bear on natural, material processes normally conceived (at least within Western modernity) only in terms of mechanistic laws of cause and effect.

A closer look at Whitehead's microcosmic analysis reveals the significance of this "aesthetic indeterminacy" within the most fundamental operations of the cosmos. The process of an actual occasion's becoming begins with the occasion's "feeling" or "enjoyment" of its (past) world. These "prehensions" are integrated by and creatively directed toward a novel aim— the "subjective aim"—unique to that occasion. The patterned becoming of each occasion or event in the cosmos is, in this way, not simply dictated by external laws but emerges in and through a space of indeterminacy in which each event freely actualizes itself—not independent of but *through* its various prehensive relationships.[21] The degree of experiential "satisfaction" each event is able to realize in the integration of its prehensions depends on its capacity to overcome discord among its various prehensions by creatively resolving conflicts into new, harmonically intense "contrasts." In short, without the language of aesthetic valuation, there really would be no way to describe the inner *telos* of each subjective aim.

The subjective aim, however, while freely self-generated by each event, is itself conditioned—indeed, initiated—by a "hybrid physical prehension" of God—also called the "initial aim" in much process theology. It is this gift of a divine "aim" that makes available a range of novel—and relevant—possibilities for each occasion's becoming. Whitehead's discussion of God's role in this process is quite nuanced and easily misunderstood. On one hand, Whitehead makes clear that the occasion's own aesthetic aim at intensity and harmony is conditioned by God's own primordial aim or appetition toward intensity. "Each occasion exhibits its measure of creative emphasis in proportion to its measure of subjective intensity. The absolute standard of such intensity is that of the primordial nature of God . . ."[22] The "primordial nature" of God is "the lure for feeling, the eternal urge of desire. His particular relevance to each creative act as it arises from its own conditioned standpoint in the world, constitutes him the initial 'object of desire' establishing the initial phase of each subjective aim."[23]

From this, however, we should not conclude that the aesthetic intensities and harmonies of the world's becoming are mere derivatives of some larger divine plan—poetic or otherwise. It can be argued that Whitehead invokes aesthetic language precisely in order to keep radically open the plurality of the world's own emergent purposes, functions, and goals. This is precisely the point Faber drives home in his theopoetic understanding of divinity. The world's own creative *poiesis* (defined by him as "any creative event of construction that can't be reconstructed out of its elements") is not merely a secondary effect of God's own theopoiesis—we are not mere "verses" in God's cosmic poem. Rather, for Faber, theopoetics implies a divine gift of "self-creativity" or, put another way, "a divine insisting on a multiplicity that saves the manifold from any controlling power of unification."[24]

In this vein, might we conceive of divine agency as that which insists that we "resonate with" something greater, something more in the cosmos, but in such a way that we become something new, something for ourselves, *through* this "something more"? Value would not be attributed to our creative becoming solely on the basis of whether or not we conform to God's larger plan or function. Each event's becoming has its own immanent value based on the unique innovations it is able to self-realize, in and through its relations. Purpose is not merely handed over to the world's occasions by God; rather, God inspires the occasion's *own* seeking after new, perhaps hitherto unrecognized problems to solve, purposes to work out. In Faber's words, "If intensity is the meaning of an event, then . . . the 'worth' of every event resides in its *aesthetic purposelessness.* In the initial aim, God grants to every event this ultimate functionlessness in which every event is bequeathed to itself; that is, here every event both is bequeathed to itself *and* is the goal of itself, never the cause of itself (*causa sui*) in an anti-divine sense."[25]

Thus far, I have discussed God's role primarily in terms of God's primordial nature; however, insofar as we understand theopoiesis as inseparable from theoplicity, God's "consequent nature" must be granted at least as prominent a role. Ultimately I want to argue that God's consequent, receptive enfoldment of the world is what allows God to relevantly impart God's vision to the world—a vision that, in turn, allows the world to generate its own ecologically diverse intensities and harmonies. Before I explore the role of theoplicity any further, however, it is first necessary to discuss some of the more macrocosmic elements of Whitehead's cosmology—in particular, Whitehead's understanding of the way mutually enfolded, interlocking structural societies create the "environment" necessary for the uniquely intense satisfactions of the "entirely living nexus." I have already pointed toward a parallel between the centrality of a certain aesthetic indeterminacy in Deleuze and Guattari's and Grosz's ecological, evolutionary framework, and the indeterminate, aesthetic drive toward intensity, or harmony, that shapes the concrescence of actual occasions on the microcosmic level of Whitehead's analysis. However, these parallels become even more striking when we move to an analysis of some of the more macrocosmic aspects of Whitehead's cosmological account, particularly his account of the complex ecological "nestings" or enfoldments of structured societies necessary for the emergence of *life*.

We have discussed how each event is "propelled" in a certain sense by its aim toward intensity and harmony—an impulse initiated by God's own quest for intensity. It turns out that the emergence of complexly interlocking ecological orders of "structured societies" of events in the cosmos can best be understood in terms of this very goal of generating greater intensities, or harmonies: "Thus God's purpose in the creative advance is the evocation of intensities. The evocation of societies is purely subsidiary to this absolute end."[26] Whitehead paints a cosmological picture from lesser to greater levels of order in the universe, each of which "enfolds" the next almost like a complexly overlapping set of Chinese boxes. As we shall see shortly, however, the evolutionary "advancement" of the cosmos is not conceived as a linear movement out of chaos toward order but actually involves increasingly complex *integrations* of chaotic spontaneity and stable orders of rhythmic repetition.

In the chapter of *Process and Reality* entitled "The Order of Nature," Whitehead provides a detailed account of the different layers of complex order that have emerged in our particular "cosmic epoch." At the base of the cosmos is a general type of relatedness that—while refusing to dictate any specific kind of order—points to the underlying reality that all events share a common world. This "extensive continuum" is described by White-head as a vast "nexus." Whitehead uses the term nexus to describe the most general mode of relationship among events—one that does not necessarily display patterns of ordered consistency as in the case of "societies."[27] This "chaotic nexus" plays a key role in Faber's interpretation of process cosmology, representing for him something akin to Plato's *khora*. The basic or chaotic nexus represents a certain "empty" capacity for truly open-ended becomings in the cosmos—becomings that at the same time don't cease to be relational in the broadest sense. Faber describes the chaotic nexus in the following terms: "The locus of actualization of potentiality as such, abstracted from actualization, articulates simply the existence of an ontological freedom of singular events that do not *have* to repeat anything. . . . Its fundamental, unique feature is to be the locus of the singular, the non-repeatable, the unpredictable."[28] The chaotic or basic nexus is identified with "empty space" in the cosmos in the sense that it represents a framework on which no particular structures are yet imposed.

Various interlocking layers of "structured societies" emerge out of the chaotic nexus, all the way from the most basic "geometric" and "electro-magnetic" societies to the inorganic societies that make up the relatively stable material structures of our cosmos. These types of societies employ a particular strategy for generating intensity, harmony, and satisfaction—namely, to block out unwelcome details in their environment by means of negative prehensions. This increases their survival value but renders them largely incapable of the kind of satisfactions that could emerge through a more positive integration of contrasting features of their environment. These structured societies, however, provide the relatively stable "environments" within which other, more specialized networks of events can emerge—including, most interestingly, the phenomenon of *life*.

Life, for Whitehead, cannot be placed under the category of a "society" insofar as the latter is defined by the repetition of certain consistent traits (whether across time or space) by its component members, for he recognizes the uniqueness of life as something like the opposite—a capacity to originate *novelty* by means of *original* "mental" reactions to its prehensions. Whitehead's refusal to define life by any consistent, underlying set of characteristics represents a radical break from both classical and modern traditions. Because he understands life in terms of its capacity to override the ordered structures and functions of the societies within which it occurs, Whitehead places it in the more general category of nexus—more specifically an *entirely living nexus*.[29] Instead of pursuing a strategy of blocking out and "abstracting from" the spontaneous chaotic flux of its larger environment, the entirely living nexus "channels" and integrates these influences into fresh contrasts of higher intensity, or harmony, allowing for far higher levels of satisfaction than its inorganic counterparts.

This unique capacity of the entirely living nexus, however, is entirely dependent on the particular "environment" provided by the complexly overlaid milieus of structured societies. Like the folded territories that Deleuze, Guattari, and Grosz describe, these nested layers of structured societies function simultaneously as a kind of "filter" that protects the entirely living nexus from chaotic vicissitudes of its larger environment, and an "amplifier" that selectively channels those chaotic inputs such that they can be utilized for the entirely living nexus's own innovations.[30] In this way, the more intense satisfaction of the component members of the entirely living nexus "arises by reason of the ordered complexity of the contrasts which the society stages for these components."[31] Without the complexly interlocking folds of the various structured societies, the entirely living nexus would be unable to constructively draw on the chaotic spontaneities of its larger world for its own radically novel becomings.

While Whitehead's discussion of structured societies in this role refers in large part to the functioning of the living organism's body, the body for Whitehead isn't strictly distinguished from the environmental layers within which the body itself is embedded. Whitehead thus describes the body as "only a peculiarly intimate bit of the world."[32] Just as the entirely living nexus is specialized to the particular environment provided by the body, the body itself is in turn specialized to the particularities of the ecosystem within which it finds its needs met. The body and the ecosystem thus function together as complementary systems of "foldings" that—together—"stage" a set of complexly contrasting inputs for the entirely living nexus. The line of influence of course doesn't just move from outside to inside—the entirely living nexus's novel concrescences also rebound outward, shaping, reorganizing and reinventing the world around it. Thus, the operations of the entirely living nexuses are not subordinate to the structural functions of the more law-abiding societies within which they occur—but, in the right contexts, might actually go on to restructure or reinvent *what those functions are*. As in Deleuze and Guattari and Grosz, it is the seeking after a certain excessive, aesthetic self-expression that precedes, indeed invents, the more "stratified" functions of living organisms, rather than vice versa.

I spoke earlier of the "chaotic nexus" at the "base" of the universe—a structure of utterly open-ended connectedness identified with the idea of empty space. It turns out that the entirely living nexus is *also* said to occur primarily in a region of empty space—this time, the empty space opened up in the "interstices" of the body and brain. It makes sense that the entirely living nexus's capacity to subvert the more rigid social orderings of the structured societies within which it is embedded would be linked to a certain "empty" interstitiality, simultaneously making available a maximally rich set of relations *and* keeping the living occasions free from having to replicate any pre-given functions or patterns of behavior. This interstitiality provides, in Whitehead's words:

> . . . intense experience without the shackle of reiteration from the past. This is the condition for spontaneity of conceptual reaction. The conclusion to be drawn from this argument is that life is a characteristic of "empty space" and not of space "occupied" by any corpuscular society. . . . Life lurks in the interstices of each living cell, and in the interstices of the brain.[33]

In a later passage, Whitehead references Christ's invocation of the "lilies" in the Sermon on the Mount in order to gesture toward the particular quality of freedom opened up within this interstitial space: "It is by reason of the body, with its miracle of order, that the treasures of the past environment are poured into the living occasion. The final percipient route of occasions is perhaps some thread of happenings wandering in 'empty' space amid the interstices of the brain. *It toils not, neither does it spin.* It receives from the past, it lives in the present."[34]

Jesus's call to "consider the lilies" occurs of course in the context of encouraging his followers to push beyond a narrow-minded preoccupation with some of the more "habitual functions" of human life. (Eating and clothing ourselves are the examples given—in other words, the securing of life's basic resources.) We might read this passage's invocation of the "uselessly" aesthetic becomings of the lily as part of a larger reminder to get in touch with the deeper, theopoetic source of life itself—a divine urge toward an aesthetic richness and enjoyment that underlies life's most fundamental processes. For Whitehead, then, the entirely living nexus—the closest that Whitehead gets to circumscribing some unique "essence" of life—is thus understood in terms of an "aesthetic purposelessness" that is at the same time not disengaged or disconnected from the larger universe within which it is nested. Like the expressive, ecologically situated territories that Grosz describes, they function on the one hand as something utterly unique for themselves, and yet this originality is precisely drawn or extracted from a selective, divinely inflected relationship with a larger chaosmos.

Like Deleuze and Guattari's refrain, the "interstitial harbors" provided by overlaid structured societies enable the spontaneous inputs of the world not just to be filtered, but "canalized" so that the originality they inspire can rhythmically build on itself from one moment to the next. The chaotic nexus, in and of itself, represents a merely centrifugal movement out toward a deterritorialized cosmos—pure exposure to it would simply rip the living organism to shreds, similar to Deleuze and Guattari's description of being hurled into a black hole by too rapid a deterritorialization. The interstitial harbor within which the entirely living nexus rests, however, *integrates* this centrifugal, dilating, chaotic force with a centripetal, contracting force, enabling the entirely living nexus to develop new projects, goals, purposes with their own internal continuities. Whitehead describes this "canalization" (a term taken from Bergson, arguably the philosopher most central to Deleuze and Guattari's biophilosophy) as a transmission of "hybrid physical prehensions" such that "the mental originality of the living occasions receives a character and a depth. In this way originality is both 'canalized'—to use Bergson's word—and intensified. Its range is widened within limits. Apart from canalization, depth of originality would spell disaster for the animal body. With it, personal mentality can be evolved."[35]

Faber's interpretation of process theology explicitly highlights this connection in Whitehead's thought between the "empty" potentiality of the larger chaotic nexus and that of the entirely living nexus:

> Here Whitehead understands the *basic nexus* both as the *fundamental relationship* of events, as the most primitive (still empty) context on whose basis *all* organisms develop their organization, and as a highly complex, non-objectifiable (i.e., not object related) form of *vitality* within the cosmos, the latter of which transcends the organizational structures of organisms. Hence, in the basic nexus one finds the convergence of, on the one hand, the empty "wherein" of the development of increasingly complex organisms, *and,* on the other, life, mind and freedom on the basis of these more complex organic levels. Because the basic nexus stands as the locus of novelty at both the *foundation* and the *peak* of every organization of the "cosmos" it acquires a fundamental significance in Whitehead's cosmology. The cosmos—as every possible form of organism in a specific stabilization of order and novelty—arises between the *basic nexus* as "chaos," that is, as the environment of every organization, and the basic nexus as the living sundering of every order.[36]

I want to build on Faber's notion of the cosmos arising *between* these two nexuses—that occurring in the empty interstices of the living organism and that occurring in the larger chaosmos. Perhaps the emergence (or creation—but only in a qualified sense) of the cosmos itself is best understood as a poiesis of folding that occurs in the interstices of these two manifestations of the basic nexus. As in Deleuze and Guattari and Grosz, it is this unique amalgamation or meeting between two principles or orders—one territorializing, one deterritorializing; one contracting/folding, one dilating/unfolding—that enables the uniquely creative capacities of life, consciousness and art. In *both* cases the relationship between these two is made possible by overlaid structures of folding that complexly mediate a larger chaosmic environment to an inner space—simultaneously protecting, or harboring, the local lifeform from the environment and amplifying and intensively overlaying selective elements of that environment. For Deleuze, Guattari, and Grosz, on the one hand, and Whitehead, on the other, the ordered, stratified structures of the cosmos should not be seen as the "foundation" of life in the sense of that to which life is ultimately reducible; rather these structures or functions arise in the first place as part of a larger strategy to enable and intensify the world's "zestfully" aesthetic "purposelessness." Ordered structures and functions coalesce out of the chaotic nexus—almost paradoxically—as part of a larger strategy for proliferating diverse, diverging experiences of intensity and harmony in the world. For Whitehead, Deleuze, Guattari, and Grosz, the basic error of a certain modern scientific reductionism is to invert this reality.

These cosmological reflections open up some new ways of considering the workings of "theopoiesis." So far I have not spoken of the role of eternal objects and God's "primordial envisagement" of them, which constitute Whitehead's metaphysical account of how novelty is woven into the world. While I can only touch on their role here, it is important to understand how the ingression of eternal objects into the world's events constitutes an insertion of divine eternity into time. Unlike Plato's account of ideal forms, however, the divine "primordial conceptual valuation" of eternal patterns does not "organize" material flows "from above" so much as enable these eventive flows to become relationally creative. Eternal objects are described by Whitehead as the "modes" or patterns by which events prehend other events—modes that, in themselves are nontemporal. However, the arrow of time in the world in which a past, present, and future can be both differentiated and connected requires these recurring patterns—they are precisely what allow the cosmos to "resonate" with itself across time and space.[37] While, historically, process theology has emphasized the role of the primordial nature of God in "attuning" eternal objects to one another and the world, perhaps God's consequent nature has as important a role.[38] I want to suggest in particular that the ecologically interlocking folds of the cosmos are only able to interdependently emerge insofar as they are *first* receptively folded inside God. The gift of God's unique vision for each event, thus, emerges from theoplicity—God's own creative receptivity to the world as it becomes in its totality from moment to moment.

I have discussed how understanding God as theopoet is tantamount to disclaiming the idea that God determines or directs creation from a position of transcendent power. In Faber's words, "A theopoetic interpretation discloses the relationship between God and the order of the world. As poet of the world, God guides the world with God's living vision, a vision that rather than imposing (orders) instead frees us (patterns for decisions)."[39] I also suggested above that God works by insisting that we open to the "more than" of the world, but in such a way that we become something unique for ourselves *through* this "more than." In my analysis of Deleuze, Guattari, and Grosz and of Whitehead, I showed how it is precisely the emergence of complexly layered ecological folds that enables this very process to happen. Perhaps God's "vision" then can best be described as a larger, concerted effort—throughout the entire cosmos—to coordinate the becoming of each event with every other event. From a creaturely perspective, the initial aim would be experienced not so much as a divine vision "beamed" directly into our reality from a place of eternal, divine transcendence, but—in a more Deleuzian vein—as a certain capacity to innovatively, virtually "refract" our own inheritance of our past. God's vision lures each occasion to realize its own aesthetic, subjective aim *precisely through* the complex folds of its interactions—folds that developed in the first place precisely in and through this process.

In this way, God's "everlasting," salvific enfoldment of the cosmos—what Faber calls theoplicity—is precisely what enables the world to extract original, "virtual" becomings from the larger temporal-spatial cosmos within which it is embedded. The world's access to God's vision depends on each event's ability to inhabit a deep "interstitiality" at the heart of the world. As creatures we must suspend our attachment to habitual drives and functions—our "toiling and spinning"—so as to open to the free, creative capacity of this interstitial "emptiness." In getting in touch with this open-ended, aesthetically driven *telos* of God's vision, a space opens up to reconsider the forces that drive the larger project of the human species. Instead of conceiving of our alliance with God as one that sets us over and against nature as its masters, we can begin to seek the divine call from within the deep interstices of the world's complex, ecological folds. God's vision in this way is not "transmitted" over and above these folds but speaks, sings, vibrates, *through* them.

God as theopoet is no ruthless director who demands that we play a preordained role in his providential drama. Creation is better understood as a kind of improvisational performance, with God in the role of the one in whom all voices become cosmically interwoven—an experience of creative receptivity that then allows God to function as a kind of inspirational "muse" for each individual. This muse deepens and creatively "refracts" what each creature is taking in, such that she is able to respond with freshly inspired innovations. In this way theopoiesis takes place as a kind of God–world synergy wherein the divine vision enables a kind of ever-differentiating manifold of intensively resonating connections. This approach can encourage ecotheology to consider God's call to environmental responsibility not as obedience to a set of eternal divine prohibitions so much as a divine insistence that we improvise synergistically with the interweaving riffs of our complexly enfolded, always shifting ecosystems. An epic poem of cosmological dimensions can thus continue to vibrate, resonate, between House and Universe, the local refrain and the infinite Plane of Composition, the world's own ecopoetic folds and divine theoplicity. . . .

Becoming Intermezzo
Eco-theopoetics after the Anthropic Principle

ROLAND FABER

The Necessity of Wildness

John Muir, the wholehearted naturalist who was instrumental in the creation of the first modern national park worldwide, Yellowstone, in the Northwest of the United States, understood the preserves of nature we create as ways to grant nature our absence. It is only when we recognize and experience the wildness of mountains, waters, and woods that we can perceive their own ways of being, beating in their own rhythms. In recognizing that *we* are the intruders, the foreigners, the strangers, we are granted the feeling of our own contingency within the necessity of wildness in return.[1] Nothing is just for our use—energy, water, and wood—but everything is a fountain of life in its own measures, rhythms, and harmonies. Only invited to listen to its own ways, the wilderness in return speaks with infinite patience, suffering our presence without being impressed by it: growing into the sky on its own, flowing down on its own, bending in the wind with its own voice.

Of course, we *can* misuse and misunderstand this patience. We *can* disturb the wilderness with our own clamor; we *can* dig tunnels through its mountains, cut its trees, and pollute its waters—and *still* it is patient, strangely reacting to our inflictions with its own rhythms of ignorance, degeneration, refusal, retreat, or disappearance.[2] We can misunderstand this patience as passivity; we can try to fill its seeming silence with our bubbles;

we can plaster it with our divisions of power; we can overlook its plenitude and mistake it for a wasteland that only waits to be filled by our human rule. We can mistake its voices as formless matter ready to be imprinted with our faces. We can waste it for our own sake. We can possess it.

I will propose that our ecological future is indispensably entangled with a very different view of nature that must become sensible to the necessity of wildness in which *we* are only strangers, guests, invited by incredible patience—*only in which* we become participants in what I will call "eco-nature." I will argue that to recognize this necessity we need shift the way we experience and frame our world in such a way that we *become contingent* upon this nature; that to homestead within the necessity of wildness means to let go of all excuses to justify the disturbance that our existence causes. I will propose that we must become an *intermezzo within this necessity* and that to become such an intermezzo we must give up on all forms of power of control, manipulation, and destruction in the name of our survival. We must become what we always have been: an expression of the rhythms of necessity in which our contingent existence is an overflow of its patient grace.

It is the *solitude* that Muir experienced in the wildness that made him feel *solidarity* with its own ways and rhythms. Maybe, then, it is precisely the colonizing logic, economy, and philosophy of the West that was resisting Muir's insight and experience. Maybe we should rather listen to the wisdom traditions of Asia: the ecological wisdom of interrelatedness with the All—as Whitehead has suggested?[3] Isn't the *dao* one of the oldest symbols of such a harmony we desperately seek: of the necessity of wildness in which everything goes by its own rhythms, even if they cross one another, complicate one another, and sometimes, tragically, cancel one another out?[4] Isn't the Buddhist realization of suchness (*tathata*) and all-relational interpenetration (*pratitya-samutpada*) a symbol for an immediate access to this emptiness of patience that harbors its own liberating plenitude?[5] Isn't the eco-wisdom of the East all we need to understand? Maybe so. I am not contesting such a view.

What complicates things, however, is the very hybridity by which we live today in this globally webbed and mapped-out world, an interpenetration of East and West that cannot be sorted out easily: technology, democracy, economy, spirituality—all mixed up. We have all lost the innocence of pure traditions both in the East and the West. And, maybe, these categories are wrong altogether, making us blind to other binary hybridities: North and South, for instance, or the "worlds" that we count so lightly with the ordinal numbers *first, second, third.* Maybe what we need is to realize our *common complex contingency* in the majestic necessity of *this* wilderness: the patience of all of these wisdom traditions for our little lives as they flow together and apart within us, between us, and among us.

All I can do is realize the *contingency* in my thought within the great streams of necessary wildness in their interflowing connections and diversions, consciously *deconstructing* my own Western baggage in the face of the confluent and diffluent, affluent and influent necessities that, from their own rhythms, connect and diverge. All I will do is, from my own location, contextualize my ecological deconstruction so as to take its contingency seriously, opening it to the patience of wildness ever beyond and, yet, always within.

The Economy of Omnipotence

Science has always had its unexpected effects. In 1847, Hermann von Helmholtz formulated the famous law of the conservation of energy. Curiously enough, he had discovered it by investigating the biological functioning of nerves. This law states that, in a process of the transmission of energy, energy is not lost but only transformed. It became a universal law of physical, chemical, and technical transformations of energy, for instance, from kinetic energy into thermal energy. It expresses an important axiom of current cosmology, namely, that there is no "free lunch," that is, that the differentiated energy in the cooling cosmos must have been the same in the point-concentration of the Big Bang.[6] It insures that there is no energy coming in from any transcendent force, such as God, acting upon the world *ex machina.* Maybe this cosmos is just borrowed from nothing as it jumped into existence from a random quantum fluctuation, its missing part being dark energy. We have only borrowed this universe, and we will eventually have to give it back. Furthermore, Helmholtz's law allows us to travel through space. When we burn the thrusters full of rocket fuel, we propagate in one direction because we leave a trail of burned waste of particles behind such that the sum of the energy in both directions is zero.

It is even more unexpected that this law became part of nineteenth-century economic theory.[7] Since there is no prescription for the form into which energy is transformed, we need not care what we leave behind as long as we gain *in* the process for what the process of transformation was invented. Since our economy can just use the sources of energy transformation, it can, like a rocket, also just carelessly leave a trail of waste behind. The world is a reservoir of energy that we transform according to our will, technology, and aims. The economic cycles are hermetically closed; we only have to sustain the process of economical transformation since the resources are either inexhaustible or replicable raw material and, after their economic transformation, only waste. Nature is a mere supply for the sustainability of an economic mechanism; it is a mere substratum, the exploitation of environments just the "outside" of economy, the mere passive material of transformation.

This mechanism is deeply ingrained in Western thought. Alfred North Whitehead, the English mathematician and American philosopher, has called its inner mechanics "substantialism" and followed it back to two of its main roots: Christianity and Greek philosophy.[8] Philosophically, it claims that the true reality is independent permanence; that is, first, it is what it is without any relation to anything else except itself and, second, it is what it is through time without being affected by changes in anything else.[9] Such substance, if it construes our understanding of reality, not only needs nothing to exist but has everything else in itself or, conversely, everything else is just a mode of dependent participation in its essence.[10] Whitehead claimed that this mode of constructing reality is deeply inscribed in languages that use a subject–predicate form such that it divides our perception of reality itself into independent existents without any inner relation but only with derivative forms of participation.[11]

Whitehead went even further and demonstrated that this installation of substantial reality, with its sole legitimate power that excluded the substratum of dead matter as a mere passive instrument to be imprinted by the activity of a substance, structured Greek society even in the form of Athenian democracy, which could only live from a substratum of slaves being the mere instrument of its own sustenance. As substances have all power of activity, so free citizens have all the power of the *polis;* and, as the material substratum is a mere supply for the imprint of the substances, so slaves are the supply for the sustenance of the free state.[12] Indeed, the economical application of Helmholtz's law is just a late insight in the substantialism that has haunted Western societies from their very beginning: that the human economy is a substance, an independent machine of the transformation of material for its own sustenance, and that the under side, the material, the slaves, the strangers, the others, are only waste products.

Theologically, Whitehead reconstructed the substantialism of the mainstream Christian notion of God as having been formulated precisely within this Greek context as the highest substance. In fact, if God is the independent permanent being, everything else can only be an inherent derivation from God, and in case of stubborn reservations, evil deviations. In fact, according to this marriage of Greek and Christian categories, the world's existence is a mixture of imperfection and evil. If substance is elevated to the eminent reality of God; that is, if it expresses the ultimate reality of everything, it must become the ultimate power from which everything else is created *ex nihilo,* out of nothing.[13] The wilderness, the chaos of a creative universe, is vampirized of its own life and bestowed to the highest substance, which as an independent being now grants existence like a substance to its accidents or the master to his slaves.

This is the economy of omnipotence: that substantialism from its barbaric origin in the relation of absolute rulers over their subjects is sublimated into "the one absolute, omnipotent, omniscient source of all being, for his own existence requiring no relations to anything beyond himself."[14] As "He was internally complete"[15] so are God's legitimate powers on earth and, finally, in ironic participation in this history of substantialism, so was humanity over against the wilderness and economy over its resources.

The Ecological Death of God

Everything changes with a different perception of an economy not based on substantialism and its philosophical and theological implications. God is dead, claims Nietzsche; meaning that the substantialist illusion that roams through our abstractions with which we order our world is obsolete.[16] Indeed, with the fall of the substantialist God *a whole cascade of deconstructions is initiated* of which we might not yet have seen a bottom.[17] Most of the atheist rhetoric in the nineteenth century might be dismissible; that is, it is not radical enough to overcome substantialism since it builds its very resistance on the same mechanicism that was the outcome of its substantialist forbearers. If we cannot experience God because we don't have any organ for it, as in Hume, referring to sense experience, then the deconstruction of this divine fantasy only furthers a mechanistic universe that, in its own turn, sustains the economical omnipotence.[18] It leaves the deep substantialism with its dualistic binary of economy and resources, inside and outside, form and matter, master and slaves, intact. Nietzsche's claim was different because it attacked the very underlying substantialism: that a God of substance is a God that upholds the regime of Being, of the economic laws of omnipotence, by granting what is life's own: its becoming, the creativity of fluctuations that always escapes substantialism: the waste, the slaves, the underside. To dethrone *this* God is to give back the *power of becoming* to what has been excluded from Being. And, in its groundlessness, *becoming* now, for the first time, appears in *ecological* terms: as "eternal return" of novelty, as recurrence of the cycle of becoming in itself, as an endless cycle of togetherness.[19]

What becomes obvious is that the *mechanicism* in which substantialism began to structure economy as independent, all-present, omnipotent, internal infinity that can ignore any "outside" or is even the creator of it in terms of divine resources given to control them (make them subjected) must be overturned. It is clear now: the very dichotomy of mind and matter in Descartes that left our bodily existence outside the mind as the mere extension and the mere coexistence of an almighty God with an infinite extended space, as in Newton, will only sustain a substantialist economy.[20] Indeed, it was the Romantic movement of the later nineteenth century that questioned this very presupposition. It found in Schelling a proponent that not only shifted the view of the mechanist universe of exploitation but expressed it with a very different notion of the divine: that of the depth of nature that, in fact, is so deep—infinitely deep—that it is even deeper than God. It was this *Ungrund,* or groundlessness, that he called the *nature* of God, that is, *that* in God that is *not* God but even God's groundless ground.[21] Here we gain a first glimpse of eco-nature in which "nature" was given back its wildness, indicating the groundlessness of everything that happens. In it, we are at home and strangers alike; in this nature, we become—with God—contingent on its necessity.

The immanent vitalism of the Romantic movement dealt with the mechanicism in such a way that a new paradigm could emerge: that of a community of becoming in cyclic fate bound together in their becoming and infinitely hovering over a wildness of which humanity is only a contingency.[22] With Whitehead, we enter a new phase of the exploration of this togetherness. Motivated by the hybrid confluence of science and religion in his philosophical encounter with mechanicism and in light of the new physics of relativity theory and quantum physics, he might have been one of the very first philosophers who systematically proclaimed a new paradigm of organic philosophy. This paradigm "is neither purely physical, nor purely biological" but is always "the study of organisms. Biology is the study of the larger organisms; whereas physics is the study of the smaller organisms."[23] His whole philosophy can be seen as making sense of an organic universe or, in more technical terms, that the universe is a groundless process of becoming and that this becoming is always an irreducible multiplicity of relations in the process of growing together and dissipating into a new multiplicity of relations.[24] In this paradigm, everything is related and nothing is without "life"; everything is a becoming of worth (inner value) and nothing is just material or waste.[25]

It was Whitehead's contention that if the universe is a process of processes of becoming relationships or relational becomings, the most fundamental characteristic of this ecological complexity must be only *one:* namely that there is no other characteristic more fundamental and, actually, groundless, than this very togetherness of relationships in becoming.[26]

He called this most profound *ecological* character of the universe—which "does not presuppose any special type of order, nor . . . any order at all pervading its members"—"the general metaphysical obligation of mutual immanence."[27] Its inner consequence, however, is the *ecological death* of the substantial God. Deeper than the death of God as Being in Nietzsche and the death of God as ground in Schelling, it *erases God's power altogether,* only leaving a trace as a warning: If "there is nothing in the Universe other than instances of this passage and components of these instances," then "the word Creativity expresses the notion that each event is a process issuing in novelty" such that its "Immanent Creativity, or Self-Creativity, . . . avoids the implication of a transcendent Creator," only in an air of paradox, or pantheism" suggesting "the [immanent] origination of novelty" instead of "Creator."[28] Strangely enough, as we will see later, this was only the birth of an ecological divine.

The Anthropic Fallacy

So deeply was the justification of substantialism ingrained into Western experience that the *fact of its very inscription* came into question.[29] Its easiest and most obvious version is this: that even the ecological death of God has left us with the dead body of this divinity,[30] namely, with power-instilled, substantialist abstractions like Subject, Right, Power, Integrity, and Humanity.[31] A case in point is Feuerbach's analysis of substantialist power as a projection onto God by social and political interests of legitimizing certain power structures. Their rupture, however, would *not* lead to the ecological death of God and, hence, a new ecological paradigm of mutual immanence but straightly into *reclamation* of the diverted powers projected as powers of the *infinite* human nature. This is the Anthropic Principle: the half-death of God *in* its corpse—the superiority, even infinity, of humanity. The Anthropic Principle reverses the necessity of wildness and our contingency into *our* necessity and the contingency of nature.[32]

This Anthropic Principle expresses itself most prominently and obviously in the form of the Anthropic Fallacy in the current ecological discourse such that to save nature *from* human influences is actually a strategy of *human survival.* We are not interested in ecological relationality in terms of Whitehead's mutual immanence in which we have to situate humanity anew by redefining what nature means for humanity and in what way it is part of its mutual environmental relations. Even Muir's "necessity of wildness," which includes the preservation of wilderness devoid of human influence, can be misunderstood as not being for nature's own sake as the fountain of life but, rather, about strategies of restoration, manipulation, or development of the environment so as to allow human persistence in it. This fallacy is *anthropocentric* insofar as its rhetoric of the integrity of nature is really about saving human existence in nature. Conversely, "nature" is not viewed from its own organic integrity in which humanity is relationally "integrated" but from *techniques* of human survival. It is *anthropomorphic* insofar as it presupposes that nature as a whole *conspires* for our survival. In such an anthropocentric condescendence, we "preserve" nature because it *needs* our preservation. Nature is not the necessity of *our* contingency but the contingency in *need* of preparation, preservation, and manipulation.[33]

The spiritual traditions have heavily contributed to this situation of the Anthropic Reversal of necessity and contingency. Again restricting myself to the Western heritage, it seems that the religious and theological discourses interested in ecological issues are still implicitly following the divine supremacy *before* the "ecological death of God" in order to establish the supremacy of their own orthodoxies. They take the environmental crisis as a chance to reintroduce the relevance of one's own religion. With strategies that want to establish that the depth of the theological traditions was *always* "ecological," orthodoxies are still following the Anthropic Reversal by claiming that it is humanity's imperative to "preserve creation." This so-called "stewardship for creation" is, however, less ecological in essence than it is concerned with the survival of humanity. Even in this new context—ecological interrelationality—the argument from "creation" is still executing the old mindset for which nature was reduced to a mere background condition of human existence and salvation. As many traditional texts attest, this nature is not an *integral* part of salvation but only humanity's background in which humans repeat the wipeout of the integral pleroma of interrelationality transforming it into a mere extension, a place to be filled with humanity. We still repeat the guilty Christian heritage of disrespecting the Earth in her own right; we still make her necessity contingent on humanity's destiny; we still "subject" her to humanity's necessity.[34]

The superiority of these "humanisms" was most prominently deconstructed by French poststructuralists since the '20s of the twentieth century—including Barthes, Levi-Strauss, Lacan, Althusser, Serres, Bataille, Kristeva, Foucault, Derrida, Lyotard, Deleuze, Irigaray, Baudrillard, Butler, Spivak, and Žižek.[35] In cascading down the ladder of deconstruction, they superseded the death of God with the "death of the subject" and "humanism"—the first one, because it is a product of power structures, that is, of subjection; the second, because it infects the world with a hidden claim to the superiority of the colonizing West. To be "human" is the *possession* of the one who is able, has the money, power, and means to "subject" the rest of the world: politically, culturally, technically, religiously. Humanism is about orthodoxies of suppression. Its deconstruction has led us a step closer to the composting of the "dead body of God."

However, the *awakening* in the midst of an "ecology of power" in which subjects are always the surface expression of social, cultural, religious power-relations has lead, fairly unexpectedly, to another omnipotence, not of "God" or "subjectivity" but the *omnipotence of power*. For Foucault, power is not unilateral, a means of suppression of the "better ones," but a relational, structural, objective infinity in which humans constitute themselves as humans. Again, as in the economic omnipotence, we end up in a *hermetic interiority of transformation*, not of economic objects, but of objects of power, which itself remains deeply (dialectically) dependent on the rejection of humanism. The problem of the Anthropic Principle is this interiority of omnipotence even in its negation of human subject; it negates the necessity of wildness and empties it into a contingency of human power relations; thereby it deconstructs *nature itself* as an essentialist illusion, as a mirage of a mirage; as a Romantic original that has been lost in all of its infinite reflections—nature as a projection of omnipotent power.[36]

Ecology Deconstructed

Still following the cascade of deconstruction of the ecological death of substantialist omnipotence downward, the appearance of philosophical reflections within the ecological movement was equally problematic. Cases in point are deep ecology and ecofeminism.[37] While ecofeminism succeeded in deconstructing the Anthropic Fallacy as an *androcentric* superiority, it is in danger of "identifying" the suppressed female with suppressed nature—suffering at the hand of unilateral, Western, male powers—such that it not only countersubstantializes the suppressed but remains within the old concept of unilateral power, overcome by poststructuralism. Its resonance with the Gaia project—first proposed by James Lovelock—which has relativized our Anthropic Condescendence in putting emphasis on the inherent integrity of the Earth as a living being in its own right,[38] unfortunately also seals our complicity with "nature" as an integrity that must be "preserved" for human survival.[39]

Deep ecology also appears as the recognition of an internal form of the self-value of nature not only in its individuals as entities of life but even more in more complex living unities such as species and ecosystems.[40] It overcomes the Anthropic Fallacy by integrating humanity within nature but, at the same time, remains complicit to it by its use of "subjectivity."

Arne Naess views ecological consciousness as a process of the widening of Self in which we overcome the egoism of human individualism in a process of identification with wider contexts: humanity, other species, ecosystems, and, finally with the whole ecosphere. But its compassionate altruism remains egoism: It becomes a new *omnipotent interiority of an infinite Self*. Despite this identification, deep ecology becomes a counterhumanism that is geared not toward the *integration* of humanity into nature but toward a *legal battle* of "natural entities" over against humanity. As Arne Naess's "deep ecology platform"[41] formulates an *equality of the right of survival* among any species, this approach shifts the discourse again into the realm of substantialism: Humanity and any other species now appear as equal subjects of "natural rights" in a fight of survival over against another.[42]

As both approaches imply a substantialism of viewing ecosystems as "subjects"—nature, Earth, species, ecosystems—they, in fact, only repeat the substantialism that *defines identities against one another:* not as relationships but in categories of war; not as mutual immanence but in terms of legal victory; not as diversity in inherent connectivity but as liberation of suppressed entities that are understood as *hermetic units.* In fact, this substantialism of the "identification" of legal, moral, or ontological unities of worth and action has pervaded ecological discourse proper and environmental ethics for a long time. While the "individualistic" approach just reduplicated the anthropomorphic reduction of humanity to individuals in viewing nature as an accumulation of individuals to be preserved, the holistic extended this individualistic view to groups of individuals like species or ecosystems as relationality between individuals. Even in the form of the acceptance of emergent features of ecosystems over against individuals, such an approach remains bound by its substantialism of *properties* that are seen as principles or aims of ecological action: Integration, balance, harmony, diversity, wholeness, and health become expressions of the new hermetic unity of ecological identification and action.

In an Anthropic Transfer, such holistic features of ecosystems widen human categories of value, integrity, stability, self-realization, and health to ecosystems as a form of universal "egology" expanded to the world as the body of such substantial properties. Nevertheless, they all remain problematic in their very substantialist independence. Integrity becomes static if we think of it as an a priori identity of any given ecosystem; it ignores interrelationality within and beyond itself and the fact that it is always in its own flux of identity. Integrity is always ecologically surprised by novelty in the system such that the new system will find a new integrity that cannot recast the old identity and, hence, also has no internal value to be "preserved." There is no wholeness to an ecosystem as its aim (fixed identity or

Idea) that can be used as a criterion of ecological action; it always changes in mutual interaction from diversity within and without.[43]

The same is true for more dynamic properties suspected to define ecosystems as an ecological action, like self-realization, diversity, or complexity. Like stability, which would motivate us to "preserve" a certain "state" as exceptional, natural, or most whole, self-realization predefines a given substance of Self to be realized and not to be disturbed by human existence. This is not Muir's fountain of life in preserved wildness—which is only a symbol of *our* contingency—but a call for the independence of such Selves in ecosystems by a projected human notion of Self-identity with its predominantly Cartesian necessity. Diversity and complexity, on the other hand, have been contested as aims because their *use* implicated the contention that if we let a system become complex enough, it will result in a certain "natural" stability of that system like a nascent Aristotelian substance that is still in the process of becoming constituted as *what* it is (if you do not hinder a seed from growing it will become a tree). Although this teleology is not about a *state* of things but is open to a *process* that we "preserve" and from which we withhold intervention that would disturb it or intervene to get it flowing again, its aim is still such a state of balance. This is the final deconstruction of the Anthropic Principle inscribed in nature: that there is no fixed, final, or ideal measure; and no such balance of states, processes, and identities.[44]

Eco-nature

Have we reached the bottom of the ecological cascade down from substantialism yet? And where do we go from here? The first question relates to the deconstruction of world-conquering omnipotence of modes of wholeness, oneness, substantiality, subjectivity, and power infliction that structures our conceptual framework and our experience in such a way that it eliminates any *outside*—as if the rocket is everything that exists and its propagation is just a matter of an *internal* transformation of a hermetic whole so that neither the acquisition of transformative energy nor the space in which it happens matter and that the propagation only leaves a wasteland behind that is not of its concern as are the wasted spaces the rocket transverses. The second question names a different *kind* of aim that we might have for such processes of transformation: nonsubstantial, nonstatic, nonwholistic (all-inclusive), nonomnipotent.

I will answer both questions with a yes if we mean that such a new approach to nature that is beyond the Anthropic Fallacy is *eco-natural* insofar as it pertains to the necessity of wildness and human contingency, and beyond that *the mutual contingency of everything within eco-nature* such that there is no overarching aim, criterion, or final state except their mutual immanence.

If we begin with mutual immanence, as suggested earlier in Whitehead,[45] the limitations of omnipotence we can discover are threefold: First, the approach to eco-nature is such that we always find a *multiplicity* of becomings that are neither reducible to one another nor to any one pre-given origin or final state, and hence, to any kind of state at all. Second, nothing in eco-nature is isolated or, conversely, everything is in a mutual process of *becoming* that is as much unification as it is diversification; simplification and complexification, reduction and unfolding—always both at the same time. Third, no synthesis, element, moment, property, feature, concept, or character is absolute in the sense of being complete; rather everything we discover about the process of mutual becoming of multiplicities is a relationality that is always *incomplete* so that no conceptuality can ever be closed because of perfection. We can restate these three criteria as: *the irreducible multiplicity of becoming in a process of mutual reciprocity, determination, and incompleteness.* The ideal of eco-nature is infinite becoming without any fixed measures of relationality, criteria for aims, and presupposed directions of harmony.[46]

Whitehead's vision of eco-nature is that of its "perfect incompleteness," that is, "complete" immanence in its becoming in which it never does become encompassing or complete but demonstrates a "necessity in universality" that is that of "relationality"[47] beyond which there is no relationality that is not already part of the openness of relational becoming toward novelty. In the framework of Gilles Deleuze's "transcendental empiricism," this formulates the conditions of a world in which novelty is possible such that the universal incompleteness of relationality is also its *rationality,* the measure by which we can understand eco-nature.[48]

While William James in his *Pluralistic Universe* had already stated that the universe is plural in such a way that any unification is always a simplification of its multiplicity in which, hence, something always escapes,[49] Whitehead, in reading James, was maybe one of the first philosophers to create an ecophilosophy of the entanglement of eco-relations and eco-events, eco-systems and eco-chaos in the mutual oscillation between organisms and environments. His "organic philosophy"[50] proposes that all relations are in becoming, in the rhythms of repetition and differentiation such that they create events of novelty and structures of repetition as they vibrate within and between processes of synthesis and deconstruction like swarms or clouds of mutually compromising complexities.[51] In always creating and recreating multiplicities on multiplicities, such processes condensate to social structures with reparative and competitive characters of survival and pleasure of organism within ever wider fields of environments *in which* they become what they are and *in which* they define their rules of ascension, existence, and fading as much as they define the processes of their environments to which they are always related in complex ways.[52]

Eco-nature, for Whitehead, is a vast interrelated multiplicity of entangled organisms and environments such that every organism is an environment for other organisms that, in its own turn, is enveloped by environments, which are themselves organisms in other environments. As all of these organisms are *not* related to one another as layers of an onion but rather in always immediately cutting through all layers, having all layers *inherent* to one another, all organisms and environments influence their mutual becoming. Insofar, however, as these organisms and environments also do not form one superorganism in which everything is balancing itself out so as to create a superstructure or supersymmetry, these organisms and environment are *externally limiting* each other as a matter of mutual enrichment by the always surprisingly unexpected other and, with equal importance, by struggling against each other for survival, attention, and satisfaction of life. The basic "relation" in Whitehead's eco-nature is neither mutually external nor mutually internal but *prehensive,* that is, reenactive and creative of its relata—in other words: Eco-nature is a process of always new configurations of multiplicities of becoming as transformation of divergences into contrasts of novelty.[53] This is the driving appetite of eco-nature: its creativeness as processes of intensification of contrast and harmonization of contrast of contrasts, infinitely recreating each other.

Beyond the Anthropic Principle, this eco-cosmos is, as Deleuze says about Whitehead's eco-nature, a *chaosmos*[54] that is not defined by any substantiality as sublimation or derivation of human proportions for measuring everything. In the ever-*disbalanced becoming* of new constellations of multiplicities of incomplete organisms and environments, humanity is interwoven as a product of serendipitous processes of precisely such constellations of the creative disequilibrium of intensity and harmony but also unhappy constellations of disintegration and chaos that together *are* eco-nature.[55] To this eco-process humanity is neither an exception nor a peak; neither an isolated entity with unique rights nor unworthy to exist. Within the necessity of the wildness of eco-chaosmos, humanity is but a contingency: a serendipitous event of intersecting environments without necessity or exception from chaosmic rhythms of becoming and fading.[56]

Becoming Animal

While deconstructing the Anthropic Exception of humanity in its relational embededness in eco-nature, we still need to address the experience of nature within us as subjects of experience of such nature. The question is: Do we, indeed, experience eco-nature and, if so, how do we understand the emergence of the Anthropic Principle? While any classical anthropology has differentiated humanity either by its capacity to think, reflect, and understand or by its subjective inwardness, its ability to differentiate itself consciously from nature—the binaries of mind and body, form and matter, master and slave are attesting to this fact—the poststructuralist deconstruction of these binaries, however, has left us with a disappearance of nature into our cultural games of omnipotent power.[57] How do we account for eco-nature in our experience as human beings, and how can we overcome the binaries such that we do not diffuse eco-nature in the fiction of a new omnipotent "subjection" to power in which humanity becomes absolute again?

Deleuze has proposed this question in the form of his provocative imperative that we must become animals again. Becoming animals, however, does not mean to literally revoke human existence as *animal rationale* (Aristotle) or the animal that knows death (Heidegger) in order to become *indistinguishably united* with nature—this would contradict the mutual incompleteness of multiplicities in eco-nature. Rather a "becoming-animal always involves a pack, a band, a population, a peopling, in short, a multiplicity"[58] that overcomes the dualistic differentiation between *res cogitans,* which is always distinctly human, and *res extensa,* which is always erasing our chaosmic, organic, and environmental heritage, such that this ecotransfer can no longer be demonized as a diabolic state of perversion—as some, especially Western, orthodoxies suggest. Becoming wolf, becoming whale, becoming multiplicities!

I will mention three aspects of what Whitehead calls the mutual "pollution"[59] of mind and body in becoming multiplicities/animals again. First, it is an appeal to a diffusion of the symbolic stasis of differences between humanity and nature in the form of recognizing our internal *presymbolic multiplicity* that always supersedes our well-defined identities.[60] Julia Kristeva has argued that our human difference from nature is the product of our birth into a world in which we seek through symbolic acts of longing, language, and stabilization to actually find our prenatal state again. Expelled from its presymbolic, bodily, material cycles of being multiple, we always substitute the impossibility to reverse this process with differentiations from it that cope with existential feelings of abjection: becoming subject, becoming substance, becoming omnipotent. She suggests that we will only overcome this move toward subjection and substantiation when we allow for the porosity in these processes of absolutism, if we grant ourselves an absolution for being abjected from the presymbolic realm of chaosmic multiplicity and invite it in in the form of *poetic inconstancy* in its material indirectivity.[61] In the *poetic break of continuity* that *excludes* this Platonic *khora* of mutual immanence and incompleteness, we will get a taste (*aesthesis*) of multiplicity beyond and before human identity.

Second, Whitehead addresses the same problem of exclusion from and of multiplicity in terms of our projective epistemologies in which, since Aristotle and with Kant, we have *closed* the human mind *off* from the pollution of the eco-chaosmos and isolated it from eco-nature with the help of its omnipotent thought-figure found in the divine realm of Ideas and Being. In breaking through such immunization tactics of omnipotence, Whitehead suggests that such isolation is an *emergent* in the evolutionary process for reasons of survival, orientation, and directionality of organisms. However, it becomes toxic when it closes itself from its primary inclusion within a realm of feelings of the multiplicity of nature in us such that it actualizes ourselves within eco-nature always before, within, beyond, and across any constitution of subjectivity, intellectuality, and superiority. In criticizing this binary isolation from multiplicity, Whitehead suggests, as Derrida would later, that we need to reconnect with the enveloping nature *beyond* all of our endeavors to constitute independent "presentational immediacy" (isolating self-presence) within ourselves, in which we become "one" *over against* eco-nature (as multiplicity in despair), elevating ourselves to the controlling kings of our desires and the eco-chaosmos.[62] It is precisely releasing this *feeling of connectivity* that leaves "us a prey to vague terrors respecting a circumambient world of causal operations," where we *become multiplicity,* finding "ourselves in a buzzing world, amid a democracy of fellow creatures."[63]

> In the dark there are vague presences, doubtfully feared; in the silence, the irresistible causal efficacy of nature presses itself upon us; in the vagueness of the low hum of insects in an August woodland, the inflow into ourselves of feelings from enveloping nature overwhelms us; in the dim consciousness of half-sleep, the presentations of sense fade away, and we are left with the vague feeling of influences from vague things around us.[64]

Third, Georges Bataille in his *Theory of Religion* develops the intense suggestion that our whole human world is an excess of the inability to reenter the animal realm in which we were and now feel, in painful absence, to have been "like water in water,"[65] that is, in an *intimacy* that is permanently lost. Instead, the human world became one of the divisions of subjects and objects in the search for meaning, although all we find are devoid of aims that are only means again. This creates our world of wars and empires as it creates religions in the place of meaning with subjectivity inscribed to objects, spirits, and gods. Meaning, which resides only in the directionless intimacy of animality, can only be returned to if we *consciously,* that is, *through* our human difference, revoke the difference of subject and object and allow ourselves to be part of the animal kingdom in the depth within us as a multiplicity of becoming: not as the "romantic object" of a para-dise—this is for him the "Poetic Fallacy of Animality"[66]—but in all of its variety of mutual immanence and the monstrosity of mutual devouring.

The Theopoetic Difference

Eco-nature in us, bursting us inside out, and eco-nature between us, im-ploding the chaosmic All within us—this is the unconquerable wildness, the necessity of which makes us its happenings, disowned of our "necessi-ties" of possession.[67] This consummation of humanity in the dispossession within eco-nature is for Bataille, after the ecological death of God, the *mystical* move of becoming-animal, becoming multiplicity.[68] This *unio mystica,* however, if it is not the unification with the omnipotent God that has to have died first in this eco-chaosmic death of substantialism, is also *not* a new indifference of the Oneness of humanity and nature but the consum-mation of all unity into the ream of multiplicity that, as Luce Irigaray puts it, is divine precisely by *not being One.*[69] It is the *khoric* realm of a paradox where we have to go through divergences, bifurcations, and antinomies *all at once;* in which we become empty and the All *at the same time* by being, as Deleuze puts it, One-All *with* multiplicity,[70] infinitely moving through ever-new multiplicities of mutual immanence and limitation, planes of immanence and consistency in constant refigurations within an infinite chaosmos of transformation.[71]

This is the realm of *poetics,* of the rupture of the continuity of unifica-tion where, as for Kristeva, meaning is indirected.[72] This is the poetics of the unprecedented in which, as Whitehead puts it, "philosophy is mysti-cal. For mysticism is direct insight into depths as yet unspoken."[73] Where the Romanticism of Bataille's Poetic Fallacy is avoided by recognizing the monstrosity of becoming—in which everything, as Deleuze says, reappears "like a single and unique 'total' moment, simultaneously the moment of evanescence and production of difference, of disappearance and appearance," "the moment at which difference both vanishes and is produced."[74] In this mystical in/difference, everything is only *in* difference.[75] Its poetics *cannot differentiate* God as cosmological function anymore. God and the world become "one" in being not differentiated *by any property* that would be *reserved* to God.[76] As Whitehead says, in *this* in/difference

> It is as true to say that God is permanent and the World fluent, as that the World is permanent and God is fluent.
>
> It is as true to say that God is one and the World many, as that the World is one and God many . . .
>
> It is as true to say that God creates the World, as that the World creates God.[77]

If, however, in this *khoric* realm God and the world are in/different as in the mystics, that is, if their difference cannot be crafted around any difference of property, why then not say that God *is* the world?[78] To be sure, many philosophers would follow such a line of thought—pantheism as last resort of divine apophasis in the world.[79] Deleuze became a Spinozist and many theologians today feel themselves to be ecstatic naturalists or mystical nihilists.[80] But if, for many, eco-nature leaves a mystery of luminescent darkness—as for Nicolas of Cusa—that cannot be reduced to *unity;* we need still to differentiate between enfolding (*complicatio*), which Cusa named "God," and unfolding (*explicatio*), which Cusa named the infinite "world" of multiplicity.[81] We will be speaking of the multiplicities of God and the world in their mutual immanence, limitation, resonance, incompleteness, and determination. We will, with Whitehead, avoid the "identification" of God and world over against another not by naming reserved properties but instead naming God and the world as *multiplicities in mutual in/difference,*[82] that is, only as *mutual embodiment.*[83] This divine (in) multiplicity will insist *on* multiplicity and only "*ex*-sist" by "*in*-sisting" *in* multiplicity.[84]

You may wonder how we got here. What does this have to do with eco-nature? I shall answer: everything! My answer follows the reasoning of the employed logic of multiplicity, namely, that in mutual immanence nothing can become complete or omnipotent, not even multiplicity.[85] If eco-nature is nothing but the mutual immanence of all becoming relationality, externally and internally, in beauty and in monstrosity, in war and peace, we need to break open once again the creeping substantialism of such a statement by differentiating the *poetry* of breaking open the chaosmos of the creative multiplicity from its closure of omnipotence. Per se, eco-nature now appears to be a universality of relationality in a twofold danger of closure: that of a liberated multiplicity that is given back its own powers of becoming and that of the monstrous multiplicity that is haunted by the clash of its own powers—because both closures live (again) from the *omnipotence of power.*

This is the reason for a *theo*poetics within the immanence of multiplicities: that, as Whitehead says, God is not identical with "creativity"—Whitehead's "ultimate" that is the *posse ipsum* that empowers the becoming of multiplicities in the fulfillment to all of their different powers and that also created the monstrosities of power against power.[86] If power is not absolute, either in the form of Foucault's power of subjection or in the form of Deleuze's (and Nietzsche's) power of becoming multiplicity, the *divine multiplicity is not identical with power.*[87] I understand Whitehead's theopoetic difference between God and creative/destructive powers as that of power and love. It is the love of multiplicity—polyphilia![88] It is the love that cannot be addressed in terms of power. It is the *subtractive affirmation* of multiplicity that hinders its closure into power.[89] *This* love is, as Whitehead says, a "reciprocal relation, [in which] the love in the world passes into the love in heaven, and floods back again into the world" so that "God is the great companion [of multiplicity]—the fellow-sufferer who understands."[90] In its reciprocity, it is the *ecotheosis*[91] of multiplicity, the mutual metabolism of the divine companionship with the chaosmos, and the *mutuality of compassion* in the midst of the powers of multiplicity, the luminescence of dispossession and nonviolence in the midst of the wars of mutual digestion.

The Wasp and the Orchid

The insight into an eco-theopoetics[92] of eco-nature after the Anthropic Principle is twofold: It is the recognition of the necessity of its wildness and our contingency in the mutual contingency of multiplicities in multiplicities; and it is the differentiation of polyphilia from power in a commitment to compassion. The first one activates us within eco-nature with eco*consciousness;*[93] the second activates us within eco-nature with ecological *conscience.*

Gilles Deleuze has conceptualized such an ecoconsciousness with the poetic of the wasp and the orchid. Both organisms follow their own paths of generation and regeneration within their respective environments without having anything in common, *except* that they share the same environment in order to follow their ecorhythms. They are not developing in their *own* stratum of a shared environment, in a parallelism of possession of substantial identity, so to say, but entirely differently: "a becoming-wasp of the orchid and a becoming-orchid of the wasp." It is an "*aparallel evolution*"[94] of entangled multiplicities without internal recognition. This is the *external* side of eco-nature, the entanglement of mutual differentiation that copies itself *only* by enacting the other, by "preserving" the other's multiplicity in its own wildness. This preservation, however, is not that of a patient that is in need, but of a cross-pollution of each other's cycles. Its enactment in human action will not lead to any aims defined for the whole of the ecoprocess but arouses a desire for differentiation and complication of different multiplicities in their mutual touch. Their mutual immanence does not reveal the *logos* of a divine plan in its preestablished harmony, but an *eros* of touch, of intercourse, of mingling without a common direction, in fact, with a divergence of directions, with an indirection of consummation that is never One.[95]

Aparallel evolution is not necessarily calm—it is wild in the sense that it can lead to a mutual occupation of the space of the others' metabolism. Viruses and bacteria use host organisms for their own generation and regeneration by virtually destroying the very environment of their proliferation. Pandemics are not only a phenomenon of human beings; they have created strange intersections and interferences between organisms as they have become a mutual environment for the respectively other. Such hostile relations are not unnatural or counter to the mutual immanence of relationships but rather show the power character of such relationships that are neutral as to their moral implications, which are usually projected by human beings and their ethical impulses.[96] An organism in its environment might function as its very nemesis insofar as an environment becomes hostile to an embedded organism without breaking the rules of external connectivity that grants mutual touch. Counterreactions of organisms in their use as environments for the becoming of other organisms as well as counterreactions of environments against destroying organisms are to be expected and are, in fact, widespread. Hence, the disturbances of any temporal organization of organisms and their environments into ecosystems is not the destruction of the value of ecological equilibrium but a *necessity of the mutual contingency* of all ecosystems in eco-nature—its wildness in constant change. The touch of ecoconnectivity is *eros* and *thanatos*.[97]

Ecoconscience, on the other hand, will address the *internal* relationship of eco-nature in its wild ecoconnectivity—as that of mixtures of war and peace—for a post-anthropic human self-understanding and activation *within* ecoconnectivity. In other words, we ask for the *transhuman* measure for a new eco-anthropic *intention* to live and act within the ecoconstellations of intensity and harmony so as to always lead to their maximal unfolding.[98] In light of the previous discussion of multiplicities, any intended *influence* of aparallel evolution in a posthuman or ecohuman sense regarding such a transhuman, postanthropic measure will be a countermovement of liberation of eco-multiplicity from substantialism and an infusion of human life within eco-nature such that its necessary disbalancing (its wildness) will foster our constitutional contingency within its wildness either by *unfolding* its polyphonic powers *or* by *limiting* these polyphonic powers by polyphilic love.[99]

Deleuze has taken the first route in grounding the valuation of the differentiation of multiplicity that always avoids a transcendent One in the very *affirmation of the All of potentials* (virtuals) of limited multiplicities in the eco-chaosmos in which its dimensions come into their own power.[100] Its ethical measure is accompanied by the avoidance of extremes in order to allow for the multiplicity in its very connectivity to organize itself regarding a polyphony of its internal and intermediate powers with other interfering multiplicities *and* by inherently including even the faintest potentials (virtuals) in the calculus, not just the overpowering potentials so as to avoid their occupying and colonizing tendencies.[101] Although such an ethical impulse will seek to unfold the "creative" powers of ecoconnectivity in their mutual beneficial or destructive determination toward a *maximum* of intensity and polyphony, it also inherently seeks to unfold the *minimum* intensities; in other words, it seeks the least, the powerless, the forgotten, the suppressed.

Whitehead follows the second path by refusing to accept the omnipotence of powers even in the form of the powers of multiplicities in their liberation from forced unifications in which they always would give up their polyphony for a forced harmony, a prestabilized harmony, or a preordained measure of harmonization.[102] Whitehead's transhuman, postanthropic measure of intensity and harmony is the *subtractive affirmation of chaosmic polyphony*—a *love* of multiplicity—that is not built on power but on its mutual limitation by, immanence in, and determination through *theo*plicity—*divine* multiplicity—that is *the transformation of relationality into compassion* and, beyond any fixed measure of intensity and harmony, of the *disequilibrium of powers toward ecotheosis* in the midst of *the potential (virtual) violence* of multiplicities. A theopoetics to this effect, I name *eco-theopoetics* after (post) the Anthropic Principle.[103]

It will not only be compassionate to the minimum of enfolded powerlessness in the midst of the polyphony of powers but also open to everything between the minimum of enfolding and the maximum of unfolding *beyond* power. This "novelty" cannot be grasped in terms of "creativity" but may be faintly approximated with a *divine poetics of salvation of multiplicities from the potential (virtual) omnipotence of their own powers.*[104] It is this divine *poiesis* that Whitehead says does *not* create—as power—but saves in compassion.[105] An ecoethics under the auspices of the eco-theopoetics of polyphilia will be the "creation" of the transhuman, post-anthropic world *from* this sense of peace in the midst of the constructive and destructive power of creativeness. Mediated by this sense, eco-human life must become *nonviolent in the midst of power.* In other words, it must become intermezzo in eco-nature.

Becoming Intermezzo

Ecoconsciousness and ecoconscience have an ethical and a spiritual dimension. Both can be characterized as "always beginning in the middle."[106] Deleuze formulates this new categoreal imperative of ecoethics as letting "your loves be like the wasp and the orchid" and, without beginning and end, as being "always in the middle, between things, interbeing, *intermezzo.*" To begin in the middle always means to follow multiplicities in their deconstructive complexity within and without, to unsettle the boundaries and clear borders of forced identities, which are always imposed measures of the One with its power-installed abstractions of unification and division. To begin in the middle is an ethical category that activates us *from* the middle of the happening of multiplicities and asks us to always *submerge* into their middle, the many folds of connectivity within and beyond, which always form *under the skin* of powers of unification and division and only come to life within, across and beyond the boundaries of power. To become interbeing, we need to leave the high states of unity to become actors of the folds *within* unties *between* their moments of unifications, and *between* unities *in the middle* of their artificial isolation. To become "in between" means to become intermezzo, that is, *less* than the abstract unifications that always feed the Anthropic Imperialism over nature, culture, and (human) Self. It means to become *minor.*[107]

To become minor does not mean to reduce to lower unities; it does not mean to atomize reality. It rather means to become *uncountable* in terms of units, to become intermezzo within and between all abstractions like Self, Culture, Nature, to undercut "identity" with diverging dimensionality—like a river, a rhizome, *a* life.[108] It is this access to becoming *within* and *between* culture, nature, and us in which we lose the Anthropic substantialism and, at the same time, become "events between" and a multiplicity of such events. However, in becoming a minority we become universal in a new sense: by becoming *ecologically connected* beyond any *structural integrity.*[109] We become *subversively distributed* among all unifications. For Whitehead, this is the eco-ethical imperative of becoming multiplicities: In the "self-correction by consciousness of its own initial excess of subjectivity" it is the task of ecophilosophy (organic philosophy) to deconstruct subjectivity's "selective character" in which "the individual obscures the external totality from which it originates and which it embodies" in order "to recover the totality obscured by the selection."[110]

For a post-anthropic ecoethics, this impulse of becoming minor implies a redirection of ecological action: With Deleuze, we have to become "molecular" not "molar"—not seeking higher or lower unifications.[111] Hence, an ecoethical imperative cannot be built on slogans such as the "preservation" of states—since their presupposed unity and identity is a mere abstraction from their becoming; or on the "reparation" of an ecological equilibrium—because it is an abstraction of a certain state of nature as ideal (especially for human survival); or on "ecojustice"—because it presupposes fixed identities with legal responsibilities; not even on "sustainability"—insofar as it might already presuppose sustenance like substances. Instead, post-anthropic ecoethics will direct us toward the compassionate life with the *multiplicities within and between*.

Post-anthropic ethics is a procedure for the emergence of "tragic beauty"[112] in which humanity falls in place, the place of *khora*, the medium of intercommunication that, if it is perused as compassion, always leads beyond any "state" and "desire" into a depth of *love of multiplicity* as such—*the* "in between" of the wildness of eco-nature and, perhaps, its divine intermezzo.[113] The emphasis on "wildness" does not seek "nature" over against "culture" as the "other" of culture that must be preserved. It is not presupposing any identity of nature *or* culture; it is in between; it is this in between as necessity in which we realize ecoconnectivity as constitutional contingency.

Mutual Suspension

In their eco*spiritual* dimension, wisdom traditions must be read from the standpoint of their ability of becoming molecular, becoming animal, becoming minor, becoming intermezzo in order to release the molar identities into their molecular connections, the subversive interaction within and between them. The new spiritual measure for religious multiplicity, beyond religious identity and plurality alike, leads *into* the differentiations of eco-nature between abstractions of self, culture, and nature and, hence, into the multiplicities within and between religions, which consciously (or, more often, in a suppressed way) *live from* their mutual incompleteness, reciprocity, determination, and becoming.

Whitehead's differentiation of the world of wisdom traditions in *Religion in the Making* is an interesting staring point. For Whitehead, three traditions have reached logocentric universality and, hence, Anthropic omnipotence as well as an obvious mutual limitation, namely, Christianity, Buddhism, and science.[114] Since these traditions are universal insofar as they give universal answers to cosmological questions,[115] they will allow us to rediscover the "totality obscured by the selection"[116] they made by imprinting their "identity" onto eco-nature, that is, the spiritual interbeing of humanity with eco-nature.

First, there is the odd dynamic of the mutual limitation of science and religion in which science has become the new "theology" of the cosmos and a medium of their cosmic, post-anthropic spirituality: eternal inflation, multiverse, quantum entanglement, chance and necessity, emergence, evolution—they cannot be ignored by religions.[117] While its very spiritual impulse is always transcending its methods, it does not overflow into an indeterminate realm of the spirit but is already awaited by wisdom traditions such as Christianity and Buddhism. Second, there is the mutual limitation of Buddhism and Christianity in their cultural diversity in which they contextualized themselves as modes of living that we abstractly meet with the typology of the East and the West. In establishing their counteridentities, their classical opposition appears in the mutual feeling of superiority regarding their respective entertainment of a personal and impersonal understanding of ultimate reality. But interfusion in dialogues and transformations alike has unearthed a mutual incompleteness within and between these traditions in their mutual mystical approximation.[118]

Third, there is the mutual limitation of all three traditions in relation to an avoidance of their omnipotence. In fact, there are the many other wisdom traditions, which are not forgotten but only obscured by the substantiation of these three. Then we can ask: Which Christianity (there is only a multiplicity)? Which Buddhism (there is only a multiplicity)? Which science (there is only a multiplicity)? Then, we can begin to see all of these obscured *molecular* connections within and between their molar unities and the wisdom traditions oppressed by their universal claims. This is the realm of eco-spirituality and its multiplicity of eco-theopoetics.

In such an eco-spirituality, many positions of ecoconnectivity can be taken within and between wisdom traditions; but all of them will want to begin in the *middle* of the ecoconnectivity as interbeing, as medium of intercommunication: *khora,* the Godhead, *pratitya-samutpada,* quantum nothingness, the enfolded multiverse, inter-carnation, *ecotheosis.* The ultimacy of such a mystery will appear as *natura naturans,* as creativity, as wonder of existence, as nothingness, as divine multiplicity. In the emptiness of becoming intermezzo, we might find its characters as wisdom and compassion: as overflow of *sunyata,* as persons of the infinite sea of the divine, as modes of creativity—Whitehead's eco-metabolism between the embodiment of God in the world and the embodiment of the world in God.[119] But, always, ultimacy will be bound back into a *mutual suspension* of their claims—redirecting us back *into the middle of becoming intermezzo.*[120]

If there is a place for eco-*theo*poetics, that is, for naming the divine in eco-nature, it will be that of polyphilia, the interval *between* power. After the ecological death of omnipotence, the divine will show its ecological traces only as divine (in) multiplicity, as being in the middle of the multiplicity of power—as love in its many folds: as *eros, philia, agape;* as *shakti* and *bhakti.* Maybe this is best addressed by the Lotus Sutra: While ultimacy of becoming intermezzo will harbor *skillful means* of the mutual suspension of ultimacy in which we become in between, a trace of the divine may be much like the appearance of *Indra/Śakti* in the midst of the infinite number of Buddhas and bodhisattvas of the infinite universes—divine but limited; in between Earth and *sunyata,* a place and a multiplicity (of mortal *devas*).[121] If *the divine (in) multiplicity* is the symbol for such mutual suspension, we might, in following its traces, become inspired by the desire to become intermezzo in the necessity of the wildness of eco-nature.

After-Word

Silence, Theopoetics, and Theologos
On the Word That Comes After

JOHN THATAMANIL

> In my *Symbolic Theology* I have discussed analogies of God drawn from what we perceive. I have spoken of the images we have of him, of the forms, figures, and instruments proper to him, of the places in which he lives and of the ornaments he wears. I have spoken of his anger, grief, and rage, of how he is said to be drunk and hungover . . . and indeed of all those images we have of him, images shaped by the workings of the symbolic representations of God. And I feel sure that you have noticed how these latter come much more abundantly than what went before, since *The Theological Representations* and a discussion of the names appropriate to God are inevitably briefer than what can be said in *The Symbolic Theology*.
>
> **—Pseudo-Dionysius, "The Mystical Theology"**

When I was a young seminarian, my first encounter with Alfred North Whitehead proved to be jarring—and not (just) because of the daunting complexity of his vision and writing. When I first read Whitehead's assertion "God is an actual entity,"[1] my reaction was one of stark aversion. My first thought was, "You cannot say that!" What prompted this allergic response? My best guess is that I found Whitehead's discourse out of keeping with the texture of theological speech I imbibed while growing up within the high liturgical milieu of the Mar Thoma Church. This Whiteheadian dictum seemed alien to the language of prayer and praise and so problematic and impermissible.

Even now I remain unsure about how best to articulate the reasons for my initial and intense (but now diminished) antipathy. As my protest was not prompted by what was then only a nascent ground of being theology, my guess is that I must have been convinced that Whitehead had made a category mistake of some kind or violated some principle of theological speech that I did not then know how to articulate. Perhaps I was persuaded that to speak of God as an "actual entity" was to violate the mystery of God, to know too much about the inner life of divinity, and say too much, or to say the wrong sort of thing.

In a theological idiom that was then only becoming available to me, I could not see how a theological apophasis was possible within a process frame. And a theology without mystery was not a theology worth having. Whitehead, at times, seemed to be a diagnostician of God's interior life. I could not then have put it this way, but my reaction was likely prompted by the following conviction: No philosophical discourse about God can be plausible if it seeks to undo or overcome the mystery of the divine life. Hence, all theological speech must emerge from and tarry in the shadowy fringes of the cloud of unknowing. Theological speech must be enshrouded by that silence from which it is born and into which it returns when confounded by depths it cannot plumb.

The questions that this book explores so subtly have brought back to mind that early moment in my theological formation because the authors are in rich and multifarious ways trying to probe the relationship between discourse in the theopoetic and theological registers. Over the last two decades, much has changed in the process-theological imagination, and a new appreciation for the darkness in which God dwells infuses the writings of many who follow in the wake of Whitehead. The reasons for this tantalizing turn are multiple, some internal to the unfolding logic of process reflection and some generated by encounters between process thought and other philosophical and theological movements.

A primary philosophical encounter that determines much of the work in this volume has been the meeting between process reflection and the poststructuralist tradition. This confluence of reflective traditions has felicitously served to introduce a new metaphysical humility as well as a linguistic creativity to process theology's God-talk. A certain theological modesty generated by an encounter with *différance* has birthed in many process theologians and fellow travelers a deeper appreciation for the theopoetic, an intuition that God-talk can best revere divine mystery by attention to evocation rather than by conceptual description (alone).

But the theopoetic turn has other sources, provocations, and meanings. A second source for the theopoetic turn is internal to developments within the process tradition. Several process thinkers have sought to reclaim for theology Whitehead's category of creativity, thereby generating a pluriform divinity that is more than an actual entity. The God who lures and listens is not erased or undone by attention to creativity. Rather, divinity acquires new depths that can hardly be sounded by the descriptive designations of a flatter discourse that takes the propositional form, "God is x" wherein x is a univocal term that can be securely grasped by mind and language. One needs a *poiesis* to plumb the unfathomable depths of divine creativity.

An especially direct provocation to theopoetics is the encounter between process thinkers and the mystical tradition, most specifically the apophatic stream of that great lineage. A fascination with Nicholas of Cusa is especially prominent in the work of Roland Faber and Catherine Keller. Keller, in particular, suggests the theopoetic turn holds great promise precisely because it has the power to lead process reflection into a deeper and felicitous kinship with apophatic theology.

A final motivation fueling the theopoetic turn is the process encounter with religious diversity. The encounter with religious diversity liberates theological imagination from the confines of Christian *mythos* alone. The promise of this encounter with religious diversity for theopoetics is noted herein in the work of Matthew LoPresti and enacted in Robert Mesle's moving and evocative description of his encounter with Brahman in the face of his grandson Elliot. Readers can see that the Whiteheadian religious imagination is enriched by this nondualist naturalism, one that is prepared to say, "Whatever is, is Brahman, including you and me, and any God or Gods there may be. The traditions of India teach us that if we all understood fully our interrelatedness in Brahman, the world would be a better place for children and other living creatures." I agree. Elliot Matters.

It is worth noting here that the intention of this volume is not to appeal theopoetics solely in order to speak of God as poet who lures and so moves the world into its own emergent loveliness but rather to speak of the world itself or rather all occasions within it as sites of creative becoming. But the creative becoming of the world is intrinsically rich with texture and quality, as Halewood's chapter insists. There is an integral world in which feeling and color dwell; they are not superimposed upon a bare world of data points by the "mind of man." What then must be the shape of a discourse that refuses "to separate the quality from the facticity, the adjectives from the nouns, the colors from the things?" What language other than poetry suffices not merely to describe but to receive and in the very act of reception augment and enrich the world's unfolding of which we are constitutively a part rather than its alienated spectators? The textured novelty of the world, whether that novelty is given with every arising actual occasion or in the exceptionally rare event—as Phelps indicates is the case for Badiou—requires a linguistic register that is richer than ordinary discursive speech. We need theopoetics not just to sing praises of the divine but also to sing the world's beauty.

The combined force of these provocations toward theopoetics suggests that theological speech must not be confined to the conceptual register alone nor should it fall too soon into silence and unknowing despite its reverence for the divine darkness. It must also be marked by an appropriate prolixity lest any narrow repertoire of images come to seem normative and final on account of repetition, inertia, and lack of imagination. Even Pseudo-Dionysius, who stands very near the fount of Christian apophatic theology, commends both silence and speech, and speech in riotous excess. The principles he follows are clear. When thought descends down the cataphatic course, talk about God proliferates. When thought ascends to the darkness beyond being, our speech about God grows sparse until it falls altogether into silence.

The way of ascent into silence and unknowing is well known, but that ascent into silence does not and cannot stand alone. Hence, the apophatic trajectory of *The Mystical Theology* must stand together with the linguistic profusion of *The Symbolic Theology*. Surely then it stands as a textual tragedy that we lack access to Pseudo-Dionysius's *Symbolic Theology* in which we would have come to know more fully this strange God who at times suffers from a hangover and is bedizened with bling.[2] Should we not recognize *The Symbolic Theology* as the mother text of theopoetics enjoying pride of place alongside the cataphatic theology of *The Divine Names* and the apophatic ascent of *The Mystical Theology*?

Of course, the theopoetic turn is hardly new to process thought. We have yet to explore in sufficient detail the relationship between metaphysical and theopoetic elements in Whitehead's own work. In stark contrast to my initial allergy toward Whitehead's description of God as actual entity, I received with great warmth Whitehead's most famous characterization of God as "the great companion—the fellow-sufferer who understands."[3] Read metaphysically or in as literal a sense as possible, this statement too is rooted within the totality of Whitehead's integral metaphysical vision and has a rather precise meaning therein. Process readers know that Whitehead speaks here of God's consequent nature as able to prehend the whole of the world, its joys and sufferings, and to offer back to the world the richness of divine vision so enriched. But who could fail to discern the felt difference between these two great Whiteheadian dicta? But how to name the difference? Is discourse about God as actual entity an instance of *theo-logos* and God as fellow sufferer who understands an instance of *theo-poiesis*? And if so, what is the relationship between these two linguistic registers? How do they hold together in Whitehead's vision? More broadly, how do or should they hold together in theological discourse as such in this or any other theology?

Does it matter that we can easily imagine integrating the latter utterance into acts of worship, prayer, and praise, whereas we cannot easily imagine ourselves praying to the God who is an actual entity? And is this not akin to the long running objection raised against Tillich's assertion that God is being-itself, namely that it would be impossible to imagine raising one's head (or lowering it, as may befit this case) in prayer to the ground of being? Just what is the relationship between theopoetics and religious utterance in its first-order registers of prayer and praise? Does the promise of theopoetics rest, in part, on its greater proximity to first order religious discourse? Might the power of theopoetics rest in its capacity to transform first order religious life more directly than any theologic can?

That hope for vital transformation of contemporary religious life and reflection is the promise that motivates Amos Wilder's brief, poignant, and now-classic plea for theopoetics. One of the fathers of mid-twentieth-century theopoetics writes,

> My plea for a theopoetic means doing more justice to the role of the symbolic and the prerational in the way we deal with experience. We should recognize that human nature and human societies are more deeply motivated by images and fabulations than by ideas. This is where power lies and the future is shaped. This plea therefore means according a greater role to the imagination in all aspects of religious life.[4]

For Wilder, the call for forging a new theopoetic is a vital cultural and ecclesiological project. Should the church attempt to live without a viable contemporary theopoetic, it will fail to capture the imagination of the age. Christian theology that lacks rooting in a biblically informed, culturally appropriate, and aesthetically rich theopoetic will be unmusical and so uncaptivating. But the danger of theology without theopoetics haunts the internal life of the church as well. Wilder's warning is stark: "When imagination fails doctrines become ossified, witness and proclamation wooden, doxologies and litanies empty, consolations hollow, and ethics legalistic."[5] Without such imagination, the church falls prey to Philistinism: "Philistinism invades Christianity from within wherever the creative and mythopoetic dimension of faith is forfeited. When this happens doctrine becomes a caricature of itself. Then that which once gave life begins to lull and finally to suffocate us."[6]

How does one generate such an animating theopoetic? Wilder calls for discipline and spirituality: "Any fresh renewal of language or rebirth of images arises from within and beyond our control. Nevertheless we can help prepare the event, both by moral and spiritual discipline and by attention to the modes and vehicles of the Word. Of first importance here are the deeper vocabulary and idiom of the Spirit, all that is suggested by such terms as primordial language and dynamic symbol."[7] This work of preparation is neither something that can be done without the work of the theologian nor something that can be accomplished by that work alone. Generating a novel theopoetic is thus a matter of prayerful waiting and discerning creativity. For Wilder, the work of theopoetics is the quest for new imaginative resources for generating a captivating and transformative discourse about divinity that while grounded in tradition has the capacity to renew the religious vision of both church and world because it has been emancipated from stale and dissipated doctrinal frameworks that no longer give life.

Wilder's understanding of theopoetics is not the only formulation operative in this book. One of the virtues of this volume is precisely that it sets the table for rich conversation about the range of possible meanings that theopoetics may bear. For all the remarkable generativity of Wilder's own formulations, there lingers in his work something of the stale air of orthodoxy he seeks to dispel. By way of contrast, whereas Wilder believes that any theopoetic can be derived from within the frame of a single tradition alone, breezes from a variety of philosophical and religious traditions blow through this volume, opening up possibilities that Wilder was only beginning to sense, albeit with some trepidation. His call for a biblical theopoetic was proffered as a discerning counter to "the current resurgence of spirituality, mysticism and phantasy."[8] Wilder was well aware that he would be "put down as a traditionalist" for expressing such worries; still, he must be commended for seeking to walk a via media between openness to the new and reverence for tradition. That desire for prudence can be found in this volume as well, but our time opens up new possibilities, especially interreligious ones, which were unavailable in Wilder's own.

But still the question remains: What is the relationship between theopoetic creativity and theological discourse in its conceptual register. Human beings cannot live by concept alone, but can we live by way of symbol alone? This is the question that I will foreground and probe in the remainder of my brief reflections.[9] I make no promise to answer this question but instead venture some reflections prompted by reading these groundbreaking chapters.

I should acknowledge that my reflections herein are inevitably conditioned by the fact that I am something of a marginal process bedfellow. While my own cosmological intuitions are shaped by process philosophy, my core theological convictions remain Tillichian in nature, even if process conceptions of creativity have persuaded me that it would perhaps be more felicitous to talk about God as becoming-itself rather than being-itself. Nonetheless, questions about theopoetics raised in this volume resonate deeply with questions that abide unresolved at the heart of Tillich's theological enterprise.

Of the essays in this volume, John Caputo's offering makes the most direct assault on this elemental question. He quite rightly frames these matters in Hegelian terms as the question about the proper relationship between *Vorstellung* (representation) and *Begriff* (concept). That question recurs in yet another guise in the work of Paul Tillich—and receives therein a different answer than the one that Caputo offers—where it is framed as a question of the relationship between symbol and ontology, most particularly about the status of the claim that God is being-itself. In what follows, I will take up the question as Caputo frames it but offer an answer that is closer to Tillich's own.

Before turning to these authors, I look briefly to the work of Harold Oliver, who has formulated the sharpest answer to questions about the relationship between these two modes of speech. In an essay aptly entitled "Myth and Metaphysics: Perils of the Metaphysical Translation of Mythical Images," Oliver issues a stark hermeneutical warning that is worth citing at some length:

> I should like to argue . . . that metaphysical discourse in its classic Western forms—from Plato through Whitehead—combined rational abstractions, like "ideas" and "entities"—with selected mythical images—like "God" and "soul" with ominous effect." The mythical images were thereby recontextualized with the result that their "meanings" became "cognitive variables" to be determined by the same means used to "set the values" of all other concepts. They were largely "devalued" so as to become "variables" which could function under the conditions of generality required for metaphysical discourse. . . . The fact of "inclusion," nevertheless meant that they were largely severed from their original place in "the symbolic world." The act of inclusion translated "symbols" into "terms"—a "translation" whose success lay in its subtlety.[10]

Oliver plainly believes that something dire, even "ominous," is at stake in a procedure that has largely been, by his own admission, commonplace in Western thought. Oliver means to apply the semantic brakes on an operation that has the weight of the whole of the Western tradition behind it in order to resolve certain recurrent problems. The deepest of the problems that follow from the metaphysical translation of mythical images is that mythical images are conscripted to perform in a fashion contrary to their intrinsic, unruly, and vital polyvalence and are instead compelled to behave in orderly fashion as is the right and proper obligation of metaphysical terms.

In fact, a mythical image is compelled to become a variable or a term when installed inside a metaphysic. For Oliver, this is a category mistake that diminishes the rich intentionality of mythic discourse and confounds the philosophical integrity of the metaphysical project. The result can only be that the richness of mythic discourse is necessarily received within a metaphysical framework as "ambiguity." Oliver specifies what follows from such inclusion: "the symbolic depth they add to such [metaphysical] discourse is bought at the risk of semantic specifiability."[11] Oliver makes his case with brevity and power:

> The propositions, "God spoke through the prophets" and "Socrates spoke through Plato," are formally identical, yet no one supposes them to be materially identical. . . . The problem—as I see it—lies in failing to fathom the intentionality of the former, and assuming as a consequence that it can only have the intentionality of the latter. Lacking any clear meaning within the domain of the latter, it is assumed to be dysfunctional, since no other domain of intentionality is envisioned. The translation of mythical-language into metaphysical discourse effects a mistranslation of its intention.[12]

For present purposes, Oliver's philosophy of myth need not be considered. It will suffice instead to hear his warning: Do not mix terms from mythic discourse with terms from metaphysical discourse because the result can only be incoherence. This assertion entails that questions such as "Is God the totality of the world?" or "Is God the ground of being?" rest on fundamental category mistakes and so are unintelligible within the domains of myth and metaphysics. These two questions are Oliver's own examples of such confusion. We might add to that list Whitehead's claim that God is an actual entity.

What are we to make of Oliver's warning? If Oliver is taken seriously—and I believe it would be foolish not to—there can be no easy and unreflective passage from theopoetics to theological discourse especially insofar as the latter is marked by the habitual conflation of mythic and metaphysical terms. But given the history of Western philosophical and theological discourse—a history with which he is intimately familiar—Oliver's prohibition risks bringing the whole theological enterprise, as customarily practiced, to a dead standstill. Wherein lies the way forward?

At the very least, Oliver's injunction against the metaphysical translation of mythical images is a plea for a deeper and sustained attention to hermeneutics. More work must be done before *God*, a term from mythic discourse, is deployed for metaphysical ends. Those who would formulate any proposition whatsoever of the form "God is *x*" wherein *x* is a metaphysical term must realize that such a proposition will likely distort and even falsify what is meant by *God* as that term is used in religious life. Understood maximally, Oliver's claim is total: Do not introduce *God* into any metaphysical discourse *whatsoever*, as the result will not only be false but incoherent. God is not being, God is not non-being, and God is not an actual entity. But can theologians and philosophers abide by this bar?

John Caputo is willing to abide by this constraint. As noted above, Caputo frames the questions under present consideration in Hegelian terms as the relationship between representation and concept. Caputo rightly summarizes Hegel's own position as a unilateral triumph of the latter over the former. What Caputo finds compelling and right about Hegel is that Hegel has no interest in a bloodless rational and natural theology. It is the very stuff of Christian discourse and its central representations that are of vital and life giving import: incarnation, cross, resurrection, Trinity, and the like. But, Caputo rightly notes that for Hegel, representational truth remains deficient and obscure. The symbols of faith await and require translation into the realm of concept, and that work of translation is the philosopher's task. Caputo's summary is elegant: "Each and every 'doctrine' of Christian revelation is true, is a stage of truth in the making, where truth is a work in progress, and so each element merits philosophical respect and demands a philosophical analysis. The truth needs philosophy, but philosophy needs religion."

Caputo respects Hegel's antisupernatural attention to the core elements of Christian myth, but he departs radically from Hegel's project in philosophical translation. Caputo characterizes his own position as a "headless Hegelianism without the Concept." His own conviction is "that religion is a *Vorstellung* of which there is no Concept, a figure that does not admit of metaphysical elucidation. My *Vorstellung* has nowhere to turn for a Final Explanation of itself." Put simply, there is no conceptual test of intelligibility than can be put to the deliverances of religion. That is not because religion bespeaks supernatural truth or discloses a world above this one. Caputo walks a subtler path by advancing a theology of the event in which revelation is understood as an in-breaking of what cannot be anticipated, the in-breaking of another way of worlding the world. The only way this event can be spoken or the way in which this eruption bespeaks itself is as a poetics. Caputo's position is captivating:

In my hybrid headless Hegelianism the *Vorstellung* is a presentation or representation, a figure or an image, not of the *Begriff*—I have no head for the *Begriff*—but of the event. A poetics is not an aesthetics of the work of art, nor a logic of the concept, but a poetics of the event. . . . A genuinely radical theology is a poetics of the event, a theo-poetics, not a theo-logic, a poetics of the event that is harbored in the name of God.

Caputo's call for a theo-poetics without a theo-logic appears to satisfy Oliver's bar against the translation of mythic images into metaphysical concepts; after all, no concept or set of concepts is adequate to what bespeaks itself in the event. Such translation is neither possible nor desirable. Caputo's theopoetics of the event offers rigorous grounds for refusing any attempt at translation. Translation is understood by Caputo as an inevitable appeal to the authority of the concept over symbol, as though symbol must be vetted and approved before the court of reason before it can accomplish its own distinctive labor. By displacing a "philosophy of the Spirit with the poetics of the event," Caputo offers a frame for theopoetics as a substitute for theology. The result is, for Caputo, a theology without theology, a theology without logos.

But can there be a theology without logos? Only if there can be an incarnation without flesh and bone. To speak of a theology without logos hardly seems congruent with the deep intuitions of a tradition that from its beginnings speaks of the logos who becomes flesh. That very claim and phrase should surely be read first as a theopoetic claim lest we fall into the wooden dogmatism that Wilder warned against, but it should also be read as an openness to the conceptual, an attempt to express a logic as well as a poetic. If the word can condescend to becoming flesh, surely it can also condescend to become concept while simultaneously exceeding it, just as the logos becomes flesh but without evacuating itself from the whole of the cosmos that it grounds and structures.

Christian theology has long been open to a host of names for divinity including what Dionysius calls "the conceptual names of God."[13] In addition to the sensible names that are treated in *The Symbolic Theology, The Divine Names* commends and explains the conceptual names such as being, life, light, God, the truth, good, beautiful, wise, and the like.[14] Of course within the Neoplatonic frame of Dionysius's theology, these conceptual names are marked as superior to symbolic names although, of course, it is worth remembering that for Dionysius *superior* must be understood to mean less inadequate; no names, conceptual or otherwise, are adequate to the one who dwells in the deep darkness.

That said, how are we to honor Caputo's deep suspicion of a tyranny of reason and concept—one in which God must appear before the bar of reason before divinity is allowed to speak? How best to register Caputo's intuition that theopoetics must have a certain pride of place in its relationship with theo-logos? The alternative may lie in the work of Paul Tillich, whom Caputo suggests may be the father of radical theology, in which case Hegel would have to be the grandfather. Tillich offers an inverse Hegelianism—but not one that is headless. With Tillich we have the possibility that religious life cannot live other than by way of *Vorstellung,* but it needs also *Begriff* and cannot do without it. The concept serves the symbol but cannot supersede it.

The symbols of faith are, if we may use Caputo's own vocabulary, evental. They participate in the power to which they point. The power of symbols rests in this: They cannot be pinned down and they continue to bear within them a power that keeps religious life open to the insistent, to what has come in revelation, but what remains also yet to come. And what has come, is now coming, and is yet to come is not a supernatural deliverance from a super-being or from a realm above this one. Tillich's ecstatic naturalism resonates with Caputo's deepest commitments. Religious life is sustained by the symbol. What role then is accorded to the concept?

Tillich was acutely aware of the Hegelian question about the relationship between the symbol and the concept. But there is ample reason to believe that he changed his mind in important respects even during the years in which he wrote his three-volume *Systematic Theology.* Exploring one such shift in Tillich's thought will prove vital to our reflection on the question of theopoetics. The matter at hand is Tillich's reflection on whether anything at all can be said about God that is not symbolic.

Readers of Tillich know well that he was consistent in asserting that God is not one being among beings. Rather, God is being itself. The question at hand has to do with the status of that assertion. What kind of statement is the claim, "God is being itself?" We know that Oliver believes that this most famous of Tillichian utterances is a conflation par excellence of the mythic and the metaphysical. But what does Tillich himself have to say on this question? As the matter at hand is quite subtle, it is necessary to quote Tillich at length:

The statement that God is being-itself is a non-symbolic statement. It does not point beyond itself. It means what it says directly and properly; if we speak of the actuality of God, we first assert that he is not God if he is not being-itself. Other assertions about God can be made theologically only on this basis. Of course, religious assertions do not require such a foundation for what they say about God; the foundation is implicit in every religious thought concerning God. Theologians must make explicit what is implicit in religious thought and expression; and, in order to do this they must begin with the most abstract and completely unsymbolic statement which is possible, namely, that God is being-itself or the absolute. However, after this has been said, nothing else can be said about God as God which is not symbolic.[15]

Tillich plainly believed, at least in his first volume, that it is possible to make one and only one nonsymbolic statement about God. After that single assertion, everything else must be symbolic. But religious life does not require the conceptual assertion; it lives by its own power and logic. At any rate, the notion that God is ground and power of being lives implicitly in religious life. *The nonsymbolic assertion serves religious life and neither transcends it nor sublates it in Hegelian fashion.* Only the symbol participates in the power to which it points; the concept does not. The human being cannot live religiously by appeal to the concept, nor does the concept master and domesticate religious life. The concept serves by attempting to clarify what is at stake in religious life, but every such attempt at seeking to understand what transpires in religious life cannot be a stand in for religious life. The human being cannot live by concept alone. There is no escape from the symbolic.

However, Tillich's own thinking about the relationship between the symbolic and the conceptual seems to have undergone notable transition. Six years later, when he writes his second volume, Tillich appears to have changed his mind about the status of the claim that "God is being itself" under the pressure of lecture audiences who pressed him on the matter:

> the question arises . . . as to whether there is a point at which a non-symbolic assertion about God must be made. There is such a point, namely, the statement that everything we say about God is symbolic. Such a statement is an assertion about God which itself is not symbolic. Otherwise we would fall into a circular argument. On the other hand, if we make one non-symbolic assertion about God, his ecstatic-transcendent character seems to be endangered.[16]

Here we have what appears to be at least a striking qualification, if not a reversal, of his earlier claim. "The one non-symbolic thing that can be said about God" is not that God is being itself but rather that "every statement about God must be symbolic." What then is the status of Tillich's prior claim that the statement God is being itself is nonsymbolic? In his first formulation, a possibility is raised that one nonsymbolic statement might tether down the unruly linguistic profusion of the symbolic. Admittedly, this tethering is profoundly un-Hegelian; after all, the gain in conceptual explication comes at the expense of religious power. Conceptual translation does not seek to produce a mastery over the symbol. The concept serves as a cataphasis for thought, venturing a fallible hypothesis about the intentionality of mythic discourse. What is at stake is not thought that seeks to master and render univocal what remains obscure and muddled in the realm of representation. Rather, thought seeks humbly to articulate what is implied in and by the symbolic.

In his second formulation, Tillich appears to have given up on the idea that any *first-order* statement about God can be literal or nonsymbolic. His second claim, contrary to his own assertion, is not a claim about God; rather, it is a claim about what sorts of statements concerning God are permissible. Only a second order claim qualifies.

Why the change? Tillich is clear: To assert that any first order statement of God can be nonsymbolic is to compromise divine transcendence. What then can we say about God? Is any nonsymbolic speech about God possible?

In the second volume, Tillich is plainly wrestling with the problem of symbolic or theopoetic speech, and the struggle feels unfinished, as it must be for us. His working answer is that nonsymbolic speech is possible and necessary when, driven by ultimate concern, human beings seek after "the content of the concern."

> This is the point at which we must speak non-symbolically about God, but in terms of a quest for him. In the moment, however, in which we describe the character of this point or in which we try to formulate that for which we ask, a combination of symbolic with non-symbolic elements occurs. If we say that God is the infinite, or the unconditional, or being-itself, we speak rationally and ecstatically at the same time. These terms precisely designate the boundary line at which both the symbolic and the non-symbolic coincide. Up to this point every statement is non-symbolic. . . . Beyond this point every statement is symbolic. . . . The point itself is both non-symbolic and symbolic.[17]

Unfolding the multiple meanings of these claims would require unpacking Tillich's system as a whole, hardly a realistic objective herein. Nonetheless, a few critical observations can be made that bear on our central question, namely the relationship between symbolic and conceptual discourse, between theopoetics and theology. First, it appears as though Tillich has given up on the idea that any speech about God as such can be entirely nonsymbolic. Nonsymbolic statements are possible only when human beings are seeking to conceptualize the content of their longings. When God is a question, one can seek to explain just what it is that one longs for.

But when asking meets receiving, when yearning meets reception, when my speech about God becomes also God speaking in me, when the subject–object character of experience is transcended, at that very point, there is a coincidence of nonsymbolic with the symbolic. At that juncture, it becomes impossible to disentangle concept from symbol, rational speech from ecstatic speech, and theology from theopoetics. Oliver's somber warnings about the risks of category mistakes and incoherence notwithstanding, Tillich argues compellingly that it is impossible neatly to sever the metaphysical from the mythic. This impossibility does not amount to an excuse for undisciplined conflation of speech domains or for hermeneutic laxity, but it does demonstrate the impossibility of a theology without a theopoetics.

But Tillich also keeps us open to both a theology that drives us toward theopoetics and a theology that humbly follows in the wake of theopoetics, seeking to articulate in the conceptual register what it is that we long for when we long for God and what it is that we have encountered when we are grasped by the event of revelation. This work of disciplined reflection is unavoidable because it is impossible to dwell in the theopoetic realm alone. In order to make the arduous ascent to the darkness where God dwells and in order also to make the descent, we must risk a more mundane and accountable prose that seeks to map the terrain of our longings and to speak faithfully and apologetically of what it is that has claimed us. The concept does not promise mastery; it promises only a vulnerable accountability and a broader sociability. We must avoid undisciplined evasions—"God cannot be spoken of other than by way of theopoetics, and so we cannot and so will not seek to explain ourselves; no logos will do,"—and we must avoid also a solipsistic recourse to a purely private, privileged speech—"You cannot understand what we say without saying it with us. You must speak as we do if you are to know as we do. Enter the world of our metanarrative, and only then you will come to know what we mean."

There is no doing without theopoetics. After reading this volume, the reader will come to feel the full force of this claim. But I would contend that there is no escaping the need for unpretentious, fallibilistic theologos—one that courts necessary failure always speaking about what exceeds speech in the discursive and conceptual register. We must again and again strive to speak about what (we believe) we have encountered when we are taken into the divine darkness.

What then are we to make of Whitehead's own discourse and even his talk about God as actual entity? Plainly Whiteheadians in this volume, most certainly Faber, Fackenthal, and Keller, read Whitehead primarily as a theopoet and not solely as a systematizer. Indeed, Oliver himself suggests that Whitehead might be best read in this fashion. In a brief and tantalizing essay entitled, "A New Approach to a Hermeneutic of Whitehead," Oliver suggests that readers ought to distinguish in Whitehead's writings between his "(1) life-long principles; (2) his deeply spiritual sentiments; and (3) his *Gedankenexperimente* (his thought-experiments) considered as experiments in speculative metaphysics."[18] Among his lifelong principles, Oliver lists Whitehead's opposition to substance metaphysics, antimaterialism, rejection of simple location, and his advocacy of "holistic organismic categories." By *sentiments,* Oliver means, "those things that he 'felt' (*sentire*) deeply, as Wordsworth—his poetic muse—felt 'the moving presence' of Nature."[19] Oliver goes on to observe that "poetic passages scattered throughout his later writings strike a chord in those who know nothing of his categories or his principles."[20]

Oliver cautions that no definitive list of such sentiments can be generated, but he includes among these

> the priority of persuasion over coercion, the feeling for "the tender elements of the world," and the feeling for compassion whose noblest expression is that of the Divine as "the fellow-sufferer who understands." . . . Most of all we think of the strong soteriological strain in his thought, captured in the Johannine phrase alluded to in the text of *Process and Reality:* "that nothing be lost."[21]

Most intriguing and provocative is Oliver's suggestion that Whitehead's various divergent attempts at metaphysical schemes were but important thought-experiments in which he sought to spell out with systematic rigor the content of his principles and his sentiments. Oliver concludes, "These experiments [*sic*] were for him 'adventures of ideas,' of spirit, which brought a measure of satisfaction. He never regarded any stage of this process as final, and seemed never to have looked back upon a previous attempt as binding upon his free spirit. The process of system-building was rather an 'advance into novelty.'"[22]

Oliver employs this threefold distinction between principles, sentiments, and metaphysical schemes to argue that there are a variety of ways in which one might be Whiteheadian. One might chose fidelity to Whitehead's principles and sentiments but refuse allegiance to any or even all of Whitehead's speculative schemes and still legitimately count oneself a Whiteheadian. Oliver suggests that this nondogmatic adherence to a theopoetic reading of Whitehead might be the deepest sort of fidelity—likely the form that Whitehead would himself commend. A great many voices in this book are Whiteheadian theopoets in this most generative and encompassing sense. Without ignoring or trivializing the ongoing significance and promise of Whitehead's metaphysical schemes, the primary focus herein remains steadfastly on the latter's principles and sentiments.

Might there be a poetics even in the workaday labor of conceptual explication and systematic reflection that Whitehead ventures and that theology is compelled to undertake? The answer must be yes: Even the humble work of explication can acquire an elegance and evocative power that befits speech about the "object" of our longings. The cumulative witness of the authors of this volume as well as the work of Wilder and Tillich suggest that we can never remain entirely in nor can we leave behind the theopoetic. Theology that is not inscribed within a theopoetic would amount to a desiccated and doctrinaire discourse that seeks to persuade without luring. How could such threadbare theological speech do justice to life in the matrix of the self-diffusing Good whose erotic lure is everywhere leading us into the cloud of unknowing? Silence, a profligate *poiesis,* logos, and then, once more, the enshrouding silence.

Notes

Introduction: The Manifold of Theopoetics
Roland Faber and Jeremy Fackenthal

1. George Santayana, *Three Philosophical Poets: Lucretius, Dante, Goethe* (New York: Barnes & Noble, 2009), 12.

2. Cf. Alfred North Whitehead, *Process and Reality,* corrected ed., ed. David Ray Griffin and Donald W. Sherburne (New York: Free Press, 1978), 350.

3. Whitehead, *Process and Reality,* 346.

4. Alfred North Whitehead, *Science and the Modern World* (New York: Free Press, 1967), 192.

5. Alfred North Whitehead, *Adventures of Ideas* (New York: Free Press, 1967), 172.

6. Raimon Panikkar, *The Rhythm of Being: The Gifford Lectures* (Maryknoll, N.Y.: Orbis Books, 2009), 200.

7. Whitehead, *Process and Reality,* 338.

8. Gilles Deleuze and Félix Guattari, *A Thousand Plateaus: Capitalism and Schizophrenia,* trans. Brian Massumi (Minneapolis: University of Minnesota Press, 1987), 20.

9. Alfred North Whitehead, *Modes of Thought* (New York: Free Press, 1938), 174.

Reality, Eternality, and Colors: Rimbaud, Whitehead, Stevens
Michael Halewood

1. A colorful edition of Rimbaud's 1871 poem "Vowels" in both English and French can be found at: http://www.doctorhugo.org/synaesthesia/rimbaud.html. All citations from this poem are taken from this website.

2. Rimbaud ends the poem with the following line: "O the Omega! The violet ray of [His] Eyes!" The capital *H* of the word *His,* along with connotations of the notion of Omega, have often been taken to signal some notion of deity. What is of most interest, however, is that he chooses the word *violet* to describe the ray of these eyes, not the word *blue,* which is his original designation of the vowel *O* at the start of the poem. Violet is at the very edge of the visible spectrum; it is where the visible world broaches the unseeable. If this is God, then Rimbaud is describing the manner in which such a deity engages with the world as an extreme example of the manner in which potentiality suffuses existence.

3. This means, approximately, "stick your finger down your throat," which is precisely the feeling one would get if the world were made up only of consonants. Clearly the letter *r* is somewhat vowely in this context. I am very grateful to Kristýna Šrejberová for her help with my Czech-language skills.

4. Alfred North Whitehead, *The Concept of Nature* (Cambridge: Cambridge University Press, 1964), 30–31.

5. Alfred North Whitehead, *Science and the Modern World* (Cambridge: Cambridge University Press, 1932), 68–69.

6. Whitehead, *The Concept of Nature,* 29–30.

7. Ibid., 29.

8. Ibid., 15.

9. Whitehead, *Science and the Modern World,* 107.

10. Alfred North Whitehead, *Modes of Thought* (Cambridge: Cambridge University Press, 1938), 237–38.

11. Whitehead, *Science and the Modern World,* 129.

12. Ibid., 207.

13. The text of *Process and Reality* was based on the Gifford lectures, which Whitehead gave in 1927–28 and was first published in 1929, three years after the publication of *Science and the Modern World.*

14. Alfred North Whitehead, *Process and Reality* (New York: Free Press, 1978), 61.

15. Isabelle Stengers, *Penser Avec Whitehead* (Paris: Editions de Seuil, 2002), 238, my translation. Isabelle Stengers is one of the world's leading philosophers of science and is also, perhaps, the foremost contemporary commentator on Whitehead. Throughout her work, she stresses the importance of taking science seriously but also challenging its attempts to claim authority for its abstractions beyond their initial field of deployment. She has developed what she terms a "constructivist" philosophy that sets out to produce novel concepts and approaches that are able to describe more of reality and not to reduce it to less, and that refuses to accede to the power of the "bifurcation of nature."

16. Whitehead is referring to a passage in book 2, chapter 2, § 1 of Locke's *An Essay Concerning Human Understanding* (London, J. M. Dent, 1988), 45.

17. Whitehead, *Process and Reality,* 59.

18. Ibid., 215.

19. Andrew Marvell, "The Garden," in *The Metaphysical Poets,* ed. H. H. Gardiner (London: Penguin Books, 1985), 257.

20. I have used the edition from Wallace Stevens, *Collected Poems* (London: Faber & Faber, 1984), 163–84. All poetry quotations in this next section are from this poem.

21. Steven Meyer, personal correspondence with author, July 4, 2006, Salzburg.

22. Whitehead, *Process and Reality,* 73.

23. Ibid, 35.

24. Ibid, 23.

25. Ibid., 51, 219, 257.

26. The proliferation of masculine pronouns in these phrases should be noted. I do not think that such an author should necessarily be conceived of as male.

27. Ibid., 50.

28. Michel Foucault, *The History of Sexuality: Volume I: An Introduction,* trans. Robert Hurley (London: Penguin Books, 1984), 93.

29. Isabelle Stengers, "A Constructivist Reading of *Process and Reality,*" in *Theory, Culture, and Society,* 25, no. 4 (2008): 95.

30. Whitehead, *Modes of Thought,* 37.

(Theo)poetic Naming and the Advent of Truths:
The Function of Poetics in the Philosophy of Alain Badiou
Hollis Phelps

1. Alain Badiou, *Handbook of Inaesthetics,* trans. Alberto Toscano (Stanford, Calif.: Stanford University Press, 2005), 10.

2. Alain Badiou, *Manifesto for Philosophy,* trans. Norman Madarasz (Albany: SUNY Press, 1999), 35.

3. Ibid., 37.

4. "Ontology and Politics: An Interview with Alain Badiou," in Alain Badiou, *Infinite Thought: Truth and the Return of Philosophy,* ed. and trans. Oliver Feltham and Justin Clemens (New York: Continuum, 2004), 191–92.

5. Ibid., 192.

6. Alberto Toscano, translator's note to *Logics of Worlds,* by Alain Badiou, trans. Alberto Toscano (New York: Continuum, 2009), xv.

7. Badiou, *Being and Event,* 4.

8. From here on out, I use *mathematics* to indicate the scientific truth procedure and *poetics* to indicate the artistic truth procedure. This is largely in keeping with Badiou's own tendency to privilege mathematics among the sciences and poetry among the arts.

9. Alain Badiou, "God Is Dead," in *Briefings on Existence: A Short Treatise on Transitory Ontology,* trans. Norman Madarasz (Albany: SUNY Press, 2006), 21–32.

10. Ibid., 24.

11. Ibid.

12. Alain Badiou, *Saint Paul: The Foundation of Universalism,* trans. Ray Brassier (Stanford, Calif.: Stanford University Press, 2003), 1.

13. Ibid., 30.

14. Alain Badiou, *Ethics,* trans. Peter Hallward (London: Verso, 2001), 25.

15. Badiou, "God Is Dead," 28.

16. Badiou, *Being and Event,* 1.

17. Ibid., 9.

18. Ibid., 9–10.

19. Martin Heidegger, "Only a God Can Save Us," trans. Maria P. Alter and John D. Caputo, in *The Heidegger Controversy,* ed. Richard Wolin (Cambridge, Mass.: MIT Press, 1988), 107.

20. Badiou, *Being and Event,* 2.

21. Badiou, *Briefings on Existence,* 29.

22. Alain Badiou, *Manifesto for Philosophy,* ed. and trans. Norman Madarasz (Albany: SUNY Press, 1999), 51.

23. Alain Badiou, *Pocket Pantheon,* trans. David Macey (London: Verso, 2009), 67.

24. Badiou, *Briefings on Existence,* 26. Cf. Alain Badiou, *Pocket Pantheon,* 67; Alain Badiou, "Definition of Philosophy," in *Manifesto for Philosophy,* 143; and Alain Badiou, *The Century,* trans. Alberto Toscano (Cambridge, UK: Polity Press, 2007), 148–64.

25. Badiou, *Briefings on Existence,* 29.

26. Badiou, "Philosophy and Mathematics," 22.

27. Badiou, "Mathematics and Philosophy," 16.

28. Ibid., 17.

29. Badiou, *Being and Event,* 8.

30. Ibid.

31. Ibid., 5.

32. Ibid., 27.

33. Ibid., 130.

34. Justin Clemens and Job Roffe, "Philosophy as Anti-Religion in the Work of Alain Badiou," *Sophia* 47 (2008): 350.

35. Given Whitehead's understanding of mathematics and his emphasis on speculative philosophy, it seems odd that Badiou hardly ever mentions him. In Badiou's work, I know of only a few passing references to Whitehead, all of which occur in the context of discussions concerning Deleuze. See Alain Badiou, *Deleuze: The Clamor of Being,* trans. Louise Burchill (Minnesota: University of Minnesota Press, 2000), 10, 15, 100; and Alain Badiou, "One, Multiple, Multiplicities," *Theoretical Writings,* 246n4.

36. Alfred North Whitehead, *Science and the Modern World* (New York: Free Press, 1967), 21.

37. Ibid., 24.

38. Ibid., 21; emphasis mine. Referring to his own metaphysical system, White-head even remarks, "The generality of mathematics is the most complete generality consistent with the community of occasions which constitutes our metaphysical situation" (Ibid., 25). However, I do not mean to suggest that Badiou's understanding and Whitehead's are exactly similar. For Whitehead, in the end, it seems that philosophy trumps mathematics in the realm of ontology, given that he understands mathematics as "an essential auxiliary mode of verification whereby to test the scope of [philosophical] generalities." See Alfred North Whitehead, *Process and Reality* (New York: Free Press, 1978), 10.

39. Badiou, *Being and Event,* 27.

40. Ibid., 3.

41. Ibid.

42. Badiou, "Philosophy and Mathematics," 36.

43. Badiou, *Being and Event,* 27.

44. Ibid., 3.

45. Plato, *Republic,* 10.603b.

46. Ibid., 10.606d.

47. Ibid.

48. Ibid., 10.605c, 607b.

49. Ibid., 10.607b.

50. Badiou, *Handbook of Inaesthetics,* 21.

51. Badiou, *Being and Event,* 26. The main problem is that Plato fails to take ontology as a situation. This is what Badiou refers to as the "Great Temptation": "To say that ontology is not a situation is to signify that being cannot be signified within a structured multiple, and that only an experience situated beyond all structure will afford us access to the veiling of being's presence. The most majestic form of this conviction is the Platonic statement according to which the Idea of the Good, despite placing being, as being-supremely-being, in the intelligible region, is for all that epekeina tes ousias, 'beyond substance'; that is, unpresentable within the configuration of that-which-is-maintained-there. It is an Idea which is not an Idea, whilst being that on the basis of which the very ideality of the Idea maintains its being, and which therefore, not allowing itself to be known within the articulations of the place, can only be seen or contemplated by a gaze which is the result of an initiatory journey."

52. See, for instance, Badiou, *Manifesto for Philosophy,* 61–77.

53. Badiou, *Handbook of Inaesthetics,* 22.

54. Immanuel Kant, *Critique of Pure Reason,* trans. Norman Kemp Smith (New York: Palgrave Macmillan, 2003), B xxx.

55. Badiou, "Philosophy and Art," *Infinite Thought,* 98.

56. Badiou, *Handbook of Inaesthetics,* 20.

57. Ibid., 29.

58. Badiou, *Manifesto for Philosophy,* 72.

59. Badiou, *Handbook of Inaesthetics,* 29.

60. Ibid., 25.

61. Ibid., 22.

62. Ibid., 23.

63. Ibid., 25.

64. Ibid.

65. Ibid., 26.

66. Badiou, *Infinite Thought*, 100.

67. Alain Badiou, *Being and Event*, 181.

68. Ibid., 202.

69. Ibid., 203.

70. Ibid., 232–52.

71. Ibid., 391–409.

72. Badiou, *Handbook of Inaesthetics*, 21.

73. Whitehead, *Process and Reality*, 346.

74. Roland Faber, *God as Poet of the World: Exploring Process Theologies*, trans. Douglas W. Stott (Louisville, Ky.: Westminster John Knox Press, 2008), 81.

75. Ibid., 81.

76. Badiou, *Logics of Worlds*, trans. Alberto Toscano (New York: Continuum, 2009), 513.

77. Faber, *God as Poet of the World*, 83.

78. Ibid., 83.

79. Badiou, however, would largely accept Whitehead's view of the world as in a constant state of flux. The difference concerning notions of events, in this sense, would primarily be one of terminology.

80. Badiou, *Logics of Worlds*, 512–13.

81. Ibid., 361.

82. See also Badiou's remarks in his "Preface to the English Edition" of *Ethics*, lvi–lvii.

83. Badiou, *Logics of Worlds*, 394, 361.

84. As Adrian Johnston has pointed out, despite adopting a new terminology, Badiou adopts in *Logics of Worlds* the same temporal structure found in *Being and Event*, "that of the future anterior, in which what happens after retroactively determines whether what came before was/is or was/is not an event." Moreover, as Johnston also points out, Badiou explicitly evokes the concept on naming in a 2006 discussion with Simon Critchley, the same year of the publication of *Logics of Worlds*. See Adrian Johnston, *Badiou, Žižek, and Political Transformations: The Cadence of Change* (Evanston, Ill.: Northwestern University Press, 2009), 33. Moreover, although I cannot discuss the details here, Badiou's notion of "resurrection" in *Logics of Worlds* bears a striking similarity to the notions of intervention and eventual recurrence as expressed in *Being and Event* and seems to require some act of nomination. For a discussion of self-reflexivity as it relates to the event in *Logics of Worlds*, see also Oliver Feltham, *Alain Badiou: Live Theory* (New York: Continuum, 2008), 103–7.

85. Faber, *God as Poet of the World*, 85.

Kierkegaardian Theopoiesis: Selfhood, Anxiety, and the Multiplicity of Human Spirits
Sam Laurent

1. Mark C. Taylor, *Journeys to Selfhood, Hegel, and Kierkegaard* (Berkeley: University of California Press, 1980), 91.

2. Ibid.

3. Ibid., 93.

4. Søren Kierkegaard, *The Concept of Anxiety: A Simple Psychologically Orienting Deliberation on the Dogmatic Issue of Hereditary Sin*, trans. Rei Thomte, Kierkegaard's writings (Princeton, N.J.: Princeton University Press, 1980), 42.

5. Taylor, *Journeys to Selfhood*, 54.

6. Ibid., 55.

7. Kierkegaard, *Concept of Anxiety*, 12–13.

8. Ibid., 13.

9. Ibid., 9.

10. Ibid., 10.

11. M. G. Piety, "The Place of the World in Kierkegaard's Ethics," in *Kierkegaard: The Self in Society*, ed. George Pattison and Steven Shakespeare (New York: St. Martin's, 1998), 24–42, here 27.

12. Alfred North Whitehead, *Process and Reality*, ed. David Ray Griffin and Donald W. Sherburne, 2nd ed. (New York: Free Press, 1979), 108.

13. Taylor, *Journeys to Selfhood*, 125.

14. Whitehead, *Process and Reality*, 7–8.

15. Søren Kierkegaard, *The Sickness unto Death: A Christian Psychological Exposition for Upbuilding and Awakening*, ed. and trans. Howard Vincent Hong and Edna Hatlestad Hong, vol. 19, *Kierkegaard's Writings* (Princeton, N.J.: Princeton University Press, 1983), 14.

16. Ibid.

17. Ibid., 29–30.

18. Ibid., 68.

19. Ibid.

20. Ibid.

21. Helene Tallon Russell, *Irigaray and Kierkegaard: On the Construction of the Self* (Macon, Ga.: Mercer University Press, 2009), 8.

22. Kierkegaard, *Sickness unto Death*, 13.

23. Russell, *Irigaray and Kierkegaard*, 8.

24. Ibid., 67.

25. Ibid., 68.

26. Ibid.

27. Søren Kierkegaard, *Fear and Trembling*, trans. Alastair Hannay (New York: Penguin Classics, 1986), 82.

28. Thanks to Derek France-Malone for sharing his 2009 American Academy of Religion paper on Kierkegaardian anxiety. In that paper, France-Malone links Kierkegaard's understanding of anxiety as an awareness of possibility without cer-

tainty to process theism, helping, in my opinion, to further humanize process theology's description of the human experience. Malone-France beautifully interprets Kierkegaard: "anxiety, then, is the slow but steady, quiet yet terrible, upwelling of the recognition of choice, which comes like a flood from which there is no escape, despite its unhurried pace, because one does not notice it until one looks around and finds water everywhere, with no dry pathway out."

29. Whitehead, *Process and Reality*, 21.

30. Kierkegaard, *Concept of Anxiety*, 43.

31. Ibid., 43–44.

32. Russell, *Irigiraray and Kierkegaard*, 11.

33. Roland Faber, *God as Poet of the World: Exploring Process Theologies*, trans. Douglas W. Stott (Louisville, Ky.: Westminster John Knox Press, 2008), 239.

34. Ibid.

35. Ibid.

36. Ibid., 240.

37. Kierkegaard, *Concept of Anxiety*, 86.

38. Ibid., 86.

39. Ibid., 89.

40. Ibid.

41. Ibid., 91.

42. Ibid., 49.

43. Ibid.

44. Russell, *Irigaray and Kierkegaard*, 11.

45. Taylor, *Journeys to Selfhood*, 257.

46. Faber, *God as Poet of the World*, 179.

47. Whitehead, *Process and Reality*, 24.

48. Alfred North Whitehead, *Adventures of Ideas* (New York: Macmillan, 1933), 203.

49. Ibid., 203–4.

50. Faber, *God as Poet of the World*, 324.

51. John Dewey, *Art as Experience* (New York: Perigee Trade, 2005), 25.

52. Thomas M. Alexander, *John Dewey's Theory of Art, Experience, and Nature: The Horizons of Feeling* (Albany: State University of New York Press, 1987), xiii.

53. Ibid.

54. Ibid., xiii–xiv.

55. Dewey, *Art as Experience*, 173.

56. Ibid., 316.

57. Ibid., 347–48.

58. Ibid., 348.

59. Whitehead, *Process and Reality*, 111.

60. Ibid.

Theology as a Genre of the Blues
Vincent Colapietro

1. See Roland Faber, *God as Poet of the World,* trans. Douglas W. Stott (Louisville, Ky.; Westminister John Knox Press, 2004), 138, 148, 156–57, 177–78.

2. In his *Zettel* (Berkeley: University of California Press, 1970), translated by G. E. M. Anscombe, Ludwig Wiggtenstein notes: "Language is variously rooted; it has roots, not a single root" (656). The same might be said of both theology and the blues.

3. As I am using the term, *experience* signifies our encounter with the world. However fragmentary, perspectival, and distorted, our experience is, in my judgment, not invincibly subjective or private. Here I am following the example of the classical pragmatists—Charles S. Peirce, William James, John Dewey, and George H. Mead—(at least) as much as that of A. N. Whitehead, Charles Hartshorne, and John Cobb Jr. For an illuminating account of the pragmatist conception of human experience, see chapter 1 ("The Reconception of Experience in Peirce, James and Dewey") in John E. Smith's *America's Philosophical Vision* (Chicago: University of Chicago Press, 1992). For a nuanced development of this understanding of experience for the explicit purpose of a philosophical theology, see chapter 1 ("The Recovery of Experience") of his *Experience and God* (New York: Fordham University Press, 1995). Even though I am so deeply indebted to the pragmatists regarding this reconception of experience, my debt in this regard to Whitehead and, in particular, Hartshorne is deep. Indeed, in the spring of 1976, when Hartshorne was present at Marquette University to present the Aquinas Lecture—*Aquinas to Whitehead: Seven Centuries of Metaphysics of Religion* (Milwaukee: Marquette University Press, 1976)—I had the great good fortune to converse with him at length. In one of our exchanges, he suggested that experience is a dialogue between self and world. It is thus in his sense no less than that of the pragmatists that I am using *experience* in this essay.

4. Albert Murray, *Stomping the Blues* (Cambridge, Mass.: Da Capo Press, 2000), 250. Cf. Eddie Glaude Jr., *In a Shade of Blue: Pragmatism and the Politics of Black America* (Chicago: University of Chicago Press, 2008), x.

5. Murray, 250–51, emphasis added.

6. In *Art as Experience* (Carbondale: Southern Illinois Press, 1989), John Dewey notes: "A work of art elicits and accentuates . . . [our sense] of belonging to the larger, all-inclusive whole which is the universe we live in. . . . We are, as it were, introduced into a world beyond this world which is nevertheless the deeper reality of the world in which we live in our ordinary experiences. We are carried out of ourselves to find ourselves" (199). Moreover, we are carried "beyond" the world in such a way that the characteristics of *this* world are brought home to us with incomparable force and salience.

7. See, however, Milan Kundera's *The Curtain: An Essay in Seven Parts* (New York: HarperCollins, 2007). He argues here for appreciating the significance of the irreducibly senseless or meaningless details of everyday life. Part of the value of the novel, as he envisions it, concerns a tutelage in such appreciation or acceptance.

8. Attention to blues is itself the example of such a hermeneutic. But, in my treatment of the blues, this genre of expression and whatever else the blues might turn out to be (e.g., a sensibility, an orientation toward the world, a style of being, or a manner of sustaining and transforming ties to others) are themselves both modes of direct experience and forms of interpretive practice. That is, the blues is at once experience and expression—including therefore the experience of expressing oneself in just this fashion, the expression of one's experience in just these forms.

9. I am deeply appreciative of encouragement offered by Paul Taylor and Robert Bernasconi, two colleagues who have a more intimate, extensive understanding of the blues (and much else) than I possess. My response to Robert Bernasconi's puzzlement regarding my failure to make more of the gospel blues deserves repetition here, since other readers will certainly be puzzled regarding this. Gospel blues easily makes it look as though the blues are derivative from a prior religious tradition rather than in its way being a source of the religious. Of course it would be a mistake—indeed a stupid mistake—to strain too hard, or to strain at all, to isolate the blues in their purity, untainted by religious traditions or theological traditions of other sorts. In sum, the actuality of gospel blues has to be taken into account and acknowledged as blues, not merely an accompaniment of what might be expressed otherwise. But the blues in the sense in which I am focusing on it here are not reducible to this specific genre; they are much more inclusive, also more complexly related to religious traditions. It is of course undeniable that certain forms of the blues are distinctive genres of religious expression. But the question for me is, rather, in what sense might theology be reimagined as a genre of the blues?

10. Charles Hartshorne, *A Natural Theology for Our Time* (LaSalle, Ill.: Open Court, 1973), viii.

11. Ibid.

12. Ibid.

13. Ibid.

14. Ibid.

15. Alfred North Whitehead, *Process and Reality*, corrected ed., ed. David Ray Griffin and Donald W. Sherburne (New York: Free Press, 1978), 324.

16. Whitehead, *Process and Reality*, 209.

17. Ibid., 208. For my purpose, the phrase "utterances of religious aspiration" is too narrow. For my main concern is with the religious expression of a wide range of human emotions and attitudes, feelings and impulses. The crucial matter is not aspiration but the historically evolved forms of distinctively religious utterance, in their thick historicity and thus textured actuality. By implication, it encompasses the forms of expression growing out of, but not reducible to, religious utterances (most evidently, the blues as rooted in the spirituals of an enslaved people). See James H. Cone, *The Spirituals and the Blues* (Maryknoll, N.Y.: Orbis Books, 1991).

18. Ibid., emphasis added. As William James, an author whom Whitehead deeply admired and even called "that adorable genius," put it in *A Pluralistic Uni-*

verse (a work directly relevant to this book), it is high time we thicken up the bases of philosophical discussion. Whitehead in his way and James in his stand for experiential thickness. This entails what might be an invincible ambivalence toward theoretical systematicity, far more obvious in the case of James than that of Whitehead (but perhaps far more central to Whitehead's project than most of his interpreters are disposed to acknowledge).

19. In advocating this, I am not implying (or committed to implying) that the best rendering of integral experience is often to be found in those arresting instances of *artistic* "utterance." Indeed, I would only argue that this is frequently the case.

20. Whitehead, *Process and Reality*, 15.

21. Ibid.

22. In *Experience and God* (New York: Fordham University Press, 1995) as well as other writings, John E. Smith forcefully makes the case for sustaining a vital connection between philosophical and theological discourse, also such a connection between theoretical discourse and the direct experience of those who define themselves in and through their participation in historical communities of religious worship. On this and a number of other points, he was influenced by (among others) Whitehead. My own acquaintance with Whitehead owes much to a summer in 1986 spent with Smith, Edward Pols, Robert Neville, Lewis Ford, Donald Sherburne, George Lucas, Jorge Nobo, and others studying Whitehead.

23. Whitehead, *Process and Reality*, 8.

24. Though there are numerous and deep differences, this reveals a philosophical kinship between Whitehead, on the one hand, and a number of influential contemporary thinkers, on the other. These thinkers include John Dewey, Ludwig Wittgenstein, Martin Heidegger, and (I would strenuously argue—see, e.g., *Positions*) Jacques Derrida. The affirmation of the *primacy of practice* resounds throughout the writings of these thinkers, but the deep significance of our quotidian practices do not on their accounts require a transcendental justification. See *The Practice Turn in Contemporary Theory* (New York: Routledge, 2001), edited by Karin Knorr Cetina, Theodore R. Schatzki, and Eike von Savigny. While being antitheoreticist, this turn is not necessarily antitheoretical. At its best, it involves envisioning theory itself as a form of practice or, more accurately, a vastly extended family of historically evolved and evolving practices.

25. Whitehead, *Process and Reality*, 13.

26. Ibid.

27. Ibid.

28. See, e.g., Whitehead, *Process and Reality*, 4.

29. Patricia Hempl, *I Could Tell You Stories: Sojourns in the Land of Memory* (New York: Norton, 1999), 18.

30. See *Event and Decision: Ontology and Politics in Badiou, Deleuze, and Whitehead*, ed. Roland Faber, Henry Krips, and Daniel Pettus (Cambridge: Cambridge Scholars, 2010).

31. This seems not only significant but, as far as humans are concerned, nothing less than the basis of significance itself. See, e.g., Whitehead's *Symbolism: Its Meaning and Effect* (New York: Fordham University Press, 1985).

32. James Agee, *Let Us Now Praise Famous Men* (New York: Library of America, 2005), 63.

33. Ibid.

34. Ibid.

35. Ibid.

36. One of the most intriguing and suggestive metaphors for experience as a medium of disclosure is that of the rainbow—in effect, the metaphor of a prism. Experience refracts reality as a prism refracts light, thereby disclosing both properties of itself and those of what is other than itself. C. S. Peirce adopts this metaphor from Kant and uses it to deconstruct the dualism between appearance and reality (phenomena and noumena). See *The Collected Papers of Charles Sanders Peirce,* vol. 5, ed. Charles Hartshorne and Paul Weiss (Cambridge, Mass.: Belknap Press of Harvard University Press, 1934), par. 283.

37. Richard Rorty, *Contingency, Irony, and Solidarity* (New York: Cambridge University Press, 1989), 6.

38. Ibid.

39. Charles Sanders Peirce, *The New Elements of Mathematics,* vol. 4 (Atlantic Highlands, N.J.: Humanities Press, 1976), 298.

40. Ibid., 299.

41. Ibid.

42. Ibid.

43. My thinking on this topic has been shaped by a variety or authors but, at bottom, most of all by my experience of listening to the blues. Such listening is clearly a mode of participation, illustrating unmistakably, because dramatically, what Christopher Small means by *musicking.* Even so, my thinking on the blues has been influenced by those who have much more intimate and incontestable ties to this mode of utterance, above all, Amiri Baraka, Ralph Ellison, James H. Cone, and Angela Davis. For an understanding of music in general but also the blues, I am also deeply indebted to Christopher Small, in particular, to his *Musicking: The Meanings of Performance and Listening* (Middletown, Conn.: Wesleyan University Press, 1998) and *Music of the Common Tongue: Survival and Celebration in African American Music* (Middletown, Conn.: Wesleyan University Press, 1999).

44. It would be an error to suppose that a resolution necessarily existed prior to utterance. Typically, the utterance is a process in and through which the resolution to carry on, to fight back, to seek escape, and to attempt countless other things takes form and focus. The blues is thus a *resolute* expression in a processual sense.

45. James Cone, *The Spirituals and the Blues: An Interpretation* (Maryknoll, N.Y.: Orbis Books, 1991), 105. Cf. Christopher Small, *Music of the Common Tongue* (Middletown, Conn.: Wesleyan University Press, 1987), 102. "The basic idea of spirituals is," according to Cone, "that slavery contradicts God; it is a denial of

God's will. To be enslaved is to be declared nobody, and that form of existence contradicts God's creation of people to be God's children. Because black people believed they were God's children, they affirmed their *somebodiness,* refusing to reconcile their servitude with divine revelation" (33). The blues are continuous with the spirituals in their unqualified affirmation, their unrestrained celebration, of the singular *sombodiness* of all those engaged in this form of musicking—in truth, nothing less than a form of life for which this mode of expression functions as a synecdoche (a part standing for the whole).

46. Cone, *The Spirituals and the Blues,* 98.

47. Quoted in Cone, *The Spirituals and the Blues,* 121.

48. Cone, *The Spirituals and the Blues,* 29.

49. Ibid., 28.

50. I take theological discourse to be rooted in, and ultimately accountable to, religious utterances in the actual contexts of their human usages. That is, religious utterance is in my judgment primary, whereas theological discourse derivative. While derivative, theology is indispensable. This is in large measure due to the critical function of theological discourse, a function most effectively and humanely fulfilled when it assumes the vital forms of immanent critique. What makes these forms vital is that they not only indicate participation in a form of life but also contribute to the vitality of the community in which they are ultimately rooted.

51. Lucille Clifton, "grandma, we are poets," in *Quilting: Poems 1987–1990* (Brockport, N.Y.: BOA Editions, 1991), 52–53.

52. I am deeply indebted to the estate of Lucille Clifton for permission to quote this poem in its entirety.

53. Clifton, "grandma, we are poets," 52–53.

54. Adam Phillips, *On Flirtation: Psychoanalytic Essays on the Uncommitted Life* (Cambridge, Mass.: Harvard University Press, 1994), 68.

55. Ibid., 68, emphasis added.

56. Ibid., 40, emphasis added.

57. Cf. Hanna Segal, "The Achievement of Ambivalence," *Common Knowledge* 1 (1992): 92–104.

58. Clifton, "grandma, we are poets," 52–53.

59. John Coltrane, *Live at Birdland,* Grp Records, 1963, compact disc. John Coltrane is on tenor saxophone; McCoy Tyner, piano; Jimmy Garrison, bass; and Elvin Jones, drums. This was in fact not one of the pieces recorded live at Birdland but rather one recorded in the studio and included on what was originally a vinyl album. This can also be found on *The Very Best of John Coltrane,* a compilation issued in 2001.

60. Langston Hughes, "Daybreak in Alabama," in *The Collected Poems of Langston Hughes,* ed. Arnold Rampersad (New York: Vintage, 1995), 220.

61. See Angela Davis, "Remembering Carole, Cynthia, Addie Mae and Denise," in *Essence* (September 1993), 122–23.

62. In his eulogy at the funeral of three of them, Martin Luther King Jr. does not refer to them by name. See "Eulogy to the Young Victims of the Sixteenth

Street Church Bombing," in *A Call to Conscience: The Landmark Speeches of Dr. Martin Luther King, Jr.*, ed. Clayborne Carson, Kris Shepard, and Andrew Young (New York: Grand Central, 2002), 89ff.; or listen to this eulogy on the Hachette Audio version (2001).

63. It is appropriate to recall that the title of Spike Lee's documentary regarding their deaths, made in 1997, is entitled *4 Little Girls*. At least three of the individuals were, however, closer to being young women than little girls.

64. George Wallace, the governor of Alabama at the time, got his wish: he had called for a few high-class funerals to put a stop to the efforts to desegregate his state. See King, "Eulogy to the Young Victims"; also James Baldwin, "A Talk to Teachers," in *The Price of the Ticket: Collected Nonfiction 1948–1985* (New York: St. Martin's Press, 1985).

65. Hughes, "Daybreak in Alabama," 220.

66. One can hear a recording of this on *A Call to Conscience: The Landmark Speeches of Dr. Martin Luther King, Jr.* (Hachette Audio, 2001).

67. I want to avoid altogether the pornography of violence, but the scene in the aftermath of the bombing was horrific beyond what we are likely to imagine.

68. Clifton, "grandma, we are poets," 53.

69. Cone, *The Spirituals and the Blues*, 114.

70. In its own way, this chapter (as it turns out) rings changes on Robert Mesle's "Elliot Matters." The mattering of this somebody is, on his account, a revelation of what matters, not just in this instance but in every one of our encounters. It presumably extends beyond—possibly far beyond—the bearers of proper names (to use the examples from his paper, the names of Elliot, Sarah, and Mark).

71. In "Notes for a Politics of Location," to be found in *Arts of the Possible: Essays and Conversations* (New York: Norton, 2001), Adrienne Rich rightly advises us: "Begin with the material. Pick up again the long struggle against loft and privileged abstractions." She warns against "abstractions severed from the doings of living people, fed back to people as slogans." But Rich is not opposed to theory, at least when this activity is properly conceived: "Theory—the seeing of patterns, the forest as well as the trees—theory can be a dew that rises from the earth and collects in the rain cloud and returns to earth over and over. But if it doesn't smell of the earth, it isn't good for the earth" (65).

72. Paul Tillich, *The Dynamics of Faith* (New York: HarperCollins, 1958), chapter 1.

73. Arguably, the poet of the world is just the chorus of voices. See Faber, *The Poet of the World*, 324.

Poiesis, Fides, et Ratio in the Absence of Relativism
Matthew S. LoPresti

1. Quoted in Roland Bleiker, introduction to *Popular Dissent, Human Agency, and Global Politics* (New York: Cambridge University Press, 2000), 50.

2. David Hoy, "One What?" in *Relativism: A Contemporary Anthology* (New York: Columbia University Press, 2010), 524.

3. It seems just as normal for scholars to use the term *soteriology* to speak of the salvific project of various religious traditions. This despite the fact that it originally meant "a study of salvation as it relates to Christ." While we are aware of the term's original meaning, it is useful in the parlance of salvific projects in general and thus has currency across traditions.

4. W. S. Merwin, interview on *PBS Hawaii, Long Story Short with Leslie Wilcox,* PBS, December 22, 2009.

5. See Matthew S. LoPresti, "Inter-religious Dialogue and Religious Pluralism: A Philosophical Critique of Pope Benedict XVI and the Fall of Religious Absolutism," in *Philosophical Basis of Inter-religious Dialogue: The Process Perspective,* ed. Mirosław Patalon (Cambridge: Cambridge Scholars Publishing, 2009), 66–94.

6. John Paul II, *Fides et Ratio,* Encyclical Letter to the Bishops of the Catholic Church on the Relationship between Faith and Reason, September 14, 1998, n. 1.

7. John Paul II, *Ad Limina Address,* October 24, 1998, n. 5.

8. Ibid.

9. John E. Fagen, "Fides et Ratio (Faith and Reason)," in *The Teachings of Pope John Paul II: Summaries of Papal Documents* (New York: Scepter, 2005), 64–71, accessed August 9, 2011, http://www.catholiceducation.org/articles/education/ed0294.htm.

10. By *heart-mind* I refer to the Chinese term *xin.* In Chinese thought, one does not merely think with one's mind, but one simultaneously feels with one's emotions; the two are inseparable. Just as there is no discrete individual who exists in isolation from one's relationships and roles, there is no discrete mind (or ideas) separate from one's heart (or emotions). See Roger T. Ames and David L. Hall, *Daodejing "Making this Life Significant": A Philosophical Translation* (New York: Ballantine Books, 2003), 26–27, 38–39. At one point (26), in explaining this concept to a Western audience, they quote Alfred North Whitehead's *Religion in the Making* (New York: Fordham University Press, 1996), 67, where he writes, "mothers can ponder many things in their hearts that words cannot express."

11. Here I find myself in happy agreement with Gwen Griffith-Dickson in *The Philosophy of Religion* (London, SCM Press, 2005), 364.

12. It can most effectively achieve this in ways that more closely resemble the sage or *zenren* in the Chinese tradition—as a person who is attenuated to the ebb and flow of things in such a way as to be efficacious in speech and action

13. I am grateful here to Eliot Deutsch's work in epistemology, *On Truth: An Ontological Theory* (Honolulu: University Press of Hawaii, 1979). I believe this would be the ideal starting point for establishing such a criteria of truth when discoursing on the myriad religious paths, ends, and expressions. Deutsch develops an idea of truth as authenticity insofar as something can be judged to be true if it is what it ought (or intends) to be. This theory is developed by way of aesthetics and has profound implications for an epistemology of world religions. For example, Deutsch argues that to determine truth in a piece of art is to discern its integrity. A work of art is authentic (true) when it is *right for itself* by the standards of its own

intentionality. Similarly, theopoetic ruminations could be judged to be authentic or inauthentic.

14. Sometimes in spite of faith and reason, in which case it would take some time to philosophically and theologically establish novel theopoetic utterances as authentic (or true) and adequately amend faith and reason to account for it in a tradition.

15. This runs contrary to much of the debate regarding religious experience: for example, Wayne Proudfoot, Steven Katz, and others write about how religious experience cannot be taken as evidence for religious beliefs, since religious beliefs shape religious experiences and vice versa (e.g., see Griffith-Dickson, *The Philosophy of Religion,* 400). This would result in circular reasoning. I do not at all mean that this is what I am talking about; rather, I am talking about religious experience and religious realizations that run counter to (or at least go beyond) dogmas that we are spoon-fed, and that surely do shape our experiences.

16. I believe that approaching the problem from a metaphysical perspective is necessary and possibly sufficient for establishing a philosophical basis for religious pluralism.

17. It is interesting to note that the higher the degree of dogmatism among a tradition's practitioners, the younger the religious movement. This seems to unsurprisingly correspond to the fact that younger religious traditions tend to promulgate more exclusivist dogmas, whereas older, more established traditions have made inroads toward pluralism in both theology and in their congregations. Only 72 percent of Orthodox, 56 percent of Muslims, 39 percent of Mormons, and 16 percent of Jehovah's Witnesses believe that there are multiple religions that can lead to salvation. This makes perfect sense since the younger the tradition, the more likely it will need to make dogmatic statements to mark its own territory and the more fervent it requires its congregations to be. This is a good survival strategy for a relatively nascent religious movement. Mainline Protestants are on average less dogmatic than Catholics, I suspect, because they, by historic fact of the Reformation, represent more liberal institutions, whereas Roman Catholicism (and later, Orthodox Catholicism) can be defined in relation to the Protestant Reformation as more conservative. Within the Protestant branch of Christianity, evangelicals then represent a more dogmatic branch of this historically liberal movement.

18. Although the cited poll only covers religious people in the United States, this and other compilations of statistics such as John L. Esposito and Dalia Mogahed's *Who Speaks for Islam? What a Billion Muslims Really Think* (New York: Gallup, 2007) and the corresponding research provided at http://www.GallupMuslim Societies.com imply similar pluralistic views around the world. The Gallup research documents positive views of religious others as well as (according to a poll of European Muslims) the widespread desire of Muslims to live in culturally and religiously diverse communities. Though the Gallup study avoided questions regarding views of the religious beliefs of others, the expressed desire to live in religiously diverse environments when combined with what is arguable an inherently

pluralistic doctrine of there being one God with many prophets (this is often expressed in a way that includes non-Islamic and sometimes even non-Abrahamic religious figures throughout history), it is not unreasonable to project widespread pluralistic meta-theological views among lay people of Islamic faith, especially among those living in culturally diverse places like Europe and the United States. The basic suggestion I am making here is that there is a correlation between cosmopolitan societies and pluralistic meta-theological views.

19. I have argued on behalf of Cobb and Griffin that Whiteheadian process metaphysics is most conducive to a genuine religious pluralism largely because it seems to be the only currently articulated system that can account for a nonhierarchical multiplicity of religious ultimates. See Matthew S. LoPresti, "Religious Pluralism in Analytic, Process, and South Asian Philosophies of Religion: An Essay Towards a Comparative Metaphysics of Religion," (PhD diss., University of Hawaii at Manoa, 2008), accessible at: http://hpu.academia.edu/MatthewLoPresti/Papers/.

20. This is at least how I make sense of religion as a matter of philosophical anthropology. By this measure theopoetics is not a relativism and does not necessarily result in relativistic speculative theology.

21. A brief (non-process-related) theological examination of this issue in Psalm 113 can be found in Siew Kiong Tham, "Theology Through the Psalms," (2000): 20–22, accessed August 9, 2011, http://www.newcreation.org.au/studies/pdf/C0068_TheologyPsalms.pdf.

22. Whitehead, *Process and Reality*, 346.

23. Ibid.

24. This particular persuasive power of deity is why Whitehead says very clearly in this sentence that "He does not create the world, he saves it: or more accurately, he is the poet of the world . . ." (Ibid.). It is Whitehead's aversion to the conception of God as a creator who employs raw causative power that informs his statement here that God is not a creator. But creation in another sense is, nevertheless, a part of what Whitehead seemingly intends here. For a clearer understanding of this and many other aspects that differentiate a process deity from other, perhaps more popular, conceptions of deity, see, for example, John B. Cobb Jr. and David Ray Griffin on God's persuasive power in their book *Process Theology* (Louisville, Ky.: Westminster John Knox Press, 1976).

25. It is important to note that this is not a view crucial to process theology itself; it is merely peculiar to Whitehead. For a more in-depth analysis of the fatal problems that face Whitehead's conception of God as a preserver of all value, see Matthew S. LoPresti, "The Inappropriate Tenderness of the Divine: *Mono No Aware* and the Recovery of Loss in Whitehead's Axiology," in *Butler on Whitehead: On the Occasion,* ed. Roland Faber et al. (Lanham, Md.: Lexington Books, 2012).

The World as an Ultimate: Children as Windows to the World's Sacredness
C. Robert Mesle

1. Roland Faber, *God as Poet of the World: Exploring Process Theologies,* trans. Douglas W. Stott (Westminster John Knox Press, 2008), 324. The italics are his in every case cited.

2. Ibid., 327.

3. Ibid., 322. The parenthetical "divine" is original.

4. In his forthcoming Japanese translation of my book *Process Theology,* To-kiyuki Nobuhara has translated this phrase delightfully. He explains, "'Taisetsu' means in modern Japanese: precious, of utmost importance. Your love might be referred to, therefore, as 'taisetsu na hito' (a precious person; a person of utmost importance)." E-mail message to author, March 2, 2010.

5. Robert McAfee Brown, "Starting Over: New Beginning Points for Theology," *Christian Century* 97, no. 18 (May 14, 1980): 546.

6. Cited by Tanaka, in "The Philosophy of Nothingness and Process Theology," 14–15, an unpublished paper given at Process, Religion, and Society, the International Whitehead Conference (January 5–9, 2009), held at Dharmaram College, Christ University, Bangalore, India.

7. Cobb returned to this theme in an essay he wrote for inclusion in the forth-coming Japanese translation, by Tokiyuki Nobuhara, of my book *Process Theology.* It is to that essay that I am immediately responding. He emailed the essay to me on August 16, 2008. While the manuscript carries no title, I will cite it as "Two Ultimates," since that is its main theme.

8. John Cobb Jr., *Beyond Dialogue: Toward a Mutual Transformation of Christianity and Buddhism* (Philadelphia: Fortress Press, 1982), 112. Later in *Beyond Dialogue* (124–27 especially), he argues that Emptiness can be understood in terms of Whitehead's creativity, as ultimately formless and without specific character. In "Two Ultimates," he adds: "Process theologians have learned the great religious values that lie in the realization that we are instances of creativity chiefly from Buddhism, especially because the Buddhist understanding of Dharmakaya is so similar to Whitehead's understanding of creativity" (6).

9. Of course, the phrase "religious naturalist" is even less clear than usual in the process-relational conversation, since nearly all process theists also reject su-pernaturalism and hence might be included as religious naturalists. Indeed, when I teach about religious naturalisms, I always include process theism as one impor-tant option. In this conversation, however, I use *religious naturalism* as shorthand for the nontheistic side of the process-relational family.

10. Paul Tillich, *The Dynamics of Faith* (New York: HarperOne, 2001), espe-cially chapter 3, "Faith and Symbols."

11. Paul Tillich, *Theology of Culture* (Oxford: Oxford University Press, 1959), especially chapter 5, "The Nature of Religious Language."

12. Tillich, *The Dynamics of Faith,* 42.

13. Rene Descartes, *Philosophical Works of Descartes,* trans. Elizabeth Haldane and G. R. T. Ross, vol. 1 (New York: Dover, 1931), 232. Descartes was quick to

point out that all created substances are dependent upon God. So, strictly speaking, only God would fully fit this definition of substance. Descartes would have us qualify the idea of created substances by saying that they exist independently except for their dependence on God.

14. Tillich, *The Theology of Culture*, 56.

15. Tillich, *The Dynamics of Faith*, 42–43.

16. Tillich, *The Theology of Culture*, 57.

17. Tillich, *The Dynamics of Faith*, 49.

18. I have found this quoted and credited to Elizabeth Stone on a wide range of websites, but so far none provide original reference to the source.

19. Tillich, *The Theology of Culture*, 59.

20. Tillich, *The Dynamics of Faith* 45, *The Theology of Culture*, 64. Also, Tillich, *Systematic Theology*, vol. 2 (Chicago: Harper & Row), 9.

21. Recall that, in *Beyond Dialogue*, Cobb made a very similar argument that God is not subordinate to Emptiness, which Cobb argues can be connected with Whitehead's notion of creativity. God is not subordinate to the Emptiness/Creativity that God manifests because God *actualizes* creativity. Indeed, God, he says, is the "ultimate *actuality*" (111–12).

22. Alfred North Whitehead, *Process and Reality*, corrected ed., ed. David Ray Griffin and Donald W. Sherburne (New York: Free Press, 1978).

23. Ibid., 18.

24. Ibid., 19.

25. Ibid., 24.

26. Ibid., 22.

27. Bernard Loomer, "Two Conceptions of Power," in *Criterion* 15, no. 1 (Winter 1976): 21.

28. Stephen Mitchell, *Bhagavad-Gita: A New Translation* (New York: Three-Rivers Press, 2000), 132–35 passim.

29. Meera Chakravorty, professor of Sanskrit at Bangalore University, suggests that it might be appropriate here to speak of Brahmanda here—Brahman expressed as the manifold of the world, as distinguished from the undifferentiated ultimate, Brahman (e-mail correspondence with author, March 19 and 21, 2010). Brahmanda is symbolized as the cosmic egg from which the world emerged. Mousumi Roy, another of my colleagues from India who attended the HIARPT conference in Assisi in 2008, argues in favor of keeping Brahman (e-mail correspondence, March 20, 2010). Overall, I think Brahman works if we keep in mind the traditional distinction between Brahman unmanifest and Brahman as manifest in the manifold. I refer to the latter here.

30. Whitehead, *Process and Reality*, 7, 20.

31. Ibid., 349.

32. Ibid., 348.

33. Ibid.

34. John B. Cobb Jr., "Two Ultimates." Cobb brings in the idea of the World as the third ultimate only at the end. I contributed a new "Spiritual Autobiogra-

phy" for the Japanese translation, which suggests the ideas I develop here. Nobuhara has also written for the book an essay that is tentatively titled "Reflections on the Three Ultimates and the Mystery of Creation: In Dialogue with John B. Cobb Jr. and Bob Mesle." He emphasizes the theme of loyalty, which also influences my thinking here.

35. Cobb, "Two Ultimates," 7.

36. Jeffrey D. Long, "A Whiteheadian Vedanta: Outline of a Hindu Process Theology," in *Handbook of Process Theology,* ed. Jay McDaniel and Donna Bowman (St. Louis: Chalice Press, 2006), 262–73.

37. Ibid., 268.

38. Ibid.

39. Yang Fubin, "Process Philosophy and Chinese Philosophy," PowerPoint slides. Yang was kind enough to give me an electronic copy of the slides. I quote from slide 19 as stored on my own computer.

40. Cobb, "Two Ultimates," 3.

41. Faber, *God as Poet of the World,* 326.

42. Mark 2:27 (RSV).

43. Matthew 22:37 (RSV). Of course, I suspect that many modern Christians, and especially process-relational thinkers, would see the whole format of commandments as anachronistic for a compassionate vision of the divine.

The Gravity of Love: Theopoetics and Ontological Imagination
Laurel C. Schneider

1. Joy Harjo, *The Woman Who Fell From the Sky: Poems* (New York: Norton, 1994), 10.

2. Jean-Luc Nancy, *Being Singular Plural,* trans. Robert D. Richardson and Anne E. O'Byrne (Stanford, Calif.: Stanford University Press, 2000), 39.

3. Ibid., 40.

4. Ibid. Miguel de Beistegui, "The Ontological Dispute: Badiou, Heidegger, and Deleuze" in *Alain Badiou: Philosophy and Its Conditions,* ed. Gabriel Riera (Albany: SUNY Press, 2005), 56; Gilles Deleuze and Félix Guattari, *A Thousand Plateaus,* trans. Brian Massumi (Minneapolis: University of Minnesota Press, 1987), 6.

5. Rosi Braidotti, *Metamorphoses: Towards a Materialist Theory of Becoming* (Malden, Mass.: Blackwell, 2002), 2.

6. Alain Badiou, *Being and Event,* trans. Oliver Feltham (New York: Continuum, 2005).

7. I am indebted to John Thatanamil for this excellent insight.

8. Deleuze, *A Thousand Plateaus.* See also J. Rajchman, *The Deleuze Connections* (Cambridge, Mass.: MIT Press, 2000), 7.

9. de Beistegui, "The Ontological Dispute," 49.

10. T. E. Reynolds, *The Broken Whole: Philosophical Steps Toward a Theology of Global Solidarity* (Albany: SUNY Press, 2006), 9.

11. B. E. Schmidt, "The Creation of Afro-Caribbean Religions and Their Incorporation of Christian Elements: A Critique Against Syncretism," *Transformation* 23, no. 4 (2006): 236.

12. Laurel Schneider, *Beyond Monotheism: A Theology of Multiplicity* (London: Routledge, 2008).

13. Chance and coincidence are important and recurrent themes in both Harjo and Vizenor's writing. The protagonist in Harjo's titular poem "The Woman Who Fell from the Sky" is named St. Coincidence (5–10). And according to Gerald Vizenor, "tribal consciousness is wonder, chance, coincidence, not the revisions of a pedate paradise." *Manifest Manners: Narratives on Postindian Suvivance,* 2nd ed. (Lincoln: University of Nebraska Press, 1999), 14ff. See also his preface and introduction to *Narrative Chance: Postmodern Discourse on Native American Literature,* ed. Gerald Vizenor (Norman: University of Oklahoma, 1989).

14. Samuel Johnson, *The Lives of the English Poets* (London: Oxford University Press, 1968), 180, quoted in Regina Mara Schwartz, *Sacramental Poetics at the Dawn of Secularism: When God Left the World* (Stanford, Calif.: Stanford University Press, 2008), 5.

15. Joy Harjo, "A Postcolonial Tale," in *The Woman Who Fell from the Sky,* 18.

16. Roland Faber, *God as Poet of the World: Exploring Process Theologies,* trans. Douglas W. Stott (Louisville, Ky.: Westminster John Knox Press, 2008), 202.

17. See Alfred North Whitehead, *Process and Reality,* corrected ed., ed. David Ray Griffin and Donald W. Sherburne (New York: Free Press, 1978), part 3, chapter 3.

18. Ibid., 246.

19. Regina Schwartz, *Sacramental Poetics at the Dawn of Secularism: When God Left the World* (Stanford, Calif.: Stanford University Press, 2008), 5.

20. Gerald Vizenor, *Manifest Manners,* vii. Vizenor does not capitalize *native, indian,* or the name of his own tribe, *anishinaabe* (*Ojibway*). I am following his usage where appropriate.

21. Louis Dupre, quoted in Vizenor, *Manifest Manners,* viii.

22. Vizenor, viii.

23. John Cobb, "Process Theology," in *Philosophy in the 21st Century,* ed. D. Z. Phillips and Timothy Tessin (New York: Palgrave Macmillan, 2001), 253.

24. Harjo, "A Postcolonial Tale," in *The Woman Who Fell from the Sky,* 18.

25. For a fuller discussion of the bifurcation of fact and fiction in the logic of the One, see Schneider, *Beyond Monotheism,* chapter 6.

26. See Mary Daly, *Beyond God the Father* (Boston: Beacon, 1973) and *Pure Lust* (Boston: Beacon, 1984). I also discuss this aspect of Daly's "elemental feminist philosophy" in "The Courage to See and to Sin: Mary Daly's Elemental Transformation of Paul Tillich's Ontology," in *Feminist Interpretations of Mary Daly,* ed. Marilyn Frye and Sarah Lucia Hoagland, Re-Reading the Canon (Philadelphia: Pennsylvania State University Press, 2000).

27. Catherine Keller, *The Face of the Deep: A Theology of Becoming* (New York: Routledge, 2003), 202.

28. Ibid., 231–32; Gilles Deleuze, *Difference and Repetition,* trans. Paul Patton (New York: Columbia University Press, 1994), 122ff.

Theopoetics as Radical Theology
John D. Caputo

1. G. W. F. Hegel, *Lectures on the Philosophy of Religion: The Lectures of 1827,* One-Volume Edition, ed. Peter Hodgson (Berkeley: University of California Press, 1988), 190–91. Hereafter "LPR."

2. Hans-Georg Gadamer, *Truth and Method,* 2nd rev. ed., trans. Joel Weinsheimer and Donald G. Marshall (New York: Crossroad, 1991), 388.

3. Jacques Derrida, "The University without Conditions," in *Without Alibi,* ed. and trans. Peggy Kamuf (Stanford, Calif.: Stanford University Press, 2002), 202–37.

4. I am making use of Derrida's elaboration of the distinction between *foi* and *croyance* in "Faith and Knowledge: The Two Sources of Faith and Knowledge at the Limits of Reason Alone," trans. Samuel Weber, in *Religion,* ed. Jacques Derrida and Gianni Vattimo (Stanford, Calif.: Stanford University Press, 1998), 1–78.

5. See Jacques Derrida, *Given Time, I: Counterfeit Money,* trans. Peggy Kamuf (Chicago: University of Chicago Press, 1991), 30.

6. See Jacques Derrida, *Rogues: Two Essays on Reason,* trans. Pascale-Anne Brault and Michael Naas (Stanford, Calif.: Stanford University Press, 2005).

7. Getting straight what Derrida means by *à venir* is crucial. Allow me to refer to my "Temporal Transcendence: The Very Idea of *à venir* in Derrida," in *Transcendence and Beyond,* ed. John D. Caputo and Michael Scanlon (Bloomington: Indiana University Press, 2007), 188–203.

8. I refer to the famous argument in Jacques Derrida, "The Force of Law: 'The Mystical Foundation of Authority,'" trans. Mary Quantaince, in *Acts of Religion,* ed. Gil Anidjar (New York: Routledge, 2002), 242–58.

9. LPR, 84–85, 92, 402–4.

10. LPR, 422–25.

11. LPR, 425–26n93.

12. Jacques Derrida, "*Avances,*" in *Le Tombeau du Dieu Artisan,* by Serge Margel (Paris: Edition de Kinuit, 1995), 38–39.

13. This notion of theopoetics is not "theopoetry," as David Miller contends, because these discursive resources are not deployed as a way to poetically ornament an established confessional faith and prior theological knowledge. On the contrary, it begins by delimiting and displacing the latter; then it produces a discourse cut to fit the events that takes place *in* confessional faith and theological knowledge. I make a distinction that parallels Miller's; between a faith (*foi*) in an event that takes its leave of any confessional *croyance* and its *credo.* Miller is right that I put myself at a distance from the theopoetics attributed to Altizer's death of God, but that is not because I reject Altizer's radical theology *tout court* but because his radical theology is up to its ears in Hegelian metaphysics. Altizer's Hegel is orthodox, whereas my theopoetics of the event represents a heretical and post-

metaphysical Hegelianism. Having said that I quite agree with Miller that theo-poetics displaces the -*ology* in *theology*, and that a theopoetics evokes events that are without author, that do not mean but be, that are chaosmic and open ended. That is very much my argument in *The Weakness of God: A Theology of the Event* (Bloomington: Indiana University Press, 2006). See David L. Miller, "Theopoetry or Theopoetics," *Cross Currents* 60, no. 1 (March, 2010): 6–23.

14. Friedrich Nietzsche, *Truth and Philosophy*, ed. and trans. Daniel Brazeale (Atlantic Highlands, N.J.: Humanities Press, 1979), 84.

15. Jacques Derrida, *Psyche: Inventions of the Other*, vol. 1, trans. Peggy Ka-muf and Elizabeth Rottenberg (Stanford, Calif.: Stanford University Press, 2007), 23–47.

Toward the Heraldic: A Theopoetic Response to Monorthodoxy
L. Callid Keefe-Perry

1. I use this term in awareness of Catherine Keller's work with the term *poly-doxy*. While I appreciate what I understand to be the thrust of that term, I am ea-ger to maintain the justified *right*ness, which *ortho*doxy conveys, while yet allow-ing for a multiplicity of what potentially constitutes that rightness. Thus, rather than *monodoxy* and *polydoxy* I employ the slightly more unwieldy *monorthodoxy* and *polyorthodoxy* in the hopes that it makes clear I have no desire to obliterate the categories of right and wrong, only to challenge who it is that interprets and polices the boundaries of those descriptions.

2. Walter Brueggemann, "Emergent Conversation" (lecture, November 10, 2007).

3. For more on how Jesus's ministry calls society toward a revisioning of power and control, see Donald B. Kraybill's *The Upside-Down Kingdom* (Scottdale, Pa.: Herald Press, 1990).

4. Edward Moore, "Kerygma and Dogma: A Post-Modern Perspective" *Thean-dros* 2, no. 2 (May 2004): http://www.theandros.com/kerygma.html.

5. Carl Raschke, *GloboChrist: The Great Commission Takes a Postmodern Turn* (Grand Rapids, Mich.: Baker Academic, 2008), 168.

6. Yoder, *The Royal Priesthood*, 256.

7. Amos B. Alcott, "Orphic Sayings," *The Dial: Magazine for Literature, Phi-losophy, and Religion* 1 (1841): 357.

8. Revelation 19:12 (ESV).

9. Russel Pregeant, "Scripture and Revelation," in *Handbook of Process Theology*, ed. Jay McDaniel and Donna Bowman (St. Louis, Mo.: Chalice Press, 2006), 74.

10. Faber, *God as Poet of the World*, 318.

11. I do not mean to suggest that the answers given within the monorthodox framework are easy to live into or to follow. In fact, often times they feel impos-sible to follow. Rather, the answer given to the earnest inquiry of religious seekers is often too pat of a response to contain within it the boundless possibility offered. These types of answers are easy for the answerer to give and can leave the seeker still dry and wanting more.

12. David V. Erdman, *The Complete Poetry and Prose of William Blake* (Berkeley: University of California Press, 2008), 691.

13. James Cone, "Martin E. Marty Award Interview with Cornell West" (Annual Meeting of the American Academy of Religion, Montreal, Canada: November 8, 2009).

14. James Cone, *Black Theology and Black Power* (Maryknoll, N.Y.: Orbis Books, 1997).

15. Daphne Hampson, *Theology and Feminism* (Oxford: Blackwell, 1990), 121, emphasis added.

16. Ibid., 122.

17. Ibid., 124.

18. David L. Miller, introduction to *Why Persimmons? and Other Poems: Transformations of Theology in Poetry,* Stanley R. Hopper (Atlanta: Scholars, 1987), 3.

19. Stanley R. Hopper, "The Literary Imagination and the Doing of Theology," in *The Way of Transfiguration: Religious Imagination as Theopoiesis,* ed. R. Melvin Keiser and Tony Stoneburner (Louisville, Ky.: Westminster John Knox Press, 1992), 207–29.

20. Ibid., 207.

21. Ibid., 218.

22. Ibid., 220.

23. Ibid., 221.

24. Ibid., 225.

25. Amos N. Wilder, *Theopoetic: Theology and the Religious Imagination* (Philadelphia: Fortress Press, 1976), 47.

26. Hopper, "The Literary Imagination," 224.

27. Emmanuel Levinas, *Totality and Infinity* (Pittsburgh: Duquesne University Press, 1969), 299.

28. Jason Derr, "In the Consideration of the Theopoetic," *CrossLeft: Balancing the Christian Voice* (December 2008).

29. Nancy M. Victorin-Vangerud, "From Metaphors and Models to Maps," in *Theology that Matters: Ecology, Economy, and God,* ed. Kathleen R. Darby (Minneapolis: Fortress Press, 2006), 76.

30. Wilder, *Theopoetic,* 2.

31. Paul Wildman, "Polyphonic Universities," *Futures* 30, no. 7 (1998): 627.

32. Scott Holland, "Theology Is a Kind of Writing: The Emergence of Theopoetics," *Cross Currents* 47, no. 3 (1997): 327.

33. Stanley Fish, *Is There a Text in This Class? The Authority of Interpretive Communities* (Cambridge: Harvard University Press, 1980), 354.

34. Ibid., 355.

35. Ibid., 342.

36. In the field of genetics, in particular the study of contained populations, there is a noted decline of genetic variation when a new population is created and/ or maintained by a significantly smaller segment of a larger population. For ex-

ample, the Afrikaners of South Africa are descendents of a small number of Dutch colonists. In contemporary times, Afrikaners have an unusually high frequency of the gene that causes Huntington's disease because some among the original colonists carried that gene with unusually high frequency and the community had limited contact with outside sources of genetic variation. This result has been clearly observed in numerous situations such as new colonies that had a fixed and small number of colonists with which to contribute to the gene pool, hence "founder" effect (Provine).

37. Dietrich Bonhoeffer, *The Communion of Saints: A Dogmatic Inquiry into the Sociology of the Church* (New York: Harper & Row, 1960), 22.

38. Pregeant, "Scripture and Revelation," 76.

39. Richard Kearney, *Anatheism* (New York: Columbia University Press, 2010), 14.

40. For more about the postcritical moment, see Paul Ricoeur's writing about "the second naivete," specifically his concluding chapter in *The Symbolism of Evil* (Boston: Beacon, 1969).

41. Sandra Schneiders, *The Revelatory Text* (San Francisco: Harper Collins, 1991), 172.

42. Yoder, *The Royal Priesthood*, 256.

43. Alfred North Whitehead, *Religion in the Making* (New York: Fordham University Press, 1996), 144.

44. Jorge L. Borges, *A Universal History of Infamy* (London: Penguin, 1975).

45. Raschke, *GloboChrist*, 153.

46. Ibid., 160.

The Sublime, the Conflicted Self, and Attention to the Other: Toward a Theopoetics with Iris Murdoch and Julia Kristeva
Paul S. Fiddes

1. Jean-Luc Nancy, "The Sublime Offering," in *Of The Sublime: Presence in Question,* Jean-Francois Courtine et al., trans. Jeffrey Librett (New York: SUNY Press, 1993), 25.

2. Jean-François Lyotard, *Lessons on the Analytic of the Sublime: Kant's Critique of Judgment,* trans. Elizabeth Rottenberg (Stanford, Calif.: Stanford University Press, 1994), 50–58.

3. Neither appear in Lyotard, *Lessons on the Analytic of the Sublime;* Courtine et al., *Of The Sublime;* Slavoj Žižek, *The Sublime Object of Ideology* (London: Verso, 2008); Clayton Crockett, *A Theology of the Sublime* (New York: Routledge, 2001); Philip Shaw, *The Sublime* (New York: Routledge, 2006). Passing references to Kristeva appear in Neil Hertz, *The End of the Line: Essays on Psychoanalysis and the Sublime* (New York: Columbia University Press, 1985), 231–33, and Christine Battersby, *The Sublime, Terror, and Human Difference* (London: Routledge, 2007), 116. More attention is given to Kristeva in some articles: see Charles I. Armstrong, "Echo: Reading The Unnamable Through Kant and Kristeva," *Nordic Journal of*

English Studies 1, no. 1 (June 2002): 173–87; Judy Lochhead, "The Sublime, the Ineffable, and Other Dangerous Aesthetics" in *Women and Music: A Journal of Gender and Culture,* 12 (2008): 63–74.

4. Immanuel Kant, *The Critique of Judgement,* trans. James Creed Meredith (Oxford: Oxford University Press, 1973), First Part, § 26 (pp. 98–109).

5. Ibid., First Part, §§ 23, 29 (pp. 91, 120).

6. Ibid., First Part, § 25 (p. 97); cf. § 29 (p. 119).

7. Ibid., First Part, §§ 1, 6, and 7 (pp. 41–42, 50–53).

8. Ibid., First Part, §§ 7–8 (pp. 51–56); § 16 (pp. 72–74); § 22 (pp. 84–85).

9. Iris Murdoch, "The Sublime and the Good" (1959), reprinted in Murdoch, *Existentialists and Mystics: Writings on Philosophy and Literature,* ed. Peter Conradi (London: Chatto & Windus, 1997), 205–20; "The Sublime and the Beautiful Revisited" (1959), reprinted in *Existentialists and Mystics,* 261–86.

10. Kant, *Critique of Judgement,* First Part, §§ 25, 29 (pp. 96, 123).

11. Iris Murdoch, *The Sovereignty of Good* (London: Routledge and Kegan Paul, 1970), 81–82.

12. Iris Murdoch, "Existentialists and Mystics" (1970), reprinted in *Existentialists and Mystics,* 233; cf. Murdoch, *The Sovereignty of Good,* 58–61, and her novels, *The Nice and the Good* (London: Chatto & Windus, 1968), 350, *The Good Apprentice* (London: Chatto & Windus, 1985), 245.

13. Murdoch, "Sublime and the Good," 215.

14. Murdoch, *The Sovereignty of Good,* 64–66, 69.

15. Lyotard, *Lessons on the Analytic of the Sublime,* 75.

16. Ibid., 180.

17. See the critique by Judy Lochhead, "The Sublime, the Ineffable, and Other Dangerous Aesthetics," *Women & Music* 2 (2008): 66–68.

18. Iris Murdoch, *Metaphysics as a Guide to Morals* (London: Chatto & Windus, 1992), 81–88.

19. Iris Murdoch, *Nuns and Soldiers* (London: Chatto & Windus, 1980), 107–8.

20. Ibid., 111–12, my italics.

21. Ibid., 292.

22. Ibid., 500.

23. Ibid., 152.

24. Ibid., 271.

25. Ibid., 154.

26. Ibid., 272.

27. Ibid., 385.

28. Ibid., 388.

29. Ibid., 400–403.

30. Ibid., 474.

31. Murdoch, "Sublime and the Good," 215.

32. Murdoch, *Nuns and Soldiers,* 129.

33. Ibid., 475.

34. Jacques Lacan, *Écrits: a Selection,* trans. A. Sheridan (London: Tavistock/ Routledge, 1977), 104–5, 218.

35. Jacques Lacan, *The Four Fundamental Concepts of Psychoanalysis,* trans. A. Sheridan (Harmondworth: Penguin, 1979), 54–55; Jacques Lacan, *The Ethics of Psychoanalysis,* vol. 7 of *The Seminar of Jacques Lacan,* trans. Dennis Porter (London: Routledge, 2008), 65–68, 130–31, 160.

36. E.g., Julia Kristeva, *Powers of Horror: An Essay on Abjection,* trans. Leon S. Roudiez (New York: Columbia University Press, 1982), 5–6; Julia Kristeva, *Black Sun: Depression and Melancholia* (New York: Columbia, 1989), 9–30.

37. Julia Kristeva, *Desire in Language: A Semiotic Approach to Literature and Art,* trans. T. Gora, A. Jardine, L. Roudiez (Oxford: Blackwell, 1980), 133–36.

38. Julia Kristeva, *In the Beginning Was Love: Psychoanalysis and Faith,* trans. Arthur Goldhammer (New York: Columbia University Press, 1987), 5.

39. Julia Kristeva, *Revolution in Poetic Language,* trans. M. Waller (New York: Columbia University Press, 1984), 25–30.

40. Ibid., 11–12, my italics.

41. Ibid., 2, 4–5.

42. Ibid., 12.

43. Jacques Derrida, *The Truth in Painting,* trans. Geoff Bennington and Ian Macleod (Chicago: Chicago University Press, 1987), 58–63. Derrida takes up the term from a passing use by Kant.

44. Kristeva, *Powers of Horror,* 9.

45. Ibid., 11.

46. This relies on the Hegelian sense of sublation (*Aufhebung*), which takes its point of departure from the Kantian *Erhebung*. In Hegelian idealism, two antitheses are sublated and the resulting synthesis takes place at a higher level. Freud, however, denies both Kant and Hegel: He disallows the raising of an individual or group onto some spiritual plane above the material.

47. Lacan, *Ethics of Psychoanalysis,* 122–23, 136–37.

48. Ibid., 305, 310.

49. So Christine Battersby, *The Phenomenal Woman* (Cambridge: Polity Press, 1998), 88–89.

50. Judith Butler, *Gender Trouble: Feminism and the Subversion of Identity* (New York: Routledge, 1990), 93.

51. Julia Kristeva, *Murder in Byzantium,* trans. C. Jon Delagu (New York: Columbia University Press, 2006).

52. Ibid., 32.

53. Ibid., 208–11.

54. Ibid., 136.

55. Ibid., 157–58.

56. Ibid., 205.

57. Ibid., 67.

58. Ibid., 68.

59. Ibid., 116.

60. Ibid., 83.

61. Ibid., 100.

62. Ibid., 51.

63. Ibid., 63.

64. Murdoch, *Nuns and Soldiers,* 45.

65. Ibid., 214.

66. Ibid., 290–91.

67. Kristeva, *Black Sun,* 98–100.

68. Murdoch, "Sublime and the Good," 213–14.

69. Ibid., 215.

70. Murdoch, *Nuns and Soldiers,* 69–70.

71. Ibid., 290–91.

72. Ibid., 419.

73. Ibid., 424.

74. Julia Kristeva, *Tales of Love* (New York: Columbia University Press, 1987), 23–30, 42–50.

75. Kristeva, *Black Sun,* 135. This must be a reference to Von Balthasar's "trinitarian self-giving"; see her footnote 42.

76. Kristeva, *Tales of Love,* 140.

77. Kristeva, *Black Sun,* 184, cf. 97–98.

78. Ibid., 185.

79. Ibid., 204.

80. Ibid., 207.

81. Ibid., 206–7.

82. Ibid., my italics.

83. Ibid., 211.

84. Kristeva, *Murder in Byzantium,* 14.

85. Ibid., 121.

86. Ibid., 172.

87. Ibid., 69, 72, 74.

88. Ibid., 119.

89. Ibid., 182.

90. Ibid.

91. Ibid.

92. Murdoch, *The Sovereignty of Good,* 75, 102–3; *Metaphysics as a Guide,* 494–96.

93. Peter J. Conradi, *The Saint and the Artist: A Study of the Fiction of Iris Murdoch* (London: HarperCollins, 2001), 142.

94. Murdoch, *Nuns and Soldiers,* 381.

95. Ibid., 368.

96. Cf. Kristeva, *Murder in Byzantium,* 224.

97. Slavoj Žižek, *Sublime Object of Ideology* (New York: Verso, 1997), 227–34.

98. Lacan, *Ethics of Psychoanalysis,* 158–59, 185–97.

99. Slavoj Žižek, *The Fragile Absolute: Or Why is the Christan Legacy Worth Fighting For?* (London: Verso, 2008), 91–92, 132–34, 136–37.

100. Žižek, *The Fragile Absolute,* 147–49; cf. Žižek, *Sublime Object of Ideology,* 227–29.

101. See Kristeva, *Black Sun,* 132: "a caesura, which some have called a 'hiatus.'" See further Kristeva, *Black Sun,* 272n28. Kristeva references *La Gloire et La Croix* (1975), 3:2 = *The Glory of the Lord: A Theological Aesthetics,* trans. Brian McNeil, vol. 7, *Theology: The New Covenant* (Edinburgh: T&T Clark, 1989); she mentions no pages, but relevant sections are on "self-abandonment" (142–61), "the time of discipleship" (188–201: see "hiatus," 190), and "trinitarian self-giving" (391–98).

102. For instance, Daniel D. Williams, *The Spirit and the Forms of Love* (London: Nisbet, 1968), 52–90; Paul Tillich, *Systematic Theology,* combined vol. (Welwyn: James Nisbet, 1968), 1:310–16; 3: 143–47.

103. Paul S. Fiddes, *The Creative Suffering of God* (Oxford: Oxford University Press, 1988), 66–68; so, in agreement, Vincent Brümmer, *The Model of Love* (Cambridge University Press, Cambridge, 1993), 237.

104. Eberhard Jüngel, *God as the Mystery of the World,* trans. D. Guder (Edinburgh: T&T Clark, 1983), 317–18.

105. For the term, see, e.g., Amos Wilder, *Theopoetic: Theology and the Religious Imagination* (Philadelphia: Fortress, 1976); Roland Faber, *God as Poet of the World: Exploring Process Theologies,* trans. Douglas W. Stott (Louisville, Ky.: Westminster John Knox Press, 2008), 14–15.

106. Augustine, *De Trinitate* 5.6: "the names . . . refer to relations"; Aquinas, *Summa Theologiae:* "person signifies relation."

107. G. Leibniz, *Die Philosophischen Schriften,* ed. G. J. Gerhardt, vol. 7 (Hildesheim: G. Olms, 1890), 389–20.

108. See Paul S. Fiddes, *Participating in God: A Pastoral Doctrine of the Trinity* (London: Darton, Longman & Todd, 2000), 28–55.

109. For example, David Bentley Hart, *The Beauty of the Infinite: The Aesthetics of Christian Truth* (Grand Rapids, Mich.: Eerdmans, 2003), 43–92; cf. John Milbank, "Sublimity: The Modern Transcendent," in *Transcendence,* ed. Regina Schwarz (New York: Routledge, 2004), 211–34.

Theopoiesis and the Pluriverse: Notes on a Process
Catherine Keller

1. Gary Dorrien, *The Making of American Liberal Theoogy: Crisis, Irony, and Postmodernity: 1950–2005* (Louisville: Westminster John Knox Press, 2006), 190.

2. Faber, *God as Poet of the World.*

3. Clement of Alexandria, *Christ the Educator,* 1.6, in *Ante-Nicene Fathers,* ed. A. Roberts and J. Donaldson (Buffalo, N.Y.: Christian Literature, 1886–1896). Reprint, Peabody, Mass.: Hendrickson, 1994. See also *Partakers of the Divine Nature: The History and Development of Deification in the Christian Traditions,* ed.

Michael J. Christensen and Jeffery Wittung (Madison, N.J.: Farleigh Dickinson University Press, 2007). See especially my colleague Michael J. Christensen's "The Problem, Promise, and Process of Theosis," 25.

4. Clement of Alexandria, *Christ the Educator,* 1.6. Cf. also the discussion of Irenaeus and Athanasius in my *Face of the Deep: A Theology of Becoming* (New York: Routledge, 2003).

5. Christensen, "The Problem, Promise, and Process," 23.

6. Quoted in the text Roland Faber chooses as epigraph to *God as the Poet of the World.*

7. Thomas Buchan, "Paradise as the Landscape of Salvation in Ephrem the Syrian," in *Partakers,* 147.

8. Michael J. Christensen, "John Wesley: Christian Perfection as Faith Filled with the Energy of Love," in Christensen and Wittung, *Partakers,* 224.

9. John 10:34.

10. Morny Joy, Kathleen O'Grady, Judith L. Poxon, eds., *Religion in French Feminist Thought: Critical Perspectives* (London: Routledge, 2003), 8.

11. Grace Jantzen, *Becoming Divine: Towards a Feminist Philosophy of Religion* (Bloomington: Indiana University Press, 1999).

12. Alfred North Whitehead, *Process and Reality,* corrected ed., ed. David Ray Griffin and Donald W. Sherburne (New York: Free Press, 1978), 346.

13. Amos Niven Wilder, *Theopoetic: Theology and the Religious Imagination* (Lima, Ohio: Academic Renewal Press, 2001), iv.

14. David Leroy Miller, "Theopoetry or Theopoetics?," *Cross Currents* 60, no. 1 (2010): 9, accessed May 16, 2012, ATLA Religion Database with ATLASerials, EBSCOhost.

15. Stanley R. Hopper and David Miller, eds., *Interpretation: The Poetry of Meaning* (New York: Harcourt, Brace & World, 1967).

16. Roland Faber, Henry Krips, and Daniel Pettus, eds., *Event and Decision: Ontology and Politics Badiou, Deleuze, and Whitehead* (Newcastle: Cambridge Scholars, 2010).

17. Miller, "Theopoetry," 8.

18. Ibid., 10.

19. Ibid., 8.

20. See Chris Boesel and Catherine Keller, eds., *Apophatic Bodies: Negative Theology, Incarnation, and Relationality* (New York: Fordham University Press, 2010). Currently I am finishing *Cloud of the Impossible: Theological Entanglements,* which continues the work of a constructive apophatic theology.

21. Jacques Derrida, *"How Not to Speak,"* trans. Ken Frieden, in *Derrida and Negative Theology,* ed. Harold Coward and Toby Foshay (Albany: SUNY Press, 1992).

22. Jacque Derrida, *On the Name* (Stanford, Calif.: Stanford University Press, 1995), 69. He explores here the Baroque apophatic poetry of Silesius, important also to Heidegger.

23. Elizabeth A. Johnson, *She Who Is: The Mystery of God in Feminist Theological Discourse* (New York: Crossroad, 2002), 44–46.

24. Cardinal Nicholas of Cusa, *Selected Spiritual Writings,* trans. H. Lawrence Bond (Mahwah, N.J.: Paulist Press, 1997), 127.

25. As in Nancy J. Hudson, *Becoming God: The Doctrine of Theosis in Nicholas of Cusa* (Washington, D.C.: Catholic University of America Press, 2007).

26. Cusa, *Selected Spiritual Writings,* 134.

27. Alfred North Whitehead, *Science and the Modern World* (New York: Free Press, 1967), 114.

28. Faber, *God as Poet of the World,* 151.

29. Ibid. *Reconciliation* is for him a metonym for the "nondifference" of the Cusan *non aliud.*

30. Ibid.

31. Ibid., 260.

32. Ibid.; emphasis mine.

33. Elsewhere I construct a political reading of the cosmologial convivencia, in the light of a millennium long crusader complex definitive of "the West," in dialogue with Enrique D. Dussel. Catherine Keller, "Peace Talk, or, the Unspeakable Conviviality of Becoming," *Process Studies* 40, no. 2 (2011): 315–39.

34. Note Faber's critique of McFague where he argues against construing "process theology as *poetic in nature." God as Poet of the World,* 322.

35. Whitehead, *Process and Reality,* 346.

36. See *Polydoxy: Theology of Multiplicity and Relation,* ed. Catherine Keller and Laurel C. Schneider (New York: Routledge, 2011).

37. Alfred North Whitehead, *Modes of Thought* (New York: Free Press, 1968), 174.

38. Ernesto Cardenal, *Pluriverse* (New York: New Directions, 2009).

39. Vandana Shiva, *Earth Democracy: Justice, Sustainability, and Peace* (Cambridge, Mass.: South End Press, 2005).

Consider the Lilies and the Peacocks: A Theopoetics of Life Between the Folds
Luke B. Higgins

1. Alfred North Whitehead, *Process and Reality,* corrected ed., ed. David Ray Griffin and Donald W. Sherburne (New York: Free Press, 1978), 346.

2. Elizabeth Grosz, *Chaos, Territory, Art: Deleuze and the Framing of the Earth* (New York: Columbia University Press, 2008).

3. Gilles Deleuze and Félix Guattari, *A Thousand Plateaus: Capitalism and Schizophrenia,* trans. Brian Massumi (Minneapolis: University of Minnesota Press, 1987).

4. Roland Faber, *God as Poet of the World: Exploring Process Theologies,* trans. Douglas W. Stott (Louisville, Ky.: Westminster John Knox Press, 2008), 317.

5. While I do not have the space in this paper to fully develop my approach, I can briefly outline it here: I assert that the *becoming* of God's consequent nature

(refracted/lured by the primordial vision), parallels the *emptying out* of creation's occasions to its virtual possibilities—which together culminate in the gift of the initial aim. Conversely, the *emptying* of God's "virtually eternal" primordial nature (to make room for the fullness of the world) parallels the *becoming* or concrescence of the plurality of the world's events.

6. Deleuze and Guattari, *A Thousand Plateaus*, 315.

7. Ibid., 311–12.

8. Ibid., 311.

9. Ibid.

10. Grosz, *Chaos, Territory, Art*, 6.

11. Gilles Deleuze and Félix Guattari, *What Is Philosophy?*, trans. Hugh Tomlinson and Graham Burchell (New York: Columbia University Press, 1984), 28.

12. Grosz, *Chaos, Territory, Art*, 9.

13. Deleuze and Guattari, *What is Philosophy?*, 186.

14. Deleuze and Guattari, *A Thousand Plateaus*, 42.

15. Grosz, *Chaos, Territory, Art*, 6–7.

16. Ibid., 30.

17. Ibid., 34.

18. Charles Hartshorne, *Born to Sing* (Bloomington: Indiana University Press, 1973), 56.

19. Grosz, *Chaos, Territory, Art*, 7.

20. Ibid., 10.

21. Following this principle, Whitehead observes a fundamental degree of indeterminacy in the emergence of even some of the most basic structures of the cosmos. So, for instance, even basic physical laws as incontrovertibly universal as those of electromagnetism are understood by Whitehead as spontaneous actualizations of order that could have emerged differently. Hence, we can characterize ourselves as inhabiting a particular "cosmic epoch" characterized by "electronic and protonic actual entities: "The arbitrary, as it were, 'given' elements in the laws of nature warn us that we are in a special cosmic epoch. Here the phrase 'cosmic epoch' is used to mean that widest society of actual entities whose immediate relevance to ourselves is traceable. This epoch is characterized by electronic and protonic actual entities, and yet more ultimate actual entities which can be dimly discerned in the quanta of energy." Whitehead, *Process and Reality*, 91.

22. Ibid., 47.

23. Ibid., 344.

24. Faber, *God as Poet of the World*, 324. The following quote from Faber drives home even further the extent to which divine poiesis must dissociate itself from any traditional concept of the divine power responsible for the world's creation: "To remind us a last time of Whitehead's line on the poet of the world, the *posse* of the divine *poiesis* must *completely subtract itself form the complicity of 'creation'*— God as being 'someone' creating, a 'self' being subject of self-creativity, a 'force-field' of creativity, a 'divine' matrix—and *affirm nothing but the salvation of the manifold, that is, insist only as/on infinite manifoldness*" (327).

25. Ibid., 101.

26. Whitehead, *Process and Reality*, 105.

27. Ibid., 96–97.

28. Faber, *God as Poet of the World*, 72.

29. Whitehead, *Process and Reality*, 104.

30. In Whitehead's words, "According to this interpretation, the human body is to be conceived as a complex 'amplifier'—to use the language of the technology of electromagnetism. The various actual entities, which compose the body are transmitted to one or more central occasions to be inherited with enhancements accruing along the way, or finally added to by reason of the final integration." Whitehead, *Process and Reality*, 119.

31. Whitehead, *Process and Reality*, 107.

32. Ibid., 81.

33. Ibid., 105–6.

34. Ibid., 339; my emphasis.

35. Ibid., 107.

36. Faber, *God as Poet of the World*, 72.

37. In Faber's words, "What, however, is the actual status of this 'potential' within events? As surprising as it may initially seem, Whitehead paradoxically defines it as the presence of the timeless within the process. In and of itself, the possible is not temporal, but rather is that which is timeless within all time. That notwithstanding, it is the ground of the temporality and status of time within the history of events and event nexuses." Faber, *God as Poet of the World*, 86.

38. I am certainly not claiming to be alone in making this point: Various Process theologians, including Marjorie Suchocki and Faber, however, also recognize that without God's consequent nature, God would not be able to adapt God's primordial vision to the particular contextual situations of each of the world's occasions in the initial aim. One passage at the very end of the chapter of *Process and Reality* entitled "God and the World" gestures toward this link. After speaking of a first phase of conceptual origination (God's Primordial nature), a second phase of physical origination (concrescence of the world's occasions), and a third phase of everlastingly perfected actuality (God's Consequent nature), Whitehead goes on to speak of a "fourth phase" in which the creative action completes itself. "For the perfected actuality passes back into the temporal world, and qualifies this world so that each temporal actuality includes it as an immediate fact of relevant experience. For the kingdom of heaven is with us today" (351). Faber gives a prominent place to this "fourth phase" of the divine-world process, identifying it with what he calls God's "primordial superjectivity," which he ends up identifying with God the Father as the "origin of the divine process." Faber, *God as Poet of the World*, 187. Along the lines of Faber's uniquely relational and processual Trinitarianism, I want to suggest that we grant God's consequent receptivity of the world a more prominent role in our conception of a larger divine–world ecology.

39. Faber, *God as Poet of the World*, 93.

Becoming Intermezzo: Eco-theopoetics after the Anthropic Principle

Roland Faber

1. See E. Teale, *The Wilderness World of John Muir* (Boston: Mariner Books, 2001).

2. For Whitehead's understanding of this "patience" of nature, see Alfred North Whitehead, *The Principle of Relativity* (New York: Cosimo, 2007), chapter 2.

3. See Alfred North Whitehead, *Process and Reality,* corrected ed., ed. David Ray Griffin and Donald W. Sherburne (New York: Free Press, 1978), 7.

4. See I. Robinet, *Taoism: Growth of a Religion* (Stanford, Calif.: Stanford University Press, 1997), 11.

5. See D. T. Suzuki, *Outlines of Mahayana Buddhism* (Chicago: University of Chicago Press, 1907), chapters 8–9.

6. See Paul Davies, *God and the New Physics* (New York: Simon & Schuster, 1983), 214–17.

7. See R. Nadeau, "The Economist Has No Clothes: Unscientific Assumptions in Economic Theory Are Undermining Efforts to Solve Environmental Problems," in *Scientific American* (April 2008): 42.

8. See Alfred North Whitehead, *Adventures of Ideas* (New York: Free Press, 1967), chapter 10.

9. See R. L. Fetz, *Whiteheads Prozeßdenken und Substanzmetaphysik* (Munich: Alber, 1981).

10. See C. Robert Mesle, *Process-Relational Philosophy: An Introduction to Alfred North Whitehead* (West Conshohocken, Pa.: Templeton Foundation Press, 2008), chapter 5.

11. See Stephen T. Franklin, *Speaking from the Depth: Alfred North Whitehead's Hermeneutical Metaphysics of Propositions, Experience, Symbolism, Language, and Religion* (Grand Rapids, Mich.: Eerdmans, 1990), chapter 13.

12. See Roland Faber, "'Amid a Democracy of Fellow Creatures'—Onto/Politics and the Problem of Slavery in Whitehead and Deleuze (with an Intervention of Badiou)," in Roland Faber, Henry Krips, and Daniel Pettus, eds., *Event and Decision: Ontology and Politics in Badiou, Deleuze, and Whitehead* (Newcastle: Cambridge Scholars, 2010), 192–37.

13. See Roland Faber, *God as Poet of the World: Exploring Process Theologies,* trans. Douglas W. Stott (Westminster John Knox, 2008), § 35.

14. Whitehead, *Adventures of Ideas,* 169.

15. Ibid.

16. See J. Thomas Howe, *Faithful to the Earth: Nietzsche and Whitehead on God and the Meaning of Human Life* (Lanham, Md.: Rowman & Littlefield, 2003), chapter 2.

17. See Gianni Vattimo, *Beyond Interpretation: The Meaning of Hermeneutics for Philosophy* (Stanford, Calif.: Stanford University Press, 1997), chapter 1.

18. See David Ray Griffin, *Reenchantment without Supernaturalism: A Process Philosophy of Religion* (Ithaca, N.Y.: Cornell University Press, 2001), chapter 2.

19. See Gilles Deleuze, *Desert Islands and Other Texts: 1953–1974* (Los Angeles: Semiotext[e], 2004), 117–27.

20. See Edward Casey, *The Fate of Place: A Philosophical History* (Berkeley: University of California Press, 1998), chapters 6–7.

21. See Joseph Bracken, *The Divine Matrix: Creativity as Link between East and West* (Maryknoll, N.Y.: Orbis, 1995), chapter 3.

22. See Alfred North Whitehead, *Science and the Modern World* (New York: Free Press, 1967), chapter 5.

23. Ibid., 103.

24. See Roland Faber, "Immanence and Incompleteness: Whitehead's Late Metaphysics," in Roland Faber, Brian Henning, and Clinton Combs, eds., *Beyond Metaphysics? Explorations in Alfred North Whitehead's Late Thought* (Amsterdam: Rodopi, 2010), 91–107.

25. See Philip Rose, *On Whitehead* (Belmont, Calif.: Wadsworth/Thomas Learning, 2002), chapter 1.

26. See Roland Faber, "Whitehead at Infinite Speed: Deconstructing System as Event," in *Schleiermacher and Whitehead: Open Systems in Dialogue,* ed. Christine Helmer, Marjorie Suchocki, and John Quiring (Berlin: de Gruyter, 2004), 39–72.

27. Whitehead, *Adventures of Ideas,* 201.

28. Ibid., 236.

29. See Judith Butler, *Gender Trouble: Feminism and the Subversion of Identity* (New York: Routledge, 1999), chapters 5–6.

30. See Thomas J. J. Altizer, *The New Gospel of Christian Atheism* (Aurora, Colo.: Davies Group, 2002), chapters 4–5.

31. See Gilles Deleuze, *Two Regimes of Madness: Texts and Interviews 1975–1995* (Los Angeles: Semiotext[e], 2006), 304.

32. See Roland Faber, "'Indra's Ear'—God's Absence of Listening" in *The Presence and Absence of God,* ed. Ingolf U. Dalferth (Tübingen: Mohr Siebeck, 2010), 161–86.

33. See Roland Faber, "Ecotheology, Ecoprocess, and *Ecotheosis*: A Theopoetical Intervention," in *Salzburger Zeitschrift für Theologie* 12 (2008): 80–83.

34. See Ibid., 75–80.

35. See Gary Gutting, *French Philosophy in the Twentieth Century* (Cambridge: Cambridge University Press, 2001).

36. See Roland Faber, "Introduction: Negotiating Becoming," in *Secrets of Becoming: Negotiating Whitehead, Deleuze, and Butler,* ed. Roland Faber and Andrea Stephenson (New York: Fordham University Press, 2011), 1–52.

37. See Christina Aus der Au, *Achtsam wahrnehmen: Eine theologische Umwelttethik* (Neukirchen-Vluyn: Neukirchener, 2003), chapters 2.1, 2.3.

38. See Rosemary Radford Ruether, *Gaia and God: An Ecofeminist Theology of Earth Healing* (New York: HarperOne, 1994).

39. See Faber, "Ecotheology," 91–95.

40. See A. Naess, *Ecology, Community, and Lifestyle: Outline of an Ecosophy* (Cambridge: Cambridge University Press, 1993).

41. See George Sessions, "Deep Ecology as Worldview," in Mary Evelyn Tucker and John A. Grim, eds., *Worldviews and Ecology: Religion, Philosophy, and the Environment* (Maryknoll, N.Y.: Orbis, 1994), 212–13.

42. Ibid., 87–88.

43. See Aus der Au, *Achtsam wahrnehmen*, chapters 2.5–6.

44. Faber, "Ecotheology," 86–91.

45. See Roland Faber, *Prozeßtheologie: Zu ihrer Würdigung und kritischen Erneuerung* (Mainz: Grünewald, 2000), § 25.

46. See Roland Faber, "Cultural Symbolization of a Sustainable Future," in *New Directions in Sustainable Design,* ed. Adrian Parr and Michael Zaretsky (New York: Routledge, 2011), 242–55.

47. Whitehead, *Process and Reality,* 4.

48. See Roland Faber, "Surrationality and Chaosmos: For a More Deleuzian Whitehead (with a Butlerian Intervention)," in *Secrets of Becoming,* 157–77.

49. See William Connoly, *Pluralism* (Durham, N.C.: Duke University Press, 2005), chapter 3.

50. See Roland Faber, "Organic or Orgiastic Metaphysics? Reflections on Whitehead's Reception in Contemporary Poststructuralism," in *Japanese Journal of Process Thought* 14 (2010): 203–22.

51. See Gilles Deleuze, *The Fold: Leibniz and the Baroque* (Minneapolis: University of Minnesota Press, 1993), chapter 6.

52. See Whitehead, *Process and Reality,* 83–109.

53. See Faber, "Cultural Symbolization," 246–48.

54. See Deleuze, *The Fold,* 81.

55. See Faber, "Ecotheology," 89.

56. See Gordon Kaufman, *In the Beginning . . . Creativity* (Minneapolis: Fortress Press, 2004), chapter 2.

57. See Michel Foucault, *Power/Knowledge: Selected Interviews and Other Writings, 1972–1977* (New York: Vintage, 1980).

58. Gilles Deleuze and Félix Guattari, *A Thousand Plateaus* (Minneapolis: University of Minnesota Press, 1996), 239.

59. Alfred North Whitehead, *Religion in the Making* (New York: Fordham University Press, 1996), 87.

60. See Roland Faber, "Bodies of the Void: Polyphilia and Theoplicity," in *Apophatic Bodies: Negative Theology, Incarnation, and Relationship,* ed. Chris Boesel and Catherine Keller (Fordham, 2010), 200–23.

61. See Julia Kristeva, *Revolution in Poetic Language* (New York: Columbia University Press, 1984).

62. See Alfred North Whitehead, *Symbolism: Its Meaning and Effect* (New York: Fordham, 1985), chapters 1–2.

63. Whitehead, *Process and Reality,* 50.

64. Ibid., 176.

65. Georges Bataille, *Theory of Religion* (Brooklyn, N.Y.: Zone Books, 1992), 19.

66. Ibid., 20.

67. See Faber, "Cultural Symbolization," 245–46.

68. See George Bataille, *Inner Experience* (New York: SUNY, 1988), part 4.

69. See Luce Irigaray, *The Sex Which Is Not One* (Ithaca, N.Y.: Cornell University Press, 1985).

70. See Gilles Deleuze and Félix Guattari, *What Is Philosophy?* (New York: Columbia University Press, 1994), 35.

71. See Tasmin E. Lorain, *Irigaray and Deleuze: Experiments in Visceral Philosophy* (Ithaca, N.Y.: Cornell University Press, 1999).

72. See Noëlle McAfee, *Julia Kristeva* (New York: Routledge, 2003), chapter 1.

73. Alfred North Whitehead, *Modes of Thought* (New York: Free Press, 1968), 174.

74. Gilles Deleuze, *Difference and Repetition* (New York: Columbia University Press, 1994), 42. See Roland Faber, "'The Infinite Movement of Evanescence'—The Pythagorean Puzzle in Plato, Deleuze, and Whitehead," in *American Journal of Theology and Philosophy* 21, no. 1 (2000): 171–99.

75. See Roland Faber, "De-Ontologizing God: Levinas, Deleuze and Whitehead," in *Process and Difference: Between Cosmological and Poststructuralist Postmodernism,* ed. Catherine Keller and Anne Daniells, University of New York Series in Constructive Postmodern Thought (New York: SUNY, 2002), 209–34.

76. See Faber, *God as Poet of the World,* § 31.

77. Whitehead, *Process and Reality,* 348.

78. See Faber, *Prozeßtheologie,* § 7.

79. See Michael P. Levine, *Pantheism: The Non-theistic Concept of Deity* (New York: Routledge, 1994).

80. See Deleuze and Guattari, *What Is Philosophy?,* 60. Cf. Robert S. Corrington, *Ecstatic Naturalism: Signs of the World* (Bloomington: Indiana University Press, 1994).

81. See Catherine Keller, *The Face of the Deep: A Theology of Becoming* (New York: Routledge, 2003), chapter 12.

82. See Roland Faber, "God's Advent/ure: The End of Evil and the Origin of Time," in *World Without End: Christian Eschatology from Process Perspective,* ed. Joseph Bracken (Grand Rapids, Mich.: Eerdmans, 2005), 91–112.

83. See Roland Faber, "God in the Making. Religious Experience and Cosmology in Whitehead's *Religion in the Making* in Theological Perspective," in *L'experience de Dieu: Lectures de Religion in the Making d'Alfred N. Whitehead: Aletheia,* ed. Michel Weber and Samuel Rouvillois (Janvier: Ecole Saint-Jean, 2005), 179–200.

84. See Faber, *God as Poet of the World,* § 40.

85. See Roland Faber, *The Divine Manifold* (forthcoming 2012), part 1.

86. See Griffin, *Reenchantment without Supernaturalism,* chapter 7.

87. See Faber, *Divine Manifold,* chapter 11.

88. See Faber, "Bodies of the Void," 217; cf. Roland Faber, "The Sense of Peace: A Para-doxology of Divine Multiplicity," in *Polydoxy: Theology of Multiplicity and Relation,* ed. Catherine Keller and Laurel Schneider (New York: Routledge, 2011), 36–56.

89. See Faber, *God as Poet of the World,* 326; cf. *Divine Manifold,* chapter 3.

90. Whitehead, *Process and Reality,* 351.

91. See Faber, "Ecotheology," 113–15; cf. *Divine Manifold,* chapter 14.

92. See Faber, "Ecotheology," 100.

93. The reference to "consciousness" is of course meant in the sense of Whitehead's insistence on the "dim consciousness" by which we reverse our basis for experience from "presentational immediacy" to "causal efficacy" and, hence, a fundamentally different opening to the feeling of eco-nature, as quoted earlier in the text. It does, therefore, not indicate an idealism of mere conscious change of direction in terms of ecological reorientation, but understands "counsciousness" in the context of Whitehead's evolutionary view in which it arises as the emergence of art and artificiality in eco-nature. See Whitehead, *Adventures of Ideas,* 269–70.

94. Deleuze and Guattari, *A Thousand Plateaus,* 10.

95. See Laurel Schneider, *Beyond Monotheism: A Theology of Multiplicity* (New York: Routledge, 2008).

96. See Faber, "Cultural Symbolization," 250–52.

97. See Faber, "Ecotheology," 105.

98. See Ibid, 89–90.

99. See Faber, *God as Poet of the World,* 325; cf. *Divine Manifold,* chapter 11.

100. See James Williams, *Encounters and Influences: The Transversal Thought of Gilles Deleuze* (Manchester: Clinamen Press, 2005), chapter 5.

101. See Faber, "Amid a Democracy," 204–11.

102. See Roland Faber, "Tears of God: In the Rain with D. Z. Phillips and J. Keller, Waiting for Wittgenstein and Whitehead," in *Metaphysics, Analysis, and the Grammar of God,* ed. Randy Ramal (Tübingen: Mohr Siebeck, 2010), 57–103.

103. See Faber, "Ecotheology," 112.

104. See *Divine Manifold,* part 3.

105. See Whitehead, *Process and Reality,* 346.

106. Deleuze and Guattari, *A Thousand Plateaus,* 17.

107. See Ibid., 470.

108. See Gilles Deleuze, "Immanence: A Life," in Gilles Deleuze, *Pure Immanence: Essays on a Life* (Brooklyn, N.Y.: Zone Books, 2005), 25–33.

109. See Roland Faber, "'O Bitches of Impossibility!'—Programmatic Dysfunction in the Chaosmos of Deleuze and Whitehead," in *Deleuze, Whitehead, Bergson: Rhizomatic Connections,* ed. Keith Robinson (New York: Palgrave Macmillan, 2009), 200–219.

110. Whitehead, *Process and Reality,* 15.

111. See Deleuze and Guattari, *A Thousand Plateaus,* 272–86.

112. Whitehead, *Adventures of Ideas,* 295.

113. See Roland Faber, "Bodies of the Void," 210–13.

114. See Whitehead, *Religion in the Making,* 139–49.

115. See Ibid., 141.

116. Whitehead, *Process and Reality,* 15.

117. See Paul Davies, *The Mind of God: The Scientific Basis for a Rational World* (New York: Touchstone Books, 1972), chapter 2.

118. See John B. Cobb Jr., *Beyond Dialogue: Toward a Mutual Transformation of Christianity and Buddhism* (New York: Wipf & Stock, 1998).

119. See Faber, *Divine Manifold,* chapter 5.

120. See Ibid., chapter 4.

121. See Gene Reeves, "Divinity in Process Thought and the Lotus Sutra," in *Journal of Chinese Philosophy* 28, no. 4 (2001): 353–87.

Silence, Theopoetics, and Theologos: On the Word That Comes After
John Thatamanil

1. "God is an actual entity, and so is the most trivial puff of existence in far-off empty space. But, though there are gradations of importance, and diversities of function, yet in the principles which actuality exemplifies all are on the same level. The final facts are, all alike, actual entities; and these actual entities are drops of experience, complex and interdependent." Alfred North Whitehead, *Process and Reality,* corrected ed., ed. David Ray Griffin and Donald W. Sherburne (New York: Free Press, 1978), 18.

2. Scholars of the Areopagite suggest either that this text is fictitious or that it has been lost to history. One cannot help but wonder what the fate of theopoetics would have been if we had enjoyed access to this text.

3. Whitehead, *Process and Reality,* 351.

4. Amos Niven Wilder, *Theopoetic: Theology and the Religious Imagination* (Lima, Ohio: Academic Renewal Press, 2001), 2.

5. Ibid.

6. Ibid.

7. Ibid., 6.

8. Ibid., 102.

9. Regrettably, there is no way to do justice to such a rich and varied slate of offerings and only a handful of authors will be directly referenced herein.

10. Harold H. Oliver, "Myth and Metaphysics: Perils of the Metaphysical Translation of Mythical Images," in *Metaphysics, Theology, and Self: Relational Essays* (Macon, Ga.: Mercer University Press, 2006), 33–34.

11. Ibid., 34.

12. Ibid., 36.

13. "The Divine Names," *Pseudo-Dionysius: The Complete Works,* 57.

14. Ibid., 55.

15. Paul Tillich, *Systematic Theology,* vol. 1 (Chicago: University of Chicago Press, 1951), 239.

16. Paul Tillich, *Systematic Theology,* vol. 2 (Chicago: University of Chicago Press, 1957), 9.

17. Ibid., 9–10.

18. Harold H. Oliver, "A New Approach to a Hermeneutic of Whitehead," *Creative Transformation* (Summer, 1993): 3.

19. Ibid.

20. Ibid.

21. Ibid.

22. Ibid., 4.

Contributors

John D. Caputo is the Thomas J. Watson Professor Emeritus of Religion at Syracuse University, where he taught from 2004 until his retirement in 2011, and the David R. Cook Professor Emeritus of Philosophy at Villanova, where he taught from 1968 until 2004. Caputo's works circulate between philosophy and theology, treating "sacred" texts and traditions as a poetics of the human condition, or as a theopoetics, a poetics of the event harbored in the name of God. His major books have attempted to persuade us that hermeneutics goes all the way down (*Radical Hermeneutics*), that Derrida is a thinker to be reckoned with by theology (*The Prayers and Tears of Jacques Derrida*), and that theology is best served by getting over its love affair with power and authority and embracing what Caputo, following St. Paul, calls *The Weakness of God*. He has also addressed wider-than-academic audiences in *On Religion* and *What Would Jesus Deconstruct?* He has an interest in interacting with church and community activists and has long been interested in Ikon. He is currently working on a book on God to be entitled *The Insistence of God: A Theology of Perhaps,* and another book on risen bodies, angelology, and technology as figures of our frail and mortal flesh, probably to be entitled *The Fate of All Flesh.*

Vincent Colapietro is liberal arts research professor of philosophy at Pennsylvania State University. His areas of specialization include American philosophy, semiotics, and Charles Sanders Peirce. His most recent book is *Fateful Shapes of Human Freedom: John William Miller & The Crises of Modernity* (2003). His most recent coedited volume is John William Miller's *The Task of Criticism: Essays On Philosophy, History & Community,* edited with Joseph P. Fell and Michael J. McGandy

(2005). His current projects include *Psyches and Their Vicissitudes*, an attempt to stage a mutual interrogation between pragmatism and psychoanalysis.

Roland Faber is the founder of the Whitehead Research Project. He is Kilsby Family/John B. Cobb, Jr. Professor of Process Studies at Claremont Lincoln University, professor of religion and philosophy at Claremont Graduate University, and codirector of the Center for Process Studies. His fields of research and publication include systematic theology; process thought and process theology; poststructuralism; interreligious discourse, especially Christianity and Buddhism; comparative philosophy of religion; philosophy, theology, spirituality, and cosmology of the Renaissance; and mysticism. He has published four books, including *God as Poet of the World: Exploring Process Theologies* (2008), and edited two.

Jeremy Fackenthal is a recent graduate of Claremont Graduate University with a PhD in philosophy of religion and theology. He is adjunct professor at Vincennes University. His fields of research include post-Holocaust philosophy and theology, critical theory and the Frankfurt School, and process philosophy and theology. He has contributed to *Butler on Whitehead: On the Occasion* (2012) and has been published in the journal *Concrescence*.

Paul S. Fiddes is professor of systematic theology and University of Oxford Director of Research at Regent's Park College. Paul Fiddes took undergraduate degrees in both English literature and theology at the University of Oxford, and he continues to have a particular interest in the interface between theology and literature. After gaining a doctorate (DPhil) in theology from Oxford, he spent a year of postdoctoral study in the University of Tübingen, Germany. He taught as a fellow of Regent's Park College from 1972 to 1989 and then became principal of the college for eighteen years, recently moving into his new position, in which he is mainly occupied with supervising postgraduate students and coordinating research projects of the college. He gained the degree of doctor of divinity (DD) of the University of Oxford for his published work in 2005. Professor Fiddes is an ordained minister of the Baptist Union of Great Britain and serves as the chair of the Doctrine Commission of the Baptist World Alliance. He is very active in ecumenical conversations and is at present the cochair of the international conversations between the Roman Catholic Church and the Baptist World Alliance, as well as an ecumenical representative on the Synod of the Church of England. This mixture of academic and church life has been focused on a double concern: to connect Christian faith with the culture of the modern world and to connect the local church with the riches of faith and tradition in the Church Universal.

Michael Halewood is a lecturer in social theory at the University of Essex, U.K. His main area of research is the relationship of philosophy to social theory. His publications include "A. N. Whitehead, Information and Social Theory," in *Theory, Culture & Society* (2005), and "On Whitehead and Deleuze: The Process of

Materiality," in *Configurations* (2007). He has also edited a collection of papers on Whitehead for a special edition of *Theory, Culture & Society* (2008). He has recently published a monograph titled *A Culture of Thought: A. N. Whitehead and Social Theory* (2012).

Luke B. Higgins received his MDiv from Pacific School of Religion in Berkeley, California and is currently writing his dissertation for a PhD at Drew University. Drawing on the philosophies of life of Bergson, Deleuze, and Whitehead, his dissertation develops an interpretation of the kenotic incarnation of the Logos that can serve as the basis for an ecological, nonanthropocentric doctrine of creation. He is also an adjunct professor of philosophy at Rockland Community College in Suffern, New York, and is director of Christian education for a United Church of Christ congregation in Cedar Grove, New Jersey.

L. Callid Keefe-Perry acts with an improv-comedy theatre group, consults on the use of the arts in classrooms, is the national coordinator of the Transformative Language Arts Network, maintains TheImageOfFish.com and Theopoetics.Net, and is a returning student at Colgate Rochester Crozer Divinity School. He travels in the Gospel Ministry within and beyond the Religious Society of Friends, often with his wife Kristina serving as elder, and he has served as a teacher of Quakerism at the Pendle Hill Retreat Center. Most of his work connects to language and how it shapes our dreams and hopes for the future. Academically, he is captivated by issues of communal hermeneutics, Ricoeur's notion of the second naivete, and Christian mysticism. Pastorally, he is committed to helping people find their own voice with which to express their experience of the divine, to exploring how expression influences experience, and to encouraging dialogue rather than debate. He believes in the possibility of a just world while he still lives.

Catherine Keller has taught for over two decades in the Theological School of Drew University and its Graduate Division of Religion. After studies in Europe and in seminary, she did her doctoral work at Claremont Graduate University with John Cobb. In her teaching, lecturing, and writing in a multiplicity of religious and secular, scholarly and activist settings, she seeks to midwife a theology of becoming. As director of the annual Drew Transdisciplinary Theological Colloquium since its inception in 2000, she works with colleagues and students to foster a hospitable local setting for planetary conversations. Her books include *On the Mystery: Discerning Divinity in Process, God and Power: Counter-Apocalyptic Journeys,* and *The Face of the Deep: A Theology of Becoming.*

Sam Laurent is a doctoral student in theology at Drew University. His work has recently focused on articulations of human creativity within theological doctrines, particularly within pneumatology. Sam's current project is a formulation of a theopoetics loosely modeled on collective improvisation, seeking to include the values of openness, creativity, and communal accountability from a musical model in a constructive description of the Spirit. Prior to studying at Drew, Sam received degrees from the Graduate Theological Union and the University of North Carolina at Chapel Hill.

Matthew S. LoPresti is visiting assistant professor of philosophy and humanities at Hawaii Pacific University. He recently received the doctorate in philosophy from the University of Hawaii at Manoa where his research in comparative philosophy and philosophy of religion culminated in the dissertation, *Religious Pluralism in Analytic, South Asian, and Process Philosophies of Religion: An Essay Towards a Comparative Metaphysics of Religion*. Matthew has contributed to academic and popular publications on process philosophy and religious pluralism and has participated in process-themed conferences in Asia and Europe, but he is honored to be included in this, his first such conference at Claremont. Currently, he is looking to publish his first book, tentatively entitled *The Philosophical Basis for Religious Pluralism*.

C. Robert Mesle sees his main contributions to the process movement in his introductory books, *Process Theology: A Basic Introduction* (also published in Korean and forthcoming in Japanese) and *Process Relational Philosophy: An Introduction to Alfred North Whitehead* (also published in Chinese). His efforts at basic introductions have led to his involvement in teaching at the Process Academies in China in 2007 and 2009, and he hopes to continue doing that. Motivated by his own children and grandson, many of Bob's more scholarly contributions are also shaped by Robert McAfee Brown's challenge that "Any future theology I do should put the welfare of children above the niceties of metaphysics." Bob serves on the boards of *Process Studies, The American Journal of Theology and Philosophy,* the Highlands Institute for American Religious and Philosophical Thought, the China Project, and others.

Hollis Phelps is a recent graduate of the theology, ethics, and culture program at Claremont Graduate University. His dissertation focuses on the role that theology plays in the philosophy of Alain Badiou. He currently teaches at Mount Olive College in Mount Olive, North Carolina.

Laurel C. Schneider is professor of theology, ethics, and culture at Chicago Theological Seminary in Chicago, Illinois. Her books include *Beyond Monotheism: A Theology of Multiplicity* (Routledge, 2008) and *Re-Imagining the Divine: Confronting the Backlash Against Feminist Theology* (Pilgrim, 1999). She is co-convenor of the Constructive Theology Workgroup and serves on the Status of LGBTIQ Persons in the Profession Committee of the American Academy of Religion.

John Thatamanil is associate professor of theology and world religions at Union Theological Seminary in New York. He has taught a wide variety of courses in the areas of comparative theology, theologies of religious pluralism, Hindu–Christian dialogue, Buddhist–Christian dialogue, the theology of Paul Tillich, process theology, and Eastern Orthodox theology and spirituality. Tying together these diverse interests is a basic commitment to a deeply metaphysical form of philosophical theology that he takes to be essential for any Christian theology that seeks to be in conversation with non-Christian religious traditions. Professor Thatamanil seeks to revive in his work a commitment to speculative reflection as found in the work of Paul Tillich and Alfred North Whitehead. Specifically, he is on the hunt for a viable "process Tillichianism."

Index

abstract, 19–23, 25–26, 37, 51, 106, 135–36, 189, 205, 232, 250; abstraction, 22, 25, 37, 51, 56, 102, 112, 147, 149, 216, 218, 232–33, 245, 256n15, 268n71

actual entity, 20–21, 51, 58, 102–3; God as, 239–40, 242–43, 246–47, 253, 293n1

actual occasion, 58, 66, 95, 118, 202, 204

aesthetic, 1, 6, 7, 8, 49, 53, 60, 61, 87, 95–96, 137–39, 159–60, 184, 192, 195–98, 200–4, 206–7, 209–10, 243, 248, 269n13; judgment, 161; theory, 6; valuation, 10, 195, 202

agency, 55, 115, 116, 119, 195, 199, 203; agent, 4, 68

anthropic: fallacy, 218, 219, 220, 222; principle, 218, 220, 222, 224, 225, 229, 231

apophatic: theology, 175, 181, 187, 188, 189, 190; theopoetics, 9, 191, 193, 194, 241, 242

Aquinas, St. Thomas, 10, 90, 116, 174, 188, 263n3

Aristotle, 1, 226

art, 1, 10, 18, 30–32, 36, 39, 44, 60–62, 89, 95, 114–17, 137, 139, 161–62, 164–65, 167, 171, 185, 192–93, 196–201, 209, 248, 292n93; artistic, 135, 198, 257n8, 265n19; artwork, 169

Augustine, 136, 174

Badiou, Alain, 2, 7, 30–46, 111–12, 140, 184, 241, 257n8, 258n35, 259n38, 260n84

Bataille, Georges, 165, 219, 226–27

beauty, 2, 4, 10, 24, 63, 70, 89–90, 159, 161, 163, 169–71, 174, 175, 187, 193, 196, 201, 228, 233, 241; truth, goodness, and, 4, 10, 43, 95, 192

Begriff, 136–37, 139, 245, 248–49

Benedict XVI (pope emeritus), 85–86

Bergson, Henri, 198, 208

bifurcation, 11, 20, 114–15, 275n25; of nature, 17, 24, 27–28, 256n15

binary, 6, 84, 88, 213, 216, 225–26

Blake, William, 147, 278

body, 54, 101, 104, 116, 165, 171, 172–74, 201, 206–8, 225, 287n30; of Christ, 55; dead body of God, 218, 220

Brahman, 83, 88, 99, 103–6, 241, 273n29

Buddhism, 8, 106, 108, 213, 234–35, 272n8; Buddhist–Christian dialogue, 99, 106

Butler, Judith, 2

Cardenal, Ernesto, 179, 191, 193–94

causal, 17, 62, 95, 271n24; efficacy, 226, 292n93

chaosmos, 10, 191, 196–97, 207, 208, 224, 227, 229, 231; eco-, 224, 226

chora. See *khora*

herald, 144–49, 151–58; heraldic, 9, 143
hermeneutics, 9, 65, 126, 128–29, 184,
    247
Hopper, Stanley, 149, 150, 184–86, 188

identity, 20, 44, 55, 63, 99, 164–65, 167,
    170–71, 183, 185, 221–22, 226, 229,
    232–34
immanence, 24, 41, 46, 55, 57, 63, 77, 94,
    112, 183, 217–18, 229, 231, 267n50; mu-
    tual, 11, 57, 59, 218, 221, 223, 226–28,
    230; plan of, 2, 136, 139–40
indeterminate, 52, 195, 199, 202, 204, 234
initial aim, 50, 196, 203, 210, 285n5, 287n38
interrelation, 8, 57, 180, 219, 221
Irigaray, Luce, 2, 52, 183, 219, 227
Islam, 93, 125, 140, 270n18, 271n18

John Paul II (pope), 85–86

Kant, Immanuel, 1, 21, 40, 100, 114, 116–17,
    119, 126, 134, 159, 160–64, 166–67, 170,
    226, 266n36
kataphatic, 115, 118, 175
khora, 129, 140, 165–66, 175, 186, 228,
    233–34; of Plato, 165, 205, 226
Kierkegaard, Søren, 7, 47–63 passim, 137,
    262n28
Kristeva, Julia, 2, 9, 159–61, 163–75 passim,
    219, 225, 227, 279n3

Lacan, Jacques, 159, 163–65, 167, 170–71,
    173, 219
Leibniz, Gottfried Wilhelm, 117, 174
Levinas, Emmanuel, 2, 150, 159
logocentrism, 6–7
logos, 6, 44, 84–85, 141, 181–83, 186, 189,
    191–92, 194, 230, 242, 248–49, 252,
    254
love, 6, 97, 99, 109–10, 118, 125, 151, 161–65,
    167–68, 170–75, 229, 231–33, 272n4;
    God and, 86, 107–8, 115, 192; science,
    art, politics, and, 30–31, 44

manifold, 3, 6, 8–9, 34, 59, 63, 97–98, 102,
    106, 143, 158, 193, 203, 211, 273n29,
    286n24; divine, 5, 118; theopoetics of,
    113, 115, 117
material, 30–31, 44, 115, 118, 199, 202, 205,
    209, 215, 217, 225–26, 268n71, 281n46;
    materiality, 1, 115, 183
mathematics, 1, 30–33, 35–38, 40–41, 43,
    112, 135, 168, 257n8, 258n35, 259n38

matrix, 58, 60, 135; divine, 48, 55–59, 97,
    286n24
metaphor, 3, 6, 16, 24, 31, 38–39, 68, 76, 87,
    115, 118, 138, 152, 175, 180, 185, 187, 189,
    191–93, 266n36
metaphysics, 2, 33–35, 50, 60, 66–68, 84,
    93, 95, 98–99, 115–16, 118, 126–27, 137,
    139, 179, 183, 189, 191, 245–46, 276n13;
    of process, 114, 117, 119, 271n19
Miller, David, 184–88, 192, 276n13, 277n13
misplaced concreteness. *See* fallacy
modernity, 17, 27, 114–19, 121, 126–27, 159,
    187, 202
monorthodoxy, 9, 142–45, 147, 151–53, 155,
    157–58, 277n1
morality, 87, 99–100, 134, 157, 161, 164, 184,
    221, 230, 243
Muir, John, 212–13, 218, 222
multiplicity, 2, 3, 5–11, 20, 41, 48–49, 52,
    53, 55, 57–59, 62, 67–70, 76, 84, 93,
    95, 97, 110–13, 116–17, 119–21, 127, 130,
    155, 161–62, 165, 185, 191, 193, 203, 217,
    223–35 passim, 271n19, 277n1; of self-
    hood, 54, 63
Murdoch, Iris, 9, 159–65, 167, 169–75
Muslim. *See* Islam
mutual immanence. *See* immanence

Nancy, Jean-Luc, 110–11, 119, 159
negative theology, 181, 187–91. *See also*
    apophatic
neoplatonism, 136, 181, 187–89, 248
Newtonian, 114–15, 118, 174, 217
nexus, 55, 58–59, 68, 115, 118, 184, 187,
    196–97, 204–9, 287n37
Nietzsche, Friedrich, 1, 33, 76, 139, 183, 187,
    216, 218, 229
novelty, 10, 11, 44–46, 54, 58, 60–62, 95–96,
    105, 196, 205, 208–9, 216, 218, 221,
    223–24, 231, 241, 253

objects, 23–24, 40–42, 60, 69, 151, 160–62,
    165–67, 173, 190, 203, 208–9, 220, 227,
    252, 254; eternal, *see* eternal; objectivity,
    26, 40–41, 49, 58, 88, 95, 114, 118, 132,
    144, 154, 169, 175, 181, 184–85, 187, 192
occasions, 21, 62, 65, 95, 203, 207, 208, 210,
    241, 259n38, 285n5, 287n30; actual, *see*
    actual occasion
Oedipal, 165, 171; pre-, 167, 170
Oliver, Harold, 245–49, 252–53
omnipotence, 214, 216, 220, 222–23, 226,
    228–29, 231, 234, 235

Perspectives in Continental Philosophy
John D. Caputo, series editor

John D. Caputo, ed., *Deconstruction in a Nutshell: A Conversation with Jacques Derrida.*

Michael Strawser, *Both/And: Reading Kierkegaard—From Irony to Edification.*

Michael D. Barber, *Ethical Hermeneutics: Rationality in Enrique Dussel's Philosophy of Liberation.*

James H. Olthuis, ed., *Knowing Other-wise: Philosophy at the Threshold of Spirituality.*

James Swindal, *Reflection Revisited: Jürgen Habermas's Discursive Theory of Truth.*

Richard Kearney, *Poetics of Imagining: Modern and Postmodern.* Second edition.

Thomas W. Busch, *Circulating Being: From Embodiment to Incorporation—Essays on Late Existentialism.*

Edith Wyschogrod, *Emmanuel Levinas: The Problem of Ethical Metaphysics.* Second edition.

Francis J. Ambrosio, ed., *The Question of Christian Philosophy Today.*

Jeffrey Bloechl, ed., *The Face of the Other and the Trace of God: Essays on the Philosophy of Emmanuel Levinas.*

Ilse N. Bulhof and Laurens ten Kate, eds., *Flight of the Gods: Philosophical Perspectives on Negative Theology.*

Trish Glazebrook, *Heidegger's Philosophy of Science.*

Kevin Hart, *The Trespass of the Sign: Deconstruction, Theology, and Philosophy.*

Mark C. Taylor, *Journeys to Selfhood: Hegel and Kierkegaard.* Second edition.

Dominique Janicaud, Jean-François Courtine, Jean-Louis Chrétien, Michel Henry, Jean-Luc Marion, and Paul Ricoeur, *Phenomenology and the "Theological Turn": The French Debate.*

Karl Jaspers, *The Question of German Guilt*. Introduction by Joseph W. Koterski, S.J.

Jean-Luc Marion, *The Idol and Distance: Five Studies*. Translated with an introduction by Thomas A. Carlson.

Jeffrey Dudiak, *The Intrigue of Ethics: A Reading of the Idea of Discourse in the Thought of Emmanuel Levinas*.

Robyn Horner, *Rethinking God as Gift: Marion, Derrida, and the Limits of Phenomenology*.

Mark Dooley, *The Politics of Exodus: Søren Kierkegaard's Ethics of Responsibility*.

Merold Westphal, *Overcoming Onto-Theology: Toward a Postmodern Christian Faith*.

Edith Wyschogrod, Jean-Joseph Goux, and Eric Boynton, eds., *The Enigma of Gift and Sacrifice*.

Stanislas Breton, *The Word and the Cross*. Translated with an introduction by Jacquelyn Porter.

Jean-Luc Marion, *Prolegomena to Charity*. Translated by Stephen E. Lewis.

Peter H. Spader, *Scheler's Ethical Personalism: Its Logic, Development, and Promise*.

Jean-Louis Chrétien, *The Unforgettable and the Unhoped For*. Translated by Jeffrey Bloechl.

Don Cupitt, *Is Nothing Sacred? The Non-Realist Philosophy of Religion: Selected Essays*.

Jean-Luc Marion, *In Excess: Studies of Saturated Phenomena*. Translated by Robyn Horner and Vincent Berraud.

Phillip Goodchild, *Rethinking Philosophy of Religion: Approaches from Continental Philosophy*.

William J. Richardson, S.J., *Heidegger: Through Phenomenology to Thought*.

Jeffrey Andrew Barash, *Martin Heidegger and the Problem of Historical Meaning*.

Jean-Louis Chrétien, *Hand to Hand: Listening to the Work of Art*. Translated by Stephen E. Lewis.

Jean-Louis Chrétien, *The Call and the Response*. Translated with an introduction by Anne Davenport.

D. C. Schindler, *Han Urs von Balthasar and the Dramatic Structure of Truth: A Philosophical Investigation*.

Julian Wolfreys, ed., *Thinking Difference: Critics in Conversation*.

Allen Scult, *Being Jewish/Reading Heidegger: An Ontological Encounter*.

Richard Kearney, *Debates in Continental Philosophy: Conversations with Contemporary Thinkers*.

Jennifer Anna Gosetti-Ferencei, *Heidegger, Hölderlin, and the Subject of Poetic Language: Toward a New Poetics of Dasein*.

Jolita Pons, *Stealing a Gift: Kierkegaard's Pseudonyms and the Bible*.

Jean-Yves Lacoste, *Experience and the Absolute: Disputed Questions on the Humanity of Man*. Translated by Mark Raftery-Skehan.

Charles P. Bigger, *Between Chora and the Good: Metaphor's Metaphysical Neighborhood*.

Dominique Janicaud, *Phenomenology "Wide Open": After the French Debate*. Translated by Charles N. Cabral.

Ian Leask and Eoin Cassidy, eds., *Givenness and God: Questions of Jean-Luc Marion*.

Jacques Derrida, *Sovereignties in Question: The Poetics of Paul Celan*. Edited by Thomas Dutoit and Outi Pasanen.

William Desmond, *Is There a Sabbath for Thought? Between Religion and Philosophy*.

Bruce Ellis Benson and Norman Wirzba, eds., *The Phenomenology of Prayer*.

S. Clark Buckner and Matthew Statler, eds., *Styles of Piety: Practicing Philosophy after the Death of God*.

Kevin Hart and Barbara Wall, eds., *The Experience of God: A Postmodern Response*.

John Panteleimon Manoussakis, *After God: Richard Kearney and the Religious Turn in Continental Philosophy*.

John Martis, *Philippe Lacoue-Labarthe: Representation and the Loss of the Subject*.

Jean-Luc Nancy, *The Ground of the Image*.

Edith Wyschogrod, *Crossover Queries: Dwelling with Negatives, Embodying Philosophy's Others*.

Gerald Bruns, *On the Anarchy of Poetry and Philosophy: A Guide for the Unruly*.

Brian Treanor, *Aspects of Alterity: Levinas, Marcel, and the Contemporary Debate*.

Simon Morgan Wortham, *Counter-Institutions: Jacques Derrida and the Question of the University*.

Leonard Lawlor, *The Implications of Immanence: Toward a New Concept of Life*.

Clayton Crockett, *Interstices of the Sublime: Theology and Psychoanalytic Theory*.

Bettina Bergo, Joseph Cohen, and Raphael Zagury-Orly, eds., *Judeities: Questions for Jacques Derrida*. Translated by Bettina Bergo and Michael B. Smith.

Jean-Luc Marion, *On the Ego and on God: Further Cartesian Questions*. Translated by Christina M. Gschwandtner.

Jean-Luc Nancy, *Philosophical Chronicles*. Translated by Franson Manjali.

Jean-Luc Nancy, *Dis-Enclosure: The Deconstruction of Christianity*. Translated by Bettina Bergo, Gabriel Malenfant, and Michael B. Smith.

Andrea Hurst, *Derrida Vis-à-vis Lacan: Interweaving Deconstruction and Psychoanalysis*.

Jean-Luc Nancy, *Noli me tangere: On the Raising of the Body*. Translated by Sarah Clift, Pascale-Anne Brault, and Michael Naas.

Jacques Derrida, *The Animal That Therefore I Am*. Edited by Marie-Louise Mallet, translated by David Wills.

Jean-Luc Marion, *The Visible and the Revealed*. Translated by Christina M. Gschwandtner and others.

Michel Henry, *Material Phenomenology*. Translated by Scott Davidson.

Jean-Luc Nancy, *Corpus*. Translated by Richard A. Rand.

Joshua Kates, *Fielding Derrida*.

Michael Naas, *Derrida From Now On*.

Shannon Sullivan and Dennis J. Schmidt, eds., *Difficulties of Ethical Life.*

Catherine Malabou, *What Should We Do with Our Brain?* Translated by Sebastian Rand, Introduction by Marc Jeannerod.

Claude Romano, *Event and World.* Translated by Shane Mackinlay.

Vanessa Lemm, *Nietzsche's Animal Philosophy: Culture, Politics, and the Animality of the Human Being.*

B. Keith Putt, ed., *Gazing Through a Prism Darkly: Reflections on Merold Westphal's Hermeneutical Epistemology.*

Eric Boynton and Martin Kavka, eds., *Saintly Influence: Edith Wyschogrod and the Possibilities of Philosophy of Religion.*

Shane Mackinlay, *Interpreting Excess: Jean-Luc Marion, Saturated Phenomena, and Hermeneutics.*

Kevin Hart and Michael A. Signer, eds., *The Exorbitant: Emmanuel Levinas Between Jews and Christians.*

Bruce Ellis Benson and Norman Wirzba, eds., *Words of Life: New Theological Turns in French Phenomenology.*

William Robert, *Trials: Of Antigone and Jesus.*

Brian Treanor and Henry Isaac Venema, eds., *A Passion for the Possible: Thinking with Paul Ricoeur.*

Kas Saghafi, *Apparitions—Of Derrida's Other.*

Nick Mansfield, *The God Who Deconstructs Himself: Sovereignty and Subjectivity Between Freud, Bataille, and Derrida.*

Don Ihde, *Heidegger's Technologies: Postphenomenological Perspectives.*

Françoise Dastur, *Questioning Phenomenology.* Translated by Robert Vallier.

Suzi Adams, *Castoriadis's Ontology: Being and Creation.*

Richard Kearney and Kascha Semonovitch, eds., *Phenomenologies of the Stranger: Between Hostility and Hospitality.*

Michael Naas, *Miracle and Machine: Jacques Derrida and the Two Sources of Religion, Science, and the Media.*

Alena Alexandrova, Ignaas Devisch, Laurens ten Kate, and Aukje van Rooden, *Re-treating Religion: Deconstructing Christianity with Jean-Luc Nancy.* Preamble by Jean-Luc Nancy.

Emmanuel Falque, *The Metamorphosis of Finitude: An Essay on Birth and Resurrection.* Translated by George Hughes.

Scott M. Campbell, *The Early Heidegger's Philosophy of Life: Facticity, Being, and Language.*

Françoise Dastur, *How Are We to Confront Death? An Introduction to Philosophy.* Translated by Robert Vallier. Foreword by David Farrell Krell.

Christina M. Gschwandtner, *Postmodern Apologetics? Arguments for God in Contemporary Philosophy.*

Ben Morgan, *On Becoming God: Late Medieval Mysticism and the Modern Western Self.*

Neal DeRoo, *Futurity in Phenomenology: Promise and Method in Husserl, Levinas, and Derrida.*

Sarah LaChance Adams and Caroline R. Lundquist, eds., *Coming to Life: Philosophies of Pregnancy, Childbirth, and Mothering.*

Thomas Claviez, ed., *The Conditions of Hospitality: Ethics, Politics, and Aesthetics on the Threshold of the Possible.*

Roland Faber and Jeremy Fackenthal, eds., *Theopoetic Folds: Philosophizing Multifariousness.*

Jean-Luc Marion, *The Essential Writings.* Edited by Kevin Hart.

Adam S. Miller, *Speculative Grace: Bruno Latour and Object-Oriented Theology.* Foreword by Levi R. Bryant.

Jean-Luc Nancy, *Corpus II: Writings on Sexuality.*

David Nowell Smith, *Sounding/Silence: Martin Heidegger at the Limits of Poetics.*